Some Wine and Honey for Simon

Some Wine and Honey for Simon

*Biblical and Ugaritic Aperitifs
in Memory of Simon B. Parker*

Edited by A. Joseph Ferrara†
and Herbert B. Huffmon
with the assistance of Sergey Kozin

☙PICKWICK *Publications* • Eugene, Oregon

SOME WINE AND HONEY FOR SIMON
Biblical and Ugaritic Aperitifs in Memory of Simon B. Parker

Copyright © 2020 Wipf and Stock Publishers. All rights reserved. Except for brief quotations in critical publications or reviews, no part of this book may be reproduced in any manner without prior written permission from the publisher. Write: Permissions, Wipf and Stock Publishers, 199 W. 8th Ave., Suite 3, Eugene, OR 97401.

Pickwick Publications
An Imprint of Wipf and Stock Publishers
199 W. 8th Ave., Suite 3
Eugene, OR 97401

www.wipfandstock.com

PAPERBACK ISBN: 978-1-5326-9296-3
HARDCOVER ISBN: 978-1-5326-9297-0
EBOOK ISBN: 978-1-5326-9298-7

Cataloguing-in-Publication data:

Names: Ferrara, A. Joseph, editor. | Huffmon, Herbert B., editor. | Kozin, Sergey, assistant editor.

Title: Some wine and honey for Simon : biblical and Ugaritic aperitifs in memory of Simon B. Parker / edited by A. Joseph Ferrara and Herbert B. Huffmon, with the assistance of Sergey Kozin.

Description: Eugene, OR: Pickwick Publications, 2020. | Includes index.

Identifiers: ISBN 978-1-5326-9296-3 (paperback). | ISBN 978-1-5326-9297-0 (hardcover). | ISBN 978-1-5326-9298-7 (ebook).

Subjects: LCSH: Parker, Simon B. | Bible—Old Testament—Criticism, interpretation, etc. | Ugaritic literature—History and criticism. | Ugaritic poetry—Translations into English. | Ugarit (Extinct city)—Religion. | Narration in the Bible.

Classification: BS1188 S61 2020 (print). | BS1188 (ebook).

Manufactured in the U.S.A.   MAY 22, 2020

Contents

Abbreviations | vii
Preface | xv
A Narrative of Simon | xvii
  —Bruce Zuckerman

1. Biblical Narrative and Canaanite Narrative | 1
  —Edward L. Greenstein

2. Baal as Warrior-King in the Baal Cycle | 23
  —Mark S. Smith

3. Baal in Boston, Bethel in Amherst | 51
  —Karel van der Toorn

4. Gods on the Mind at Ugarit | 65
  —Steve A. Wiggins

5. The Rumpelstiltskin Factor: Explorations in the Arithmetic of Pantheons | 88
  —Nicolas Wyatt

6. To Be or Not To Be a Proverb: When Water Flows Beneath Straw (and Don't Think It Doesn't) | 129
  —Katheryn Pfisterer Darr

7. The Birth Announcement: A Masoretic Note on Naming | 168
  —David Marcus

8. 1 Kings 13: A Story of Two Prophets United | 175
  —Herbert B. Huffmon

9   "Enthroned upon Donkeys": The Entry of Divine Jesus into
    Jerusalem according to Matthew | 189
        —Bernard F. Batto

10 Narrative-Ancestry-Dot-Com: The Gettysburg Address,
    Descendant of the Book of Jonah | 205
        —Tim Koch

11 A Song of Love: Isaiah 5:1–7 | 218
        —F. W. Dobbs-Allsopp

    Appendix: Isaiah 5:1–7 | 243

    Simon Bruce Parker: A Bibliography | 253
        —Amy Limpitlaw and Herbert B. Huffmon

Abbreviations

GENERAL

Aq	Aquila's translation
Ant.	Josephus, *Jewish Antiquities*
Arad	Arad inscriptions (see HI)
ArBib	The Aramaic Bible
BH	Biblical Hebrew
BHS	Biblia Hebraica Stuttgartensia
BM	tablets in the collections of the British Museum
G	Greek Bible
Gez	Gezer Calendar
EA	registration number of tablets from El Amarna
HB	Hebrew Bible
KJV	King James Version
Lach	Lachish letters (see HI)
M, MT	Masoretic text
MH	Mishnaic Hebrew
Mf	Masora finalis
Mm	Masora magna
Mp	Masora parva
Mur	Murabba'at papyrus (see HI)
NIV	New International Version

NJPS	Tanakh: The Holy Scriptures: The New JPS Translation according to the Traditional Hebrew Text
NRSV	New Revised Standard Version
QH	Qumranic Hebrew
RIH	field number of tablets excavated at Ras Ibn Hani
RS	Ras Shamra text number
Sym	Symmachus
S, Syr.	Syriac
T	Targum
Theod	Theodotion
TIM	texts in the Iraq Museum
V	Vulgate

REFERENCE WORKS

AB	Anchor Bible
ABD	*Anchor Bible Dictionary*. 6 vols. Edited by David Noel Freedman. New York: Doubleday, 1992
AEM	Archives épistolaires de Mari
ALASP	Abhandlungen zur Literatur Alt–Syrien–Palästinas und Mesopotamiens
ANEP	*The Ancient Near East in Pictures Relating to the Old Testament*. 2nd ed. Edited by James B. Pritchard. Princeton: Princeton University Press, 1994
ANET	*Ancient Near Eastern Texts Relating to the Old Testament*. 3rd ed. Edited by James B. Pritchard. Princeton: Princeton University Press, 1969
AnOr	Analecta Orientalia
AO	*Der Alte Orient*
AOAT	Alter Orient und Altes Testament
AoF	*Altorientalische Forschungen*
ARM	Archives royales de Mari
AuOr	*Aula orientalis*

ABBREVIATIONS

BA	*Biblical Archaeologist*
BAR	*Biblical Archaeology Review*
BASOR	*Bulletin of the American Schools of Oriental Research*
BASORSup	Bulletin of the American Schools of Oriental Research Supplements
BETL	Bibliotheca ephemeridum theologicarum lovaniensium
BDB	F. Brown, S. R. Driver, and C. A. Briggs, *A Hebrew and English Lexicon of the Old Testament*. Oxford: Clarendon, 1907
BFCT	Beiträge zur Förderung christlicher Theologie
BJS	Brown Judaic Studies
BibB	Biblische Beiträge
BibS	Biblische Studien
BKAT	Biblischer Kommentar, Altes Testament
BRev	*Bible Review*
BSac	*Bibliotheca Sacra*
BZAW	Beihefte zur Zeitschrift für die alttestamentliche Wissenschaft
CAD	*The Assyrian Dictionary of the Oriental Institute of the University of Chicago*. 21 vols. (A–Z). Edited by A. L. Oppenheim, et al. Chicago: Oriental Institute, 1956–2011
CANE	Sasson, J., ed. *Civilizations of the Ancient Near East*. 4 vols. New York, 1995
CBQ	*Catholic Biblical Quarterly*
CBQMS	Catholic Biblical Quarterly Monograph Series
CM	Cuneiform monographs
ConBOT	Coniectanea biblica: Old Testament Series
COS	*The Context of Scripture*. 3 vols. Edited by William W. Hallo. Leiden, 1997–2002
CTU	*The Cuneiform Alphabetic Texts from Ugarit, Ras Ibn Hani, and Other Places*. Edited by Manfred Dietrich, Otto Loretz, and Joaquín Sanmartín. Abhandlungen zur Literatur Alt-Syrien-Palästinas 8. Münster: Ugarit-Verlag, 1995
CUSAS	Cornell University Studies in Assyriology and Sumerology

DDD	*Dictionary of Deities and Demons in the Bible.* 1st ed. Edited by Karel van der Toorn, Bob Becking, and Pieter W. van der Horst. Leiden: Brill, 1995
DULAT	*A Dictionary of the Ugaritic Language in the Alphabetic Tradition.* 2 vols. Edited by Gregorio del Olmo Lete and Joaquín Sanmartín. HdO 112. Leiden: Brill, 2003. 3rd revised ed. 2015
EG	A. H. Gardiner, *Egyptian Grammar.* Oxford: Griffiths Institute, 1927. 2nd ed., 1950; 3rd ed., 1957
EI	*Eretz-Israel: Archaeological, Historical and Geographical Studies*
FAT	Forschungen zum Alten Testament
GBS	Guides to Biblical Scholarship
GUS	Gorgias Ugaritic Studies
HALOT	*The Hebrew and Aramaic Lexicon of the Old Testament.* Ludwig Koehler, Walter Baumgartner, and J. J. Stamm. Translated and edited under supervision of M. E. J. Richardson. 5 vols. Leiden: Brill, 1994–2000
HAT	Handbuch zum Alten Testament
HdO	Handbuch der Orientalistik
HI	*Hebrew Inscriptions: Texts from the Biblical Period of the Monarchy with Concordance.* Edited by F. W. Dobbs-Allsopp et al. New Haven: Yale University Press, 2005
HO	Handbuch der Orientalistik
HSM	Harvard Semitic Monographs
HS	*Hebrew Studies*
HSS	Harvard Semitic Studies
HTR	*Harvard Theological Review*
IEJ	*Israel Exploration Journal*
ICC	International Critical Commentary
IM	Museum siglum of the Iraq Museum in Baghdad
IOS	*Israel Oriental Studies*
JAH	*Journal of Ancient History*
JANER	*Journal of Ancient Near Eastern Religions*

JANESCU	*Journal of the Ancient Near Eastern Society of Columbia University*
JAOS	*Journal of the American Oriental Society*
JBL	*Journal of Biblical Literature*
JEA	*Journal of Egyptian Archaeology*
JNES	*Journal of Near Eastern Studies*
JNSL	*Journal of Northwest Semitic Languages*
JPS	Jewish Publication Society
JRAS	*Journal of the Royal Asiatic Society*
JSOT	*Journal for the Study of the Old Testament*
JSOTSup	Journal for the Study of the Old Testament: Supplement Series
JSS	*Journal of Semitic Studies*
KAI	H. Donner and W. Röllig, *Kanaanäische und aramäische Inschriften*. 2nd ed. Wiesbaden: Harrassowitz, 1966–69
KAR	E. Ebeling, ed., *Keilschrifttexte aus Assur religiösen Inhalts*. Leipzig: Hinrichs, 1919–23
KTU	*Die keilalphabetischen Texte aus Ugarit*. Edited by Manfred Dietrich, Otto Loretz, and Joaquín Sanmartín. AOAT 360. Munster: Ugarit-Verlag, 2013. *KTU* [=*CTU*]
LHB/OTS	Library of Hebrew Bible/Old Testament studies
LQ	*Lutheran Quarterly*
L&N	Johannes P. Louw and Eugene A. Nida, eds., *Greek-English Lexicon of the New Testament: Based on Semantic Domains*. 2nd ed. New York: United Bible Societies, 1989
MC	Mesopotamian civilizations
NEA	*Near Eastern Archaeology*
NCBC	New Century Bible Commentary
NIB	*The New Interpreter's Bible*. 12 vols. Edited by Leander E. Keck. Nashville: Abingdon, 1994–2004
NICOT	New International Commentary on the Old Testament
OBO	Orbis biblicus et orientalis
OLA	Orientalia Lovaniensia Analecta

Or	*Orientalia* (Nova Series)
OrAnt	*Oriens Antiquus*
PEQ	*Palestine Exploration Quarterly*
RA	*Revue d'assyriologie et d'archéologie orientale*
RB	*Revue Biblique*
RBS	Resources for Biblical Study
RelSRev	*Religious Studies Review*
RINA	Royal Inscriptions of the Neo-Assyrian Period
RSP	*Ras Shamra Parallels: The Texts from Ugarit and the Hebrew Bible*. 3 vols. Edited by Loren R. Fisher (vol. 1–2) and Stan Rummel (vol. 3). AO 49–51. Rome: Pontifical Biblical Institute Press, 1972, 1975, 1981
SAA	State Archives of Assyria
SAAS	State Archives of Assyria Studies
SANER	Studies in Ancient Near Eastern Records
SBLDS	Society of Biblical Literature Dissertation Series
SBLRBS	Society of Biblical Literature Resources for Biblical Study
SBLSCS	Society of Biblical Literature Septuagint and Cognate Studies
SBLSP	Society of Biblical Literature Seminar Papers
SBLSymS	Society of Biblical Literature Symposium Series
SBLWAW	Society of Biblical Literature Writings from the Ancient World
SemeiaSt	Semeia Studies
SHBC	Smyth & Helwys Bible Commentary
SHR	Studies in the History of Religions (supplements to *Numen*)
SMEA	*Studi Micenei ed Egeo-Anatolici*
TAD	*Textbook of Aramaic Documents from Ancient Egypt*. 4 vols. Edited and Translated by Bezalel Porten and Ada Yardeni. Jerusalem: Hebrew University, 1986–99
TDOT	*Theological Dictionary of the Old Testament*. 16 vols. Edited by G. Johannes Botterweck, Helmer Ringgren, and Heinz-Josef Fabray. Grand Rapids: Eerdmans, 1974–2018
UBL	Ugaritisch-biblische Literatur

UF	*Ugarit-Forschungen*
UNP	*Ugaritic Narrative Poetry.* Edited by Simon B. Parker. SBLWAW 9. Atlanta: Scholars, 1997
VT	*Vetus Testamentum*
VTSup	Vetus Tetamentum Supplements
WBC	Word Biblical Commentary
WO	*Die Welt des Orients*
ZAW	*Zeitschrift für die alttestamentliche Wissenschaft*
ZÄS	*Zeitschrift für ägyptische Sprache und Altertumskunde*

Preface

SEVERAL YEARS AGO I got a phone call from A. J. (Joe) Ferrara, to the effect that we needed to take some initiative in preparing a Festschrift honoring our dear friend from the old days (mid-60s) in Baltimore. For various reasons an earlier plan for such a volume had not gotten underway. So we undertook the project. But, sadly, A. J. himself unexpectedly—like Simon—died in the fall of 2017, before he was able to complete his own contribution.

Both A. J. and myself had coauthored an article with Simon, as noted in the Bibliography, and we kept in touch in spite of geographical separation. Simon spent most of his academic career at Boston University and its School of Theology, which, earlier, A. J. Ferrara had attended. A. J., while continuing in Sumerological work, was a prominent trial attorney in Albuquerque and I was teaching at Drew University. The last time the three of us were together was again in Baltimore in late September 1999, on the sad occasion of the memorial service for our friend, classmate, and former colleague or teacher, Delbert Hillers. (Simon himself had visited Del in Baltimore a few months prior to the memorial service.)

What Simon represented was not only being a quiet, content, and charming person, with a ready smile and a quick wit, but also being an outstanding teacher and colleague. Simon got special awards for his teaching, and impressed all who met him with his intellect, his inherent kindness and his capacity, when disagreeing with you on some point, to leave you feeling better. Simon also excelled as an academic administrator, to which he gave his primary efforts for several years—note the gap of many years in his publications. His special calling, however, was that of a teacher, a role to which he was able to return. The carry-over was that he also excelled as a scholarly leader in his role for several years as the General Editor of the outstanding series, Writings from the Ancient World, for the Society of Biblical Literature. Simon was more than equal to whatever task he undertook—as a classical pianist, an administrator, a teacher, and of course as a scholar. Above all, he was a very genuine person.

We are especially grateful for the copyediting by Sergey Kozin, the technological assistance of Helen Hong and Milton Eng, and the guidance of Jim Eisenbraun. The senior editor thanks Katharine Sakenfeld for a critical reading of an earlier form of his own essay. We are especially grateful to K. C. Hanson of Wipf and Stock Publishers for taking on the publication of this volume in their Pickwick Publications imprint.

Readers are advised that these essays were submitted a few years ago and were up-to-date as of that time. The death of one of the editors, together with a change in publishers, has led to a delay in publication.

This volume represents the desire of the contributors and the editors to honor a dear friend, a wonderful, gracious person, by offering him some "wine and honey" to mark a life well lived.

A. Joseph Ferrara†
Herbert B. Huffmon

A Narrative of Simon[1]

Bruce Zuckerman

WHEN WE LEARNED THE distressing news that our long-time friend and colleague, Simon Parker, had been felled by a brain hemorrhage, the first thing I thought of was a line from one of the Phoenician inscriptions he loved and studied so avidly: *ngzlt bl 'ty*, literally, "I was torn away—not my time." The bluntness and anguished surprise embodied in this ancient lament of the Sidonian King Eshmunazar seems to capture precisely how so many of us felt when the word came of Simon's unexpected death. It did not seem possible that someone as vibrant and hale as he had always seemed to be could be so suddenly and irrevocably taken from us.

Simon was there at the creation of *Maarav*—indeed, before the creation. When *Maarav* was being established, one of the first things that was required was the formation of a credible editorial board. My hope, of course, was that, if people thought the editorial board was made up of serious people, they might also be inclined to take *Maarav* seriously as well. The first person I thought might be of help in this regard was Simon Parker. And to be frank, it was not easy to get Simon to agree to join the board. He was highly skeptical and questioned—rather sharply—why I thought there was a need for yet another journal in our areas of academic interest. Fortunately, Simon did see the point of developing a journal with specific focus on Northwest Semitic studies, and he served for a number of years as a primary shaper of our editorial policy and arbiter of the quality of the articles that we published.

Over the years, I have come to think of Simon as the kind of scholar who is absolutely indispensable in our field of Northwest Semitic studies

---

1. Originally published as "Parker, Simon B, 1940–2006," *MAARAV* 13.2 (2006): 279–80.

because he always did things the way they ought to be done. First and foremost he built his theoretical interpretations from the words up. That is, he began any analysis by looking closely, even minutely, at the texts themselves—their words, their structures, their nuances—and used these as the elemental building blocks of his higher critical conclusions. Moreover, in a field where arcane jargon often tends to obscure meaning, his scholarly presentations were always lucid and easy to follow. Most importantly, the way he developed his concepts was so naturally convincing that one found oneself immediately incorporating them into the fabric of one's own way of thinking. As if to say: well, of course, I knew that—except one really did not know it until Simon had stated it.

I particularly loved those occasions when I had a chance to bat ideas back and forth with Simon. I still remember one time over lunch how we scribbled Ugaritic on paper napkins and fought over how to interpret the syntax of an especially tricky phrase. Neither of us was quite satisfied with what the other thought might be the way to read the text, but in our efforts to convince each other we finally came to a better synthesis—a reading that we both finally thought was better than what either of us had originally proposed. That's the way it always seemed to be when one was in dialogue with Simon: his stimulating thinking made you want to reach beyond where you were to gain a new perspective, a better insight.

One's first impression of Simon, when he greeted you with that clipped British accent, was of a man perhaps more reserved and cool than warm and friendly. But the amused half-smile he always seemed to wear soon betrayed that he had a sly and companionable sense of humor. In the last exchange I had with him by email before his death, I sent him a recently written draft of an article—knowing that I could count on a frank appraisal. When he did not respond right away, I sent another somewhat nervous note: "So what do you think?" He replied with a single phrase: "It was unexceptionable." My first reaction was shock: how could he imagine that my work—which I had labored so hard upon—could be so pedestrian as to be labeled unexceptional? But, of course, I had jumped to conclusions and had not read his response closely enough. He had said the work was "unexceptionable," which, as a quick check in the dictionary affirmed, is hardly the same thing as "unexceptional." In fact, he was paying me the nicest of compliments by noting that he could find no objections to my entire line of reasoning. But even as I warmed to the notion that my work might be—at least from the Parker perspective—without exception, I also ruefully concluded that this was a typical bit of Simon's droll humor. He *knew* I would misread what he wrote and jump to the wrong conclusion and he probably even knew that I would have to run to a dictionary to make sure I understood precisely what he meant to say. I could imagine his smile as he laid his clever semantic trap for me to trip into.

As I think of Simon and how much we miss him, it occurs to me that turn-about is fair play: Perhaps in his last communication to me he gave me (once again) the key insight for characterizing his life and his scholarly work. In a word: unexceptionable.

1

Biblical Narrative and Canaanite Narrative[1]

Edward L. Greenstein

LITTLE TIME HAD PASSED since the first discoveries of literary texts in the excavations of Ras Shamra—the site of the ancient north Syrian metropolis of Ugarit—before Umberto (Moshe David) Cassuto made a fairly bold claim concerning the relationship between this north Canaanite literature and the literary compositions of ancient Israel, dating hundreds of years later:

> When we examine the initial stages of Biblical literature, we are struck by a fact that, at first, appears surprising: they do not give the impression of being "first steps" or "first-fruits," and they

---

1. *Author's note*: This essay is a revised version of a Hebrew essay published in *Essays on Hebrew Literature in Honor of Avraham Holtz* (ed. Z. Ben-Yosef Ginor; New York: Jewish Theological Seminary of America, 2003) 9–29. I thank the Jewish Theological Seminary for permission to publish an English adaptation of that essay. The Hebrew essay was based on a presentation I made at a symposium of the Hebrew University Department of Bible in 1992. It followed upon a number of presentations on the subject in the Ugaritic Studies section of the Society of Biblical Literature annual meetings, the first of which was a prepared response to an excellent paper on the composition of the Ugaritic epics given by Simon Parker in 1984. My work on the art of Canaanite narrative, still in progress, received support from the John Simon Guggenheim Foundation, the National Endowment for the Humanities, and the Memorial Foundation for Jewish Culture in 1991–1993. In the present essay I have changed little but have added some pertinent references, especially to the important work of my former student, Dr. Shirly Natan-Yulzary.

show no signs of experimental groping or of searching for techniques. On the contrary, they are perfected and polished writings, which bear witness to the existence of an artistic tradition that had evolved in the course of many centuries.[2]

How might such a phenomenon be explained? Cassuto asked, and he answered his own question:

> Now the problem is easily solved if we assume that the Bible is but a continuation of Canaanite literature, which antedates the former. Just as the Hebrew language is simply one of the dialects that grew from the ancient Canaanite stem, and just as it continues ... the oldest and most homogeneous Canaanite idiom, so Hebrew literature is heir to the Canaanite literary tradition, which had already taken shape among the Canaanite-speaking populations before the people of Israel had come into being.[3]

In the view of many, if not most, scholars in the field, Cassuto's thesis has the merit of explaining the correspondences between early Hebrew poetry and the Syro-Canaanite poetry that was unearthed at Ugarit. Scholars recognize the many resemblances between Israelite poetry and Ugaritic verse both in the vocabulary and in the diverse and well-known forms of parallelism that they share.[4] Cassuto, however, discerned a historical link between Israelite and earlier Canaanite literature not only in their poetry but also in the area of prose. In this regard Cassuto cited in particular "rhetorical forms and ways of expression."[5] In the style of Biblical narrative he found distinctive signs of Canaanite epic style, and these features he tended to attribute to the early epic poetry of Israel, which has survived only in various embeddings within Biblical prose and in disparate verses within Biblical poetry.[6] Cassuto, however, paid little attention to the narrative

---

2. U. Cassuto, "The Relationship between Ugaritic Literature and the Bible," in *The Goddess Anath: Canaanite Epics of the Patriarchal Age* (trans. I. Abrahams; Jerusalem: Magnes, 1971) 18.

3. Cassuto, "The Relationship," 19.

4. See, e.g., Y. Avishur, *Stylistic Studies of Word-Pairs in Biblical and Ancient Semitic Literatures* (AOAT 210; Kevelaer: Butzon & Bercker, 1984); S. B. Parker, *The Pre-Biblical Narrative Tradition* (SBLRBS 24; Atlanta: Scholars, 1989); D. Pardee, *The Ugaritic Texts and the Origins of West-Semitic Literary Composition* (The Schweich Lectures of the British Academy 2007; Oxford: Oxford University Press, 2012).

5. Cassuto, "The Relationship," 18.

6. U. Cassuto, "The Israelite Epic," in *Biblical and Oriental Studies* (Vol. 2; trans. I. Abrahams; Jerusalem: Magnes, 1975) 69–109. On Canaanite epic formulae incorporated within Biblical prose narrative, see further, e.g., F. Polak, "Epic Formulas in Biblical Narratives and the Roots of Early Hebrew Prose," *Te'uda* 7 (1991) 9–53 (in Hebrew);

devices of Biblical prose, nor did he delineate the narrative strategies of the Ugaritic epics.

There is a tendency among scholars to see an unbridgeable gap between Canaanite epic and Biblical prose narrative. A line is drawn between them, analogous to the boundary that is marked between the literary modes of verse and prose. Scholars regard Biblical narrative written in prose as a revolutionary or at the very least innovative literary form in the ancient Near East. Some go so far as to ascribe to this putative revolution ideological motives. According to one view, ancient Hebrew prose was developed in an attempt to present the personalities of God and the human characters in their full complexity.[7] This point of view rests on the assumption that Canaanite epic, in which characters are often described by means of formulaic epithets, without regard to their placement in the narrative, are lacking in complex, round personalities. In the Bible, by contrast, it is maintained, the character of the protagonists evolves in the course of a narrative, by way of their actions and their discourse.

According to another view, the ancient Hebrew scribes rejected the poetic form of epic that had served as the typical medium of pagan myth and replaced it with prose narrative, in order to relate the deeds of YHWH in a form distinct from the one that served the pagan bards.[8] Yet a third view points out that the Biblical narrator leaves gaps in the course of a story concerning the motives and reasons for characters' behaviors, gaps which the reader must fill in. The extra-Biblical narrator, by contrast, reveals the inner life of the protagonists by means of direct description.[9] It follows from this contention that the Hebrew storyteller was interested in the moral character of the individual, while the pagan bard was interested in events that were thrust forward by an apparent fate or the diffidence of the gods.

Scholars adopting these views, or views similar to them but more nuanced,[10] find a substantial difference in kind between Biblical narrative

---

F. Polak, «וישתחו: קבוצת נושאות בשירה ובסיפורת שבמקרא» in *Sha'arei Talmon: Studies in the Bible, Qumran, and the Ancient Near East, Presented to Shemaryahu Talmon* (ed. M. Fishbane and E. Tov with W. W. Fields; Winona Lake, IN: Eisenbrauns, 1992) *81–*91; F. Polak, "On Prose and Poetry in the Book of Job," *JANESCU* 24 (1996) 61–97.

7. See, e.g., R. Alter, *The Art of Biblical Narrative* (New York: Basic Books, 1981) 25–26; Alter, *The Art of Biblical Poetry* (New York: Basic Books, 1985) 50; cf. R. Kawashima, *Biblical Narrative and the Death of the Rhapsode* (Bloomington: Indiana University Press, 2004).

8. Sh. Talmon, "Did There Exist a Biblical National Epic?," in *Literary Studies in the Hebrew Bible* (Leiden: Brill, 1993) 91–111.

9. See, e.g., M. Sternberg, *The Poetics of Biblical Narrative* (Bloomington: Indiana University Press, 1985) 12.

10. E.g., D. Damrosch, *The Narrative Covenant: Transformations of Genre in the*

and extra-Biblical or pre-Biblical narrative. One can hardly deny the obvious differences between the styles of Biblical prose and those of ancient Canaanite verse. For example, in Ugaritic epic the language of a command repeats virtually verbatim in the execution of that command, while in Biblical narrative it is customary to vary the wording. Even in a classic instance of repetition, such as the narrator's repetition of Jezebel's letter concerning Naboth (1 Kgs 21:9ff.), the language is altered and expansions are made, in a manner that is unparalleled in Ugaritic epic.

An even sharper illustration: in Ugaritic epic the poet describes the recurrent actions of a protagonist day by day in precisely the same language. Here, for example, is how the pious Danel (*Dana'ilu*) is described at the beginning of the Aqhat Epic (*CTU* 1.17 ii 30–40):

> (He) dines the Katharat,[11] / and wines the moon's[12] radiant[13] daughters.
> One day, and a second,
> He dines the Katharat, / and wines the moon's radiant daughters.
> A third, a fourth day,
> He dines the Katharat, / and wines the moon's radiant daughters.
> A fifth, a sixth day,
> He dines the Katharat, / and wines the moon's radiant daughters.
> Then on the sevenh day,
> The Katharat leave his house, / the moon's radiant daughters (leave his house).[14]

The Biblical narrator, by contrast, writing in prose, abridges and summarizes instead of reviewing a description of action repetitively.[15] An excellent example of synopsis in place of repetition is Josh 6:8–15:

Growth of Biblical Literature (San Francisco: Harper & Row, 1987); and see my discussion of this book: E. L. Greenstein, "On the Genesis of Biblical Prose Narrative," *Prooftexts* 8 (1988) 347–54.

11. The Katharat are goddesses who assist a woman in childbirth; see, e.g., D. Pardee, "Kosharoth," in *DDD*, cols. 915–17.

12. Literally, "the daughters of Helel," the new moon or morning star, known from Isa 14:12; see, e.g., W. G. E. Watson, "Helel," in ibid., 746–50.

13. Or "swallows," Heb. סנונית; the goddesses are imaged as birds.

14. Translation from S. B. Parker, "Aqhat," in *Ugaritic Narrative Poetry* (ed. S. B. Parker; SBLWAW 9; Atlanta: Scholars, 1997) 57.

15. See M. H. Lichtenstein, "Episodic Structure in the Ugaritic Keret Legend" (Ph.D. diss., Columbia University, 1979).

It happened, when Joshua spoke to the (fighting-)people[16] and the seven priests carrying seven rams' horns in the presence of YHWH crossed over and blew on the rams' horns ... He had the Ark of YHWH circle the city one time round; they came back to the camp and they spent the night. Joshua arose early in the morning, the priests carried the Ark of YHWH ..., they blew the rams' horns ..., they circled the city on the second day one time, and they returned to the camp. Thus did they do for six days. Then on the seventh day ...

In contrast to the well-known style of the ancient epic, the Biblical narrator abbreviates the description of the events on the second day and sums up the subsequent cycles, until arriving at the climax of the events on the seventh day, on which the people encircle the city seven times. Only then, in describing the seventh circling, does the narrative expatiate on the miraculous doings: "Then on the seventh day, they arose with the dawn, they encircled the city in the established manner seven times; only on that day did they encircle the city seven times" (Josh 6:15).[17]

One cannot, then, deny the evident differences between the features of Biblical narrative and those of Canaanite epic. And yet, if we set aside for a moment the formal distinctions between the parallelistic structures that characterize the latter and the prose discourse that characterizes the former, and if we take into account the many hundreds of years that divide the Canaanite narrative of the mid-second millennium BCE and the earliest Biblical prose that originated some time during the Israelite monarchy, we may sustain Cassuto's hypothesis that Hebrew narrative is an outgrowth of the Canaanite narrative that preceded it. All the major features of narrative that scholars discern within Biblical storytelling can be identified in early Canaanite storytelling.[18]

16. So E. Fox, *The Early Prophets: Joshua, Judges, Samuel, and Kings* (Schocken Bible 2; New York: Schocken, 2014) 35.

17. For the epic background of the seven-day count in Biblical narrative, see, e.g., G. del Olmo Lete, "La conquista de Jerico y la leyenda ugaritica de KRT," *Sefarad* 25 (1965) 3–15. See further Parker, *The Pre-Biblical Narrative Tradition*, 46–52; E. L. Greenstein, "Ugaritic Literature," in *The Literature of the Hebrew Bible: Introductions and Studies* (ed. Z. Talshir; 2 vols.; Jerusalem: Yad Ben-Zvi, 2011) 2:510–11.

18. S. B. Parker contends that in early Canaanite epic such features as prolepsis (foreshadowing) and analepsis (flashback) are absent ("The Literatures of Canaan, Ancient Israel, and Phoenicia: An Overview," in *Civilizations of the Ancient Near East* [ed. J. M. Sasson; 4 vols.; New York: Scribner's, 1995] 4:2402). However, these devices of Biblical prose narrative are found in Ugaritic epic. Prolepsis occurs in the Kirta Epic, for example, when Kirta's military campaign is fully previewed to him in a dream (*CTU* 1.14 ii-iii). Analepsis occurs at the beginning of the Kirta Epic, when the deaths of Kirta's wife and children are recounted (*CTU* 1.14 I 12–21). Cf. M. H. Goshen-Gottstein,

It is clear that at least some Biblical authors knew some of the ancient Canaanite stories. Ezekiel, for example, alludes to the Ugaritic epic of Aqhat in two places (Ezek 14:14, 20; 28:1–3).[19] Israelite poets of all periods drew directly on the epics of Baal and Aqhat,[20] and perhaps even Kirta.[21] Dozens of similar narrative patterns have also been enumerated.[22] Moreover, if we carefully examine the techniques of ancient Canaanite narrative we may conclude that the same devices that served the storytellers in ancient Canaan served those in ancient Israel as well. It is true that the best of the Biblical narratives reach a level of literary sublimity that is achieved by few works from the elsewhere in the ancient Near East. Nevertheless, we shall see below that one can analyze and interpret Canaanite epic employing the same tools by which we analyze and interpret Biblical prose narrative.[23]

The corpus of ancient Canaanite narratives includes the narrative compositions from Ugarit—epic tales and mythological stories written down between the fourteenth and thirteenth centuries BCE—as well as compositions written in Akkadian that are from a literary and cultural point of view Canaanite, such as the pseudo-autobiographical tale of Idrimi, king of Alalakh in northern Syria, from the mid-fifteenth century BCE,[24] and brief and occasional episodes incorporated within the El Amarna correspondence,

---

"Afterthought and the Syntax of Relative Clauses in Biblical Hebrew," in *Text and Language in Bible and Qumran* (Jerusalem: Orient, 1960) 149. For the different types of prolepsis and analepsis in Bibical narrative, see F. Polak, *Biblical Narrative: Art and Design* (Jerusalem: Mossad Bialik, 1994) 167–91 (in Hebrew); and cf. M. Weiss, "More on the Art of Biblical Narrative," in מקראות ככוונתם (Jerusalem: Mossad Bialik, 1987) 314 with n. 8 there (in Hebrew).

19. See E. L. Greenstein, "Tales from Ugarit Solve Biblical Puzzles," *BAR* 36/6 (Nov.–Dec. 2010) 48–53, 70.

20. See my "The Canaanite Literary Heritage in Ancient Hebrew Writing," *Michmanim* 9 (1996) 19–38 (in Hebrew).

21. Compare *CTU* 1.16 vi 45–50 to Job 22:6–9; see E. L. Greenstein, "Wisdom in Ugaritic," in *Language and Nature: Papers Presented to John Huehnergard on the Occasion of His Sixtieth Birthday* (ed. R. Hasselbach and N. Pat-El; Chicago: Oriental Institute of the University of Chicago, 2012) 74–75.

22. See, e.g., S. Rummel, "Narrative Structures in the Ugaritic Texts," *RSP* 3:221–332; Parker, *The Pre-Biblical Narrative Tradition*.

23. For a full-fledged study of this type, see the still unpublished dissertation of S. Natan-Yulzary, "Narrative and Characterization in the Epic of Aqhat from Ugarit" (PhD diss., Tel Aviv University, 2010; in Hebrew); see for now her semi-popular translation and commentary: *The Aqhat Epic: An Ancient Narrative Poem from Ugarit* (Tel Aviv: Resling, 2015; in Hebrew).

24. See E. L. Greenstein, "Autobiographies in Ancient Western Asia," in *CANE* 4:2421–32.

written primarily in Syro-Canaan in the mid-fourteenth century BCE.[25] In both the Idrimi inscription and in the Amarna letters from Syro-Canaanite proveniences, one finds manifest signs of West Semitic literature as well as West Semitic language.[26] The tell-tale features indicate that the texts belong to the Canaanite culture of the late Bronze Age.

In the present discussion I will focus on three narratives as representative of the variegated and far-flung corpus of ancient Canaanite storytelling: the epics of Aqhat and of Kirta, two Ugaritic tales formulated in verse; and the pseudo-autobiography of Idrimi from Alalakh, which is very important for our purposes because it is composed in prose,[27] like many of the early Egyptian tales and like those West Semitic narratives that are included within royal inscriptions, such as the eighth century BCE Phoenician inscription of Azatiwada,[28] and the mid-ninth century BCE Moabite inscription of Mesha—these latter texts from the period of the Hebrew Bible.[29]

However, before proceeding to discuss ancient Canaanite narrative and its relationship to Biblical prose, it behooves us to address the long-entrenched scholarly tradition of contrasting the ancient Greek epics of Homer, which allegedly abound in lengthy description, and Biblical narrative, in which facts are presented without elaboration. Thus, for example, writes Chateaubriand in the eighteenth century:

> The descriptions of Homer are prolix, whether they be of pathetic or terrible character, melancholy or cheerful, energetic

---

25. Cf. W. L. Moran, *The Amarna Letters* (Baltimore: Johns Hopkins University Press, 1992) xxxii–xxxiii. Parker restricts the corpus of Ugaritic narrative poems to Aqhat and Kirta because he excludes those mythological texts that involve the gods alone. For my purposes here I take a much broader view of narrative—any sequence of actions that are related across a spectrum of time (*The Pre-Biblical Narrative Tradition*, 4); cf. N. Wyatt, "Epic in Ugaritic Literature," in *A Companion to Ancient Epic* (ed. J. M. Foley; Malden, MA: Blackwell, 2005) 246–47.

26. See, e.g., E. L. Greenstein and D. Marcus, "The Akkadian Inscription of Idrimi," *JANES* 8 (1976) esp. 62–63; A. F. Rainey, *Canaanite in the Amarna Tablets* (4 vols.; HdO 25; Leiden: Brill, 1996).

27. There is no foundation to de Moor's claim that Idrimi is written in verse; see J. C. de Moor, "The Poetry of the Book of Ruth, Part 1," in *Verse in Ancient Near Eastern Prose* (ed. J. C. de Moor and W. G. E. Watson; AOAT 42; Neukirchen: Neukirchener Verlag, 1993) 269.

28. For a rhetorical analysis, see Greenstein, "Autobiographies"; and K. L. Younger, Jr., "The Phoenician Inscription of Azatiwada: An Integrated Reading," *JSS* 43 (1998) 11–47.

29. See S. B. Parker, *Stories in Inscriptions and Scripture: Comparative Studies on Narratives in Northwest Semitic Inscriptions and the Hebrew Bible* (Oxford: Oxford University Press, 1997). Parker's study includes analysis of the Mesha inscription, pp. 44–58.

or sublime. The Bible, in all its different species of descriptions, gives in general but one single trait; but this trait is striking and distinctly exhibits the object to our view.[30]

Such a dichotomy between Homeric and Biblical narrative has been adopted by many writers dealing with ancient Hebrew storytelling.[31] Some of them assume that the manner of description in Homeric epic holds for Canaanite epic as well[32]—but that is not the case.

First, it should be remarked, elaborate description is quite uncommon in Homer. The Greek narrator tends to rest content with a concise two-phrase epithet such as "Achilles, the beloved of Zeus," or "Achilles, the fleet footed,"[33] and with relatively brief similes to add color.[34] There are, however, some long descriptions that stand out, and in looking at them one sees how different is the case of Canaanite epic. Both the Greek bard and his Ugaritic counterpart image the march of the hero's army as a movement of a horde of locusts or flies. Homer, however, describes in vivid detail:

> Like the multitudinous nations of swarming insects
> Who drive hither and thither about the stalls of the sheepfold
> In the season of spring when the milk splashes in the milk pails:
> In such numbers the flowing-haired Achaians stood up
> Through the plain against the Trojans, hearts burning to break them.[35]

This description, moreover, follows an even lengthier image comparing the Achaian army to flocks of diverse birds.

30. F. de Chateaubriand, *The Beauties of Christianity* (trans. F. Shoberl; London: Colburn, 1813) 2/2:207.

31. Biblical scholars have been excessively taken by the famous essay of E. Auerbach, "Odysseus' Scar," in *Mimesis: The Representation of Reality in Western Literature* (trans. W. Trask; Princeton: Princeton University Press, 1953) 3–23. Compare, e.g., P. Merchant, *The Epic* (London: Methuen, 1970) 9–15; and cf. Sh. D. Goitein, "אמנות הסיפור במקרא" [The Art of Biblical Narrative], in *Studies in the Bible* (Tel Aviv: Yavneh, 1957) 25 (in Hebrew); J. Licht, *Storytelling in the Bible* (Jerusalem: Magnes, 1978) 31–32; A. Berlin, *Poetics and Interpretation of Biblical Narrative* (Sheffield: Almond, 1983) 137–39.

32. E.g., Sh. Talmon, דרכי הסיפור במקרא (Jerusalem: Hebrew University, 1965) 32.

33. Cf., e.g., G. S. Kirk, *Homer and the Epic* (Cambridge: Cambridge University Press, 1965) 4; C. M. Bowra, *Homer* (London: Duckworth, 1972) 18–24. With respect to epithets, the Ugaritic epics can be compared; cf., e.g., W. Burkert, "Near Eastern Connections [to Greek Epic]," in *A Companion to Ancient Epic* (ed. J. M. Foley; Malden, MA: Blackwell, 2005) 297.

34. See, e.g., Bowra, *Homer*, 60–66.

35. *The Iliad of Homer* (trans. R. Lattimore; Chicago: University of Chicago Press, 1961) 88 (book 2, lines 469–73).

By contrast, the narrator in the Ugaritic epic of Kirta describes a forced march of the entire population of Kirta's town using a single, concise image:

> Like a locust swarm, they inhabit the steppe;
> Like crickets, the desert's edge (*CTU* 1.14 iv 29–31).[36]

This figure more resembles several similar images in Biblical prose than it does the Homeric description that was cited above.[37] The image in Kirta also harks back to the beginning of the passage, in which the narrator merely hints at the figuration of the king's army as a swarm of locusts. There (lines 17–18) he relates:

> They march by the thousand, in rows,
> In myriads, by rank arrayed.[38]

The language recalls the description of a locust swarm in Prov 30:27: "Locusts have no king, / Yet they all advance arrayed." The use of an apparently cognate verb in Kirta (Heb. חצץ = Ugar. *ḥdd*) evokes the same image, especially once one hears the explicit imagery in the lines that follow. After opening the passage with the merest hint of an image, the narrator shifts to an entirely prosaic discourse: "After two, two more march; / After three, all of them" (lines 19–20).[39]

The poet has still not developed the image to which he began alluding at the outset. On the contrary, he enumerates the participants in the march, and, instead of simply saying that the entire population of the town was mobilized—the elderly, women, and apparently children as well (who would watch them were they to remain home?)—or instead of making use of a merism such as "from your cutter of trees to your drawer of water" (Deut 29:10), which resembles a literary topos serving the poet in a nearby context,[40] he

---

36. E. L. Greenstein, "Kirta," in *Ugaritic Narrative Poetry* (ed. S. B. Parker; SBLWAW 9; Atlanta: Scholars, 1997) 19.

37. See, e.g., Judg 6:5, 7:11; and cf. Parker, *The Pre-Biblical Narrative Tradition*, 152. On the comparison of an army to a swarm of locusts in ancient Near Eastern and Biblical literature, see J. A. Thompson, "Joel's Locusts in the Light of Near Eastern Parallels," *JNES* 14 (1955) 52–55.

38. Greenstein, "Kirta," 19. For the interpretation, see H. L. Ginsberg, *The Legend of King Keret: A Canaanite Epic of the Bronze Age* (BASORSup 2–3; New Haven: American Schools for Oriental Research, 1946) 37. Scholars who interpret *ḥdd* and *yr* (dividing *kmyr* into *km yr* in spite of the lack of a word divider) fail to understand that in ancient Canaanite poetry (which is for the most part the Hebrew Bible) rain is used figuratively not of something that occurs in abundance but of something that occurs in due season.

39. Greenstein, "Kirta," 19.

40. Kirta (*CTU* 1.14) iii 7–10: "Sweep from the well the women drawing water, / From the spring, the women filling jars!" (Greenstein, "Kirta," 16; cf. also iv 51–52

specifies a number of types within the population of King Kirta who would ordinarily be exempted from military duty—but not in this instance.[41] The roster includes the only son of his mother, the widow who hires on as a soldier, the ill who is carried in bed, the blind who finds his way by blinking.[42] Even the bridegroom, who is customarily exempted from service (cf. Deut 20:7; 24:5), is counted. The narrator develops the hyperbole in this detail and amuses the audience by expanding on the bridegroom's enthusiasm in leaving his bride to join the king's campaign: "To another man he drives his wife; / To a stranger, his own true love" (*CTU* 1.14 iv 27-28).[43] The poet, then, begins his list of participants with the simplest case—the only son who is capable of fighting but is exempted as a rule; moves on to the more serious cases—such as a blind man who is normally not conscripted; and then adds the comical case of a groom who cuts his ties with his bride—whom he explicitly loves—in order to take part in the campaign.

There is a double irony in this scene. The poet's language and the words "bridegroom" (*trḫ*) and "wife" (*aṯt*) allude to a scene near the beginning of the epic in which we are told of the death of Kirta's first wife and the grief he suffered over her loss (*CTU* 1.14 i 12-15, 26-35). By divorcing his beloved wife, the new bridegroom, who joins the king's campaign, recapitulates Kirta's loss. Moreover, because the purpose of Kirta's great march is to obtain a new wife who will be suitable for him, the bridegroom is, in a real sense, sacrificing his own wife for the sake of the king—like a poor man who would slaughter his only ewe for the sake of his liege. Such a personal sacrifice is extreme, of a piece with the sense of the entire passage. The hyperbolic

---

(ibid., 20). Compare too Josh 9:21, 23, 27; and see E. L. Greenstein, "YHWH's Lightning in Psalm 29:7," *Maarav* 8 (1992) 52.

41. *CTU* 1.14 ii 43-50; iv 21-28. See esp. J. Finkel, "The Expedition of the Ugaritan King Keret in the Light of Jewish and Kindred Traditions," *Proceedings of the American Academy for Jewish Research* 23 (1954) 1-28.

42. For the interpretation of the verb *mzl* "to blink," compare *rmz* in Rabbinic Hebrew, in Targumic Aramaic, and in Arabic; e.g., A. Kohut, הערוך השלם (repr.: Jerusalem: Makor, 1969) 7:280. Ginsberg compares Rabbinic Hebrew *pzl* (*Legend of King Keret*, 38).

43. Concerning the evident hyperboles in this passage, see, e.g., W. G. E. Watson, "An Unrecognized Hyperbole in Krt," *Orientalia* 48 (1979) 112-17. Elsewhere Watson says he has difficulty accepting the general understanding of this passage, according to which the new bridegroom leaves his wife in the hands of another because, if all the men of the town participate in Kirta's march, there will be no one to receive the abandoned bride; see his "Ugaritic and Mesopotamian Literary Texts," *UF* 9 (1977) 278. One may answer Watson's objection by recalling that in legendary literature such as this, such precisely logical considerations are not maintained. For example, in Genesis 4 Cain expresses his fear of being killed by another man, but according to that narrative, there are no other men who could do so.

description of Kirta's all-encompassing army, of course, underscores the importance of the central concern of the epic: the acquisition of a wife who could produce an heir to the throne.

Elias Canetti, a Nobel laureate in literature, wrote that the Greeks favored the eye whereas the Hebrew favored the ear.[44] If this generalization carries any merit, it should be clear that Canaanite epic belongs to the tradition favoring the ear; there is little regard for the eye. As in Biblical narrative there is virtually no description for its own sake; every description touches on and meshes with a theme of the story at hand.

The point is even clearer in the Canaanite narrative prose represented by the so-called autobiography of Idrimi. There, there is no superfluous description. The first-person narrator relates, for example, that he "spent a night" among the nomadic Sutu people "in the midst of my covered chariot" (lines 13–17).[45] If this reading of the text is correct,[46] the construction of the chariot is what enables the hero to spend the night in it. The significance of this detail becomes evident as the story further unfolds (see further below). There is only one seemingly superfluous visual description in the epic of Kirta. The narrator describes the future princess bride of Kirta with only one detail. He compares her eyes to the precious stones representing the eyes of the goddess in her sculpted likeness (*CTU* 1.14 iii 41–44; vi 26–30).[47] Homer, too, is wont to describe goddesses concisely by characterizing their eyes, e.g., "Lady Hera, the ox-eyed" (i.e., having large eyes) and "Athena, the blue-eyed." Such descriptions recall the exceptional mention of the Biblical narrator in Gen 29:17: "Now Leah's eyes were soft but Rachel was fair of form and fair of looks." In the Jacob story this detail goes far in explaining the patriarch's special love for her.

The description of the bride's eyes in Kirta is no less significant in deepening the sense of the narrative.[48] The comparisons between the eyes of

---

44. See S. Sontag, "Mind as Passion," in *Under the Sign of Saturn* (London: Vintage, 1996) 196.

45. For the reading and interpretation, see Greenstein and Marcus, "Idrimi," 64, 73.

46. Oller reads this way but hesitates to translate; G. H. Oller, "The Autobiography of Idrimi" (Ph.D. diss., University of Pennsylvania, 1977) 34–35. Dietrich and Loretz read differently; M. Dietrich and O. Loretz, "Die Inschrift der Statue des Königs Idrimi von Alalaḫ," *UF* 13 (1981) 213.

47. Cf. I. Engnell, "The Figurative Language of the Old Testament," in *A Rigid Scrutiny: Critical Essays on the Old Testament by Ivan Engnell* (ed. and trans. J. T. Willis; Nashville: Vanderbilt University Press, 1969) 254. For the text and translation, see Greenstein, "Kirta," 17, 23.

48. See E. L. Greenstein, "The Role of the Reader in Ugaritic Narrative," in *"A Wise and Discerning Mind": Essays in Honor of Burke O. Long* (ed. S. M. Olyan and R. C. Culley; Brown Judaic Studies 325; Providence: Brown University Press, 2000) 150–51.

the bride and the eyes of the goddess are placed in the speech of the patron god, El (*'Ilu*). This El, the old man of the pantheon, is revealed to be a father figure by the fact that he compares the eyes of the king's future bridge to two goddesses who are younger than he: Anath and Ashtarte (*'attartu*). The comparison expresses the male perspective of the paternal deity. On the other hand, the supernatural beauty of the bride destined for Kirta helps account for the reluctance of her compatriots, the citizens of Udum, to let her go. When she actually leaves Udum, the poet adds to his description of her outer beauty a detail that epitomizes her inner beauty: "The hungry she'd take by the hand,/ The thirsty she'd take by the hand" (*CTU* 1.15 i 2).[49] This detail characterizes the future bride by way of her behavior and at the same time explains the sadness suffered by her father, the King of Udum.

In Canaanite narrative the epithets attached to the protagonists' names convey thematic meaning. In the epic of Kirta, for example, the god El is first presented as "The Father of Humanity" (*ab adm*; *CTU* 1.14 i 37). This epithet signifies the relationship of this god to humanity in general and to the miserable king in particular. El reacts to the king's pain and descends to him in a dream to give him courage and direction on how to overcome his severe personal loss. When El addresses Kirta and asks how he is faring, he calls him "the pleasant one" (*n'mn*), one who has it well (ibid. line 40). Like Naomi in the Bible, whose name does not suit her at the beginning of the action, as she herself points out (Ruth 1:21), but who in the course of the narrative comes to conform to her given name, so does Kirta in his story reach a situation in which his name, "the pleasant," is appropriate. In the same encounter the god El addresses Kirta with another epithet—"Lad of El" (*ġlm il*; ibid. lines 40–41). This moniker seems calculated to boost the king by suggesting that he is not too old to venture out on a campaign, to acquire a new wife, and to produce additional sons and daughters. His virility is intact.

In the prose tale of Idrimi as well epithets carry significance. In the inscription's opening Idrimi introduces himself in a relatively curious fashion: instead of making use of the customary epithet, "the king," he characterizes himself as the "servant" (*abdu*) of the various gods. This characterization reflects the themes and perhaps even one of the main objectives of the text. For example, Idrimi attributes his ability to return to and conquer the land from which he fled years before to his restoration by the storm-god Teshub (lines 28–30).[50] Near the end of the inscription, where Idrimi recounts his achievements in the city of Alalakh, he enumerates the innovations he

---

49. Greenstein, "Kirta," 24.
50. See, e.g., Greenstein and Marcus, "Idrimi," 64–66; Oller, "Autobiography," 9–18.

made in the local cult and mentions his son Teshub-nirari, whom he had appointed to oversee the cult (lines 87–91); but does not mention his son Niqmepa, who inherited the kingship from him, even though the latter is far more important from a historical perspective.[51]

Furthermore, Idrimi describes the Mittani king Barattarna using the epithet "the strong (or legitimate) king" (*šarru dannu*; line 51). Although this is a conventional epithet for a great king, in this context the moniker takes on special significance. Idrimi explains that he ascended the throne of Alalakh with the support of "the strong king" Barattarna, but he also explains that it was by the power of "the strong king" that he was prevented from returning to north Syria (lines 42–44). When the narrator asserts that "the strong king" enabled Idrimi to take the throne after hearing about the "strong covenant" (*māmīta danna*) that was made between his ancestors and Idrimi's (lines 49ff.), he seems to be creating a word-play on the order of a name-midrash, a widespread phenomenon in Biblical Hebrew literature.[52]

The appositive that Idrimi uses repeatedly for the city of Alalakh, "my city" (*ālīya*), is superfluous with regard to content but is meaningful within the inscription. On account of a terrible event—which is never specified, but almost certainly involved a takeover by Mitanni and the execution of the king, Idrimi's father (see below)—Idrimi and his brothers fled from their native Aleppo and stayed with relatives to the east in the city of Emar. Idrimi continued alone—or almost alone (he took a servant)—to the land of Canaan. The story structure very much resembles the narratives of various "fugitive heroes" (as I call them) in the ancient Near East and especially in the Hebrew Bible, stories such as those of Jacob, Moses, and David.[53] For

---

51. See, e.g., Greenstein and Marcus, "Idrimi," 92; Oller, "Autobiography," 118, 154–55. For Niqmepa as Idrimi's successor, see ibid., 152–54; E. von Dassow, *State and Society in the Late Bronze Age: Alalaḫ under the Mitanni Empire* (Studies on the Civilization and Culture of Nuzi and the Hurrians 17; Bethesda, MD: CDL Press, 2008) 45–64. My work on the "fugitive hero pattern," to which Idrimi's story belongs, shows that the establishment or renewal of a cult or cultic practice is crucial; see E. L. Greenstein, "The Fugitive Hero Narrative Pattern in Mesopotamia," in *Worship, Women, and War: Studies in Honor of Susan Niditch* (ed. J. J. Collins, T. M. Lemos, and S. M. Olyan; Brown Judaic Studies 357; Atlanta: Society of Biblical Literature, 2015) 17–34.

52. See, e.g., M. Garsiel, *Biblical Names: A Literary Study of Midrashic Derivations and Puns* (trans. P. Hackett; Ramat Gan: Bar-Ilan University Press, 1991). For similar name-play in Ugaritic epic, see M. O'Connor, "The Human Characters' Names in the Ugaritic Poems: Onomastic Eccentricity in Bronze-Age West Semitic and the Name Daniel in Particular," in *Biblical Hebrew in Its Northwest Semitic Setting: Typological and Historical Perspectives* (ed. S. E. Fassberg and A. Hurvitz; Winona Lake, IN: Eisenbrauns, 2006) 269–83.

53. Several of the parallels have been pointed out for decades, but for the most specific study, and the most comprehensive bibliography to date, see now Greenstein,

seven years (evidently a round number)[54] Idrimi wanted desperately to return home and claim his legacy. But when he realized he could not conquer Aleppo, which was located east of Alalakh and was probably governed directly by Mitanni, Idrimi adopted Alalakh as his city and home. For that reason Idrimi keeps referring to it as "my city."[55]

The theme of being forced away from home and then returning home plays a central role in the story of Idrimi.[56] The theme is highlighted by means of two leading words, the noun *bītu*, "house," and the verb *ašābu*, "to dwell."[57] In his classic article on the leading word (*Leitwort*) as a literary device, Buber explains this function: "A connection is established between one passage and another, and thus between one stage of the story and another—a connection that articulates the deep motive of the narrated event more immediately than could a pinned-on moral."[58] An excellent example is adduced by Bar-Efrat in 2 Sam 7.[59] The chapter opens by indicating that King David dwells (ישב) in a "house (בית) of cedar wood" while the Ark of YHWH who "had relieved him of his enemies all around . . . dwells inside a tent" (vv. 1–2). The king seeks authorization from the prophet Nathan to construct a "house" for YHWH. That night YHWH reveals himself to Nathan, telling him: "For I have not dwelt in a house from the day I brought Israel up out of Egypt until this day" (v. 6). In spite of this, YHWH consents to David's proposal so long as his son, and not he, builds him the house. In exchange for this house, YHWH will fortify his kingdom and raise up for him a "house" or another kind: "YHWH has told you that he will make for you a house (i.e., dynasty)" (v. 11). The prophet reiterates: "Your house and your kingdom will be established for you forever" (v. 16). The leading word "house" has three senses in this passage: a. the king's palace; b. the future temple; and c. the royal dynasty. By means of the leading word the narrator suggests a thematic relationship among the three "houses."

"Fugitive Hero."

54. See Greenstein and Marcus, "Idrimi," 77–78.

55. Greenstein, "Autobiographies," 2425–26.

56. This theme plays a role in classical Greek literature as well, of course; see, e.g., M. Alexopoulou, *The Theme of Returning Home in Ancient Greek Literature: The Nostos of the Epic Heroes* (Lewiston, NY: Mellen, 2009). However, Greek stories like Homer's *Odyssey* do not have the specific features of the "fugitive hero" pattern that the stories of Idrimi and several other ancient Near Eastern narratives do.

57. Alexopoulou, *The Theme of Returning Home*.

58. M. Buber, "*Leitwort* Style in Pentateuch Narrative," in M. Buber and F. Rosenzweig, *Scripture and Translation* (trans. L. Rosenwald with E. Fox; Indiana Studies in Biblical Literature; Bloomington: Indiana University Press, 1994) 115.

59. Sh. Bar-Efrat, העיצוב האמנותי של הסיפור במקרא [The Artful Shaping of Biblical Narrative] (Tel Aviv: Sifriat Poalim, 1979) 19.

The leading words "house" and "dwell" (see above), cognate to the Biblical terms used in the passage about David and Nathan, serve the narrator of Idrimi's story in a similar way. Once the hero, Idrimi, returns from his exile in Canaan and conquers his homeland in north Syria through an alliance with Barattarna, his Hurrian overlord, he remarks (lines 54–56) that he "restored to him" (Barattarna) "a lost house." The restoration of a lost house is very important to Idrimi. Once he completes his military campaigns, he will use the spoil he looted to build himself "a house"—a palace (lines 78–80). Building the palace is the very first civic project he undertakes. The permanent house he erects in Alalakh, his adopted city, stands in stark contrast to the temporary shelter in which he lodged among the Sutu—his "covered chariot" (see above). The chariot's narratological function as the symbol of Idrimi's homelessness in exile is reinforced by the verb that is used to relate his stay among the Sutu—*bītāku*, "I spent the night." The verb is of the same root as the word for house, *bītu*. In the course of the story the hero moves from an unfit house to a "house" deserving of the name.

The significance of the leading word "house" becomes even clearer once we consider the other recurrent word in the inscription, the verb "to dwell" (*ašābu*). This verb appears in the Idrimi story in three different senses: to dwell, to reside; to spend time, to stay, somewhere; and to be situated in a place. The last meaning is influenced by West Semitic usage, for in Akkadian the notion of being situated is expressed by the verb *šakānu* (cognate to Heb. שכן) and not by *ašābu* (cognate to Heb. ישב). Accordingly, we find in the inscription the following statement: "The town of Ammiya is situated (*ašbu*) in the land of Canaan" (lines 19–20).[60]

In the first part of his narrative, Idrimi relates how he fled from Aleppo and "stayed" in four different locations. Regarding the first and last of these he employs the verb *ašābu* (lines 5–8, 27–28). The hero exhibits his distress at having to sojourn in strange places far from home, even though he found there other refugees from his homeland, who paid him respect and appointed him their leader. Later, after establishing his kingship in Alalakh, he reports on only one beneficence that he performed for his people: "The inhabitants (lit., dwellers) who were in my land I made to dwell securely (lit., dwell a secure dwelling), and even those who did not have a dwelling (lit., a dwelling did not dwell), I settled (lit., made to dwell)" (lines 84–86).[61] The stem *ašābu* occurs six times in this sentence. It is true that other kings pride themselves on finding a home for the populations they govern, but

---

60. See Greenstein and Marcus, "Idrimi," 74. For the parallel use of ישב to indicate the situation of a city in Biblical Hebrew, see, e.g., Ezek 16:46; Nah 3:8.

61. Greenstein and Marcus, "Idrimi," 67–68.

for them this is only one of the public services they record. Idrimi thinks of nothing else. It seems clear that he emphasizes the settling of his people in secure locations because he himself suffered dislocation for many years. The hero compelled to wander builds a permanent residence for himself and finds homes for all his people.

Buber writes: "The *Leitwort* rhythm is a genuinely epic rhythm."[62] Nevertheless, this "rhythm" is not only epic; it characterizes both Canaanite and Biblical narrative, whether it is composed in verse or in prose.

As Idrimi prepares for the return to his homeland and to the restoration of the home from which he had been severed, he reveals his intentions by expressing them. While he was staying with his older brothers in Emar, with family, he says that he "was thinking (things) no one (of them) was thinking":

> (Thus) said I: "One who [seeks?] the house of his father is the foremost, great son, and one who [stays] among the sons of the city of Emar is a servant" (lines 7–12).[63]

The narrator's penetration of the protagonist's psyche, by means of direct discourse, is very important to my argument because, in contrast to the Greek bard, the Biblical narrator only rarely reveals a character's thinking directly, and even then, it is usually done in abbreviated form.[64] Some good illustrations are found in the story of the rape of Dinah (Genesis 34),[65] where it is explicitly stated that Shechem son of Hamor "loved the maiden" (v. 3) and Jacob's sons spoke to Shechem and his father "with guile" because Shechem had "profaned their sister Dinah" (v. 13). It is also related there that Shechem promptly agreed to the terms set by Jacob and his sons "because he was desirous of Jacob's daughter" (v. 19).

The description of the protagonist's psyche in Homeric epic tends to be far more elaborate. The following example is not unusual:

> And Achilles took no joy at all when he saw them.
> These two terrified and in awe of the king stood waiting

---

62. Buber, "*Leitwort* Style," 116.

63. For the text, see Greenstein and Marcus, "Idrimi," 64; for the translation, Greenstein, "Autobiographies," 2426. Note that Idrimi's direct discourse is formulated in parallelism, in a manner that anticipates a widespread phenomenon in Biblical narrative as well; see E. L. Greenstein, "Direct Discourse and Parallelism," in *Discourse, Dialogue and Debate in the Bible: Essays in Honour of Frank Polak* (ed. A. Brenner and F. Polak; Hebrew Bible Monographs 63; Sheffield: Sheffield Phoenix, 2014) 79–91.

64. See, e.g., Bar-Efrat, *Artful Shaping*, 48–53; Sternberg, *Poetics of Biblical Narrative*, 191.

65. See, e.g., Sternberg, *Poetics of Biblical Narrative*, 447.

quietly, and did not speak a word at all nor question him.
But he knew the whole matter in his own heart, and spoke first.[66]

Such an exposure of the character's interior is rare in Biblical narrative. We do encounter it, however, in the story of Dinah (Gen 34:7):

> Now when they heard, Jacob's sons came in from the field; the men were aggrieved and very angry, for someone had done a perverse act in Israel, laying down with a daughter of Jacob, and such must never be done.

This description is a departure from the habits of the Biblical narrator, who tends to delineate the inner life of the characters by way of their external behaviors. The Biblical norm, however, conforms to the conventions of Ugaritic epic, where only rarely are a protagonist's thoughts externalized. The Ugaritic storyteller, like his Hebrew counterpart, tends to confine himself to such brief indications as: "Anat laughed out loud, / but inwardly she plotted" (*CTU* 1.17 vi 41–42";[67] "Yassib, too, sits in the palace, / and his spirit instructs him this way" (to say what he is about to say; *CTU* 1.16 vi 25–26).[68]

The Canaanite bard is wont to reveal the inner life of his characters by describing their outer behavior even more than his literary heir, the Biblical storyteller. In order to portray fear, tranquility, or joy, the Canaanite poet makes use of fairly fixed topoi, which relate to the physical expressions of those emotions.[69] Like the Biblical narrator, the Canaanite storyteller reveals his character's thoughts and feelings by indirection, employing a variety of strategies.[70] Like the first-person narrator in the Idrimi inscription, and like the Biblical narrator as well,[71] the Canaanite bard exposes the inner life of his characters by directly reporting their speech. The protagonists articulate

---

66. *The Iliad of Homer*, 68 (book one, lines 330–333).

67. Parker, "Aqhat," 62; and see S. Natan-Yulzary, "Divine Justice or Poetic Justice? The Transgression and Punishment of the Goddess 'Anat in the 'Aqhat Story: A Literary Perspective," *UF* 41 (2009) 583.

68. Text and translation in Greenstein, "Kirta," 40. See the notes there (p. 47) for the reading *g<n>gnh* and its interpretation as "spirit" (lit., "throat").

69. For a summary, see, e.g., Parker, *Pre-Biblical Narrative Tradition*, 18–26. For a classic detailed study, see D. R. Hillers, "A Convention in Hebrew Literature: The Reaction to Bad News," *ZAW* 77 (1965) 86–90. Cf., e.g., G. del Olmo Lete, "Frases y formulas ugaritico-hebreas," in *Mélanges bibliques et orientaux au l'honneur de M. Mathias Delcor* (AOAT 215; Neukirchen-Vluyn: Neukirchener, 1985), 79–95.

70. For the range of devices employed by the Biblical narrator, see Polak, *Biblical Narrative*, 270–78.

71. See, e.g., Bar-Efrat, *Artful Shaping*, 89–99.

their feelings aloud, like singers in an opera. When, for example, the Ugaritic poet relates that the righteous judge Danel wants desperately to bring down the vultures flying above so that he can cut open their bellies and see if there are any remnants of his son Aqhat in them, he has Danel cry out (*CTU* 1.19 iii 30–34):

> Let Baal break (the vulture) Samal's wings, / Let Baal break her pinions,
> So she falls beneath my feet.
> I'll split her belly and look: / If there's fat, / <if> there's bone.[72]

The thoughts of the characters are provided by the Canaanite narrator, as by his Hebrew colleague,[73] by describing the scene from the character's point of view. Idrimi, for example, relates that many refugees from his homeland gathered to him "when they saw that I was the son of their lord" (lines 24–26).[74] In the Ugaritic epic of Kirta, the poet does not come out and say that the king realized that his children and dynasty had been lost; rather, the narrator relates this by giving expression to the king's point of view: "He sees his progeny, Kirta, / He sees his progeny ruined, / His dynasty utterly destroyed" (*CTU* 1.14 i 21–23).[75]

The Canaanite epic poet, like the Biblical narrator, as was said, describes the inner life of characters by means of their outward actions.[76] A choice illustration may be found in the continuation of the Kirta narrative. After the bard has related that, from the hero's point of view, he seems to have no legacy, he shows us, from his own perspective, how deeply this perception troubles the king. He achieves this through a detailed delineation of Kirta's actions (*CTU* 1.14 i 26–32):

> He enters his chamber, he cries; / An inner alcove (?), and weeps.
> His tears are poured forth
> Like shekels on the ground, / Like five-weights on the couch.
> As he cries, he falls asleep; / As he weeps, there's slumber.[77]

---

72. Parker, "Aqhat," 73–74.

73. See, e.g., Berlin, *Poetics and Interpretation*, 43–82.

74. Text in Greenstein and Marcus, "Idrimi," 64; trans. Greenstein, "Autobiographies," 2426.

75. Greenstein, "Kirta," 12. Cf. F. Polak, "Some Aspects of Literary Design in the Ancient Near Eastern Epic," in *Kinattūtu ša dārâti: Raphael Kutscher Memorial Volume* (Tel Aviv: Tel Aviv University Institute of Archaeology, 1993) 140–41.

76. See, e.g., Bar-Efrat, *Artful Shaping*, 99–107.

77. Greenstein, "Kirta," 13.

The king keeps crying until he falls asleep. The meaning of this sequence is clear.

The Canaanite poet describes the characters' state of mind in even subtler ways. In the Aqhat Epic, after Aqhat is born, the crafts god brings him an extraordinarily unique bow as a gift. Once the hero has grown, the goddess Anath, goddess of love and war, confronts him and demands that he give her the bow. At first, the goddess speaks brusqely:

> Attend, now, [Aqhat the Hero].
> Ask me for silver—I'll give it, / [For gold and I'll end]ow you:
> Give [Anat the Girl] your bow, / The sister of LIMM your arrows (*CTU* 1.17 vi 16–19).[78]

The hero does not immediately refuse. Instead, he enumerates the special features of his bow and suggests that the goddess order another bow from the crafts god. One may reasonably surmise that the goddess is frustrated and enraged; but instead of describing her state of mind directly, and instead of representing it by means of her physical responses, the narrator alludes to it by elaborating her rhetoric:

> Anat the Girl answers:
> Ask for life, Aqhat the Hero,
> Ask for life, and I'll give it, / Deathlessness—I'll endow you.
> I'll let you count years with Baal, / Count months with the offspring of El.
> As Baal revives, then invites, / Invites the revived to drink,
> Trills and sings over him, / With pleasant tune they respond;
> So I'll revive Aqhat the Hero. (*CTU* 1.17 i 25–33)[79]

One may interpret that in the wake of her initial failure and her frustration, Anath adopts a more expansive and sympathetic rhetorical ploy. The narrator need not divulge the goddess's thinking explicitly because he can represent it indirectly, by way of the character's discourse. The audience completes the picture with the aid of the strokes the poet supplies.[80]

Literary theorists like Meir Sternberg remark upon the Biblical narrator's tendency to leave gaps in the text under the assumption, or the conventional understanding, that the reader will fill them in the course

---

78. Parker, "Aqhat," 60.
79. Ibid., 61.
80. See Greenstein, "Role of the Reader."

of reading.[81] Because the motives and intentions of the characters remain implicit in the literary work but emerge in the imagination of the audience, characters often appear to be round, complex, and sometimes even opaque. Following the famous essay of Erich Auerbach, "Odysseus' Scar,"[82] many scholars maintain that the Biblical narrator delves deeply into the psyche of the protagonists, in contrast to the narrator of Greek epic, who does not develop the actors in the narrative—their behavior is fixed and consistent.[83]

It must be admitted that the protagonists in Canaanite epic do not undergo much transformation in the course of a narrative; but that does not mean that they are flat. In not a few instances it is difficult to divine the motives and intentions of the leading characters, and it is difficult to anticipate their actions and sometimes to understand them. There is irony, for example, in the fact that King Kirta, who bewails his loss of children at the beginning of the epic, winds up bittterly cursing his elder son, the presumed heir to the throne, at the end of the epic (or of what remains of it).[84] Kirta asks a god of destruction to smash his son's head (*CTU* 1.16 vi 54–58). Moreover, the same pious monarch, who took pains to follow the instructions of the father-god El and even adds to them a vow of his own, forgets to fulfill the vow and is severely punished.[85]

Gaps like these, so common in Biblical narrative, are found in early Canaanite narrative, too, albeit less abundantly. Idrimi does not indicate the reasons for which he was compelled to flee his birthplace, Aleppo. He does not spell out what "evil" event (line 4) took place that set him on his flight.[86] A clue to the missing details can be found further on in the story, when the narrator remarks that he "stayed for seven years" "in the midst of the troops of the 'Apiru" (lines 27–28) and that "for seven years Barattarna, the mighty king, king of the troops of Hurri, was hostile toward" him (lines 42–44).[87]

81. Sternberg, *Poetics of Biblical Narrative*; and see the additional literature referenced in Greenstein, "Role of the Reader."

82. See n. 31 above.

83. For a contrary view of Homeric narrative, see, e.g., Kirk, *Homer and the Epic*, 97–101.

84. Cf., e.g., G. Hens-Piazza, "Repetition and Rhetoric in Canaanite Epic: A Close Reading of *KTU* 1.14 III 20–49," *UF* 24 (1992) 103.

85. See E. L. Greenstein, "Wisdom in Ugaritic," in *Language and Nature: Papers Presented to John Huehnergard on the Occasion of His Sixtieth Birthday* (ed. R. Hasselbach and N. Pat-El; Studies in Ancient Oriental Civilization 67; Chicago: Oriental Institute of the University of Chicago, 2012) 78–79. For thematic ambiguity in Kirta, see G. N. Knoppers, "Dissonance and Disaster in the Legend of Kirta," *JAOS* 114 (1994) 572–82.

86. Greenstein and Marcus, "Idrimi," 64; translation of Greenstein, "Autobiographies," 2426.

87. See Oller, "Autobiography," 205.

One may well put two and two together and conclude that these seven years are identical to those seven years. In that case, it was Barattarna who had attacked and overtaken Aleppo, probably slaying the king, Idrimi's father, in the process. In the wake of that onslaught, Idrimi and his brothers fled to a more secure location, and Idrimi remained in exile until he found an occasion to collaborate with Barattarna as an ally.[88]

An even more mysterious gap in Ugaritic narrative surrounds the making of Kirta's vow in the course of his march to Udum.[89] Until that point the king had followed the god El's instructions to the letter.[90] Yet, in the middle of his campaign to fetch his bride, he stops at the shrine of the goddess Asherah. Kirta enters and unpredictably vows that if he may have the princess of Udum for his own, he would donate a statue of her, two parts in silver and a third part in gold.[91] The vow attains a great deal of significance later on in the epic, when Kirta forgets to fulfill the vow and is afflicted with a near-fatal illness by the goddess (see above). The fatefulness of the vow piques an inordinate interest in Kirta's motive for having made it. Did he do it out of enthusiasm or a surfeit of piety? Did he perhaps approach Asherah, the consort of the patron god El, because he did not fully count on the counsel and/or power of the elderly god? The motive is an intriguing gap a serious audience would want to fill in.

If we recall the description of the princess bride's eyes, another explanation may come to mind. El had likened the face of the bridge to the image of a goddess sculpted in a statue. It makes sense that when Kirta entered the shrine of the goddess Asherah, where an image of the goddess surely stood, he would have thought of the image of his bride-to-be, causing him a flush of excitement and leading him almost uncontrollably to utter a vow.[92] The fact that the vow takes the form of the gift of a statue reinforces this interpretation (he was shown a statue-like image, he encountered a statue, he vowed a statue).

---

88. Greenstein, "Autobiographies," 2425.

89. See Greenstein, "Role of the Reader," 150–51. For the text (*CTU* 1.14 iv 31–43) and translation, see Greenstein, "Kirta," 19–20.

90. On Kirta's deviation from divine instruction, see S. E. Loewenstamm, "On the Theology of the Keret-Epic," in *From Babylon to Canaan: Studies in the Bible and Its Oriental Background* (Jerusalem: Magnes, 1992) 185–200; E. Greenstein, "The Ugaritic Epic of Kirta in a Wisdom Perspective," *Te'uda* 16–17 (2001) 1–13 (in Hebrew).

91. See T. W. Cartledge, *Vows in the Hebrew Bible and the Ancient Near East* (JSOTSup 147; Sheffield: Sheffield Academic, 1992) 111; S. B. Parker, "The Ancient Near Eastern Background of the Old Testament," in *NIB* 1:239.

92. So T. H. Gaster, *The Oldest Stories in the World* (New York: Viking, 1952) 194.

In bringing this essay to a close, I would observe that without illustrating every one of the devices of the Biblical narrator in both the prose and verse of ancient Canaanite narrative, I have, I believe, compared a sufficient number to sustain the thesis that in spite of the formal difference between Canaanite epic and Biblical prose narrative, the two bodies of literature share not only similar contents, language, and phrasing, but more sophisticated narratological techniques as well.[93] Canaanite narrative can, and I would add should, be read using the same literary tools by which we read Biblical Hebrew narrative.

I do not mean to belittle the blatant differences in form between the epic poetry and prose narrative.[94] Nevertheless, we have seen that the differences between ancient Canaanite epic and Biblical prose narrative are not nearly as distinctive as the differences between Homeric epic, on the one side, and Canaanite epic and Biblical prose, on the other.[95] Biblical prose narrative operates along similar lines to both Ugaritic epic and the prose narrative of Idrimi. It is an outgrowth of the Canaanite literary tradition, just as Cassuto had presciently discerned.[96]

---

93. For in-depth and broad analysis of the many devices of characterization in Ugaritic epic, similar to the wide range found in Biblical prose, see S. Natan-Yulzary, "Characterization in the Epic of Kirta from Ugarit" (MA thesis, Tel Aviv University, 2005; in Hebrew); S. Natan-Yulzary, "Narration and Characterization in the Epic of Aqhat." For an excellent study of contrast in Ugaritic epic, analogous to the use of contrast in Biblical narrative, see S. Natan-Yulzary, "Contrast and Meaning in the 'Aqhat Story," *VT* 62 (2012) 443–49.

94. See my "Direct Discourse and Parallelism." On the other hand, there is, I have suggested, a parallel between the use of the Ugaritic present-future *yaqtulu* verb form to relate foregrounded action and the past *qatala* verb form to indicate backgrounded action, on the one hand, and the contrast between the Hebrew *wa-yiqtol* preterite and *qatal* past tense to indicate foreground and background, respectively, in Biblical prose, on the other hand; see my "Forms and Functions of the Finite Verb in Ugaritic Narrative Verse," in *Biblical Hebrew in Its Northwest Semitic Setting*, esp. 91–102.

95. In saying this, I take issue with Gordon, who contended that Ugaritic epic constitutes a bridge between classical Greek epic and Biblical narrative; see C. H. Gordon, *The Common Background of the Greek and Hebrew Civilizations* (New York: Norton, 1965), esp. 128–205. For a critique of Gordon's approach, see P. Walcot, "The Comparative Study of Ugaritic and Greek Literatures," *UF* 1 (1969) 111–18.

96. Cf. the conclusions of S. Natan-Yulzary, e.g., "Divine Justice or Poetic Justice?: The Transgression and Punishment of the Goddess 'Anat in the 'Aqhat Story," *UF* 41 (2009) 595 [581–99].

2

Baal as Warrior-King in the Baal Cycle[1]

MARK S. SMITH

INTRODUCTION

As Simon B. Parker's work beautifully explicated, at the heart of the Ugaritic corpus lie four major works of Ugaritic poetic narrative: (1) the Baal Cycle

---

1. *Author's note*: For decades Simon B. Parker was a leader in Ugaritic and biblical studies. Beginning with his 1967 dissertation on the grammar of Ugaritic prose texts ("Studies in the Grammar of Ugaritic Prose Texts" [Ph.D. diss., Johns Hopkins University, 1967]), his works were models of precision as well as insight. His book, *The Pre-Biblical Narrative Tradition: Essays on the Ugaritic Poems Keret and Aqhat* (SBLRBS 24; Atlanta: Scholars, 1989), remains a landmark study for the field. He was also the driving force behind the well-known translation of "literary" texts, entitled *Ugaritic Narrative Poetry* (ed. Simon B. Parker; SBLWAW 9; Atlanta: Scholars, 1997). As a beneficiary of Simon's scholarship and friendship, I am honored to contribute a study dedicated to his memory.

(*KTU* 1.1–1.6);[2] (2) Kirta (*KTU* 1.14–1.16);[3] (3) Aqhat (*KTU* 1.17–1.19);[4] and (4) the *rp'um* texts, more generally known as the Rephaim Texts (*KTU* 1.20–1.22).[5] While these four texts have been amply discussed, it has been noted only rarely that all four often focus on warrior figures and their heroic actions.[6] To be sure, these works do not involve only warrior figures

---

2. The Ugaritic passages mentioned in this essay can be found in Parker, *Ugaritic Narrative Poetry*, unless indicated otherwise. For basic surveys and studies of the Baal Cycle, see M. S. Smith, *The Ugaritic Baal Cycle*, vol. 1: *Introduction with Text, Translation and Commentary of KTU 1.1–1.2* (VTSup 55; Leiden: Brill, 1994); M. S. Smith and W. T. Pitard, *The Ugaritic Baal Cycle*, vol. 2: *Introduction with Text, Translation and Commentary of KTU 1.3–1.4* (VTSup 114; Leiden: Brill, 2009); D. Pardee, *The Ugaritic Texts and the Origins of West-Semitic Literary Composition* (The Schweich Lectures of the British Academy 2007; Oxford: Oxford University Press, 2012) 41–77; A. Tugendhaft, "Unsettling Sovereignty: Politics and Poetics in the Baal Cycle," *JAOS* 132 (2012) 367–84; and F. R. Darder, "Introducció a la Mitologia Ugaritica: El Cicle de Ba'alu/Anatu," *Comun* 130 (2014) 71–84. See further N. Ayali-Darshan, "The Death of Mot and his Resurrection (*KTU*³ 1.6 II, V) in the Light of Egyptian Sources" (in preparation; cited with the author's gracious permission). Note also G. del Olmo Lete, "El Ciclo Mitológico de Baal: Nuevas perspectivas de interpretación," *Historiae* 7 (2010) 73–90, republished in *Estudios de Lingüística Ugarítica: Una Selección* (Aula Orientalis - Supplementa 30; Sabadell: Editorial AUSA, 2016) 263–73. This essay is largely a response to M. S. Tarazi, "A Cloud Roams and Beautifies by Spiting Out Her Brother: *KTU* 1.96 and Its Relation to the Baal Cycle," *UF* 36 (2004) 445–510.

3. For some recommended studies of Kirta, see Parker, *The Pre-Biblical Narrative Tradition*, 145–216; G. N. Knoppers, "Dissonance and Disaster in the Legend of Kirta," *JAOS* 114 (1994) 572–82; E. L. Greenstein, "The Ugaritic Epic of Kirta in a Wisdom Perspective," *Te'uda* 16–17 (2001) 1–13 (Heb.), and "New Readings in the Kirta Epic," *IOS* 18 (1998) 105–23. An up-to-date book-length analysis of Kirta remains a desideratum.

4. For some recommended studies of Aqhat, see Parker, *The Pre-Biblical Narrative Tradition*, 99–144; K. T. Aitken, *The Aqhat Narrative: A Study in the Narrative Structure and Composition of an Ugaritic Tale* (JSS Monograph 13; Manchester: University of Manchester, 1990); D. P. Wright, *Ritual in Narrative: The Dynamics of Feasting, Mourning, and Retaliation Rites in the Ugaritic Tale of Aqhat* (Winona Lake, IN: Eisenbrauns, 2001); C. Sun, *The Ethics of Violence in the Story of Aqhat* (Gorgias Dissertations 34; Near Eastern Studies 9; Piscataway, NJ: Gorgias Press, 2008); and S. Natan-Yulzary, "Contrast and Meaning in the 'Aqhat Story," *VT* 62 (2012) 433–49, and *Narration and Characterization in the Epic of Aqhat from Ugarit* (Piscataway, NJ: Gorgias, in press).

5. For some recommended studies, see W. Pitard, "A New Edition of the 'Rāpi'ūma' Texts: *KTU* 1.20–22," *BASOR* 285 (1992) 33–77; T. J. Lewis, "Toward a Literary Translation of the Rapiuma Texts," in *Ugarit: Religion and Culture. Proceedings of the International Colloquium on Ugarit, Religion and Culture, Edinburgh, July 1994. Essays presented in Honour of John C. L. Gibson* (ed. N. Wyatt et al.; Ugaritisch-Biblische Literatur 12; Münster: Ugarit-Verlag, 1996) 115–49; and D. Pardee, "Nouvelle étude épigraphique et littéraire des textes fragmentaires en langue ougaritique dits «Les Rephaïm»" (*CTA* 20–22)," *Or* 80 (2011) 1–65. For the sake of convenience, Rephaim is used for Ugaritic *rp'um/rp'im*.

6. See M. S. Smith, *Poetic Heroes: The Literary Commemoration of Warriors and Warrior Culture in the Early Biblical World* (Grand Rapids: Eerdmans, 2014) 5–6,

or actions; rather, these represent a major feature in all four. As a corollary, virtually all of the main human warriors involved in Kirta and Aqhat are male, including Kirta and Aqhat (the exception being Aqhat's sister, Pughat) and virtually all of the divine warriors that the Baal Cycle and the Rephaim Texts focus on are male, including Baal and the Rephaim (the exception being Anat).[7] Moreover, for several commentators the male human and divine warriors are parallel literary figures, as are the two critically important female exceptions, Pughat and Anat.[8]

This essay surveys select aspects of kingship and warriorship in the Baal Cycle, in light of heroic and royal figures in the other major Ugaritic poetic narratives and in West Semitic inscriptions. The initial section offers some general remarks about the Baal Cycle, including some relatively recent developments in its scholarship. An overview of the cycle follows, ending with a reconsideration of the narrative end in *KTU* 1.6 VI 42–53. A final section concludes this essay with some further considerations.[9]

99–182.

7. For these warriors, see Smith, *Poetic Heroes*, 162–208. For Yamm, see further A. Tugendhaft, "On *ym* and ᵈA.AB.BA at Ugarit," *UF* 42 (2010) 698–712; for Mot, see S. U. Gulde, "Der Tod als Figur: Eine motiv- und religionsgeschichtliche Untersuchung zum Alten Testament und seiner Umwelt" (Ph.D. diss., Eberhard-Karls-Universitäts Tübingen, 2005). For the female warriors (except Athtart), see the survey of J. F. Parker, "Women Warriors and Devoted Daughters: The Powerful Young Woman in Ugaritic Narrative Poetry," *UF* 38 (2006) 557–75. The survey of Anat in the Baal Cycle and related literature by N. H. Walls remains standard; see Walls, *The Goddess Anat in Ugaritic Myth* (SBLDS 135; Atlanta: Scholars, 1992) 77–185; see also J. -M. Husser, "Anat and the Warriors: Gender Definition and the Ambivalence of the Feminine in Ugaritic Mythology," in *Abigail, Wife of David, and Other Ancient Oriental Women* (ed. D. Bode; Hebrew Bible Monographs 60; Sheffield: Sheffield Academic, 2013), 96–106. For a recent survey of Athtart, see A. M. Wilson-Wright, "Athtart: The Transmission and Transformation of a Goddess in the Late Bronze Age" (Ph.D. diss., University of Texas at Austin, 2016), to appear in the FAT. Note also minor warriors in the Baal Cycle, discussed by S. Y. Ho, *Lesser Deities in the Ugaritic Texts and the Hebrew Bible* (Deities and Angels of the Ancient World 2; Piscataway, NJ: Gorgias Press, 2007) 202–18.

8. Parker, "Women Warriors," 562, 565–66; Natan-Yulzary, "Contrast and Meaning," 433–49; and Smith, *Poetic Heroes*, 114, 115, 119, 120, 125–26.

9. At this point, one preliminary issue may be noted. The precise boundaries between the three major parts of the cycle are not entirely clear. In part the issue depends on the question of the continuity among the six tablets as well as the connection of some further fragments associated historically with the Baal Cycle. For these questions, see Smith, *The Ugaritic Baal Cycle*, vol. 1, 12–19; Smith and Pitard, *The Ugaritic Baal Cycle*, vol. 2, 9–10; Pardee, *The Ugaritic Texts*, 61–72; and N. Wyatt, "The Evidence of the Colophons in the Assessment of Ilimilku's Scribal and Authorial Role," *UF* 46 (2015) 407–11. See also J. Yogev, "How Wide Should a Column Be?," *UF* 42 (2010) 847–51. If *KTU* 1.3 I may be regarded as Baal's victory feast, it may represent the end of the first major section. *KTU* 1.3 II-III, which involves Anat's battling and its cessation, may offer a transition between the first and second parts of the Baal Cycle. Similarly,

INTRODUCTORY REMARKS ABOUT THE BAAL CYCLE

The Baal Cycle (*KTU* 1.1-1.6), the longest work in Ugaritic, was not composed as a complete work in its presently attested form. The break in the narrative at *KTU* 1.4 V 42-43 as marked by scribal lines provides an instruction for additional recitation not included in this written edition of the cycle. According to this break, the reciter is instructed to add the traditional description of the sending of messengers and their delivery of their message to craftsman god, Kothar wa-Hasis.[10] Thus the Baal Cycle in its written form is not a complete literary work. Rather, it would be more accurate to characterize the written version as an aide for learning and reciting the composition known as the Baal Cycle, a point pursued further below.

The cycle relates three major sets of episodes: (1) Baal's defeat of Yamm (Sea), in *KTU* 1.1-1.2; (2) Baal's quest for a palace and its eventual realization, in 1.3 + 1.8[11] - 1.4; and (3) Baal's struggles with Mot (Death), in 1.5-1.6. The conflicts between Baal and Yamm on one side of the Baal Cycle and between Baal and Mot on the other hand frame the central event, the general recognition and manifestation of Baal's kingship represented in and through his palace. The palace is organically linked to victory in combat.[12]

---

with its exchange between Baal and Mot on the heels of the former's successful celebration of his victory in his palace in *KTU* 1.4 VII, *KTU* 1.4 VIII-1.5 I offers a transition between the second and third parts of the cycle. These considerations suggest that the seams of the three major parts of the Baal Cycle were perhaps not marked distinctively, but instead display narrative continuity, despite the various traditions or materials that may have been incorporated. For further discussion of this latter point (in particular pertaining to Anat), see below.

10. Smith and Pitard, *The Ugaritic Baal Cycle*, vol. 2, 549, 574-76, with further possible cases involving scribal lines. For this scribal demarcation, see F. J. Mabie, "The Syntactical and Structural Function of Horizontal Dividing Lines in the Literary and Religious Texts of the Ugaritic Corpus (*KTU* 1)," *UF* 36 (2004) 294 n. 10 and 297. For recitation, see also Pardee, *The Ugaritic Texts*, 47.

11. So Pardee's brilliant join, summarized and presented in Pardee, *The Ugaritic Texts*, 62-66. By contrast, the proposal to view RS 94.2953 as an Ugaritic syllabic text describing the construction of the window for Baal's house has not met with acceptance. For the text along with this proposal, see D. Arnaud, *Corpus des textes de bibliothèque de Ras Shamra-Ougarit (1936-2000) en sumérien, babylonien et assyrien* (Aula orientalis Supplementa 23; Barcelona: Editorial AUSA, 2007) 201-2, and G. del Olmo Lete, "Una 'ventana' en el temple de Baal," *AuOr* 24 (2006) 177-88. For critique, see Smith and Pitard, *The Ugaritic Baal Cycle*, vol. 2, 580-81. For the text instead as an episode from Gilgamesh, see A. Cavigneaux, "Les oiseux de l'arche," *AuOr* 25 (2007) 319-20.

12. For this point not only in the Baal Cycle, *Enuma Elish* and biblical sources such as Exodus 15 and Psalm 29, but also in Inanna and Ebih as well as Assyrian royal inscriptions, see V. Hurowitz, *I Have Built You an Exalted House: Temple Building in the Bible in Light of Mesopotamian and Northwest Semitic Writings* (JSOTSup 115; JSOT/

The Baal-Mot material parallels the Baal-Yamm section, as suggested by the similarities between these two major parts.¹³ Yamm may have been the more traditionally known enemy,¹⁴ while Mot comes to loom large in the Baal Cycle, with the Baal-Mot section informed by royal funerary ritual.¹⁵ The cycle presupposes some similarities between Yamm and Mot. They both

---

ASOR Monograph Series 5; Sheffield: Sheffield Academic, 1992) 82 and 93; see also Hurowitz, *I Have Built You*, 175 n. 1: "building a palace in itself is a sign of monarchic stability." Note further B. Pongratz-Leisten, *Religion and Ideology in Assyria* (SANER 6; Berlin: de Gruyter, 2015) 258–59.

13. Smith, *Ugaritic Baal Cycle*, vol. 1, 17–19, and *The Origins of Biblical Monotheism: Israel's Polytheistic Background and the Ugaritic Texts* (Oxford: Oxford University Press, 2001) 130–31. See also J. F. Healey, "Mot," in *DDD* 601, and his comment about Mot on 599: "he is not a deity in the full sense."

14. For the traditions about Sea, see Stolz, "Sea," 740; M. Dijkstra, "Ishtar Seduces the Sea-Serpent: A New Join in the Epic of Ḫedammu (KUB 36, 56 + 95) and its Meaning for the Battle between Baal and Yam in Ugaritic Tradition," *UF* 43 (2011) 53–83; N. Ayali-Darshan, "The Story of the Combat between the Storm-God and the Sea: Its Origin, Dispersion and Diffusion in the Ancient Near East" (Ph.D diss., Hebrew University of Jerusalem, 2012; Heb.), and "The Other Version of the Story of the Storm-god's Combat with the Sea in the Light of Egyptian, Ugaritic, and Hurro-Hittite Texts," *JANER* 15 (2015) 20–51. The closest thematic parallel of divine battle is not *Enuma Elish*, as is commonly thought; on this point, see W. G. Lambert, *Ancient Mesopotamian Religion and Mythology: Selected Essays* (ed. A. R. George and T. M. Oshima; Orientalische Religionen in der Antike 15; Tübingen: Mohr/Siebeck, 2016) 228; and W. T. Pitard, "The Combat Myth as a Succession Story at Ugarit," in *Creation and Chaos: A Reconsideration of Hermann Gunkel's Chaoskampf Hypothesis* (ed. J. A. Scurlock and R. H. Beal; Winona Lake, IN: Eisenbrauns, 2013) 200–202. A closer parallel to Baal's combat against Yamm is the storm-god's defeat of the Sea in a Mari prophecy, first published by J.-M. Durand, "Le mythologème du combat entre le dieu de l'orage et la mer en Mésopotamie," *MARI* 7 (1993) 41–61; see also P. Bordreuil and D. Pardee, "Le combat de Baʻlu avec Yammu d'après les texts ougaritiques," *MARI* 7 (1993) 63–70; Pardee, *The Ugaritic Texts*, 26–28; and Tugendhaft, "On *ym* and ᵈA.AB.BA at Ugarit," 697–712, and "Politics and Time in the Baal Cycle," *JANER* 12 (2012) 145–57. In the later tradition of Philo of Byblos, the conflict between Baal versus Sea appears in a narrative form, but Death's conflict with Baal does not. For the text, see H. W. Attridge and R. A. Oden, Jr., *Philo of Byblos. The Phoenician History: Introduction, Critical Text, Translation, Notes* (CBQMS 9; Washington, DC: Catholic Biblical Association of America, 1981) 52–55 and 56–57. By contrast, a reference to Mot's defeat of Baal has been claimed for a North Arabian inscription by A. Al-Jallad, "Echoes of the Baal Cycle in a Safaito-Hismaic Inscription," *JANER* 15 (2015) 5–19; the inscription is rendered: "Mot has celebrated a feast; the scorner eats/established is the succession of his nights and days/and behold, Baal is cut off; cut off indeed, but not dead."

15. See below, especially with respect to *KTU* 1.161 (see the studies cited in note 63). This is not to claim that Mot was not attested as a god otherwise; for his name as the theophoric element in Ebla personal names, see Lambert, *Ancient Mesopotamian Religion*, 221.

manifest destructive power[16] (attested for each of them elsewhere).[17] They also bear related titles of "beloved of El,"[18] perhaps expressive of (or corollary to) their role as enemies of the warrior storm-god, Baal, who meet him in individual combat.[19]

Most centrally, the battles between Baal and his two enemies tie their conflicts to kingship,[20] as do the processes involved in the achievement of Baal's palace. In each of the three major parts of the cycle, kingship is named as the point of the conflicts between the divine warriors.[21] Baal's might as a warrior and king reaches a crescendo at the end of each of these three parts, each one also evoking imagery of the late summer-early fall when

---

16. Cross (*Canaanite Myth and Hebrew Epic: Essays in the History of the Religion of Israel* [Cambridge: Harvard University Press, 1973] 162) lists Yamm, Leviathan, and Mot under the rubric of "chaos" (see also *Canaanite Myth*, 58). Stolz ("Sea," in *DDD* 739) also refers to Yamm in terms of "chaos." (A better candidate for "chaos" is *bĕlî-mâ*, literally, "nothingness" in Job 26:7.) R. E. Averbeck goes further in characterizing Yamm as "the evil god"; see Averbeck, "A Literary Day, Inter-Textual, and Contextual Reading of Genesis 1–2," in *Reading Genesis 1–2: An Evangelical Conversation* (ed. J. D. Charles; Peabody, MA: Hendrickson, 2013) 15. A positive view of Yamm is held by Tugendhaft, "On *ym* and ^{d}A.AB.BA at Ugarit," 698–712; and B. C. Benz, "Yamm as the Personification of Chaos? A Linguistic and Literary Argument in a Case of Mistaken Identity," in *Creation and Chaos: A Reconsideration of Hermann Gunkel's Chaoskampf Hypothesis* (ed. J. A. Scurlock and R. H. Beal; Winona Lake, IN: Eisenbrauns, 2013) 127–45.

17. For Sea, it is implied in *KTU* 1.14 I 19–20. For Mot, see his monstrous appetite in 1.5 II 2–4; cf. Hab 2:5 and implied in Isa 25:8. See Healey, "Mot," 599–601, for further discussion.

18. For these titles, see A. Rahmouni, *Divine Epithets in the Ugaritic Alphabetic Texts* (trans. J. N. Ford; Handbook of Oriental Studies I/93; Leiden: Brill, 2008) 212–14 and 217–18. Note also Wyatt, "The Religious Role," 711 n. 63 (citing his prior study on the titles). Cf. the two sons by Kronos and Astarte called "Desire and Love," in Philo of Byblos? For the text, see Attridge and Oden, *Philo of Byblos*, 52–53.

19. For an iconographic parallel for the single combats of Baal against Yamm and Mot, see J. Vidal, "Ugarit at War (2)," *UF* 38 (2006) 707–12.

20. For the possible political background of Baal's battles against Yamm and Mot, see Smith, *The Ugaritic Baal Cycle*, vol. 1, 105–10. See the comparable observations for Mesopotamian combat myths made by Pongratz-Leisten, *Religion and Ideology in Assyria*, 232–38, 258–59.

21. For kingship in the Baal Cycle, see Smith, *The Ugaritic Baal Cycle*, vol. 1, 58–114; and A. Tugendhaft, "Baal and the Problem of Politics" (PhD diss., New York University, 2012). Tugendhaft considers several aspects of the cycle as not merely a reflection of Late Bronze Age politics, but further as a critique of traditional notions of kingship. For him, the Baal Cycle calls into question royal claims made in other texts that would depict the divine world in such a way as to serve their earthly political agenda. According to the Baal Cycle, royal power does not arise as a matter of clear cosmic order and divine legitimacy as kings elsewhere claim. See further Tugendhaft's articles cited in notes 9, 16 and 18.

Baal's power is most evident. First, armed with his meteorological weapons, Baal's victory over Yamm (1.2 IV) parallels the arrival of the fall rains over the Mediterranean (cf. Psalm 29). Second, the window in Baal's palace permits his voicing of his thunder (1.4 VII 25–31); prior to that event, the rains are lacking (1.4 V 6–9). Third, following Baal's disappearance El has a dream[22] about Baal's fertility, indicating his return to life (1.6 III). Moreover, the struggle between Baal and Mot (1.6 VI) may draw on the alternation of the western rainy storm and eastern dry storm at the end of the summer dry season (sometimes called "the fall interchange period").[23] Correspondingly, at the end of all the three parts, Baal's kingship is affirmed: Baal is proclaimed king (1.2 IV); Baal's palace is completed and he manifests his meteorological power (1.4 V-VII); and Mot concedes the throne to Baal (1.6 VI). Signs, perhaps "omina," of Baal's power could be seen writ into the very text of the world, expressed also by the incantations pronounced over his meteorological weapons (1.2 IV)[24] and by his cosmic "word" (*rgm*) conveyed to Anat (1.3 III 20-28).[25]

KTU 1.1–1.2: BAAL VERSUS YAMM

In El's early speech to Yamm, kingship is named as the stakes of the upcoming conflict: "Drive him from [his royal] thr[one,] [From the resting place, the throne] of his dominion" (*KTU* 1.1 IV 24–25; see also lines 26–27).[26] Yamm and Baal appear to be competing for the throne in question, and so El's words to Yamm evidently represent a cliché advising him to dispose of

22. For a comparison with Elqunirsha's title, "lord of dreams," in a Hittite prayer (CTH 342.2), see M. Dijkstra, "Let Sleeping Gods Lie?," in *Reflections on the Silence of God: A Discussion with Marjo Korpel and Johannes de Moor* (ed. B. Becking; Oudtestamentische Studiën 62; Leiden: Brill, 2013) 71–87.

23. Smith, *The Ugaritic Baal Cycle*, vol. 1, 98, 347. For biblical imagery associated with the "fall interchange period," see A. Fitzgerald, *The Lord of the East Wind* (CBQMS 34; Washington, DC: The Catholic Biblical Association of America, 2002). A work rich with observations about weather in the Baal Cycle is J. C. de Moor, *The Seasonal Pattern in the Ugaritic Myth of Ba'lu: According to the Version of Ilimilku* (AOAT 16; Neukirchen-Vluyn: Neukirchener, 1971). For criticism, see Smith, *The Ugaritic Baal Cycle*, vol. 1, 63–69; note also Pardee, *The Ugaritic Texts*, 73–74. For a proposed ritual reflex at Ebla, see A. Archi, *Ebla and Its Archives: Texts, History, and Society* (SANER 7; Berlin: de Gruyter, 2015) 508.

24. Smith, *The Ugaritic Baal Cycle*, vol. 1, 98, 341–42. See below.

25. For "the mantic/incantational subtext of Baal's speech to Anat" in *KTU* 1.3 III 20–28, see Smith and Pitard, *The Ugaritic Baal Cycle*, vol. 2, 229–34, comparing the "secret of Baal" (*prtt b'l*) in *KTU* 1.179.16 (labelled a "mythic-magical text" by *KTU*). For the incantational force of the Baal Cycle's ending, see below.

26. Smith, *The Ugaritic Baal Cycle*, vol. 1, 153–54.

his rival, Baal. Accordingly, Wayne T. Pitard has suggested viewing El as an old royal patriarch seeking his younger successor from among his children to act as co-regent.[27] Alternatively, Noga Ayali-Darshan views El and Athirat making an effort to depose Baal as king,[28] which does not stack up well with the same cliché that appears in Kothar's prediction to Baal that he will drive Yamm from the throne of kingship in *KTU* 1.2 IV 12–13, 20. Instead, both Yamm and Baal seem to be competitors for the same throne, and neither yet has gained the upper hand despite El's support for Yamm. The kingship that Yamm attempts to win is to issue in a palace to be built for him by Kothar (*KTU* 1.2 III 7–11).[29] Baal is proclaimed as king following his defeat of Yamm in *KTU* 1.2 IV 31–37.[30] Thus kingship and the palace that it represents are named as the stakes in the battle between Baal and Yamm in *KTU* 1.2 IV.

Moreover, this victory is "performed" verbally before Baal's divine peers, namely Kothar in *KTU* 1.2 IV 7 and 11 and Astarte in *KTU* 1.2 IV 2. Kothar predicts Baal's kingship (*KTU* 1.2 IV 7–10) and another deity, perhaps Astarte, declares it as well (*KTU* 1.2 IV 32 and possibly to be seen in the damaged lines 34 and 36–37). Between these utterances is the narrative of conflict between Baal and Yamm. In this engagement Baal is critically aided by the weapons[31] provided to him by Kothar, themselves enhanced by the words that he pronounces over them, that for decades have been compared with incantations.[32] This victory realized with the help of Kothar's weapons stands in contrast with weapons given by Kothar in the story of Aqhat. There the weapons are intended as a blessing to Danil (1.17 VI) and presumably to his son, Aqhat, who wields them. Instead, they become a source of conflict with the goddess, Anat, who later has the young Aqhat executed.[33] Both Baal and Aqhat face a divine warrior with these weapons

---

27. Pitard, "The Combat Myth," 199–205. The analogy cited is 1 Kings 1.

28. Ayali-Darshan, "The Death of Mot."

29. For the palace-building theme here and in the middle section of the Baal Cycle, see M. Dietrich, "Beschreibungen transzendenter Wohnstättnen von ugaritischer Gottheiten: Die Paläste Yammus und Baals und die Schreine Anats," *UF* 45 (2014) 389–412.

30. See the interesting observations made by J. Yogev and S. Yona, "Visual Poetry in *KTU* 1.2," *UF* 46 (2015) 447–53.

31. See M. Dietrich and O. Loretz, "ṣmd I 'Paar' und ṣmd II 'Axt, Doppelaxt' nach *KTU* 4.169, 4.363, 4.136, 1.65," *UF* 41 (2009) 165–79.

32. See J. Obermann, "How Baal Destroyed a Rival," *JAOS* 67 (1947) 195–208, noting also the later "Phoenician" tradition of Chousor as an expert in spells, attested in Philo of Byblos. For the text, see Attridge and Oden, *Philo of Byblos*, 44–45.

33. See S. Natan-Yulzary, "Divine Justice or Poetic Justice? The Transgression and Punishment of the Goddess 'Anat in the 'Aqhat Story. A Literary Perspective," *UF* 41 (2009) 581–99; and Smith, *Poetic Heroes*, 99–136.

An important question involves the degree of similarity or identification among these various enemies of Baal and Anat, and what it may mean in the context of Baal's emerging kingship. A good contextual argument has been made for identifying Yamm with Tnn and Arsh in 1.3 III 38-43.[43] As inhabitants of the sea, they would be regarded as alternative forms of Yamm, but they are more expressly monstrous enemies in the sea. Yet elsewhere Yamm seems to be distinguished from Tnn in both the Ugaritic Baal Cycle and in the Bible. For example, Arsh and Tnn are apparently said to be "in the sea"[44] (*KTU* 1.6 VI 51; cf. Isa 27:1). That Yamm and Tannin are distinguished is arguably the case also in Job 7:12, where they are presented as alternatives: "Am I Sea or Tannin that you set a guard over me?"[45] As expressed in the developed tradition of Dan 7:3, later forms of such monstrous figures "emerge from" the Sea (see NJPS). Still in some contexts it is possible that these monstrous enemies could have been conflated with Yamm. For example, in *KTU* 1.83 the distinction between Yamm and Tnn is not clear.[46] However, the most that biblical or Ugaritic texts indicate explicitly is that Yamm can stand in parallel (and thus apposition) with the monstrous enemies.[47] In Isa 51:9-10 Yamm appears appositionally in a list of clauses about cosmic enemies, but it is not clear that they are to be identified. In sum, there is arguably some explicit evidence distinguishing Yamm from enemies that are in the sea, but there is no explicit evidence for their identification, only for their standing in apposition.[48]

---

43. Pitard, "Just How Many," 75-88; and Smith and Pitard, *The Ugaritic Baal Cycle*, vol. 2, 251-58. G. del Olmo Lete refers to "the Dragon" in *KTU* 1.83.8 as "Yam's hypostasis." See del Olmo Lete, *Incantations and Anti-Witchcraft Texts from Ugarit* (SANER 4; Berlin: de Gruyter, 2014) 93. For this text, see W. T. Pitard, "The Binding of Yamm: A New Edition of the Ugaritic Text 1.83," *JNES* 57 (1998) 261-80.

44. The translation of *ym* as "sea" or "day" is debatable. In view of the references to both Arsh and Tnn, "sea" appears preferable (so Pardee, *COS* 1.273). See the judicious consideration of Pitard, "Just How Many," 84.

45. Cf. Pitard, "Just How Many," 83. For the theme, cf. Job 38:10-11.

46. See Pitard, "Just How Many," 81.

47. According to Cross (*Canaanite Myth*, 120), "there is full identification between Yamm and the dragon (Isa 27:1, and especially Isa 51.9-10)." Cf. the extensive and careful discussion of Pitard, "Just How Many," 75-88. Pitard ("Just How Many," 86) concludes that Yamm and Tnn may or may not be identified in *KTU* 1.3 III 38-47. See also the highly qualified characterization about such an identification by F. Stolz, "Sea," in *DDD* 739, and N. Wyatt, "The Religious Role of the King in Ugarit," *UF* 37 (2005) 706. For a recent reevaluation, see Benz, "Yamm as the personification of Chaos?" 127-45.

48. There is also a related question regarding the relative antiquity of the traditions regarding these enemies. A serpentine enemy is known earlier at Ebla, identified by Archi, *Ebla and Its Archives*, 587-89; cf. Pardee, *The Ugaritic Texts*, 28 esp. n. 58; see also R. D. Miller II, "Tracking the Dragon across the Ancient Near East," *Archiv Orientální*

In the context of Anat's speech, these figures represent known enemies that she declares that she previously battled, perhaps echoing an old parallel tradition of battle on the goddess's part. The foe that has risen against Baal, to echo the goddess's question that frames this speech (*KTU* 1.3 III 36–38 and 1.3 IV 4), is Yamm and no other. This figure is the first in the speech, and by order and perhaps rank Yamm is the prior and perhaps the more threatening, watery personification compared with the other aquatic enemies named in the speech. By way of presentation, Sea appears as their primordial predecessor and perhaps ancestor. It is possible further that Anat's speech presupposes that when the first and foremost, Yamm, is defeated, the others are at least reduced as a threat. Without Sea there is no sea to serve as the home for the other aquatic figures. In any case, Anat's speech appears to highlight the primordial enemy that she perhaps overcame in the past and yet remained for Baal to defeat. In the narrative of the Baal Cycle, he has since done so.

Baal's further interaction with Athirat introduces a new theme that his emergent kingship entails, namely his conflict with her sons (*KTU* 1.4 II 24–26). The goddess asks if he is the slayer of her sons, betraying a direction that his warrior nature may potentially take in the wake of his victory. While this theme is not pursued any further, it signals that the fall-out from his victory over Yamm could entail not only his kingship but further violence potentially taken against any opposed to him in the family of the goddess.[49]

---

82 (2014) 225–45. According to Lambert (*Ancient Mesopotamian Religion*, 222), Yamm does not appear (so far) in documents from Ebla. See also the seven-headed dragon in Early Dynastic and Akkadian-period art, in A. Green, "Myths in Mesopotamian Art," in *Sumerian Gods and Their Representations* (ed. I. L. Finkel and M. J. Geller; CM 7; Groningen: Styx, 1997) 141 and 155 figs. 13–14. These data may point to a tradition of a serpentine monster earlier than Sea as an enemy. However, it is not known in the record from Ebla or in Mesopotamia whether the two were not identified; and if not, the apparent difference may be only a matter of a lack of attestation and not the relative antiquity of the traditions as such. The important issue about the cultural significance and meaning of the forms of deities and cosmic enemies lies beyond the scope of this essay.

49. For the motif of the seventy children of Athirat, see F. C. Fensham, "The Numeral Seventy in the Old Testament and the Family of Jerubbaal, Ahab, Panammuwa and Athirat," *PEQ* 109 (1977) 113–15; J. C. de Moor, "Seventy!" in *"Und Mose schrieb dieses Lied auf": Studien zum Alten Testament und zum Alten Orient. Festschrift für Oswald Loretz zur Vollendung seines 70. Lebensjahres mit Beiträgen von Freunden, Schülern und Kollegen* (ed. H. Schaudig et al.; AOAT 250; Münster: Ugarit-Verlag, 1998) 199–203; and M. J. Suriano, "The Apology of Hazael: A Literary and Historical Analysis of the Tel Dan Inscription," *JNES* 66 (2007) 167–68. The number has variants, for example seventy-seven parallel to eighty-eight in *KTU* 1.12 II 48–49 apparently also opposed to Baal (cf. Judg 8:14). Cf. the seventy-five that belongs to the family of the serpent, in the Egyptian tale of the Shipwrecked Sailor (M. Lichtheim, *COS* 1.84).

Following Athirat's proclamation of Baal's kingship before El, this god gives his permission for the building of Baal's palace (*KTU* 1.4 IV 45–46 and 1.4 IV 62-V 1), an indicator of his acquiescence to Baal's kingship. To celebrate the construction of his palace, Baal hosts a massive feast for Athirat's divine family (1.4 VI 38–59), called "the seventy, the sons of Athirat" (1.4 VI 46).[50] This act marks their recognition of his kingship with Baal, reversing the fear that she had expressed about Baal's potential destruction of her children (1.4 II 21–26). Baal then undertakes what may be called a victory tour on earth (1.4 VII 7–14), signaling his dominion over the earth. Here again kingship is tied to military victory. With his theophanic "voice" uttered from his palace, his enemies flee (1.4 VII 25–39), once again marking the link between Baal's meteorological power expressed from his royal home and his warrior nature. This is the highpoint of his power before the figure of Mot enters the story.

KTU 1.5–1.6: BAAL VERSUS MOT

The Baal-Mot section of the cycle likewise ties divine conflict to kingship. This final major section of the Baal Cycle not only parallels the Baal-Yamm section, as noted above; it also echoes the middle part of the cycle at a number of points bearing on Baal's kingship.

Baal asserts his kingship in proclaiming to Mot the successful construction of his royal palace (*KTU* 1.4 VIII 35–37) and perhaps more in the broken lines that follow (*KTU* 1.4 VIII 38–47). Baal's speech opens with his parallel titles "Mighty Baal" (*al'iyn b'l*) and "Mightiest of Warriors" (*al'iy qrdm*),[51] particularly suitable in this context as he now stands at the high point of his power (1.4 VIII 32–35; cf. later in 1.5 II 10–11, 18, used ironically when he stands at a very low point). Baal calls the palace "my house" that "I built" (1.4 VIII 37). Baal's words are not only an expression of what he himself managed; they also convey the consolidation of his kingship.[52] The silver and gold also said by Baal here to be the materials for the palace (1.4 VIII 35–37) mark it as a royal accomplishment, echoing Anat's claims about conquest for silver and gold (1.3 III 46–47, mentioned above).[53]

50. For comparison with dedication festivities in Enki's Journey to Nippur and *Enuma Elish*, see Hurowitz, *I Have Built You*, 95, 102.

51. For these titles, see Rahmouni, *Divine Epithets*, 49–63. Note the parallelism in *KTU* 1.5 II 17–18, apparently used ironically as Baal expresses his surrender to Mot.

52. So too Bar-Rakib's statement that "I built this house" (*'nh bnyt byt' znh*, KAI 216.20; K. L. Younger, Jr., *COS* 2.161), observed above in n. 37.

53. Cf. the silver and gold mentioned by the Sidonian king, Tabnit (KAI 13:4–5; P. K. McCarter, *COS* 2.182).

Mot's response following in 1.4 VIII (and reconstructed on the basis of his messenger's extant speech to Baal in 1.5 I 12–35) in effect ignores Baal's claims. Instead, Mot focuses on how he intends to tear Baal to pieces and devour him. As an object lesson to Baal, Mot here evokes the figure of Ltn (1.5 I 27–31),[54] much as Anat had earlier in her response to Baal's messengers, as discussed above. Mot's allusion to Baal's defeat of Ltn (1.5 I 1–4) suggests that it was an event of cosmic significance, since as a result "the heavens . . . withered."[55] Mot intends nothing less in the defeat that he plans to inflict on Baal (1.5 I 4–8).

In his speech Mot also raises a concern about feasting with his brothers (*KTU* 1.5 I 22–25), a topic that returns later in their exchanges (1.6 V 19–25 and VI 9–15).[56] Indeed, this motif frames the Baal-Mot section.[57] In 1.5–1.6 it is not merely a matter of social etiquette, but a conflict over dynastic politics[58] (cf. *KTU* 1.12 II; 1 Sam 20:29 and 1 Kgs 1:25–26).[59] The

54. For various translations of *KTU* 1.5 I 1–4, see W. D. Barker, "'And thus you brightened the heavens . . .': A New Translation of *KTU* 1.5 I 1–8 and its Significance for Ugaritic and Biblical Studies," *UF* 38 (2006) 41–52. It is unclear what the basis is for Barker's statement that "Litan must have served in some way as a protector of Mot" (Barker, "'And thus you brightened the heavens . . . ,'" 47).

55. Smith, "The Baal Cycle," in *UNP* 141. Similarly in Pardee, *COS* 1.265.

56. The motif also seems to inform the highly damaged two columns of *KTU* 1.5 III-IV, on which see the judicious comments of Pardee, *COS* 1.266 nn. 223–224. A further feast may also inform one of the subsequent lacunas, according to Pardee's reconstruction for the setting of 1.148 (*Ritual and Cult at Ugarit* [ed. T. J. Lewis; SBLWAW 10; Atlanta: Society of Biblical Literature, 2002] 102 n. 36) "the gathering would plausibly have occurred at the time of the winter solstice (or near the end of winter if the obverse-reverse orientation of the tablet is the opposite). The only concrete proposal for the function of the rite with which I am acquainted is to link it to *Baʿlu*'s vicissitudes when he was defeated by *Môtu* and buried on Mount Sapunu <dotted S> . . . Though there are no explicit links between the mythological account and the sacrificial rite, it is not difficult to imagine a rite that would have brought the gods together to commemorate *Baʿlu*'s demise at the winter solstice (or to solicit his return a month later a month before the vernal equinox, if this rite was in fact situated after *Ḫiyyāru* rather than before." In theory, such a feast could fall in the lacuna at the end of 1.5 V, at the beginning of 1.6 I, or thematically more fittingly, at the end of 1.6 IV.

57. Also framing the Baal-Mot section is the expression of divine "fear" (**yrʾ//*ttʿ*), first Baal's in 1.5 II 6–7 and then Mot's in 1.6 VI 30–31. See J. C. Greenfield, '*Al Kanfei Yonah: Collected Studies of Jonas C. Greenfield on Semitic Philology* (ed. S. M. Paul et al.; 2 vols.; Leiden: Brill, 2001) 2:226.

58. For competing dynastic lines as an issue, see Suriano, "The Apology of Hazael," 167–68.

59. For the brothers opposed to Baal in *KTU* 1.12 II, see J. D. Schloen, "The Exile of Disinherited Kin in *KTU* 1.12 and *KTU* 1.23," *JNES* 52 (1993) 209–20. Note the Sefire inscription addressees or royal "brothers" in a case of vengeance for royal assassination (KAI 224:9, 18) and in a dispute over royal succession (KAI 224:18); see the citation

motif of Mot and his brothers standing in opposition to Baal also echoes Athirat's perception that Baal poses to her family in the middle part of the Baal Cycle (*KTU* 1.4 II 21–26). The recurring motif of Mot's brothers in 1.5–1.6 is not unlike Athirat's earlier concern for her own offspring, as Baal is a threat to both. Later the Baal-Mot section narrates Baal's conflict with the sons of Athirat (1.6 V 1–4), issuing in Baal's return to the royal throne (1.6 V 5–6). Thus family members constitute a central concern for two of Baal's opponents, Athirat and Mot. Initially in the Baal Cycle, kingship is the outcome of Baal's warrior engagement; later kingship inspires further acts of martial engagement.

On this score, the story of Kirta (*KTU* 1.14–1.16) offers some helpful comparisons. The beginning of this story presumes that Kirta has established his dynasty. His loss of family at the story's outset (1.14 I) inspires him to seek the help of El (1.14 I 26–37). El initially asks if Kirta wants kingship like his very own (1.4 I 38–43), with riches galore (as indicated by Kirta's response quoting El's offer, in 1.14 I 51–II 3), but what the human king desires is sons. The narrative undertakes a long recitation by El about how to acquire a wife (1.14 II 6–IV 49). The final couplet of this speech indicates the purpose of this new wife, "to bear an scion to Kirta, a lad for the servant of El." A son as heir is the concern here, and the means for acquiring this new son is outlined: it is a matter of a new wife to be acquired through warfare. Thus the king is to undertake a military campaign, not unlike Baal following his defeat of Yamm and his assumption of kingship. In Kirta's case, it is the male heir that is centrally important to his military campaign, while for Baal his battle is not centered on securing an heir.[60]

Yet the two stories share a deeper core meaning: Kirta's campaign provides the path ultimately leading to securing an heir needed for re-establishing his dynasty and thus his kingship; and Baal's battle secures his own kingship. In terms of life and death, Baal's kingship mirrors Kirta's. Though Baal is a god and Kirta a mortal, their kingship is each threatened by death. Kirta, as a son of El, should not die (*KTU* 1.16 I 17–23, II 40–44);

---

in *COS* 2.217. For brothers as alike in nature, see the "brothers" of Chousor in Philo of Byblos; see Attridge and Oden, *Philo of Byblos*, 44–45.

60. Note *KTU* 1.5 V 17–22 where Baal's sexual relations with a heifer yields a newborn, which one might think is an heir. According to Neal Walls, this incident "provides an effective metaphor for Baal's fertilizing power over livestock and wild herds." See Walls, "The Gods of Israel in Comparative Ancient Near Eastern Context," in *The Wiley Blackwell Companion to Ancient Israel* (ed. S. Niditch; Malden, MA: Wiley Blackwell, 2016) 266. Any more specific meaning of this incident remains unclear (for example, what does it mean that Baal apparently clothes the newborn, according to line 23?). The episode seems comparable to scenes in *KTU* 1.10 III and perhaps 1.11, themselves very difficult to interpret.

and Baal, though divine, is subject to the power of Mot. Both survive the threat of death, reigning once again as kings. Aqhat's story is no less a reflection on death for a warrior figure, as it entails a threat of death that is not reversible. This death transpires through the hands of Anat, the very goddess who is Baal's stalwart support in the Baal Cycle. Baal's rains cease at the time of Aqhat's death (*KTU* 1.19 I 42–46), just as in the Baal Cycle his rains and other means of precipitation are suspended (*KTU* 1.5 V 6–17) and he is dead (1.5 VI 8–10). Thus in both narratives the demise of the land is linked to the demise of the hero. Kirta, Aqhat, and the Baal Cycle all show a concern for life and death on the natural, human and divine levels of reality that a hero in a sense is supposed to sustain. The concern over life and death in the dynasty perhaps lies just beneath the surface of these texts. Indeed, as commentators have long noted, the narrative of burial and lament over Baal in 1.5 VI–1.6 I compares closely with the royal ritual including lamentation in *KTU* 1.161 invoking Rephaim and dead kings.[61]

The end of the Baal Cycle narrates a rematch between Baal and Mot (*KTU* 1.6 VI 16–22), ending in a draw,[62] as the final line indicates that each has "fallen" (*ql*). This root is commonly used to denote a figure's demise or death (see 1.114.21), whether in a curse (1.2 I 9//1.16 VI 57), a prayer (1.19 III 3, 9, 18, 23, 32 and 37), or a prediction (1.103.1). The language signals that Baal and Mot have defeated each other thoroughly. At this point Shapshu's intervenes voicing a curse against Mot (1.6 VI 22–29), just as she does against Athtar in the Baal-Yamm section (1.2 III 17–18).[63] In both, she declares that El will overturn "the throne of your kingship," a motif that appears in a curse also in the sarcophagus inscription of the Byblian king, Ahiram.[64] A fearful Mot (1.6 VI 30–31) apparently concedes the throne to Baal (1.6 VI 33–35). The speech here draws on the clichés noted above for kingship expressed in El's command for Yamm to drive Baal from his throne

---

61. The critical study on this comparison was B. A. Levine and J.-M. de Tarragon, "Dead Kings and Rephaim: The Patrons of the Ugaritic Dynasty," *JAOS* 104 (1984) 649–59. For discussion of this comparison, with further scholarship, see M. S. Smith, *The Origins of Biblical Monotheism: Israel's Polytheistic Background and the Ugaritic Texts* (Oxford: Oxford University Press, 2001) 120–29.

62. For this point, see S. B. Parker, "The Use of Similes in Ugaritic Literature," *UF* 36 (2004) 366–67.

63. See W. G. E. Watson, "A Formulaic Curse in Ugaritic," *UF* 39 (2007) 665–68. For Shapshu in the Baal Cycle, see J. Kutter, *nūr ilī: Die Sonnengottheiten in den nordwestsemitischen Religionen von der Spätbronzezeit bis zur vorrömischen Zeit* (AOAT 346; Münster: Ugarit-Verlag, 2008) 141–84; and O. Wikander, *Drought, Death, and Sun in Ugaarit and Ancient Israel: A Philological and Comparative Study* (Winona Lake, IN: Eisenbrauns, 2014).

64. KAI 1:2; see Greenfield, *'Al Kanfei Yonah*, 2:705–8.

(1.1 IV 24–25), in Kothar's command to Baal to do likewise to Yamm (1.2 IV 12–13), and finally in Anat's concern that Baal has not been so driven from his throne (1.3 IV 2–3). Baal's throne is used literally as a physical symbol for Athtar's failure to measure up as king (1.6 I 56–62).[65] Kingship expressed in the throne is central to all three parts of the Baal Cycle, including the conflicts between the male divine warriors.

The text at the end-point of the story (*KTU* 1.6 VI 35) becomes very damaged and it is unclear what transpires from the end of line 35 to line 42. One apparent word, *qb'at*, is a verb for summoning,[66] perhaps a performative perfect ("you are summoned"),[67] possibly in reference to the feast mentioned in lines 42–45. At line 42 the text resumes apparently in a speech (indicated by second person singular suffixes in lines 48–50 and the possibly second-person forms in lines 42–45). It is not entirely clear whether or not the speech forms part of the narrative, but given the lack of scribal lines until after line 53, it should be presupposed that the speech is part of the narrative. If correct, this speech would constitute the last piece of the narrative. It has been thought quite reasonably by some to be addressed to Shapshu,[68] yet as the final portion of the Baal Cycle, it may well be imagined that this speech is directed to its hero, Baal himself. The speech seems to contain three main parts: (1) the invitation to the feast (lines 42–45); (2) the governance role of Shapshu with respect to the Rephaim of the underworld (lines 45–49); and the evidently magical role of Kothar apparently deployed with respect to the realm of the sea (lines 49–53).

Lines 42–44 would express the wish that the addressee go to such a feast where he may eat and drink. The only word surviving line 42 is the well-known verb for self-transport, *ltštql*, probably second person masculine singular ("may you surely/surely you will betake yourself . . . ").[69] Elsewhere this verb appears in the second line in a poetic couplet (the B-line),[70] in some instances for travel to a feast (*KTU* 1.3 II 17–18; 1.17 II 24–25)

---

65. Greenfield, *'Al Kanfei Yonah*, 2:892–97.

66. See J. G. Taylor, *Newsletter for Ugaritic Studies* 32 (1984) 13, and *DULAT* 681.

67. Cf. the arguably performative perfects with the same root in *KTU* 1.161.2, 10.

68. Pardee, *COS* 1.273; see also Smith, "Kothar wa-Hasis," 397. Cf. Smith, "The Baal Cycle," in *UNP*, 164.

69. I leave untranslated the apparent last word in this line, *try*, in line 43. For proposals, mostly "fresh food" or the like, see *DULAT* 877. To make sense of the verb here, various proposals have been offered to fill the lacuna with a suitable object (see Smith, "Kothar wa-Hasis," 399–400).

70. For examples, see *KTU* 1.3 II 17–18, 1.17 II 24–25, 1.19 IV 8–9, 1.100.67–68, 1.114.17–18; see Greenfield, *'Al Kanfei Yonah*, 2:732. For a different understanding of the root, see *DULAT* 688.

or from one (1.114.17–18). Thus it may be suspected that the preceding lacuna contained a first line (the A-line) telling the addressee to go to the feast. The terms used for this feast sound sacrificial ("the sacrificial [me]al" and "the offertory wine").[71] The meal evoked in lines 42–45 is followed by the mention of the divine Rephaim in lines 45–49 in association with Baal, which may be compared with one part of the so-called Rephaim Texts (*KTU* 1.20–1.22). These are largely dedicated to a series of invitations made to the Rephaim to come and feast.[72] These Rephaim are repeatedly called *'ilnym* in the Rephaim Texts just as they are at the end of the Baal Cycle (1.6 VI 45–47, as noted above), and they are further called "Rephaim of Baal, warriors of Baal, warriors of Anat" (1.22 I 8–9).[73] The six-day feast that they celebrate in this context takes place "in the house of eating, on the summit,//in the strait, in the heart of Lebanon" (1.22 I 24–25).[74] This geographical setting is followed by a reference to the next narrative action: "Then, on the seventh [day], then Mighty Baal . . . " (lines 25–26; cf. 1.17 II 32–40).[75] Unfortunately the following lines 27–28 are unclear and the text breaks off. The geography of this passage is terrestrial compared with the "landscape" of the Baal Cycle's ending. What seems comparable is the Rephaim's identification with Baal as well as his involvement with them in the context of a feast. Just as Rephaim celebrate in a setting involving Baal in 1.22 I, in 1.6 VI 42–53 Baal is invited to partake of a feast, one that later mentions the Rephaim. This constellation of narrative features in the Rephaim Texts may also inform the end of the Baal Cycle. The Rephaim are Baal's company, and perhaps then he is in some sense represented as their leader (cf. 1.108.18–27, where Baal is invoked in association with Rp'u and the Rephaim).[76] At heart, Baal is a warrior like them. Without regarding Baal specifically as a chthonic god

---

71. See H. L. Ginsberg, "The Rebellion and Death of *Ba'lu*," *Or* 5 (1936) 198; M. Held, "Rhetorical Questions in Ugaritic and Biblical Hebrew," *EI* 9 (1969 = The W. F. Albright Festschrift) 75 n. 37; and Pardee, *COS* 1.273 n. 278.

72. For a survey of texts involving the feasting of the dead in the Ugaritic texts as well as other Syro-Mesopotamian texts, see N. Wyatt, "After Death has us parted: Encounters between the Living and the Dead in the Ancient Semitic World," in *The Perfumes of Seven Tamarisks: Studies in Honour of Wilfred G. E. Watson* (ed. G. del Olmo Lete et al.; AOAT 394; Münster: Ugarit-Verlag, 2012) 259–92.

73. The construct nouns may be singular referring to a particular *rp'u*. See the discussion below in note 79.

74. Smith, *Poetic Heroes*, 149. See Pardee, "Nouvelle étude," 45: "replis"). Cf. J. C. de Moor, "Concepts of Afterlife in Canaan," *UF* 45 (2014 = *In memoriam Oswald Loretz*) 380.

75. See D. Freedman, "Counting Formulae in the Akkadian Epics," *JANESCU* 3/2 (1970–71) 64–81.

76. See the full reconstruction and translation of Pardee, *Ritual and Cult*, 194–95.

or a *rp'u*,⁷⁷ in this context he is invited to exercise authority in conjunction with these underworld denizens through the sun-goddess's aid, much as he exercises martial prowess over the rest of the cosmos in the Baal Cycle, specifically with the aid of the craftsman-god as seen in 1.2 IV. As noted above, Baal cannot defeat Mot in their final engagement (1.6 VI 16–22), and Baal gains the upper hand only through the intervention of Shapshu (1.6 VI 22–35), when Mot appears to concede. Here again in lines 45–47 this goddess serves to aid Baal.

The sun-goddess's role here has been compared to Shamash's as judge over the dead in Mesopotamian texts.⁷⁸ The significance of Shapshu's rule of the Rephaim is not entirely clear, but it might be surmised that Baal is empowered in the underworld via the aid of the sun-goddess,⁷⁹ as these divine

77. Some scholars take *rp'u b'l* in *KTU* 1.22 I 8 as a title of Baal: J. Aistleitner, *Die mythologischen und kultischen Texte aus Ras Schamra* (2nd ed.; Budapest: Akadémiai Kiadó, 1964) 85; J. de Moor, "Rāpi'ūma–Rephaim," *ZAW* 88 (1976) 328–29; K. Spronk, *Beatific Afterlife in Ancient Israel and in the Ancient Near East* (AOAT 219; Neukirchen-Vluyn: Neukirchener, 1986) 171, 173; and Doak, *The Last of the Rephaim*, 170; note also *rp'u* in *KTU* 1.108.1, taken as a title of Baal by M. Dietrich and O. Loretz, "Baal RPU in *KTU* 1.108; 1.113 und nach 1.17 VI.25–33," *UF* 12 (1980) 179, 181. For an alternative view of this phrase *rp'u b'l* in 1.22 I 8 as "the Rephaim of Baal," see the discussion above. The phrase is taken as a singular by Rahmouni, *Divine Epithets*, 219–22. However, the contextual parallel between *KTU* 1.22 I 88–9 and 1.22 II 7–8 suggests a plural (see Lewis, "the Rapiuma," *UNP* 201, 203). Thus Baal may be in some sense "aligned" with Rp'u and the Rephaim in *KTU* 1.108.18–27 and perhaps in 1.22 I 21–26 (see Smith, *Poetic Heroes*, 140, 150), contrary to the generalization of F. Stavrakopoulou, *Land of Our Fathers: The Roles of Ancestor Veneration in Biblical Land Claims* (LHB/OTS 473; London: T. & T. Clark, 2010) 19: "they [the dead] were unlikely to have been aligned with 'high gods' such as El, Baal and Yhwh."

78. See J. F. Healey, "The Sun Deity and the Underworld: Mesopotamia and Ugarit," in *Death in Mesopotamia* (ed. B. Alster; Mesopotamia 8; Copenhagen: Akademisk Forlag, 1980) 239–42, and "Ugaritic HTK: A Note," *UF* 12 (1980) 408–9; cf. T. J. Lewis, *Cults of the Dead in Ancient Israel and Ugarit* (HSS 39; Atlanta: Scholars, 1989) 36 n. 155. It is sometimes claimed that line 45–46 is to be translated "O Shapsu, the Rapiuma are under you" (or the like). See Kutter, *nūr ilī*, 175 n. 868; C. B. Hays, *A Covenant with Death: Death in the Iron Age II and Its Rhetorical Uses in Proto-Isaiah* (Grand Rapids: Eerdmans, 2015) 124 n. 176. As acknowledged by Kutter and by Pardee (*COS* 1.273 n. 279), a nominal sentence would take the nominal plural case ending and not the oblique case ending as appears here in *rp'im*, which points to a direct object governed by a transitive verb (as in the translation of Ginsberg, *ANET* 141: "Shapsh shall govern . . ."; cf. the older scholarship in support of this view in Smith, "Kothar wa-Hasis," 403). It is to be observed that Kutter (*nūr ilī*, 184) acknowledges here Shapshu's "'ordnende' Funktion."

79. Cf. Barker ("'And thus you brightened the heavens . . . ,'" 51) "Shapsh rules over the *rp'um* and the dead (*KTU* 1.6 VI 46–48), presumably because of Baal's victory over Mot." To my mind, Shapshu rules the Rephaim because this is one of her roles, not because of what Baal may have accomplished. Indeed, in 1.6 VI 16–35, Baal is not particularly victorious over Mot; their conflict ends in a stalemate (as noted above).

Rephaim appear to be called Baal's company in the following bicolon. Lines 48–49 inform the addressee that his company involves "the gods" (*'ilm*), also called in parallelism "the dead" (*mtm*).[80] This couplet in lines 45–47 may echo Shapshu's earlier role in helping to recover Baal's body from the underworld (1.6 I 8–15).[81] As she passes through the underworld at night, she is a regular, yet "temporary resident"[82] there. The sun-deity exercises her role in both the upper and nether worlds, passing through the former by day and the latter by night.[83] Accordingly, she is, to use Neal Walls's phrase, an "arbiter of magical powers."[84]

The next bicolon in lines 49–50 introduces the figure of Kothar wa-Hasis, here said to be either the addressee's companion and friend[85] or his

---

Baal gains his superior status at this point, with Shapshu's warning to Mot about El's lack of support for him and Mot's subsequent fear and apparent concession to Baal. Barker also suggests that Shapshu's welfare in *KTU* 1.6 is tied to Baal's survival ("'And thus you brightened the heavens . . . ,'" 44); while possibly true, the point of the narrative representation of Shapshu in *KTU* 1.6 seems to be that she seeks to aid Baal's proper burial as well as his return to life. It does not seem particularly "a self-interested move for Shapash" that "by securing Ba'al's life and settling the conflict, Shapash comes to rule among the living and the dead (*KTU* 1.6 VI 23–49)." Her "interest" (if there is one) seems to be the cosmic balance in favor of Baal as expressed by her view of El's will. Finally, *KTU* 1.3 V 17–18 stands outside of the Baal-Mot conflict and therefore is not to be explained "as a result of the Ba'al-Mot conflict" (Barker, "'And thus you brightened the heavens . . . ,'" 45).

80. The parallelism of these four terms has been recognized; see N. J. Tromp, *Primitive Conceptions of Death and the Nether World in the Old Testament* (Biblica et Orientalia 21; Rome: Pontifical Biblical Institute, 1969) 177; Lewis, *Cults of the Dead*, 36 n. 157, and "Dead," *DDD* 227; M. J. Suriano, *The Politics of Dead Kings: Dynastic Ancestors in the Book of Kings and Ancient Israel* (FAT 2/48; Tübingen: Mohr/Siebeck, 2010) 152; B. R. Doak, *The Last of the Rephaim: Conquest and Cataclysm in the Heroic Ages of Ancient Israel* (Ilex Foundation Series 7; Cambridge: Harvard University Press, 2012) 166 n. 59; Hays, *A Covenant with Death*, 107, 115. For the dead as divine, see also Stavrakopoulou, *Land of Our Fathers*, 19.

81. See del Olmo Lete, *Incantations*, 90.

82. The expression comes from the discussion of astral deities, including the sun-deity, in P. Steinkeller, "Of Stars and Men: The Conceptual and Mythological Setup of Babylonian Extispicy," in *Biblical and Oriental Essays in Memory of William L. Moran* (ed. A. Gianto; Biblica et Orientalia 48; Rome: Pontificio Istituto Biblico, 2005) 21.

83. Cf. Steinkeller, "Of Stars and Men," 23. For comparison of Shamash with Shapshu, see T. J. Lewis, *Cults of the Dead in Ancient Israel and Ugarit* (HSS 39; Atlanta: Scholars, 1989) 35–46; Kutter, *nūr ilī*, 178–80.

84. Walls, "The Gods of Israel," 267.

85. So Ginsberg, *ANET* 141, and other scholars listed in Smith, "Kothar wa-Hasis," 406, and Rahmouni, *Divine Epithets*, 182 n.1. See also Pardee, *COS* 1.273.

magician//diviner[86] (literally, "knower").[87] In either case, this bicolon may serve to express Kothar's help to Baal, just as Kothar had helped him earlier in the story in his defeat of Yamm in 1.2 IV. Kothar's role here perhaps parallels Shapshu's here. Both perhaps support Baal just as they had helped him earlier in the cycle. Before the scribal lines and the following colophon in lines 54–58 is a tricolon in lines 51–53 that elaborates on Kothar's role. Here, either on "the day" but more likely "in the sea"[88] of Arsh and Tnn, Kothar will act. The verbs predicated of Kothar (*yd//ytr*) are debated.[89] The root *ydy in the sense "to expel" is used elsewhere for magical action (parallel with *grš in *KTU* 1.16 V 11, 18, 21, 27;[90] *KTU* 1.169.1, with *grš in line 9),[91] which would suit the context here. Under this interpretation, Kothar would be attributed the capacity to expel hostile entities in the waters, perhaps analogous in power to his first magical weapon designed to "expel" (*grš) in *KTU* 1.2 IV 11–13. In any case, presumably Kothar is represented as acting with respect to the waters in a manner helpful to the addressed figure of Baal. The allusion to Arsh and Tnn echo the earlier speech of Anat's, where she mentions these two figures as well as a number of others. Once again this later part of the cycle echoes an earlier section. It may be that this final section serves to bring together a number of different thematic strands running through the cycle.

---

86. For this view, with support from the same terms in *KTU* 1.169.9–10, see M. S. Smith, "The Magic of Kothar wa-Hasis, the Ugaritic Craftsman God, in *KTU* 1.6 VI 49–50," *RB* 91 (1984) 377–80; Smith, "Kothar wa-Hasis," 407–9; Lewis, *Cults of the Dead*, 36–37 n. 158; O. Loretz, "'Schwarze Magie' des Tages in Hi 3,8 und *KTU* 1.6 VI 45b–53; 1.14 I 19–20; 1.4 VII 54–56. Zur Überlieferung der 'schwarzen Magie' in Altsyrien-Palästina," *UF* 32 (2000) 279–81; Kutter, *nūr ilī*, 175, 181–83; and Rahmouni, *Divine Epithets*, 182, 201–2, 266–68. For studies of the terms in *KTU* 1.169.9–10, see M. Dietrich and O. Loretz, "Sprecher und Gegner in den Schlangenbeschwörungen *KTU* 1.169 (RIH 78/20) und *KTU* 1.178 (RS 92.2014)," *UF* 43 (2011) 41–51; and H. D. Dewrell, "A Ugaritic Incantation against Gonorrhea," *UF* 44 (2013) 23–46, esp. 37–38. Note also the later "Phoenician" tradition of Chousor as an expert in spells, attested in Philo of Byblos. For the text, see Attridge and Oden, *Philo of Byblos*, 44–45.

87. For this word in this sense in *KTU* 1.178.9, see Pardee, *COS* 1.327 n. 1: "the term *d'tm* designates a category of sorcerer." See also Rahmouni, *Divine Epithets*, 182.

88. Kutter, *nūr ilī*, 176.

89. For a survey of older scholarship on this matter, see Smith, "Kothar wa-Hasis," 411–17. Here I follow Pardee, *COS* 1.273 n. 280.

90. For what he calls "El's magic" in this scene, as well as the verbal roots, see H. L. Ginsberg, "Ugaritico-Phoenicia," *JANESCU* 5 (1973) 132–34, 147; note also Cross, *Canaanite Myth*, 181.

91. See *DULAT* 945 (see also its use for Baal's role as divine warrior in driving away the enemy from the city walls in *KTU* 1.119.28, 35). Correspondingly, *DULAT* takes the parallel verb *ytr* from *ntr and translates, "to banish."

The further meaning of this final section of the narrative in lines 42–53 is difficult to gauge, apart from the general point that Baal's dominion is to extend now in some fashion to the waters and underworld, just as his power earlier in the text is to extend over the figures of Sea and Death. Baal's kingship is realized in some sense in the sea and underworld as it is in the rest of the Ugaritic cosmos. Kothar's possible role as diviner on behalf of Baal may be suggestive of magical practice.[92] It has been noted that the storm-god Adad is associated with divination. According to Daniel Schwemer, this association follows from the storm-god's attributes of lightning, thunder and rain as standard omina.[93] Suggesting that it is specifically the storm-god's wind that interacts with the sun-god in such divinatory contexts, Piotr Steinkeller notes that Adad is commonly associated with the sun-god in divinatory practice, with "Adad acting as an assistant of the sun-god. Thus, Adad helps the sun-god to transport ghosts and undesirable elements to the netherworld."[94] The crucial elements of the storm-god acting in tandem with the sun-deity in the context of divinatory practice may be similarly operative in the final section of the narrative of the Baal Cycle. Here the focus falls, however, on the storm-god and not on the sun-goddess, and it seems quite possible that the traditional motif of the sun-deity being helped by the storm-god as found in divinatory practice is shaped to exalt Baal, since here he is not only the addressee but also the focus. In this view, the sun-goddess and the craftsman-god serve to support Baal in relation to the underworld and its denizens, the divine Rephaim. This final speech to Baal is to suggest that he has power to exercise in the realms of his enemies fought earlier in the Baal Cycle, namely the sea and the underworld, in no measure thanks to the help exercised by Kothar and the sun-goddess. This concluding piece addressed to Baal (*KTU* 1.6 VI 42–53) perhaps suggests what power Baal can exercise in the realms of Yamm and Mot also with the help of Shapshu as well as Kothar.

In his reflections on Sumerian literary works, Thorkild Jacobsen characterized them as "works of praise,"[95] whether in narrative form as myth or epic, or in descriptive form as hymn. This notion of the Baal Cycle as

---

92. Cf. del Olmo Lete, *Incantations*, 16–17.

93. D. Schwemer, *Die Wettergottgestalten Mesopotamiens und Nordsyriens im Zeitalter der Keilschriftkulturen: Materialen und Studien nach den schriftlichen Quellen* (Wiesbaden: Harrassowitz, 2001) 221–26, 327, 687–94, noted and discussed by Steinkeller, "Of Stars and Men," 43.

94. Steinkeller, "Of Stars and Men," 43.

95. T. Jacobsen, *The Harps That Once . . . : Sumerian Poetry in Translation* (New Haven: Yale University Press, 1987) xiii.

narrative praise is quite suitable to Baal's achievements in this work.[96] In addition, the Baal Cycle, like other myths and epics, evokes divine presence in a human world. In the cycle, this presence is marked by famous places both at home (Sapan) and afar (Egypt and Crete), as well as the cosmic sites of the divine council and the home of El and the realms of Yamm and Mot; by contrast, rituals invoke deities into the human world.[97] The concluding address to Baal does not appear to maintain this distinction, but seems to blur narrative evocation and ritual invocation. For understanding the Baal Cycle's ending, another of Jacobsen's intuitions may be cited. He suggested that these "genres all seem to derive ultimately from incantations."[98] Whether or not such a textual genealogy can be affirmed as a historical-cultural matter, it captures the crucial performative dimension inhering in a text such as the Baal Cycle. As a whole it is a text of performance, as signaled explicitly by the instructions to reciters in 1.4 V 42–43[99] demarcated by scribal lines (as noted above). It appears designed to exercise a participatory effect on audiences. Indeed, the closest analogy for the instructions to reciters is found in a ritual prescription about recitation.[100] Recitation as a matter of performance is, in a sense, ritualistic.

This performative character may be signaled also by the Baal Cycle's ending. Lines 42–53 conjure up an incantational power on Baal's behalf, marked most explicitly by its magical representation of Kothar. Perhaps lying beneath the surface of the Baal Cycle is an "incantational world" (e.g., in *KTU* 1.82), possibly informing the helping roles of Shapshu and Anat as well as the threats posed by Mot and other enemies.[101] Indeed, as Dennis

---

96. Cf. the fourth-century Aramaic coin inscription of the priest Manbog, "servant of Hadad ... who sings of Hadad, his lord (*b'lh*)." The iconography includes a double-axe. See Greenfield, *'Al Kanfei Yonah*, 1:296–304 (with its periphrastic rendering of the verb ("praises the might ... ").

97. For this contrast, see M. S. Smith, *The Priestly Vision of Genesis 1* (Minneapolis: Fortress, 2010) 151–52.

98. Jacobsen, *The Harps That Once* ... , xiii.

99. See Smith and Pitard, *The Ugaritic Baal Cycle*, 2:576, also noting the similar instruction along the side of the tablet at *KTU* 1.19 IV.

100. *KTU* 1.40.35 in Pardee, *Ritual and Cult*, 80 and 83.

101. Anat figures as a source of help with Baal in the incantational text, *KTU* 1.82.38–40, according to the rendering of del Olmo Lete, *Incantations*, 111–13; see also G. del Olmo Lete, *Canaanite Religion according to the Liturgical Texts of Ugarit* (2nd ed.; trans. W. G. E. Watson; AOAT 408; Münster: Ugarit-Verlag, 2014) 320–26. Baal (lines 1, 10), Mot (line 5), and Shapshu (line 6) also play roles in this text, as do the Rephaim (see line 32). Shapshu plays a significant role in a number of incantational texts. Tnn has also been seen in 1.82.1 (*DULAT*, 860; cf. del Olmo Lete, *Incantations*, 113–14, 116, 123). Note also the reference to Baal in association with the "fleeing" (serpent) in *KTU* 1.82.38, associated by commentators with the fleeing serpent of 1.5 I 1 (del Olmo Lete,

Pardee has noted,[102] this "incantational world," with its demonic threats and its magical aid, was the world of the famous Ilimilku, named as the scribe of both the Baal Cycle and the difficult incantation text, *KTU* 1.179.[103] The matters of these textual worlds were of no less concern to his royal patron.[104] In sum, the initial call to feast as well as the roles of Shapshu and Kothar in 1.6 VI 42–53 may evoke a ritualized "textual moment" when Baal may enjoy power over realms both "naturally"[105] his (the heavens and the earth[106]) and not "naturally" his (the sea and the underworld). For ritually eternal "textual moments" such as the Baal Cycle's conclusion, Baal can be, perhaps paradoxically, *bʻl* over all.

CONCLUDING REFLECTIONS

The Ugaritic literary texts discussed above largely constitute heroic literature dedicated to warriors. The themes that they share in common serve to point up various aspects of Baal as warrior in the Baal Cycle. The story of Kirta operates at the level of human kingship, while the Baal Cycle presents the warrior conflicts as a matter of competition for divine kingship. Both of these kings also face threats to their kingship and surmount them. Beyond their battles that they wage, the two stories share the deeper commonality of the paradox of the king's life and death. In arguably the "most heroic" of the Ugaritic stories, Aqhat, life and death are likewise central. The reality of the deceased, divinized heroes in the Rephaim Texts explicitly links to the final part of the Baal Cycle. A similar paradox of life and death informs these texts as well, as they are concerned with the life that the Rephaim enjoy in death. At stake with all of the male heroes are life and death. Death

---

Canaanite Religion, 321 n. 147 and *Incantations*, 112, 122).

102. Pardee, *The Ugaritic Texts*, 46.

103. See the colophons in *KTU* 1.6 VI 54–58 and 1.179.40–43. For Ilimilku and these two colophons, see Pardee, *The Ugaritic Texts*, 41–48. Pardee has lowered the date of Ilimilku toward the end of the thirteenth century.

104. For death and the royal palace of Ugarit, see H. Niehr, "The Topography of Death in the Royal Palace of Ugarit: Preliminary Thoughts on the Basis of Archaeological and Textual Data," in *Le Royaume d'Ougarit de la Crète à l'Euphrate: Nouveaux Axes de Recherche* (ed. J.-M. Michaud; Proche-Orient et Littérature Ougaritique 2; Sherbrooke, Québec: GGC, 2007) 219–42. For a comparison with Ebla, see Archi, *Ebla and Its Archives*, 546–69.

105. For this cultural sense of "natural," see M. Douglas, *Natural Symbols: Explorations in Cosmology* (New York: Pantheon, 1970).

106. See his titles, "rider of the clouds" (*rkb ʻrpt*) and "lord of the earth" (*bʻl ʼarṣ*), in Rahmouni, *Divine Epithets*, 162–64 and 288–91.

potentially decimates that life (Aqhat) or will commemorate it (Kirta among the Rephaim, noted below); Baal partakes of both. Yet it is not only the life of each individual male hero that is at stake. It also means life for those around them. The web of relations involved in all four literary texts is largely a matter of family, whether human or divine.[107]

All four literary texts evoke warriors at different stages of life. Aqhat presents a younger figure that unlike Baal fails to become a hero. His family can provide aid only up to a point, culminating in the vengeance that his sister can take against his murderer. By contrast, Baal is the successful warrior albeit in need of the help provided by various deities. Overall, the deities of the Baal Cycle play out divine ideals for warriors and their conflicts over divine kingship. King Kirta is the embodiment of the heroic royal ideal; he is a warrior-king already successful in achieving kingship and a king who can conquer, rather like Baal. The Rephaim Texts present heroes who have passed from life to death. They also represent the long lineage of deceased, divine heroes that a king such as Kirta could aspire to join (*KTU* 1.15 III 2–4, 13–15): "May you be much exalted, O Kirta,/Among the Netherworld's shades/In the midst of Ditana's company!"[108] The royal funerary ritual mentions this company in framing the names of specific *rpʾu*s preceding references to more recent kings (1.161.3, 10). The name of Ditanu (with the variant, Didanu) evokes high antiquity for ancient Ugarit, with his name going back to the ancient Amorite lineage of Didanu/Tidanu.[109] The name further denotes divine status, as Ditana appears at Ugarit also as a source of ritual inquiry (1.124.2, 4, 11, 14).[110] Lineage is further evoked in the Rephaim Texts with the references to "your son(s)" and "your grandson(s)" in 1.22 I 2–3.

Taken together, the Ugaritic literary texts offer human and divine models of warriors. They also sound cautionary notes about royal life and intimate the destiny of death. At the same time, each of the texts is unique in representing warrior themes. The Baal Cycle departs from all of the others on many levels and in many details, but most especially with the figure of Baal himself, signaled by the prose superscription for the text, *lbʿl*

---

107. For the Baal Cycle on this score, note Pardee, *The Ugaritic Texts*, 75–77.

108. Parker, "Kirta," in *UNP*, 26–27.

109. As observed by many scholars, such as Pardee, *COS* 1.358 n. 5; Smith, *The Ugaritic Baal Cycle*, vol. 1, 112–13, and *Poetic Heroes*, 460 n. 132, with further data and prior bibliography. See also P. Steinkeller, "Early Semitic Literature and Third Millennium Seals with Mythological Motifs," in *Literature and Literary Language at Ebla* (ed. P. Fronzaroli; Quaderni Semitistica 18; Florence: Dipartimento di Linguistica, Università di Firenze, 1992) 261–62.

110. Parker, "Kirta," in *UNP*, 45 n. 69.

(*KTU* 1.6 I 1).¹¹¹ The Baal Cycle focuses on Baal's victories and setbacks. He alone wields meteorological power particularly manifest from his heavenly palace on Sapan (1.4 VI 27–37), providing agricultural fertility and life to the world (see 1.4 V 6–9), in other words, "a touch of Eden" (to use Jonas Greenfield's expression for **'dn* in this passage).¹¹² Baal claims in terms that sound like a royal boast¹¹³ that only he can provide for gods and men and satisfy the multitudes of the earth (1.4 VII 49–52). Unlike the other figures, Baal is a god with a story that in the extant text is relatively unconcerned with dynasty and descendants. Instead, this warrior-king can provide life for deities, humans and the world, thanks to his particular sort of meteorological warriorship.

Baal's story is, in several ways, also the story of other deities, helping him at any number of critical points, as he rises, falls and returns to kingship. Baal has a unique relationship with his ally and sister, Anat, who aids him in several ways (*KTU* 1.3 II and 1.5 VI–1.6 II). The destruction of Mot at her hands, in other words, the "death of death" (1.6 II), permits Baal's return to life. She herself is a source of life for Baal's own life.¹¹⁴ While in conflict with Yamm and Mot (1.2 IV and 1.5 VI), Baal is also aided by Kothar (1.2 IV) and Shapshu (1.6 I, IV, and VI). Baal also stands at the center of interaction with El and Athirat, each of whom initially opposes him.¹¹⁵ Baal can defy

---

111. It is unclear why this same superscription does not appear at *KTU* 1.5 I 1, as observed by commentators (e.g., Pardee, *COS* 1.268 n. 241, and *The Ugaritic Texts*, 42 n. 4).

112. Greenfield, *'Al Kanfei Yonah*, 219–24, in reference to this passage. See also del Olmo Lete, *Incantations*, 89.

113. Cf. the form of Esarhaddon's claim in Ass. F (lines 9–12) "I am also the one who knows how to greatly revere the gods and goddesses of heaven and the netherworld." See E. Leichty, *The Royal Inscriptions of Esarhaddon, King of Assyria (680–669 BC)* (RINA 4; Winona Lake, IN: Eisenbrauns, 2011) 151. Note also the claim of Hadadyith'i who sets up his stela "so that his word may be pleasing to gods and to people" (A. Millard, *COS* 2.154). Cf. the work of the junior gods in Atrahasis I line 339, "For food for the peoples, for the sustenance of [the gods]"; see W. G. Lambert and A. R. Millard, *Atra-Ḫasīs: The Babylonian Story of the Flood* (Oxford: Clarendon, 1969) 66–67.

114. Cf. Wyatt's characterization of Anat as "a kind of *Anima* to Baal himself" (Wyatt, "The Religious Role," 707; Wyatt's italics). Note the titulary devoted to Anat at the head of the inscription on a stele of Ninurta-kudurri-uṣur of Suhu dedicated to the goddess (see K. L. Younger, Jr., *COS* 2.283).

115. A critical issue is the historical importance of Baal relative to El. While the Baal Cycle seems to depict Baal as a newcomer relative to El, the historical situation has been thought by Alfonso Archi to be the opposite. Adda (Baal-Hadad) is a main god at Ebla already in the second half of the third millennium. As for El, Lambert (*Ancient Mesopotamian Religion*, 78–79, 221) detects possible evidence for this god in personal names from Ebla, Abu Salabikh, and Mari, while Archi (*Ebla and Its Archives*, 223, 570–91, 638–55) does not believe that El exists until the second millennium (see also

the force of El's decree (1.2 I 36–38), and then win over a reluctant El (1.4 V 62-V1); his death later induces El's lamentation for him (1.5 VI 11–25), and the prospect of his return to life even inspires joy in El (1.6 III 14–21). In the end, the threat of El's lack of support for Mot translates into Baal's return to his throne (1.6 VI 22–35). Athirat, initially fearful of Baal (1.4 II 12–26), is induced to help him (1.4 II 26-IV 57), and Baal includes her children in his feast inaugurating his palace (1.4 VI 44–46); at this point in the narrative they are included with the rubric of "his brothers." Still she may revert to her prior negative attitude in nominating Baal's successor in 1.6 I while he is dead.[116] In the Baal Cycle, the lives of the deities revolve around Baal, and his is critically dependent upon theirs.

In Aaron Tugendhaft's terms,[117] the Baal Cycle presents a prescriptive political vision of about Baal and about kingship (in other words, a vision that its monarchic sponsors want audiences to believe). To be Baal in the Baal Cycle is to provide life and to engage the forces of destruction and

---

W. Herrmann, "El," in *DDD* 275; for different views of the Mari evidence of *ilum* as El or "the god", see Hurowitz, *I Have Built You*, 333). If Archi were correct, the emergence of El perhaps on the model of Ea/Enki (attested at Ebla) might serve to explain their similar natures as wise and kindly, senior gods with watery abodes, as long observed; see M. H. Pope, *El in the Ugaritic Texts* (VTSup 2; Leiden: Brill, 1955) 43, 45, 71–72; Greenfield, *'Al Kanfei Yonah*, 2:895; and Lambert, *Ancient Mesopotamian Religion*, 78–79. W. Dietrich ("Enki/Ea und El—Die Götter der Künste und Magie," in *Studien zu Ritual und Sozialgeschichte im Alten Orient: Tartuer Symposien 1998-2004* [ed. T. R. Kämmerer; BZAW 374; Berlin: de Gruyter, 2007] 93–126) regards El as the Ugaritic "pendant" of Ea (cf. Ea and El also in Hurrian offering lists at Ugarit, e.g., *KTU* 1.110.3, 6, and 1.111.4, 9, 10). By contrast, the correspondence between Ea and Kothar especially in the god-lists at Ugarit has been emphasized by E. Lipinski, "Éa, Kothar and El," *UF* 20 (1988) 137–43. For further discussion, see I. Yakubovich, "The West Semitic God El in Anatolian Hieroglyphic Transmission," in *Pax Hethitica: Studies on the Hittites and Their Neighbours in Honour of Itamar Singer* (ed. Y. Cohen, A. Gilan, and J. L. Miller; Studien zu den Boğazköy-Texten 51; Wiesbaden: Harrassowitz, 2010) 385–98, esp. 390–94. The thrust of the suggestions made by Archi and Lipinski would be to view El (the wise, high level god) and Kothar (the wise, divine craftsman) as differentiations of the wise god, Ea/Enki, and possibly as divine instantiations of their very names (*'wl, "to be strong," and *ktr, "to be skillful"), not unlike the names of Baal, Yamm and Mot as well as Shapshu and Yarih. With respect to Kothar, the differentiation of a named specialized divine craftsman would fit the observation by Avigdor Hurowitz that having specialized named human craftsmen is a feature of West Semitic tradition and is not Mesopotamian; see Hurowitz, *I Have Built You*, 102–3, and "The Priestly Account of Building the Tabernacle," *JAOS* 105 (1985) 21–30. If correct, the differentiation of Kothar would be prior to El's, if the former is the god attested at Ebla under the name, ^{d}ka-ša-lu as thought by scholars (e.g., Lambert, *Ancient Mesopotamian Religion*, 221). The issues are complex and largely remain *sub iudice*. As suggested by the study of Yakubovich, the study of El in the first millennium also remains a desideratum.

116. Perhaps caution is in order; see Pardee, *COS* 1.269 n. 244.

117. For Tugendhaft's work, see above notes 9, 16, 18 and 23.

death, on the natural, human and divine levels. The vision that the Baal Cycle is designed to convey is that Baal's warrior kingship is not simply for himself, but crucially also for others.[118] This is what the "might" of Baal the warrior-king ultimately means in the Baal Cycle. After all, "Mighty Baal" (*ʾalʾiyn bʿl*) is not only the god's most common epithet;[119] it is also the most common epithet of any deity in the Ugaritic corpus.[120] Furthermore, it is only in the Baal Cycle (*KTU* 1.3 III 1, IV 7–8, VI 25 [reconstructed]; 1.4 VIII 34–35, 1.5 II 10–11, 18) that he is called "mightiest of warriors" (*ʾalʾiy qrdm*). The cycle represents Baal as the deity that embodies warrior-kingship for the world. In turn, for its scribal producers and oral performers, its sponsors and audiences, it encodes the world with this heroic vision of the god.[121]

---

118. What Baal provides as warrior-king in the Baal Cycle compares also with the benefits granted by Baal and "by the grace of Baal and the gods" to Azatawada for his kingdom (*KAI* 26; K. L. Younger, *COS* 2.148–49). These include "abundance and luxury" and the defeat of rebels, as well as the "ease (*nḥt*) of heart" similar to El's rest (**nwḫ*) for his spirit that he expresses about Baal in *KTU* 1.6 III 18–19 (cf. *lb nḫtk* [?] in *KTU* 2.103.10, but compare 2.103.31, and thus emended by P. Bordreuil and D. Pardee, with R. Hawley, *Une bibliothèque au sud de la ville: Textes 1994-2002 en cunéiforme alpha-bétique de la Maison d'Ourtenou* [Ras Shamra-Ougarit 18; Lyon: Maison de l'orient et de la Méditerranée, 2012] 187).

119. Seventy-two times by the count of Rahmouni, *Divine Epithets*, 61.

120. So Rahmouni, *Divine Epithets*, 61.

121. I wish to thank Aaron Tugendhaft and Michael Davis for their comments on an earlier draft of this essay.

3

Baal in Boston, Bethel in Amherst[1]

Karel van der Toorn[2]

BETHEL IN THE AMHERST PAPYRUS

FOR MANY YEARS, SCHOLARS knew little more about Bethel than his name. The deity is mentioned once in the Bible as the god on whom the House of Israel relied, the way the Moabites relied on the god Chemosh (Jer 48:13). The most significant extrabiblical evidence was the occurrence of Bethel and Anat-Bethel in a list of divine witnesses in two treaties of Esarhaddon.[3] Since the discovery and decipherment of an Aramaic papyrus from Egypt—Aramaic in language, Egyptian in script—we have gained access to a prime source of knowledge about Bethel. Papyrus Amherst 63, as the text in question is known to the scholarly world, dates back to

---

1. *Editor's note*: Due to delays in publication of the present volume, Prof. van der Toorn's book-length treatment of this papyrus appeared prior to this essay; see van der Toorn, *Papyrus Amherst 63* (AOAT 448; Münster: Ugarit-Verlag, 2018).

2. *Author's note*: Though I recall Simon Parker first of all for his humor and his kindness, as a scholar I honor him especially for his contributions on Ugarit and the Bible. He was my Baal in Boston—and somehow still is because I encounter his name almost daily on the cover of some of the books that I use. This contribution in honor of his memory looks at a deity that is in many ways the successor of Baal—the god Bethel. I also owe a debt of gratitude to Mark S. Smith, New York, for his comments on an earlier version of this paper.

3. See S. Parpola and K. Watanabe, *Neo-Assyrian Treaties and Loyalty Oaths* (SAA 2; Helsinki: Helsinki University Press, 1988) no. 5:iv 6'–7'; no. 6:467–68, "May Bethel and Anat-Bethel deliver you to the paws of a man-eating lion."

the late third century BCE.[4] It is the literary heritage of a predominantly Aramean community; its members were the descendants of the soldiers who once formed the core of the "Syenean garrison" stationed at Syene and Elephantine in southern Egypt.[5] The principal god of these Aramean soldiers was Bethel, venerated along with his consort "Queen-of-Heaven;" Nabu and Banit were the other divine couple receiving worship from the Aramean community. Both Bethel and Queen-of-Heaven, on the one hand, and Nabu and Banit, on the other, had temples in Syene.[6] In the Amherst papyrus the same deities play a role, with a leading part for Bethel. Bethel—more commonly referred to with his epithet "Lord," Mār—is the number one of the Amherst Papyrus and the community to which the papyrus gives witness.[7] A perusal of the data the papyrus provides about Bethel yields the contours of his portrait. Anticipating the discussion of the evidence, we may say that, by the middle of the first millennium BCE, Bethel had inherited most of the traits that Baal had had since the second millennium.

Though Bethel is the deity that dominates papyrus Amherst 63, his name occurs only seven times in the 23 columns of the papyrus; the name of his consort Anat just once or twice.[8] However, the relative infrequency of the names Bethel and Anat is deceptive; the papyrus refers to him as Mār, "Lord," and to her as Māra, "Lady" (possibly to be read as Mārī, "my Lord," and Mārtī, "My Lady.")[9] The fact that Mār is the epithet of Bethel is particu-

---

4. The most accessible presentation and translation of the papyrus is available in R. C. Steiner, "The Aramaic Text in Demotic Script (1.99)," in *COS* 1:309–27. The transliterations and translations offered in this contribution are based on two sets of photographs of the texts, the one set from 1901 kept at the Oriental Institute, University of Chicago, the other set from a few years ago, from the text as currently preserved in the Pierpont Morgan Library. I thank the librarians and curators involved for their kindness in providing me with excellent digital copies of these photographs.

5. For the expression *ḥylʾ swnknyʾ* see B. Porten and A. Yardeni, *Textbook of Aramaic Documents from Ancient Egypt* (4 vols.; Jerusalem: Hebrew University Press, 1986–1999) C3.14:32. The most thorough study of the Jewish colony at Elephantine is still B. Porten, *Archives from Elephantine: The Life of an Ancient Jewish Military Colony* (Berkeley: University of California Press, 1968).

6. Known from the so-called Hermopolis letters, see *TAD* A2.1–7, esp. A2.1:1 (Temple of Bethel and Temple of the Queen of Heaven); A2.2:1, 12 (Temple of Banit, 2x); A2.3:1 (Temple of Nabu); A2.4:1 (Temple of Banit).

7. The premier position of Mar and Mara is clear from the list of divine blessings preserved in VIII 1–7, where Mar and Mara open the list; they are followed by Baal and Pidray; Bel and Belet; Nabu and Nanay; Yaho and Asherah.

8. Bethel occurs by name in VI 22; VIII 13; IX 9, 13; X 9; XII 18; XVII 15. The only sure occurrence of the name Anat is found in VIII 9; possibly in X 8. Note the occurrences of Eshem-Bethel in XVI 1, 14, 15; and of Herem-Bethel in XVII 14.

9. In my transliteration of the text I have adopted—with a few minor modifications—the system followed by Sven P. Vleeming and Jan Wim Wesselius, presented in

larly clear in the cycle of psalms in X 9–XI 16; the first psalm opens with the invocation of Bethel (X 9: "Bethel, God on high"), a god addressed in the next line and throughout the psalms as Mār (X 10: "Do let it rain, Lord"). According to the list of divine blessings, Mār blesses "from Rash" (VIII 2; see also XVII 15); which implies his identity with Bethel because Rash is the home address of Bethel, "the God of Rash."[10] In the Amherst Papyrus, Mār does not occur as an epithet of other gods. The only exception to that rule is more apparent than real; in the three Israelite psalms contained in the papyrus (XII 11–19; XIII 1–10; XIII 11–17), Yaho is also referred to as Mār (XII 15, 17, 18; XIII 8, 16, 17), but this is based entirely on the identification of Yaho and Bethel (see XII 18). Richard Steiner, in his translation of the papyrus in the *Context of Scripture,* leaves both Mar and Mara untranslated. He has a good reason to do so: for all practical purposes, the epithets Mār and Māra do duty as proper names, in a way that is very similar to the use of Adonay for Yahweh, Baal for Hadad, and Bel for Marduk. Wherever we encounter "Mār" in our texts, then, the reference is to Bethel.[11] "Bethel" occurs seven times in the texts; "Mār" over forty times.[12] His consort Mara is also very present with some 20 appearances.[13] Further references to Bethel are extant in such designations as "the God of Rash," "the Resident of Hamath," "the Guardian of Seyan," and—perhaps—Mār Shamayin, "the Lord of Heaven."[14]

The Amherst papyrus is a collection of hymns, laments, rituals, and historical narrative.

Myth in the sense scholars traditionally assign to that term is absent from the Amherst papyrus; there is nothing like the Baal Cycle or *Enūma*

---

their *Studies in Papyrus Amherst 63: Essays on the Aramaic/demotic Papyrus Amherst 63* (Vol. 2; Amsterdam: Juda Palache Instituut, 1990) 109–11; hence mry.C and mrty.C. In the translations, however, I render these epithets as "Lord" and "Lady," since I agree with Steiner that the epithets, for all practical purposes, do duty as personal names. May the inconsistency be forgiven.

10. For references to "the God of Rash" see VI 15; VII 7, 11; IX 3, 16, 18 [2x], 20; X 15, 22; XI 6, 14.

11. The one apparent exception is the reference to Yaho as Mar (XII 15, 17, 18; XIII 8, 16, 17) however, this designation is based on the implied identification of Yaho and Bethel (see XII 18).

12. See I 1, 9; III 7; VI 1; VII 2, 7, 11, 13; VIII 2, 8, 10, 11, 12, 13, 14, 15, 20; IX 8, 11, 16, 20; X 3, 10, 15, 17, 20, 23; XI 1, 2, 5, 13, 15, 16, 17, 19; XII 15, 17, 18; XIII 8, 16, 17; XIV 9; XVI 8; XVII 15.

13. See II 13, 17; III 5; IV 5, 10, 14, 15, 18; V 2; VII 13; VIII 2; X 4; XIV 1, 2; XV 7; XVII 16 [2x].

14. For references to "the God of Rash" see VI 15; VII 7, 11; IX 3, 16, 18 [2x], 20; X 15, 22; XI 6, 14; Resident of Hamath in IX 6, 10; Guardian of Seyan in X 14, 22; XI 14; Mār Shamayin in VIII 17.

eliš. In these Aramaic texts the mythology presents itself in the shape of hymns—quite like it does in the Hebrew Bible.[15] Various mythological motifs occur in theophany descriptions and in celebrations of the power, past and present, of the gods. A fine illustration of the transposition of myth into hymn is found in a cycle of four songs linked to one another by a chorus (X 9-17, 17-24; XI 1-8, 8-16). Two passages merit special attention; I offer them here in transliteration and translation.

^{9} ʾbytlG ʾlh ʿl.C
mr₂yʾm | yʾmʾ |
tʾlʾ | t₅ry.C
k₂l | ⌒{|}by | ^{10} r₂y | bʾny + ʾ₂ʾt |
lʾky | dmmʾr₂ʾn |
∞₂mʾtʾrʾ + nʾ | mry.C
^{11} bmn₄ m₃qm.C šʾḫt₂
lʾkʾ + ksʾpʾn | wʾd₂ʾhʾb{|}n₂ʾnʾ |
lʾk | ^{12} mʾlw₂ + kw₂hʾynʾ |
lʾkʾ | tʾwʾr₂yʾnʾ |
ʾnm + bʾky{| ^{13} }r₂ʾyn (X 9-13)

Bethel, God on high,
Who sweeps up the sea,
Who holds the mountains—
You create all the rainclouds.
We praise your might!
Please let it rain, Lord,
In vessel, place, and cistern.
For you is our silver and our gold;
For you is the fullness of our possessions;
For you is our bulls, yeah, our first-born.

^{1} mn₂.C lʾbʾnʾnʾ | mry.C mn + rʾšʾH
ʾr₂ᵒᶜ + kʾl | tʾkʾ |
^{2} šʾmyGʾm + m₄ Ctʾḫt | mry C
kw₂kʾbʾnL zᵒᶜ | tʾdʾr₂ʾ |

---

15. The formal distinction between myth and hymn is not absolute; in fact, both the Ugaritic Baal Cycle and *Enuma Elish* close on a hymn, the one with a hymn to Shapshu (*KTU* 1.6 vi 42-53, see the observations by M. S. Smith in *UNP*, 175 n. 202), the other with a hymn exalting Marduk under his fifty names (*Enuma Elish*, VI 121-VII 144).

³ bkl + rʾšʾ + mᵃt | ʾlhᵃnᵃ |
yʾr₂g₂ᵃm | yʾr₂ᵃmᵃ |
bᵃ{| ⁴ }qᵃlᵃwhy | yᵃrm |
yʾr₂ᵃg₂ᵃm | bᵃqᵃlᵃwhy |
m₃nhr₂ᵃ | ⁵ bᵃš
mr₂wᵃt | ymᵃ | tᵃnhᵃr₂
wᵃymr₂ᵃ | ᶜd | yqᵃdᵃnw₂ + mry.C
⁶ yᵃqdᵃnw₂ + ᵃlhrršᵃH
kᵃ + pṣy + tᵃ + nᵃr (XI 1–6)

From the Lebanon, Lord, from Rash,
You strike the entire earth;
You have stretched out the skies, o Lord,
You put the stars into trembling
in all of Rash, the land of our God.
He howls and he hurls,
With his thunders he hurls,
With his thunders he howls,
Lighting everything up with fire.
The Sea's dominions are set alight.
And He speaks till they catch fire, Lord,
Till they catch fire, God of Rash,
Like shattered sparks of light.

It is clear from these two passages that Bethel is a Storm god with two faces: As the one who "creates all the rainclouds," he has the benign face of the god who brings rain and bestows fertility on the land; but as the one who hurls his thunderbolts, he also has the terrifying face of the god who puts all of nature in disarray. His aggression is directed more specifically at the Sea. The choice of words here is striking: Bethel sets the Sea's "dominions" alight. The word is *mārût*, literally "lordship" or "kingship;" in this context, the term has a topographical connotation, designating the area over which the Sea exercises its rule.

The focus on the confrontation between Bethel and the Sea is very reminiscent of the combat of Baal against the Sea as we know it from Ugaritic sources. The one most significant difference is the emphasis on "fire" as the weapon the Storm god employs against the Sea. In the Ugaritic Baal cycle the Storm god defeats Yamm with two specially designed weapons (*ṣmd*) whose exact nature is hard to determine; it is only said that they "leap" (*rqṣ*, Gt) from Baal's hand like birds of prey (*km nšr*) and "strike" (*hlm*) Yamm; the one his torso, between the arms (*KTU* 1.2 iv 13–17), the other Yamm's head, hitting him between the eyes (*KTU* 1.2 iv 20–25).[16] Are they arrows, or spears perhaps? Quite likely these weapons are modeled on the natural phenomenon of lightning bolts, but the description of the combat is thoroughly anthropomorphized. In a similar manner, the weapon that Marduk uses to kill Tiamat is an arrow (*mulmullu*)—though Marduk also employs a net (*saparru*), and an "evil wind" (the *imḫullu*, see *Enuma Elish*, IV, 95–104).[17] Here, too, the atmospheric conditions of a storm inform the choice of weapons, but the combat is between two human-like warriors.

The Ugaritic texts do contain references to Baal casting "lightning bolts" (*brqm*) and thundering, thus wreaking havoc in nature's realm, but the notion of fighting the Sea with fire is not attested.[18] On the other hand, the theme of fire from heaven as a divine weapon does occur with some frequency in the Hebrew Bible. In the contest between Elijah and the Baal prophets, Yahweh proves himself to be "the God who answers with fire" (1 Kgs 18:20–46, quote v. 24). While Baal remains deaf to the invocations of his servants, "the fire of Yahweh (ʾēš-yhwh) descended and consumed the sacrifice, the wood, the stones, and the earth; and it licked up the water that was in the trench" (1 Kgs 18:38). Theophany descriptions in the Psalms describe Yahweh as a God who is armed with fire.

² ʿānān waʾărāpel sĕbîbâw (. . .)

³ ʾēš lĕpānâw tēlēk

ûtĕlahēṭ sābîb ṣārâw

⁴ hēʾîrû bĕrāqâw tēbēl

rāʾătâ wattāḥēl hāʾāreṣ

⁵ hārîm kaddônag nāmassû millipnê yhwh

millipnê ʾădôn kol-hāʾāreṣ (Ps 97:2–5)

Dense clouds are around Him, (. . .)
Fire marches in front of Him
Burning His enemies on every side.
His bolts light up the world;

---

16. For the various attempts at identifying the type of the weapons see M. S. Smith, *The Ugaritic Baal Cycle: Volume 1* (VTSup 55; Leiden: Brill, 1994) 338–41.

17. For a presentation of *Enuma Elish* see W. G. Lambert, *Babylonian Creation Myths* (Winona Lake, IN: Eisenbrauns, 2013) 3–144.

18. For a survey and discussion of the most relevant texts see F. M. Cross, *Canaanite Myth and Hebrew Epic* (Cambridge: Harvard University Press, 1973), 147–51.

The earth sees it and is convulsed;
Mountains melt like wax before Yahweh,
Before the Lord of all the earth.

Similar references to Yahweh's lightning bolts causing fire and lighting up the world occur in other biblical theophanies.[19] Such theophanies are qualitatively different from mythological narrative; whereas the former are poetic interpretations of natural events, the myths tell a story in which the supernatural actors are cast in human roles. But even so—the focus on fire as an arm of the god is largely absent from Ugaritic literature, while it is prominent in the Amherst psalms to Bethel and the biblical psalms to Yahweh.

Another distinct echo of the Ugaritic Baal mythology resonates in a hymn—or a series of related hymnic fragments—originally designed for the occasion of the "elevation" of a maiden as the annual bride of Bethel (IX 1–X 8). The girl in question—the beauty queen of the year—was chosen during a beauty contest; whereupon the god would manifest his approval; after which the girl, adorned as the god's bride, was to play the part of the god's consort Anat.[20] The symbolic marriage of Bethel and Anat—Mār and Māra—was celebrated as a demonstration of Bethel's pre-eminence over all the other gods. His heroism earned Bethel the right to marry Anat—formerly the spouse of Baal, and uncontestably the most desirable among the goddesses.[21] In the context of this marriage celebration, the hymn also touches upon other aspects of Bethel's mythology. There are references to his awesome interventions on earth and to his palace in the skies.

^{8} mry.C mn nḥ^{ʾ}r$_2$ʾtʾkʾ | t$_2$ʾdmʾ | kʾl + ʾpʾrʾ |
kʾtʾnʾnʾ | lʾbw$_2$nʾ | mn rw$_2$ḥʾtkʾ |
^{9} t$_2$ʾt$_2$ʾsʾ | ʿl + ʾrwyʾkʾ |
t$_3$šq$_2$qʾp | kʾnšʾr | w$_2$ʾ$_2$yq$_2$w$_2$mw$_2$ (. . .)
^{11} yʾdmʾ | mry.C ksšʾ.C
wʾdʾnʾḥʾ | ksʾnʾ |
^{12} kʾsʾn | bʾrk | šʾmʾwhy

---

19. See Ps 29:7 ("the voice of Yahweh kindles flames of fire"); 46:7; 68:2–3; 77:17–20.

20. A lot of elements are reminiscent of the selection and investiture of the NIN. DINGIR (*ittu*, from *entu*) known from the Emar tablets, see D. E. Fleming, *The Installation of Baal's High Priestess at Emar* (HSM 42; Atlanta: Scholars, 1992).

21. In the list of gods invoked for their blessings, the pair Mār and Māra is directly followed by Baal Zaphon and Pidray (VIII 2–3). According to the Ugaritic mythology, Pidray is not Baal's spouse but his daughter. But since Anat is now the consort of Bethel, Baal is demoted and left with a daughter for a wife.

Lord, through your snorts you set all the reed marshes alight,
Like the smoke of incense, through your breaths.
You fly over the places you saturated (with water),
You move your wings like an eagle and they spring back again. (IX 8–9)
The Lord turns red like the sun,
And he shines like the moon,
Like the moon along the path of heaven. (IX 11–12)

⁹ + gšw₂r₂y + bytʾkʾ | bytlG <u>mn</u>ⁿ lʾbʾnʾn |
¹⁰ <u>mn</u>ⁿ lʾbʾ₂ʾnʾnʾ | {w}ʾgʾnky | yʾnʾʾn (. . .)
¹² | ʾ₂hʾ + yʾb<u>nw</u> + bʾšʾmynG bytʾkʾ |
ḫ₂ʾrtʾ | ʿm | kw₂kʾbʾnʾ |
¹³ yrmw₂ + bʾpʾpʾ | ʿr₂ʾsʾkʾ |
bhykʾlykʾ | yʾb<u>nw</u> lʾbytlG ʾlp + <u>mn</u>₂.Cdʾbḥʾ | (. . .)

The beams of your temple, Bethel, are from the Lebanon;
From the Lebanon, your garden, are they. (IX 9–10)
Yes, let them build your house in the heavens,
A dwelling place with the stars.
Let them set up your bed in the inner sanctuary.
Let them build in your palace
A thousand altars for Bethel. (IX 12–13)

The first part of the theophany describes a storm over the reed marshes (*ʾpr*) causing fire to erupt among the canes; after the storm, as the raging winds have turned into a breeze, the bended reeds spring back again.[22] In keeping with Bethel's role as a Storm god, the winds are interpreted as the god's "snorts" (*nḥrtk*) and "breaths" (*rwḥtk*).[23] In the quiet after the storm,

---

22. The correct interpretation of the word *ʾpr* is crucial for the understanding of this passage. For the translation of this text in COS 1.99, Richard Steiner emended the Aramaic into *kʾl* + <ʿ>ʾpʾrʾ = *kl ʿpr*, "all the dust" > "earth," hence the translation "Mar, from your snorts all the <ea>rth perishes." But the text is not in need of emendation. The word *ʾpr* is related to Akkadian *appāru*, which goes back to Sumerian ambar, "reed marsh, reed bed, canebrake, lagoon," see CAD A/2 179–81 (compare Jewish Aramaic *ʾăpar*, "meadow," always situated out of town). The word Steiner translates as "perish" is *tʾdm*, literally: "You color (the reed lands) red," meaning that lightning bolts have caused the canebrake to catch fire. Also, it is only with reference to reeds that it makes sense to say that, after the storm, they "stand up (again)" (*wyqwmw*, line 9). For the image compare Job 41:12 "Out of his nostrils (*minnĕḥîrâw*) comes smoke, like a steaming cauldron in the reeds (read *bĕʾagmôn* for *wĕʾagmôn*)."

23. On the writing of *nḥrt*, "snort" (cf. Arabic *naḥīr*), see Richard Steiner, "Ḥ>H in

the god flies over the land he has drenched (*rwyk*, cf. Ps 65:11 *tĕlāmêhā rawwēh*, "drench its furrows"). Once again, Bethel is pictured as a god who sets fire to the realm of nature; the reeds burn and produce smoke "like the smoke of incense" (*ktnn lbwnʾ*, line 8). It is as though the god has kindled his own incense. The second part of the theophany likens Bethel to the sun and moon; he "turns red" (*yʾdm*) like the sun and "shines" (*wdnḥ*) like the moon. Apparently, the change of day to night is taken as another epiphany of Bethel.

The god came to the ceremonies in his (portable) shrine (*ʾrn*, line 3); but he is entitled to a "house," a "palace" befitting him.[24] The parallel with the Ugarit Baal cycle is evident. After Baal's defeat of Yamm, he is entitled to a house like the other gods. El gives his permission. "Let a house be built for Baal like for the (other) gods, a court like Athirat's (other) sons (have)."[25] The very formulation of the command in the Ugaritic text (*ybn . bt. lbcl*) has an echo in the Amherst hymn (*ybnw bšmyn bytk*, line 12). Like Baal's house, the house of Bethel is "in heaven" (*bšmyn*) and "with the stars" (*cm kwkbn*, line 12). Another parallel is the material out of which the house is drawn up. In the Baal Cycle, the god who is building Baal's house (Kothar) "sends to Lebanon for its wood, to Siryon for its choicest cedar" (*KTU* 1.4 vi 18–21). The beams of Bethel's house are from the Lebanon as well, "from the Lebanon, your garden, are they" (mn^n lʾb$_2$ʾnʾnʾ | {w}ʾgʾnky | yʾnʾʾn, IX 10). And in both cases, the dimensions of the heavenly palace are stunning; in Bethel's house there will be room for "a thousand altars for Bethel" (*lbytl ʾlp mndbḥ*, IX 13); Baal's house is to "cover a thousand fields, and his palace a myriad hectares" (*alp . šd . aḥd bt / rbt . kmn . hkl*, *KTU* 1.4 v 56–57). The use of the plural for palaces, both in the Ugaritic and in the Aramaic text, is a grammatical expression of the grandeur of the god's mansion.[26]

Assyria and Babylonia," in *A Common Cultural Heritage: Studies on Mesopotamia and the Biblical World in Honor of Barry L. Eichler* (ed. Grant Frame et al.; Bethesda, MD: CDL, 2011) 195–206, esp. 195.

24. Lines 3–8 read in translation: "Let your shrine be brought out, my God, open it and let your mouth command your food. Let your table be full of fat, full of deer. Let butchers stand in attendance upon him, all of them with skillful hands. Every bull is becoming weak. You empty your drinking bowl, Resident of Hamath, it will be poured out and they shall fill (it). And butlers stand in attendance upon him, all of them standing straight and saying: You are at a banquet! Lift your eyes, my God, behold, and drink it!" Note that the contrast between a (portable) shrine and a temple of cedar wood also commands the perspective of 2 Samuel 7.

25. *KTU* 1.4 iv 62–v 1, and see also *KTU* 1.3 v 38–39; *KTU* 1.4 i 9–11 (reconstructed); iv 50–51. On the theme of Baal's palace in heaven see also Manfred Dietrich, "Beschreibungen transzendenter Wohnstätten von ugaritischen Gottheiten: Die Paläste Yammus und Baals und die Schreine Anats," *UF* 45 (2014) 389–412, esp. 395–96.

26. In *KTU* 1.4 the occurrence of *hklm* (in parallelism with *bhtm*) is frequent, see

Bethel is a god of rain, storm, and fire; but he also is a protector of the weak. The classic formulation of this idea takes the orphan and the widow as the paradigmatic cases of people without defense. Gods and kings throughout the ancient Near East, from Mesopotamia to Egypt, cast themselves in the role of protector of the orphan and the widow. In the cycle of four Bethel hymns, hymn #2 presents Bethel as a real "father of the orphan, judge of the widow" (X 17–24, quotation line 17). Here is my transliteration and translation of the hymn, minus the chorus.

^{17} <u>mry</u>.C ʾlh | bʾ + yt{|}mʾ |
d$_4$ynʾ | ʾ$_2$rₐʾmmʾ{|}lʾt |
^{18} d$_3$ᶜlykʾ | nʾst | yʾdyhʾ |
t$_3$sšʾbr$_3$ | bmr$_2$p + w$_2$ḥyḥʾ |
^{19} hʾ | nʾst | ʾ$_2$ydyhʾ |
t$_3$šbr$_3$ <b>mrp + w$_2$ḥyḥʾ |
^{20} mʾšʾpʾl + ytʾr$_2$ + [ʾl] |
<u>mry</u>.C ṣ$_3$qʾtʾhn | yʾ[. . .]

Lord, my God, father of the orphan,
Judge of the widow!
When to you she lifts up her hands,
She becomes instantly hopeful and laughs;
Yeah, she lifts up her hands,
Becomes instantly hopeful and laughs.
God protects the lowly ones,
The Lord will [take away] their distress.

In his capacity as a Storm god, Bethel inherited most of his traits from Baal. Yet nowhere in the Ugaritic texts do we encounter Baal as a beneficent deity defending the cause of the orphan and the widow. Does this mean that the humanitarian side of Bethel is particular to him in distinction from Baal? Hardly so. While the Ugaritic texts do not speak about Baal's care for orphans or widows, the topos as such does occur in both *Kirta* and *Aqhat*. It is a king's duty to "judge the case of the widow," and to "feed the orphan" and "the widow" (*KTU* 1.16 vi 33, 45–46, 48–50). As a model of the righteous king, Daniel "sits by the gateway, among the chiefs on the threshing floor; takes care of the case of the widow, defends the needs of the orphan" (*KTU*

KTU 1.4 v 51–54, 61–62, 64–65; vi 5–33; vii 17–19, 25–27. For the occurrence of the plural of *hykl* in the Amherst papyrus see *bhyklyk* in IX 13; X 6, and *bhyklwhy* in IX 17.

1.17 v 6–8; 1.19 I 19–23, in the translation of Simon B. Parker).[27] Since the behavior of kings is to replicate the behavior of gods, we should expect to find similar concerns for the orphan and the widow ascribed to Baal. In fact, there is significant indirect evidence that Baal was indeed "the father of the orphan, the judge of the widow." It is found in Psalm 68. Verses 5–6 of the psalm are slightly edited quotes from a Baal hymn.

> Sing to God, chant his name,
> Extol the one who rides the steppes—
> BĕYāh is his name!
> Exult in his presence,
> The Father of orphans and the Judge of widows,
> God in his holy habitation.

Who is the "Father of orphans and the Judge of widows" (*'ăbî yĕtômîm wĕdayyan 'almānôt*)? In the biblical version of the hymn it is Yah—short for Yahweh. But in the pre-biblical version it is Baal. One of Baal's epithets ("Rider-of-the-Clouds," *rkb 'rpt*), and his very name (*b 'l*), are still discernible in verse 5, as though in a palimpsest. The biblical editor changed *rkb ʿrpt* into *rkb bʿrbt*, and turned *bʿl* into *byh*; originally, the phrases were about Baal: "Extol the Rider-of-the-Clouds—Baal is his name!"[28] The preservation of the sound of the phrases, while changing their meaning through slight but significant adaptations, is typical of scribal interventions in texts received from earlier, non-Judean, traditions.[29]

Since at least this part of Psalm 68 was originally addressed to Baal, there is good reason to suspect that the phrase "father of orphans and judge of widows" did initially apply to him. The similarity of the phrasing in the Bethel hymn is striking. This is hardly a coincidence: the phrase originally

---

27. The care of the orphan and the widow is also a recurrent theme in the professions of innocence made by Job, see Job 29:12–13; 31:16–22.

28. Commentators have devised different ways of solving the problematic *byh* of the Hebrew text of v. 5; emendation of the text as we find it—and more specifically deletion of the *beth*—is often part of that solution. See, by way of example, E. S. Gerstenberger, *Psalms, Part 2, and Lamentations* (Forms of Old Testament Literature 15; Grand Rapids: Eerdmans, 2001) 36. In the present context, the *beth* seems indeed superfluous; but the fact that it is nevertheless there signals respect for a preceding version of the text; a version that was subtly reinterpreted but not forcefully altered.

29. For a striking example of the procedure see the changes to the text of the Aramaic forerunner of Psalm 20, in column XII 11–19 of our papyrus, made by the editor of the biblical version. Aramaic $š^{ɔ}l^{ɔ}ḥ^{ɔ}$ | $ṣ_3y^{ɔ}r_2^{ɔ}k$ | $\underline{mn}^n\ k^{ɔ}l$ | $^{ɔ}_2r_2^{ɔ}š^{ɔ}H\ w^{ɔ}\underline{mn}$ + $ṣ_3p^{ɔ}n^{ɔ}$ | $\underline{yhw}G\ y^{ɔ}s^{ɔc}d^{ɔ}n^{ɔ}$ (XII 13–14) became *yišlaḥ-ʿezrĕkā miqqōdeš ûmiṣṣiyyôn yisʿādekā* (Ps 20:3).

expressed a quality of Baal and was later transferred to Bethel. Also for his humanitarian side, then, Bethel is indebted to Baal.

BETHEL AND YAHWEH

So far, this contribution has focused on the relationship between Bethel and Baal. The evidence from the Amherst papyrus shows that—for the community that venerated him as their main god—Bethel was in many ways the successor of Baal as Storm god and as King of the gods; Bethel inherited most of his traits from Baal; he also took over Anat as his consort; the one characteristic that might distinguish him from Baal is the emphasis on fire as the god's weapon. Papyrus Amherst is not exclusively concerned with Bethel and Anat; it also contains three Israelite psalms addressed to Yaho (XII 11–19; XIII 1–10; XIII 11–17). While I plan to discuss these texts more extensively elsewhere, they need to be brought into the present discussion since they identify Yaho with Bethel.

Though Yaho is the dominant god of the three Israelite psalms—his name occurs 15 times, his epithet Adonay nine times—there is also mention of other gods. In these psalms, Bethel occurs both under his proper name (once) and under his epithet Mār, Lord (six times). In addition, there are references to Baal-shamayin (XII 18) and Baal-Zaphon (XIII 15)—which names I take to be references to the one god Baal, to be distinguished from Bethel and Yaho.[30] While these psalms treat Yaho and Bethel as equals, Baal finds himself in a position of inferiority. Yaho and Bethel are equals; more to the point, they are identified with each other; so much so that the texts shift almost imperceptibly from the one divine name (or epithet) to the other. In Psalm #1—the forerunner of Psalm 20—it is Bethel who will "answer us" in the morning (XII 17–18); and at various places, Mār has come to serve as an epithet of Yaho by virtue of the identification of Yaho with Bethel. Baal, on the other hand, cannot be identified with either Bethel or Yaho; he is a deity of inferior rank. Baal "blesses" either Mār (XII 18: "May Baal-shamayin bless Mār") or Yaho (XIII 15–16: "May Baal-Zaphon bless Yaho"). The lower ranking deity pays homage to his superior; by "blessing" Yaho (Bethel), Baal acknowledges his kingship.

---

30. On this score I disagree with Herbert Niehr, who argues that all the divine names and epithets of the Aramaic forerunner of Psalm 20, including the name Baal Shamayin, are in fact addressing the one and the same high God, see H. Niehr, *Der höchste Gott: Alttestamentlichen JHWH-Glaube im Kontext syrisch-kanaanäischer Religion des 1. Jahrtausends v. Chr.* (BZAW 190; Berlin: de Gruyter, 1990) 33–34, 100–101.

The identification of Yaho with Bethel in the Amherst papyrus is consonant with the earlier evidence of the Elephantine papyri. Although the identification between Yaho and Bethel is never explicit in these fifth century BCE texts, it is implied by the parallel occurrence of Anat-Bethel (*TAD* C3.15:125) and Anat-Yaho (*TAD* B7.3:3); and by the fact that the contributions to the Yaho temple are divided over Yaho, Eshem-Bethel, and Anat-Bethel (*TAD* C3.15:123–125). The veneration of Bethel at Elephantine—implicit because of the identification with Yaho, but visible through the references to Anat-Bethel, Eshem-Bethel, and Herem-Bethel (*TAD* B7.2:7–8)—attests to the presence of Israelites (Samarians) among the "Judean" colony. Bethel was a god in whom Israelites put their trust (Jer 48:13). Recent evidence on the Judean exiles in Babylonia shows that a number of deportees in Āl-Yāḫūdu and other places with Judeans had names with Bīt-il (=Bethel) as theophoric element; it is a reflection of the fact that the exiles from Judah were an admixture of Judeans, on the one hand, and Samarians who had fled to Judah in the wake of Samaria's fall, on the other.[31] There is no reason to doubt the "Northern" character of the Israelite worship of Bethel. The three Israelite psalms of the Amherst papyrus display unmistakable traces of a northern origin as well (such as the designation of Yaho as "our bull," *trn*, in XII 17).

It is hardly shocking to say that the biblical portrait of Yahweh has borrowed a significant number of traits from the mythology of Baal as we know it from the Ugaritic literature.[32] However, the role of Bethel in this transfer of mythological lore from the one god to the other has failed to receive proper notice. It is usually assumed that the transfer was, more or less, direct. The distance in time and culture militates against this assumption: more than half a millennium separates the Ugaritic texts from the bulk of the Hebrew Bible. And if the Bible as we know it is indeed a product of the scribal workshop of the Jerusalem temple, the cultural distance with respect to a fourteenth century city on the Syrian coast must be acknowledged, too. The evidence from the Amherst papyrus shows that in the first millennium BCE, Aramaic speakers from the Lebanon worshipped a god who had in effect taken the place of Baal. Bethel is Baal's successor, and the inheritor of much of his mythology. He is the missing link in the process by which much

---

31. See L. E. Pearce and C. Wunsch, *Documents of Judean Exiles and West Semites in Babylonia in the Collection of David Sofer* (Cornell University Studies in Assyriology and Sumerology 28; Bethesda, MD: CDL Press, 2014) 13.

32. For major contributions on this subject see F. M. Cross, *Canaanite Myth and Hebrew Epic: Essays in the History of the Religion of Israel* (Cambridge: Harvard University Press, 1973) 147–94; M. S. Smith, *The Early History of God: Yahweh and the Other Deities in Ancient Israel* (2nd ed.; Grand Rapids: Eerdmans, 2002) 65–101.

of the Baal mythology ended up in the hymnic celebration of Yahweh's power. It is possible that some of the Northern psalms in the Bible—Psalm 29 is the most significant and undisputed instance—were originally addressed to Baal. It is quite possible, too, that they were originally addressing Bethel.

The role of Bethel as mediator in the transfer of Baal lore to Yahweh may go some way to explain the biblical ambivalence about Baal. Whereas the similarities between Baal and Yahweh are incontrovertible, the prevalent attitude of biblical authors toward Baal is polemic. Except for Jer 48:13, such a polemical stance is not taken toward Bethel. Extrabiblical evidence—the Israelite psalms of the Amherst papyrus, the Elephantine papyri, and the onomastic evidence from the Judean exiles in Babylonia—actually attest to the acceptance of Bethel as an alter ego of Yahweh (or Yaho). Why should Bethel have received such a friendly reception? The clue to this question most likely has to do with Bethel's iconography. By the witness of his name, Bethel was venerated under the form of a standing stone—known as a *sikkanu* in the Emar texts, as a *maṣṣēbâ* in the Bible, and as a *baitylon* in the later Greek texts.[33] Such worship of stones was not offensive to most Israelites, since this was also the form under which many of them worshipped Yahweh. It facilitated the identification of the two gods to a considerable degree. But in trying to explain why many Israelites had no qualms about accepting Bethel, we are leaving the realm of facts and enter the domain of speculation. So let us refrain from further speculation and be content with the conclusion that Bethel was the stepping-stone by which important aspects of the Baal mythology came to enrich the theology of Yahweh.

---

33. For the use of erected stones as symbols of divine presence see conveniently T. N. D. Mettinger, *No Graven Image? Israelite Aniconism in Is Ancient Near Eastern Context* (ConBOT 42; Stockholm: Almqvist & Wiksell, 1995). The most significant extrabiblical evidence is discussed by J.-M. Durand, *Le Culte des pierres et les monuments commémoratifs en Syrie amorrite* (Mémoires de N A B U. 9, Florilegium Marianum 8; Paris: SEPOA, 2005), esp. 1–91 (Mari); P. M. Michel, *Le culte des pierres à Emar à l'époque Hittite* (OBO 266; Göttingen: Vandenhoeck & Ruprecht, 2014). On the personification of the cult symbol, and its elevation to the status of a god in his own right, see K. van der Toorn, "Worshipping Stones: On the Deification of Cult Symbols," *JNSL* 23 (1997) 1–14 (reprinted in van der Toorn, *God in Context: Selected Essays on Society and Religion in the Early Middle East* [FAT 123; Tübingen : Mohr/Siebeck, 2018]).

4

Gods on the Mind at Ugarit

Steve A. Wiggins

MODERN LITERARY STANDARDS PLACE a high value on consistency.[1] It is one of the milestones of logic, and it is essential in order to achieve an accurate rendition of what actually happened in any historical sense.[2] Modern literatures and religions are weighed against the standard of consistency; believability suffers if it is absent. In the case of ancient mythology—or any mythology—the issue under consideration is not what actually happened, nor is it believability in a modern sense.[3] Recognizing

---

1. *Author's note*: When Herbert Huffmon honored me with an invitation to contribute to this Festschrift, my thoughts turned to this paper, largely written for Congrès International Sherbrooke in 2005. As I do not have an academic appointment and little time to devote to research, I had to return to a project mostly composed for a contribution. Although belief in omens is not a regular habit of mine, I had to take it as a sign that upon opening this file after a decade I found this opening footnote, written and forgotten for ten years: "This study is dedicated to the memory of Simon B. Parker, a colleague whose contribution to Ugaritic studies has been essential and whose insight will be greatly missed." As I originally wrote the paper in his honor, despite its age, it seems fitting to offer it in this tribute to a friend and scholar who is still much missed.

2. As recognized by J. N. Bremmer in the context of Greek mythology. See "Myth, Mythology, and Mythography," in *The Oxford Handbook of Hellenic Studies* (ed. B. Graziosi, P. Vasunim, and G. Boys-Stones; Oxford University Press, 2009) 681. The seminal treatment remains G. S. Kirk, *Myth: Its Meaning and Function in Ancient and Other Cultures* (Berkeley: University of California Press, 1973). Many more recent treatments have appeared, notably D. E. Callender Jr., ed., *Myth and Scripture: Contemporary Perspectives on Religion, Language, and Imagination* (SBLRBS 78; Atlanta: Society of Biblical Literature, 2014).

3. The complications with mythological texts are legion. First is perhaps the

this, Barber and Barber name the various goals of mythology the "Multiple Aspects Principle."[4] Ancient mythographers were not writing with a modern readership in mind. If Baal is not always the son of Dagan, for example, this creates no crisis. The crisis arises when the material is forced into an artificial system.[5] Such an artificial system becomes another layer of contamination in the effort to understand what the Ugaritians actually believed. Epigraphy has revealed that not all Ugaritic mythology was written by the same scribe, but the actual process of composition remains unclear. If mythological stories originated from more than one source, which is certainly the case,[6] some inconsistency should be expected. Our need to have a systematic, consistent story does violence to the ancient context. Classical scholars have long reconciled to this in Greek mythology.[7]

This paper explores some of the difficulties involved in trying to understand the divine world of Ugarit on its own terms. Our modern, logical, consistent minds bristle at the thought of gods acting in contrary ways between stories; for decades it has been debated what the true nature of El is, for example.[8] Is he feeble before Anat's violent request? Does he seduce

---

tendency to view Greek mythology as the primary exemplar, although since as early as the work of Cyrus Gordon it has been clear that much was borrowed from the Semitic world. See, conveniently, C. H. Gordon, *Common Background of Greek and Hebrew Civilizations* (New York: Norton, 1965); M. C. Astour, *Hellenosemitica: An Ethnic and Cultural Study in West Semitic Impact on Mycenaean Greece* (Leiden: Brill, 1965); D. R. West, *Some Cults of Greek Goddesses and Female Daemons of Oriental Origin* (AOAT 233; Kevelaer: Butzon & Bercker,1995). More commonly, extra-biblical texts were disparaged as inferior; cf. Ulf Oldenburg, *The Conflict between El and Ba'al in Canaanite Religion* (SHR 3; Leiden: Brill, 1969) is perhaps the best, but certainly not the only example.

4. E. W. Barber and P. T. Barber, *When They Severed Earth from Sky: How the Human Mind Shapes Myth* (Princeton: Princeton University Press, 2004) 53–70.

5. We are aware that no one may have two biological fathers; however, Baal had no biological fathers at all!

6. It is widely recognized that some of the texts have a foreign origin. *KTU* 1.24, for example, likely derives from a Hurrian source. See M. Dietrich and W. Mayer, "The Hurrian and Hittite Texts," in *Handbook of Ugaritic Studies* (ed. W. G. E. Watson and N. Wyatt; HdO 39; Leiden: Brill, 1999) 58–75.

7. See, conveniently, W. Burkert, *Greek Religion: Archaic and Classical* (Malden, MA: Blackwell, 1985) 119; "Myth and Mythology," in *The Oxford Dictionary of the Classical World* (ed. John Roberts; New York: Oxford University Press, 2005) 490–91. Analysis of mythology is constantly growing more sophisticated.

8. Differing conclusions concerning El may be found in M. H. Pope, *El in the Ugaritic Texts* (VTSup 2; Leiden: Brill, 1955); F. M. Cross, *Canaanite Myth and Hebrew Epic: Essays in the History of the Religion of Israel* (Cambridge: Harvard University Press, 1973); N. Wyatt, *Myths of Power: A Study of Royal Myth and Ideology in Ugaritic and Biblical Tradition* (UBL 13; Münster: Ugarit-Verlag, 1996).

younger goddesses? Is he impotent or omnipotent? Is he powerful or weak? The evidence at hand—the Ugaritic texts—suggests that it depends upon the situation.

Recognition of our own biases as we approach a set of ancient texts illuminates the situation. We can know our biases, and we have been trained to be objective and dispassionate. Nevertheless, we are subject to the belief that forming working hypotheses and gathering evidence will lead to consistent results. In the case of Ugarit the evidence is often atomistic. Small fragments of myths that cannot be placed in a consistent pattern with other clearly related stories create tensions frustrating to any attempted empirical approach. Yet this is what the Ugaritic material, taken at face value, discloses.[9]

At the outset it must be recognized that this paper is not intended as an exercise in futility, but rather suggests an honest approach to otherwise hotly disputed trouble-spots in ancient texts. What I suggest is that tolerance for texts that do not always make sense from a modern point of view is necessary. Ancient texts should be accepted as actual portraits of ancient ideas, as inconsistent as they are.[10]

Anthropological studies have demonstrated that in traditional cultures inconsistencies are less troubling to the members of that society than they would be to someone reared in a culture which expects a logical consistency between accounts.[11] In his classic study of Nuer tribal religion, for example, Sir E. E. Evans-Pritchard noted:

> The great variety of meanings attached to the word *kwoth* in different contexts and the manner in which Nuer pass, even in the same ceremony, from one to another may bewilder us. Nuer are not confused, because the difficulties which perplex us do not arise on the level of experience but only when an attempt is

---

9. As will be discussed below, the Baal Cycle is a case-in-point. It is not obvious that all the texts associated with the cycle belong together. See M. S. Smith, *The Ugaritic Baal Cycle*, Vol. I, *Introduction with Text, Translation and Commentary of KTU 1.1.–1.2* (VTSup 55; Leiden: Brill, 1994) and M. S. Smith and W. T. Pitard, *The Ugaritic Baal Cycle*, Vol. II, *Introduction with Text, Translation and Commentary of KTU/CAT 1.3–1.4* (VTSup 114; Leiden: Brill, 2009).

10. This was recognized in a preliminary way by E. Lohse, *The New Testament Environment* (trans. J. E. Steely; Nashville: Abingdon, 1974) 21: "As the Greeks sought to develop a train of thought in conversation and through the interplay of question and answer to find the solution to a problem, so now the Jews also learned to debate and, in didactic conversation, to inquire about and to attempt to clarify the truth of the divine will."

11. Barber and Barber, *When They Severed*, 53–70.

made to analyze and systematize Nuer religious thought. Nuer themselves do not feel the need to do this.[12]

It is *our* expectation that is not met. The issue is how such unexpected incongruities can be fruitfully understood.

The first step must be the admission that our cultural expectations are not the same as the Ugaritic cultural expectations. Understanding a premodern culture on its own terms requires special attention to problems in the texts, coupled with the realization that the problem may rest with our presuppositions and not within the texts themselves.

This willingness to accept difficulties must be balanced by a recognition that internal consistency within a single literary work would be generally expected, otherwise it would be impossible to make sense of the story-line. Even accomplished modern writers sometimes lapse into inconsistency, and since writing is a human enterprise, we should not be surprised to find some difficulties even within a working unit of texts. Length of text alone cannot determine whether or not consistency will be found, but the more texts that are added to multi-tablet sets like Kirta, Aqhat, and the Baal Cycle, the greater will be the likelihood that major inconsistencies will emerge. To keep major difficulties from developing because of present-day reconstructions, care must be taken in delineating the limits of ancient sets.

Kirta is an example of a fairly well-defined unit. It begins by setting the scene, it develops the main action despite the damaged state of *KTU* 1.15,[13] and concludes the story with a reasonable resolution and a colophon. Within these limits the story appears to be fairly consistent. This is evidence that internal consistency was achieved at least in self-contained stories of human proportions. The corollary is that internal consistency was recognized and valued within literary units composed as a set.

At least two factors complicate this observation, however; it is not always possible to delimit literary units precisely, and the fickle nature of deities may lead to even internal inconsistencies. I would propose, nevertheless, that when an intentional literary unit is discerned the logic of the plot will be tractable. When stories are stretched beyond their original limits, the accumulation of inconsistent elements will eventually lead to confusion if these disparate units are forced together. Compounding this,

---

12. E. E. Evans-Pritchard, *Nuer Religion* (Oxford: Oxford University Press, 1956) 106.

13. Convention has tended to shift from *KTU* numbers to *CAT* numbers. The shift took place after this paper had been written, so I have decided to keep the original numbering system used. (*CAT* is simply the 2nd ed. of *KTU*, in English.) Ugaritic studies, as a discipline, has been vexed with competing numbering systems from nearly the very beginning.

the utter conceptual freedom of divinities adds a further layer of complexity, especially in stories where the main characters are gods and goddesses. The basic constraints of credulity should, however, apply. The credulity sought is ancient and therefore may not meet present-day expectations.

Since the brain is the gateway to all human experience (thought, belief, emotion), understanding how it worked in the past would give us insight into what ancient people produced and what their expectations of literary sources may have been.[14] Applying this principle to the Ugaritic material may help to account for some of the puzzling aspects long noted in the texts. This is a problematic venture: we have no ancient Levantine individuals from whom we might study brain structures. Neuroscience is also a developing field for which there are many unanswered questions. Human brains are the most complex entities in the known universe,[15] and any applications proposed to the understanding of Ugaritic mythology must remain provisional. At the same time, ignoring what is known of human brain functions runs the risk of locking the entryway to all human experience.

Brain processes are subject to environmental pressures and may change several times in a lifetime.[16] In responding to the stimuli that impact it, the brain develops patterns of thought through its trillions of synaptic connections. These patterns of thought fall under the rubric of cultural evolution as opposed to biological evolution. While the mechanism of cultural evolution is debated, the concept of the meme is a useful analog for discussing how ideas either survive to be carried on to a new generation

---

14. A. Newberg et al., *Why God Won't Go Away: Brain Science and the Biology of Belief* (New York: Ballantine, 2001); D. H. Hamer, *The God Gene: How Faith is Hardwired into Our Genes* (New York: Doubleday, 2004); J. W. Bowker, *The Sacred Neuron: Extraordinary New Discoveries Linking Science and Religion* (London: Tauris, 2005); A. Newberg and M. R. Waldman, *How God Changes Your Brain: Breakthrough Finding from a Leading Neuroscientist* (New York: Ballentine, 2009). From the side of religious studies, see G. R. Peterson, *Minding God: Theology and the Cognitive Sciences* (Theology and the Sciences; Minneapolis: Fortress, 2003).

15. G. Cziko, "Without Miracles: Brain Evolution and Development: The Selection of Neurons and Synapses," cited 12 May 2016. Online: http://faculty.ed.uiuc.edu/g-cziko/wm/05.html.

16. N. Calder, *Magic Universe: A Grand Tour of Modern Science* (New York: Oxford University Press, 2003) 91–94 (Brain Wiring); D. J. Levitin, *This Is Your Brain on Music: The Science of a Human Obsession* (New York: Dutton, 2006) 191. For brain development over time, W. H. Calvin: *A Brief History of the Mind: From Apes to Intellect and Beyond* (New York: Oxford University Press, 2004) is a good introduction. See also A. Zeman, *A Portrait of the Brain* (New Haven: Yale University Press, 2008). None of this suggest that brain developments can be passed on via a Lamarckian evolutionary process. The suggestion is merely that brain structures change more quickly than it is often supposed.

or fade into oblivion.[17] The meme is a cultural analogue to the gene, the unit of biological evolution. The memes referred to in this article are the mythological stories of Ugarit.

As an entry point into ancient thinking patterns, a basic consideration of neurological studies offers considerable insight. Although ancient brain patterns cannot be directly mapped, studies of modern brain patterns provide evidence for the fact of the brain's ability to adapt on a fairly rapid scale.[18] Human brains respond to the environment by developing the structures required to perform the tasks of that environment.[19] This rapid adaptation responds to the stimuli deemed to be important for survival, in evolutionary terms. Language is one such necessary survival skill.[20] There is no doubt that human survival in the long-term has been made possible by highly refined communication adaptations. Perhaps less obvious, but clearly also important for survival, is the ability to make music.[21] Studies of how music affects the brain, as an analogue to religious thought, have demonstrated that even in middle-aged subjects, sections of the brain specializing in musical performance increase in size with repeated use. Animals that make music appear to have survival factors in play, beyond the human concept of making music for pleasure.[22]

---

17. The concept of the meme was introduced by R. Dawkins in *The Selfish Gene* (2nd ed.; Oxford: Oxford University Press, 1989), 189–201. The concept was introduced in the first edition (1976, chapter 11).

18. V. S. Ramachandran, *The Tell-Tale Brain: A Neuroscientist's Quest for What Makes Us Human* (New York: Norton, 2011) 12–14.

19. C. Gaser and G. Schlaug, "Brain Structures Differ between Musicians and Non-Musicians," *Journal of Neuroscience* 23(27) 9240–9245; Levitin, *This Is Your Brain on Music*; W. L. Benzon, *Beethoven's Anvil: Music in Mind and Culture* (New York: Basic Books, 2001) 71–74, contra Barber and Barber, *When They Severed*, 152: "Our brains are still the same."

20. L. Shlain, *The Alphabet versus the Goddess: The Conflict between Word and Image* (New York: Viking, 1998). Although his conclusions are extremely questionable, Shlain's neurological analysis does demonstrate that language, in the form of reading, does "reprogram" the brain.

21. See Benzon, *Beethoven's Anvil*, throughout. Since this paper was originally written, the literature on music and the brain has also grown. See also Levitin, *This Is Your Brain on Music*; and O. Sacks, *Musicophilia: Tales of Music and the Brain* (New York: Knopf, 2007).

22. J. McDermott and M. D. Hauser, "Probing the Evolutionary Origins of Music Perception," in *The Neurosciences and Music II: From Perception to Performance* (ed. G. Avanzini et al.; Annals of the New York Academy of Science 1060; New York: New York Academy of Science, 2006), 6–16. See also Levitin, *This Is Your Brain on Music*.

Musicologists have long noted the cultural connections between religion and music.[23] Music is tied to religious experience in many cultures; often it is essential to the religious experience. This observation warns against dismissing results of musical research as irrelevant to investigation of religions. Cognitive scientist William Benzon has addressed how memes pass from generation to generation in the case of music.[24] Ritual, mutually related to music and religion, is another example of a cultural meme to which Benzon makes explicit connection.[25] Since detailed study has been undertaken in the fields of neurology and music, the latter serves as an analogue for applying results to religious thought and practice. The study of neurology and religion is still in its infancy.[26] Also, unlike music—which is well defined in terms of when it is being practiced—religion is not well-defined and what constitutes a religious activity remains debated.

This is what Benzon observes about the brain and music:

> Once mimesis has been initiated by adults, who did not themselves grow up in a mimetic culture, it becomes part of the external environment that shapes the nervous systems of infants and children as they mature. Of course, their actions can only be shaped to the models provided by adults, but if these actions are learned earlier in life they will be more deeply embedded in the microstructure of the children's brains, which means that the neurodynamics may be more stable. Thus the mimetic capacities of adults will show incremental improvement from one generation to the next as their brains become more intimately sculpted to the requirements of the task.[27]

Religious ideas are also memes that are passed on by learning from others, often from parents. Although experience and intellectual analysis may lead to the rejection of the earliest patterned religious learning, at root it is still a brain function which differs little from the learning undergone

---

23. Michael Graziano, "Why is Music a Religious Experience?," cited 28 November 2015. http://www.huffingtonpost.com/michael-graziano/why-is-mozart-a-religious_b_875352.html. This connection has been made at a very early level of human development. See S. Mithen, *The Singing Neanderthals: The Origins of Music, Language, Mind, and Body* (Cambridge: Harvard University Press, 2006) 266.

24. Benzon, *Beethoven's Anvil*, 219–21.

25. Benzon, *Beethoven's Anvil*, 194.

26. Newberg, D'Aquili, and Rause, *Why God Won't Go Away*; Hamer, *The God Gene*; Bowker, *The Sacred Neuron*; Newberg and Waldman, *How God Changes Your Brain*.

27. Benzon, *Beethoven's Anvil*, 182–83.

with music. Religious concepts are functional for survival.[28] They are mediated by human brains which are the gateways to all human experiences.

When approaching ancient myth, trying to determine how the brains of ancient writers functioned is essential. The impossibility of certainty is obvious, but clues remain from the texts ancient writers have left, as well as from indicative artifacts and what we know of ancient societies. These pieces of evidence must, however, be treated in an intellectually honest way, and not forced into a preferred interpretative system which seems logical or inevitable to our way of thinking. The result will be considerably more complex than a simple story line. Perhaps there will be no one canonical version of events. Is it not possible that "official theology" is no more than one competing image, among many, of the world of the gods? Even today thinkers on religious subjects seldom come to the exact same conclusions. Neurology may enlighten the divine world of Ugarit, when the human brain is considered.

Since the waning of the last great glaciation, human civilization sped from "hunter-gatherer" to a highly technological, globally-linked nervous system of a virtual collective consciousness[29] which includes instant sharing of information and transfer of goods in just 11,000 years. Early in this period myths were used to explain the sometimes uncanny realities experienced by human groups.[30] This mythopoetic method of understanding the world dominated civilization for thousands of years, and it still exists within social groups otherwise integrated into a technological setting.[31]

From myth-making to space travel, human culture developed in a brief period of time. Neurological science indicates how brains work and reveals how quickly they change over time.[32] The frequently asked ques-

28. W. Burkert, *Creation of the Sacred: Tracks of Biology in Early Religions* (Cambridge: Harvard University Press, 1996); D. S. Wilson, *Darwin's Cathedral: Evolution, Religion, and the Nature of Society* (Chicago: University of Chicago Press, 2002) 125–60.

29. For the religious collective as an entity, see Wilson, *Darwin's Cathedral*, 1–4. The implications of Göbekli Tepe for this collective activity are profound. See S. Scham, "The World's First Temple," *Archaeology* 61/6 (2008) 22–27. The collective consciousness is, of course, the Internet. It is clear that not all human populations share in this global nexus, but this serves to illustrate the point that it is not biological evolution, but cultural evolution which occurs at such a pace.

30. Barber and Barber, *When They Severed*, 120.

31. One has only to consider the frequent outbreaks of "creationism" in public schools to see that mythology still exerts a powerful hold on many people in the United States.

32. A number of studies written by neurological specialists have been written for the benefit of laypeople. Benzon, *Beethoven's Anvil*; Newberg et al., *Why God Won't Go Away*; A. Damasio, *Descartes' Error: Emotion, Reason, and the Human Brain* (New York: Quill, 2000), and *The Feeling of What Happens: Body and Emotion in the Making of*

tion (often in the context of Greek mythology) of whether ancient, intelligent people actually believed these stories of gods and fantastic beasts illustrates this.[33] No one ever saw a winged horse or a snake-haired woman who turned people to stone, and yet they preserved stories of such creatures alongside what is considered the beginning of historically accurate accounts. The same characteristics occur in ancient Semitic thought, but the fragmentary remains of many texts often complicate the issue even further. Understanding how brain structures influence belief systems is important in approaching ancient myth. (Also important is incorporating what we are learning from social memory theory. Anticipated readers of texts were few, illiteracy was high. These texts were single copies perhaps, not produced for wide distribution. They were written as memory aids and not literature to be read by the fireside on a winter's night. All of this affects interpretative structures.)[34]

We know that human brains have a node that allows us to believe information that we rationally know to be false.[35] If this applies to modern humans, it is reasonable to believe that this same physical structure existed in the brains of ancient peoples. Ancient peoples may have been less-than-systematic in their approaches to the numinous; brain structure continues to allow for this in the current day. When we seek structure in an ancient mythic outlook, it must be acknowledged that structures are creative overlays placed artificially on the material to help make sense of it. When constructing systems, it is natural to believe that they are actual descriptions of the realities with which they deal, as well as the correct interpretation of those realities. This outlook is problematic since there are conflicting systems and we cannot overcome our mental limitations to see the whole picture in order to determine which system is "correct."[36] Ancient religious thought is the result of the functioning of human brains at an earlier period. By attempting to understand how brains construct religious worlds, we are

---

Consciousness (San Diego: Harvest, 1999); and Shlain, *The Alphabet versus the Goddess* are examples of such studies. More recently, Ramachandran, *The Tell-Tale Brain*; and Newberg and Waldman, *How God Changes Your Brain*.

33. As asked in Barber and Barber, *When They Severed*, 1.

34. These points are discussed in A. Kirk and T. Thatcher, eds., *Memory, Tradition, and Text: Uses of the Past in Early Christianity* (SemeiaSt 52; Atlanta: Society of Biblical Literature, 2005). Substantial work continues to be done in this field. See I. D. Wilson, *Kingship and Memory in Ancient Judah* (Oxford: Oxford University Press, 2016).

35. P. A. Williams, *Doing without Adam and Eve: Sociobiology and Original Sin* (Theology and the Sciences; Minneapolis: Fortress, 2001) 46–47; Barber and Barber, *When They Severed*, 2–3.

36. This is true even today. Our brains do not represent "reality." See, for example, Ramachandran, *The Tell-Tale Brain*, 54; and Levitin, *This Is Your Brain on Music*, 96–99.

adding an overlay, but one which is informed by the final arbiter, the brain itself. If an experience is beyond the brain's ability to process it, human reason cannot access it.

Without an acute dissonance when contradictory material appeared between texts, I suggest, ancient writers and readers or hearers simply accepted multiple versions as valid. Modern analysis of ancient texts is often approached from the mind-set of historical reading. Conditioned by approaching the Bible as an historical document, whether it is conscious or not, modern readers tend to weigh material historically.

If ancient myths were composed before a meme of consistency between variant accounts was developed and applied to religious stories, it might have been predicted that inconsistency and questionable logic would have appeared in such stories. Modern interpreters, on the other hand, having been taught to look at religions systematically, examine ancient myth intent on finding logical order in it. This is our approach to the natural world; it is the method of science which helps us to make sense of our surroundings. When such methods of thinking encounter a religiously-generated conflict of outlook there are several responses possible. For the ancient brain which had not yet acquired a modern outlook, inconsistency in a mythological setting was not problematic. Baal could be both Dagan's son and El's son, without having been adopted. Both David and Elhanan killed Goliath on separate occasions. Such basic disconnects encourage modern readers to construct artificial superstructures which force the component parts into a consistent system. Ancient myths, however, do not insist on complete agreement between stories.

Beyond the oral stage stylus was put to clay or reed to parchment, and written versions preserved a fixity that oral retelling lacked. A new synaptic connection was forged: this particular story goes like *this*. Some of these written documents were edited, passages were excerpted and reused. New literary frameworks were used to house fragments of older tales and these may have been redacted. The editing process could have conceivably continued until some event forced an end to the process. In the case of Ugarit, with clay tablets, the destruction of the city led to the covering and preservation of the tablets, beyond which the stories contained on them no longer changed. In the case of the Hebrew Bible, the believing community eventually recognized it as an inspired document and took care to preserve it at that stage of its development.

Such delimiters fixed the forms of the documents. Working backward from this point, editing allows a means of explaining contradictions and inconsistencies. For the Ugaritic corpus it is more difficult to find a system. A precise date as to when each tablet was composed is lacking, making a precise reconstruction of the chronological development impossible. Careful study reveals palimpsests,[37] erasures and inserted words.[38] Such information adds valuable data that reveal how scribes operated, and in the case of the same scribe, perhaps which tablets belong together. This does not, of course, prove the relationship of tablets to each other in a cycle, but it does offer insight into such issues as consistency.

Since the Ugaritic texts are autographs written in clay, an editing process beyond the life of the original document does not exist. Some of the myths were signed by the scribe Ilimilku, and enough texts by him have been recovered to allow for recognition of his handwriting. Documents inscribed by Ilimilku form a set. Within that set subsets exist of texts which belong to an established cycle, such as Kirta or Aqhat. Isolating these subsets from each other we should find a relatively high level of internal consistency. The most we might hope to gain from this information at this point is that common authorship is one potential piece of evidence in helping to define a unit.

Mythology was originally written or orally composed for a specific set of circumstances. Individual tales could have been based on individual situations, but they are only later constructed conscientiously into a larger corpus such as Ugaritic clay tablets. Ugaritans never gathered "Scriptures" in the sense that Israel eventually did. Even when Israel compiled documents into the three sections of the Tanak, it was done at the level of allowing conflicting viewpoints to be included in each section. This arrangement allows for the examination of smaller, coherent units while realizing that a larger context exists.

The concept of a set of Scriptures, a canon, came later than the biblical period and appears not to have existed when earlier religious writings were completed.[39] If texts were not composed to be a corpus of scripture, then placing them into a collection becomes a hermeneutic tool. Essentially a new meme is created. Once the meme of "Scriptures" had been born, it forever changed the way the texts would be viewed in the future. Scriptures provide a source of purpose for life; the human mind requires a sense of purpose to operate effectively.[40]

A system which allows blatantly contrary religious thought into its interpretative model is sorely needed. What is done with this conflicting

---

37. M. Dietrich and O. Loretz, "*KTU* 1.114: ein 'Palimpsest,'" *UF* 25 (1993) 133–36.

38. Pitard's careful studies of the texts have often revealed these features. See, for example, Smith and Pitard, *The Ugaritic Baal Cycle: Vol. II.*

39. J. W. Miller, *How the Bible Came to Be* (Mahwah, NJ: Paulist, 2004), for example.

40. Damasio, *Descartes Error*, 125–64.

information is testimony to the continuation of cultural evolution to a point where religious thought must be solidly consistent and systematized, otherwise human brains conditioned by scientific and logical thought, may reject religious propositions as internally inconsistent.[41] Ancient texts do not share this anxiety.

In this light, ancient myth may have been practically believed, although known to be factually incorrect.[42] This distinction allows contradictory stories to be justified and canonized together. It appears that human brains have developed the capacity, or perhaps the need, to believe memes which are simply not factual.[43] When inconsistencies appear in ancient myth, harmonization is not the correct approach to deciphering the story line. When multiple versions exist, the better literary fit may be noted, but variant texts are also memes that have survived in written form.

Myth has survived and continues to play a role in advanced societies. The benefits of mythopoesis should be capable of isolation. Even the increased role of factual reality as the basis of society has not caused the extinction of myth.[44] As Barber and Barber demonstrate, myth is grounded in human experience.[45] We are hampered from seeing unexplained events the way that ancient mythographers did by the fact of neurological developments in the intervening centuries. Memes that reflect factual reality are generally the basis of formal educational systems today. At the same time it is recognized that belief in factually uncertain constructs is vitally important.[46]

By closely examining individual mythological units of antiquity, with an informed knowledge of their background, a snapshot of the neural weather[47] of the writer may be obtained. With this information adaptive

---

41. As will be explored further on, human brains have the capacity for accepting non-factual information as true, while being aware that at some level it does not make sense. This does not, however, mean that people are generally able to trust in internally inconsistent narratives which leave more questions than answers.

42. If Barber and Barber, *When They Severed*, are correct, there is a factual correctness in myths which has to be teased out in order to be comprehended.

43. Wilson, *Darwin's Cathedral*, 229; Ramachandran, *Tell-Tale Brain*, 70–71.

44. Religion is not, despite predictions, in a state of decline. See for example, Jeannie Banks Thomas, "Introduction," in *Putting the Supernatural in Its Place: Folklore, the Hypermodern, and the Ethereal* (ed. J. B. Thomas; Salt Lake City: University of Utah Press, 2015) 1.

45. Barber and Barber, *When They Severed*, throughout.

46. Newberg, D'Aquili, Rause, *Why God Won't Go Away*; Hamer, *The God Gene*; Bowker, *The Sacred Neuron*.

47. Benzon, *Beethoven's Anvil*, 71, 237.

causes for such a snapshot may be considered, answering the question of the adaptive function of that particular unit.

Aspects of all the major units of extant Ugaritic mythology survived the destruction of the city and the literal burial of the texts from human sight. When the texts were recovered, beginning in the late 1920s, memes known from the Hebrew Bible and other surviving ancient literature were recognized. This is a bold illustration of the utility of the memes found in these texts. Even if some of the memes were buried with the city, apparently forgotten by neighboring cultures, they had an original function or utility that caused them to be committed to writing. When the texts were rediscovered the memes once again generated enough cultural interest to survive.

APPLICATION TO UGARIT

Turning specifically to the Ugaritic texts, the above suggests, individual units must be isolated and the complexities between units must be allowed to stand. The first step is to delimit the units.

In the Hebrew Bible divisions of pentateuchal material into the four major sources J, E, D and P were attempts to isolate strands which sometimes appear as doublets with contradictory information. Although the classical documentary hypothesis has rightly been challenged, the basic premise is sound—a single unified source is likely to be generally consistent. With older material, such as the Ugaritic myths, it might be expected that the level of consistency might be lower, since as time elapses and literate populations preserve documents, higher levels of sophistication would also emerge. Among the Ugaritic texts there is no question of source hypothesis in the written form of single documents; any change of hand is obvious. None of the myths approach the length of Genesis, let alone the Pentateuch. At the same time, separate documents narrate stories of Kirta, Aqhat, and Baal. Other deities are the subject of tablets outside the provisional Baal Cycle. Some appear within that Cycle as well. Their actions and characteristics may not be consistent between separate sources.

To illustrate how this applies to the divine world at Ugarit, two specific aspects of that world will be considered: the assembly of the gods and their inter-relationships, and secondly, divine relationships in stories of human interaction with the divine world.

The Assembly of the Gods

How was the divine world of Ugarit organized? It does not seem to fit any human governing system particularly well.[48] Perhaps the reason is that one scheme does not cohere across all myths. There is clearly a god at the top, but even he can be threatened or cajoled into making unwanted decisions. He sublets his authority to squabbling lesser gods who have direct influence over the human world. These lesser gods seem to have some difference in status, but rank per se does not appear to enter into the picture. Rank implies an acknowledged line of authority, but when Baal is missing in *KTU* 1.5 and 1.6, for example, the choice of ruler is a matter of debate between El and Athirat. Neither of the divine parents suggests that the replacements have the same rank as the missing Baal, and when Athtar is chosen, he descends from the throne with an acknowledgment of his own inferiority complex. Baal challenges Yamm and Yamm's demand for Baal's submission is effected because other gods are afraid rather than because of a recognition of Yamm's superior rank. Even messengers and crafty gods are not demeaned as having a lesser rank. All are gods, but their functions differ. At times one is superior, at other times another is superior. This feature might only apply, however, to the texts about Baal.[49]

These texts may not construct a pantheon, but they do illustrate the basic Ugaritic concept of deities. They are obviously not obsessed with humans. Gods are presented in daily activities: making war, making love, washing clothes, building houses, drinking, struggling with death and chaos. The status of the king of the gods is "catch as catch can" for the strongest of the gods. The difference appears not as rank but as might or the ability of ones' allies. This is clearly demonstrated in the kingship being decided by individual combat between the gods claiming sovereignty, at least in the Baal Cycle. All the while El remains king. This Picasso-esque view of kingship does not neatly fit into effective governance systems.

The scenario sketched here rings of anarchy. Perhaps the one factor that prevents degeneration into chaos is the underlying assumption by the human author that Baal ought to be in charge. From the perspective of the inhabitants of Ugarit this would be ideal: the patron god of their city rules the cosmos. Baal, however, has trials through which he must pass.

---

48. Not that this has not been tried. Two fairly thorough attempts are C. E. L'Heureux, *Rank among the Canaanite Gods: El, Ba'al, and the Repha'im* (HSM 21; Missoula: MT: Scholars, 1979); and L. K. Handy, *Among the Host of Heaven: The Syro-Palestinian Pantheon as Bureaucracy* (Winona Lake, IN: Eisenbrauns, 1994).

49. The same organization of gods across texts, in other words, should not be assumed.

An assumption brought to the text by modern readers is that the story of Baal will have a natural cohesion. This assumption might be insightfully challenged by the practice of some current religious traditions using a lectionary to direct their readings. The committees responsible for lectionaries surely attempt to bring some unifying factors to bear on disparate and discrete readings from the Hebrew Bible, the Gospels, and the Epistles. Often the readings in this liturgical practice have no organic connection, even though they are part of a common service. The suggestion here is not that Baal stories formed part of a lectionary, nor that they were necessarily read liturgically. Rather, an analogy is being drawn to the practice of present-day religious communities to demonstrate that story-line is not always the guiding factor in religious texts. To a far-distant future civilization, the discovery of a lectionary with no explanatory text would likely be a puzzling document indeed. The stories of Baal likewise come from a foreign context. Parts of the stories obviously come from an internally coherent story-line; other parts, however, fit only with difficulty or appear not to fit at all. Harmonizing fragments from texts not written together may provide an intellectual satisfaction of having overcome the chaos of unorganized texts. The problem is that chaos may have been part of the original context. Complexity is inherent in the system.

The natural starting-point for considering the cohesion of the stories of Baal is with the texts commonly referred to as the "Baal Cycle," *KTU* 1.1–1.6. The Baal Cycle is unique in presenting a multi-tablet narration focused solely on the world of the gods. Although convenient for literary discussions of the text, it has long been noted that problems underlie the cyclical arrangement.[50] Specifically, while Ilimilku is associated with these tablets, common scribal origin does not necessarily point to a cycle. The pattern of events as generally reconstructed, Baal defeating Yamm and building a palace, fit a mythic pattern widely recognized as appropriate to the divine world. The reconstruction itself, however, raises serious questions. The events on text 1 fit uneasily with those on tablet 2 requiring differing writing patterns for the columns on the tablets in order to wrest some sense from them.[51] The fragmentary nature of both tablets does not inspire great confidence in reconstructions of their place in the "Cycle."

Within this expected series of events, the tablets must be adjusted to fit the scheme since it is not clear from the texts themselves that they were

---

50. See Smith, *The Ugaritic Baal Cycle*, vol. I, for a discussion.

51. A cursory examination of translations of the Baal Cycle reveals multiple ways of arranging texts 1 and 2. J. C. L. Gibson, *Canaanite Myths and Legends* (2nd ed.; Edinburgh: T. & T. Clark, 1977), splits text 2 to accommodate text 1.

written as a cycle. If the cycle has been falsely construed, problems reconstructing the divine world presented therein would be predicted.

Consistency among the gods should not be expected between these compositions. Additionally, there are many smaller mythological tablets with some of the same deities which do not appear to fit into any overarching system. These texts appear to be truly miscellaneous. In the systematic mindset of present-day thinkers, such small, potentially contradictory tablets may be counted as variants to a main tradition. We are unaware of how these pieces all fit together, or even if they were ever intended to. Several of these smaller pieces narrate events from the life and times of Baal or Hadad. They do not fit the anticipated larger plot that can be found in tablets 1 through 6. A number of scholars have tried to include some of these smaller texts in the cycle,[52] raising once again the question of authorship and continuity of plot and characters.

It must be considered not just how, but whether all the information on Baal fits together. The same complexity must be allowed between the various mythological cycles. If the brain patterns requiring a systematic, structured divine world had not yet developed, the dissonance experienced by those whose brains are so patterned would not have existed. If enough disconnects are present in the mythology of a given culture, evidence accumulates that such thought patterns had not yet coalesced. Mythological fragments may be just as important as large cycles.

If the Ugaritic material was unique in this respect, it might be considered simply an anomaly, perhaps based on its cosmopolitan environment. Other ancient documents, however, notably the Hebrew Bible, also display a comfort level with contradictory material which simply does not fit a modern worldview: for example, either David killed Goliath or he did not. The world was created in six days or just one. Biblical doublets are not harmonized, but simply juxtaposed. The question of which is correct seems unavoidable to a present-day reader. For a culture in which strong systematization had not been applied to the divine world, such questions simply would not have been formulated. Human brains allow for belief in phenomena which they rationally know to be false.[53] Daily life may be lived according to consistent principles, while the mythic mind believes what it does not see or something which contradicts what it does see.

Difficulties also attend the transition from *KTU* 1.3 to 1.4. The focus of these texts, however, is a palace for Baal, giving them a thematic cohesion.

---

52. N. Wyatt, *Religious Texts from Ugarit: The Words of Ilimilku and His Colleagues* (Biblical Seminar 53; Sheffield: Sheffield Academic, 1998); see Smith, *The Ugaritic Baal Cycle*, Vol. I, for others.

53. Williams, *Doing Without Adam and Eve*, 46-47.

The introduction of Mot into the story in 1.4 vii bridges the gap to text 5. *KTU* 1.5 and 1.6 fit precisely, providing a useful point of comparison. It is clear that a basic consistency holds individual story-lines together in the latter part of the Baal Cycle. Such consistency does not apply across all material concerning Baal or any other deities featured in *KTU* 1.1–1.6. The basis for comparison for how gods interact should be coherent units in order that the internal development may become evident. How do we define a coherent unit? The only witness is the texts, and it is these very texts which are not fully understood. How much deviation from current rational standards would the stories bear? How far could consistency be stretched in a mythological cycle?

In order to answer such questions, the texts must direct our reconstructions. Evident multi-tablet units may be classified together when it is evident that they were intended to belong to a set. Although ancient intention may be technically impossible to discern, the labeling of texts, direct continuity,[54] and colophons are useful evidence. These factors demonstrate that stories continued from tablet to tablet, and therefore possess some measure of consistency. Unfortunately in the Baal Cycle *KTU* 1.1, 1.2, 1.3, and 1.4 lack the opening of the tablet, and any label that may have been written is missing. A partial colophon is preserved on text 4, and the content of text 4 matches fairly well with the material in text 5. Texts 5 and 6 are clearly consonant, and text 6 preserves a label for the series and the extended colophon marking the end of the set. As Margalit recognized, *KTU* 1.4–1.6 form a fairly coherent unit.[55]

Individual units compared to each other, however, may yield differing results. The gods may interact differently in other textual units than might be expected should the "Baal Cycle" be considered normative or canonical. For example, other texts concerning Baal, such as *KTU* 1.7, 1.8, 1.9, 1.10, 1.11, 1.12, 1.101, or 1.133 might be considered variants,[56] or might be incorporated into the plot.[57] They may not impinge on *KTU* 1.4–1.6 at all. Such decisions should not be arbitrary, but based on an analysis of how such

---

54. As in the rare case of *KTU* 1.5 and 1.6 where the standard description of mourning rituals continues from an undamaged tablet end to an undamaged tablet beginning.

55. B. Margalit, *A Matter of "Life" and "Death": A Study of the Baal-Mot Epic (CTA 4-5-6)* (AOAT 206; Kevelaer: Butzon & Bercker, 1980).

56. Such as 1.8 and 1.133 are in S. B. Parker, ed., *Ugaritic Narrative Poetry* (SBLWAW 9; Atlanta: Scholars, 1997), 177–80. Wyatt (*Religious Texts from Ugarit*) treats *KTU* 1.7–1.13 separately from the Cycle without listing them as variants.

57. As in J. C. deMoor, *An Anthology of Religious Texts from Ugarit, vol. 1* (Leiden: Brill, 1987) 1–116. DeMoor treats *KTU* 1.101 as part of the Baal Cycle, and 1.10 and 1.11 as part of a separate document called "Loves."

texts interact. Were all Baal texts relatively brief, episodic accounts that fit together only loosely? *KTU* 1.4–1.6, as well as the epics of Kirta and Aqhat, would seem to gainsay this suggestion, but only partially. Where is the line to be drawn between individual episodes and coherent plot? With so much material missing, it is difficult to determine just how well the episodes in the Baal Cycle cohere.

More complete renditions of various myths might be found, throwing light from a new angle onto these stories. What I am suggesting is that with the lacunae in our knowledge it is best to treat separate stories discretely when attempting to develop a picture of the Ugaritic divine world. Such an approach requires a comfort level with complexity and inconsistency, recognizing that logical systems are a relatively recent development in human religious thought. It has been persuasively suggested that religion itself is a western, Christian phenomenon which does not sufficiently describe the belief systems of more ancient peoples.[58] In the light of such observations, attempts to systematize that which was recorded in an *ad hoc* manner only generate frustration since there is no system to be found.

Looking at the Baal Cycle in this way, it is easily broken down into at least two major sections, perhaps originally separate cycles or individual stories. The first section, Baal's conflict with Yamm (*KTU* 1.1–1.2) is fragmentary, but enough remains to discern that Baal overcomes Yamm in single combat. These two tablets may not fit together and could be smaller, somewhat parallel episodes. *KTU* 1.4–1.6 clearly belong together, and enough common themes and developments between texts 3 and 4 perhaps tether *KTU* 1.3 to the series. Between these two sections of the overall "Cycle" some common themes occur: Athtar's lack of regal status, Baal's threats from other gods, and the image of Baal victorious. These common elements may justify a cycle, but there are also inconsistencies. In *KTU* 1.3 Anat claims to have defeated Yamm.[59] This is a task assigned to Baal in *KTU* 1.1–1.2. The two Athtar episodes, one in each section, may be doublets explaining his lesser prestige than Baal, but in each section Athtar cites differing reasons for his descent. Between the two parts of the cycle complexity applies and consistency may not be evident. The success of untangling the common themes is naturally more difficult because of the fragmentary state of texts 1 and 2.

Even if both sections of the Baal Cycle are treated as separate literary units, they were both preserved in the same historical cross-section of Ugarit's history. The texts may not have fit together with any kind of

---

58. D. Dubuisson, *The Western Construction of Religion: Myths, Knowledge, and Ideology* (Baltimore: Johns Hopkins University Press, 2003).

59. N. Wyatt, "Who Killed the Dragon?," *AuOr* 5 (1987) 185–98.

consistency, but both were preserved. Perhaps they were read as part of a collection, but, if so, it would have been at a stage in which comfort with inconsistency applied. No one set of events outweighed another.

Human Interaction with the Divine World

The most complete sources for human interaction with the divine world of Ugarit are the epic tales of Kirta and Aqhat. Both are individually unified compositions. Within them it is reasonable to expect internal consistency, but between them aspects of the situational functions of deities, based on the demands of the stories, may be glimpsed. For such an analysis special attention must be given to the scenes in which divinities appear. Such scenes, compared across stories, show both congruence and divergence. Divine activity in these compositions is based on human activity; gods act in response to human requests or they respond to human situations.

In Kirta the protagonist is human. Kirta experiences interactions with deities, but the story presents him in realistic terms—he is not aware of what the gods are doing behind the scenes. Lacunae obscure some of the action, and it is uncertain what the gods may have orchestrated or accomplished in these lacunae.

Kirta's first extant interaction with the divine world comes in the form of a dream, a liminal state,[60] in which El provides instructions for Kirta to reestablish a family. The dream instructions include the directions to make a sacrifice to Baal, setting the stage for a second divine interaction. This simple episode indicates subtleties of divine relationships: El requests a personal sacrifice, but also an adoration to Baal. This would seem to indicate that El cannot wave a magic wand and solve Kirta's problem, but that he has to go through proper channels. Are the gods constrained by custom, or are specific requests under the purview of specific gods? Speculation suggests that Baal is singled out as a kind of co-regent with El, indicating an official relationship. This co-regent arrangement, however, is not explicit in Kirta, but implicit in one interpretation of the instruction El gives. Other possible reasons may be marshaled for Baal's distinction: is he associated with fecundity? Perhaps since Kirta is a king, Baal is to be involved. In *KTU* 1.15 ii it is Baal who suggests to El that he bless Kirta. It is El who blesses with

---

60. K. Bulkeley, "Dreaming and Religious Conversion," in *The Oxford Handbook of Religious Conversion* (ed. L. R. Rambo and C. E. Farhadian; New York: Oxford University Press, 2014) 257–58; C. McGinn, *The Power of Movies: How Screen and Mind Interact* (New York: Vintage, 2005) 100–157. While about films, McGinn's book illustrates well the liminal nature of dreams.

children, at the proposal of Baal. Once again the question arises of what exactly this relationship is: El, who originally responded to Kirta's distress, waits for Baal's advice before meeting the needs of Kirta for children. Baal does not do the actual blessing, but defers to El. El, on the other hand, does not bless until Baal asks him to do so. Throughout a fine interplay between El and Baal addresses Kirta's concerns. No matter what the exact nature of the relationship may be, the divine world receives a new anaglyph of cooperation between Baal and El.

Difficulties soon attend any attempt to unravel divine interactions as Kirta makes a stop, not in his instructions, to make a vow to Athirat. No account remains to chronicle if Athirat is the cause of Kirta's illness in text 15 or if there was any godly disagreement about it, if she was. With her indignant recollection of the vow in 15 iii, just prior to the onset of Kirta's illness, it would seem a natural conclusion that she brought it on.[61] Lacking, however, is any reaction on the part of any of the deities who attended Kirta's party or blessed him. The situation itself does throw more divine interaction into relief: even though El has blessed Kirta, other gods may take exception to this exalted conferral of status. The unfortunate state of text 15 leaves many details beyond anything but educated guesses.

The episode of Kirta's healing also brings gods into parley in 16 v. El seeks a champion of healing among the assembled gods, only ultimately to take on the task himself. Creating the healer, Shataqat, El's action counteracts the illness. Since it is not certain that Athirat brought on the disease, it cannot be definitively stated that El's action contradicts Athirat's. Nor can it be asserted with any force that other deities dare not take on the healing role since Athirat was behind the illness. Once again, motive is lacking, nevertheless, when the gods interact as a group to heal Kirta, it is El who does the physical work of producing a healer.

The epic of Kirta thus raises many questions on how deities interact, partly since important events are obscured by lacunae. Overall the impression appears to be one of cooperation between Baal and El, and perhaps some intrigue on the part of Athirat. Perhaps, as in the Baal Cycle, gods sometimes work at cross-purposes.

The story of Aqhat also preserves examples of divine interaction based in response to human activity. Noting Danel's worthy service to the gods, Baal, as in Kirta, asks El to bless Danel with a son. A spirit of cooperation between El and Baal also appears in this episode, as El does as Baal requests. On the larger question of how gods interact, Baal refers to El as "my father"

---

61. So it is stated, for example, in Greenstein's translation "Asherah punishes Kirta for failing to remember and fulfill the vow he made" (Parker, *UNP*, 27).

(*aby, KTU* 1.17 i 23). It might be argued that this is an honorific title appropriate for any deity to El since Baal is elsewhere referred to as the son of Dagan. A similar argument might be made for the title "son of Dagan," however. This title might be honorific to a deity associated with storms. Another solution to this dual paternity is the recognition that logical, genealogical relationships among the gods did not exist. The parentage of any one god might depend upon the circumstances of the myth. Problems with a fully-developed lineage apply to a modern approach to the material, not to the ancient texts themselves. For the purposes of Aqhat, El is Baal's father.

The Katharat, like Shataqat in Kirta, seem to effect the wishes of El. Since the crucial middle of text 17 is missing, any divine negotiations over the bow given to Aqhat are inaccessible. Since Anat is enamored of the bow and it seems to have been the handiwork of Kothar wa-Hasis, within this story it seems possible that some divine discussion of the fabulous bow might have taken place. Without direct evidence, however, only speculation informs this reconstruction. Kothar wa-Hasis delivers the bow and is honored with a banquet by Danel and Danatiya.

When Anat's anger is aroused, she journeys to El's tent and addresses him with threatening words similar to those used in the Baal Cycle. In this episode, El does not resist Anat's violent request, although El supported Baal's suggestion of blessing Danel at the outset of the story. El's permission is required, but he recognizes the futility of refusal. This type of relationship reflects a family dynamic more than a formal bureaucracy, although even in bureaucracies personality pressures may be an important factor. El replies to Anat's proposed bloodlust with the familial term *bt*, "daughter." Herein lies one of the most difficult aspects of interpreting the divine world: does the use of familial terms indicate a supposed "biological" relationship?

Phrased in larger literary terms, the question is one of figurative usage and whether it is part of Ugaritic divine relations. Human characters in Kirta and Aqhat are naturally treated as biological relatives. Does the Ugaritic divine world operate in the same fashion? Apart from the obvious difficulty of Baal's "paternity," it is obvious that gods engage in sexual intercourse and reproduce. Their "biological" life is based on that of universal human experience, there is no reproduction by "grok" here.[62] Human reproductive processes are overlaid on the divine world. Although El may create Shataqat without intercourse, it is obvious that the deities of Ugarit engage in sexual

---

62. Recourse to science fiction (R. L. Heinlein, *Stranger in a Strange Land* [New York: Putnam, 1961]) is appropriate in this context. The concept of asexual reproduction, although understood from a scientific perspective, is radically foreign to human life experience. To an author living prior to the discovery of asexual reproduction, few other options appear to be available for gods to reproduce.

activity and treat each other as family members. Ultimately the question is how to clarify the Ugaritic concept of divine consanguinity. Whether terms of relation may be treated figuratively or not is one of the greatest obstacles to understanding divine relationships in Ugaritic thought.

Literary analysis for such early texts requires particular finesse. Techniques specialized for pre-biblical material must be appropriate to the demands of such challenging literature. When many lacunae exist, speculation is unbridled and few checks or balances exist against which such speculation may be reigned in. These lacunae present an obstacle to any system of literary analysis. A second barrier to a fully developed literary system is the pre-scientific *Weltanschauung* of the Ugaritic population. This particular concern also applies to other ancient literature, including the Bible. The standards that are universally accepted today,[63] such as consistency, logical development, and empirical evidence, simply do not apply. The literature reflects a world in which shifts between pieces of literature may ignore the details of other pieces of literature, much as cartoons or situation comedies today sometimes overlook developments in previous episodes—even the death of a character—yet continue with the same characters reappearing. Complexity underlies this world and when it encounters our systematic world, a disconnect occurs. The resulting dissonance is evident in the present-day literature on the divine world.

The unconstrained Ugaritic imagination is herded into an ordered march. Inconsistencies are harmonized in order to reestablish the connection with modern expectations. What is suggested here is that the divine world of Ugarit included inconsistency and ambiguity. As the ancients knew, interviewing deities was not a possibility. Their world reflected a power and imagination beyond rational limits. The literary texts reveal that Ugaritians did not insist on a systematic theology in order to recognize and worship the beneficial divinities.

CONCLUSION

The Ugaritic texts which focus directly on divine interaction, as well as texts which highlight human interaction with gods, when taken together display glaring inconsistencies. One response to this state of knowledge is the attempt at a harmonization of the material, smoothing over contradictions and inconsistencies until a somewhat even depiction of the divine world

---

63. "Universally" is used here to represent established scientific and philosophic thought. There are individuals and groups who outwardly reject the tenets of scientific thought, although often their lifestyles indicate their tacit acceptance of the same.

emerges. Disparate material may then be considered variant from an "official" outlook.

Neuroscientific research suggests a different avenue of approach. Until relatively recent times, the state of brain studies and the assumed supernatural aspect of religion kept these disciplines widely separated. Psychologists since Freud have attempted to integrate religion into what is speculated about the mind, but the empirical results of neuroscience were not available. The perspective being suggested here is that brain studies have become advanced enough to demonstrate that the concern with systematic, consistent theology may not have been a factor for the people of Ugarit who have left this archive. Taken as a whole the divine world represented in the Ugaritic tablets is inchoate and malleable. A carefree liberty of expression concerning the gods defies a rigorous systematization reflecting the state of educated brains at that point in history. When the freedom of the Ugaritic imagination collides with the modern educated brain a disconnect results. Human brains, however, must supply a reason.[64] A reasonable approach would seem to be the law of averages: splitting differences into separate schools and then extrapolating common elements to form an "orthodox" view while the remaining differences settle out as variant traditions. Some form of this approach has held sway over the interpretation of Ugaritic religion since the site was discovered.

After more than eighty-five years of research during which great strides in understanding the gateway to all human experience, the brain, have been made, it is time to raise the question of Ugarit's state of mind. A complex world may result as the components of a provisional divine sphere are teased apart. In this divine world logic may not have the force to bring all elements into line, the areas of the brain that formulate contradictory explanations may have been prominent in the formulation of the mythological realm. In this world the meme for systematic theology had not yet evolved and the concept of religion as a separate domain did not exist.[65] In this realm the gods did as they would and humble human scribes recorded the traditions, regardless of how they corresponded to past, present or future reconstructions.

---

64. Barber and Barber, *When They Severed*, 14.
65. Dubuisson, *Western Construction of Religion*.

5

The Rumpelstiltskin Factor
Explorations in the Arithmetic of Pantheons

Nicolas Wyatt[1]

> One need not resort to fuzzy ideas of the numinous or treat religion as *sui generis* and thus not amenable to the normal tools of critical evaluation brought to bear on other spheres of human activity... This study treats "secret knowledge" entirely as a human construct...
>
> —A. Lenzi, *Secrecy and the Gods*

Michael Hundley began a recent article on much the same theme as I am addressing here with the following observation:

> The divine is seemingly ubiquitous in Mesopotamian society, yet despite its all-pervasiveness, it remains conceptually elusive. The divine sphere is vast and complex, such that it is hard to delimit and to distinguish between its various parts. In fact, there is no simple answer to even the most basic question: what

---

1. *Author's note*: It gives me great pleasure to offer this paper in memory of Simon Parker, who contributed significantly to our understanding of the Ugaritic literary tradition.

is a god? The divine world is also characterized by a fluidity not found in modern western religions.[2]

The same may be said of most, if not all ancient Near Eastern theological "systems." They are generally not bound by the same concern as that of modern religions for orthodoxy.

During his Areopagus speech in Athens, Paul famously spoke of the cult of "the unknown god," ἄγνωστος θεός (Acts 17:23). Apart from a developing interest in classification and organization of ideas, one of the principles behind such an institution may have been fear in a polytheistic culture of what we may call the wicked fairy factor: fear of inadvertently omitting a deity whose involvement was crucial for a particular rite. Pantheon-lists could help priesthoods avoid such contingencies. Theological diplomacy. Another aspect of the institution—the possibility of deities willfully withholding their name, remaining autonomous, and thus remaining intractable to human desires through the cult—is also of interest, in showing another motivation for lists: this will be the backdrop of the present paper. This I dub the Rumpelstiltskin factor.[3] There is a double-edged element here: priesthoods would want to know all the divine names necessary to perform an effective cult; at the same time, they might well be concerned to prevent uninitiated persons from knowing them, to preserve their monopoly of the cult.

The modern academic debate on the historical reality of monotheism in early Israelite and Judahite religion is really an old debate, though still alive and well. And it is not simply a modern concern: ancient religious literature, and particularly biblical literature, was also much exercised with the problem. But we also find substantial evidence of speculation and enquiry in other cultures which do not appear to have embraced it, or approached at it by other routes. Monotheism has always been the culmination of a long historical process,[4] so that to understand it in context we must always start with an understanding of polytheistic world-views (and any serious

2. Hundley 2013:68.

3. Rumpelstiltskin also has various folklore doubles, for instance Tom Tit Tot. A useful article will be found at https://en.wikipedia.org/wiki/Rumpelstiltskin. With regard to the "wicked fairy factor," in writing of the cult in Heliopolis, Katherine Eaton (Eaton 2015:27) observed that "before opening the shrine, *the priest covers all his bases* by addressing the gods and goddesses who are in Karnak, Thebes, Heliopolis, Memphis, the south, the north, the east, and the west . . ." (my emphasis).

4. Wilhelm Schmidt's attempt to reconstruct an *Urmonotheismus* (Schmidt 1912) must be judged a failure. See Evans-Pritchard 1987:104–5. The idea of a historical Abrahamic or Mosaic monotheism (that is, from the middle or late second millennium) is likewise not to be taken seriously as a historical position, whatever may be its function in contemporary religious belief.

engagement with the problem should take into account recent work on the early development of human consciousness). This is not to deny that there are early intuitions in many cultures, which we may think of with hindsight as groping, perhaps unconsciously, towards monotheism, and we shall see some examples of this in the ensuing discussion.

A useful starting point is to be found in an area perhaps unfamiliar to this readership,[5] the thought-world of the early Upaniṣads from India (*Meluḫḫa* in the Mesopotamian world, *Mleccha* in Sanskrit).[6] Consider the following conversation from *Bṛhadāraṇyaka Upaniṣad* 3.9.1:

> Then Vidagdha Śākalya asked him, "How many gods are there, Yājñavalkya?" He answered in accordance with the following *nivid* [invocation of the gods]: "As many as are mentioned in the *nivid* of the hymn of praise to the Viśvedevas, namely, three hundred and three, and three thousand and three."
>
> "Yes," he said, "but how many gods are there really, Yājñavalkya?"
>
> "Thirty three."
>
> "Yes," he said, "but how many gods are there, Yājñavalkya?"
>
> "Six."
>
> "Yes," he said, "but how many gods are there, Yājñavalkya?"
>
> "Three."
>
> "Yes," he said, "but how many gods are there, Yājñavalkya?"
>
> "Two."
>
> "Yes," he said, "but how many gods are there, Yājñavalkya?"
>
> "One and a half."
>
> "Yes," he said, "but how many gods are there, Yājñavalkya?"
>
> "One."[7]

---

5. Though the term *mleccha/mlechcha* in Sanskrit meant something like the Greek βάρβαρος, denoting people of incomprehensible foreign speech, it was probably a loan-word from the (Dravidian?) language of the Indus culture, denoting themselves. While unfamiliar to modern perceptions, it should be remembered that a considerable number of Vedic divine names appear in western Asiatic documentation. Perhaps the most important single context is the Hurro-Hittite treaty between the Mitannian and Hittite empires (*ANET* 205–6; Beckman 1999:41–48). It lists among the gods of Mitanni, Mitra, Varuṇa, Indra and the Nāsatyas (sc. the Aśvins).

6. Extensive trading took place between Mesopotamia and the Indus civilization, and with precursor cultures in both regions dating back to the seventh millennium (see Jane McIntosh, "The First Civilizations in Contact: Mesopotamia and the Indus," http://www.cic.ames.cam.ac.uk/pages/mcintosh.html), so while I am not basing my argument here on contact between East and West, it is possible that there is a genetic link between the Indian and Ugaritic evidence, especially given the intermediate Indo-Iranian dimension (Burrow 1973) and the mediating role of the Hurrians (n. 4 above).

7. Radhakrishnan 1953:234–35. Olivelle 1998:511, enlarged on the context:

This narrative is probably to be dated at some time around the seventh century BC (certainty is impossible), and reflects a richly diverse situation in which the old Vedic (Indo-Āryan) religion was blending with native pre-Āryan beliefs reflected in Buddhism and Jainism, and exhibiting a highly-developed ritual tradition and the beginnings of serious philosophical enquiry. It may be understood as a humorous response by Yājñavalkya (especially the reference to one and a half), but has a serious side to it. The larger number (3,306) is supposedly the number of different divine names occurring in the Viśvedevas hymns of the *Ṛgveda* and is clearly to be understood as all-embracing. And we may notice how our passage plays with various combinations of the number three. At the same time, the point of the story is the reluctance of the sage to reveal sacred and implicitly secret knowledge to the enquirer. We may take it as axiomatic that an answer like this, and indeed most of the clever computations we shall come across in this discussion, is designed as much to disguise as to reveal the "truth": in short, to keep it hidden from profane persons.

The number thirty-three is however particularly interesting in our present context,[8] as it corresponds to the number of entries listed (some in

---

ritual invocation [nivid]: part of a recitation of praise (*śastra*) to the All-gods. The invocation gives the number of the gods comprehended by the term "All-gods" [*Viśvedevas*]. A *śastra*, which is recited by the Hotṛ and his assistants (BU 3.1.2–6 n.), is distinguished from *stotra*, which is sung by the Udgātṛ and his assistants (BU 1.3.28 n.), and always follows the latter. The invocation given in the *Śāṅkhāyana Śrautasūtra* (8.21) reads: "You who are three and eleven; and three and thirty; and three and three hundred; and three and three thousand." Our text refers to only the last two numbers.

My thanks to Paul Dundas of Edinburgh University for this reference.

8. There are already many references to thirty-three gods in the *Ṛgveda*: 1.34.11 ("thrice eleven"), 1.45.2 (the three groups, Vasus, Rudras, and Ādityas of v. 1), 1.140.11 (three groups of eleven), 8.28.1, 8.30.2, 8.35.3, 8.39.9, 9.92.4 ("thrice eleven"), and even "thrice ten," which adds up to only thirty. *Ṛgveda* 10.55.3 has the figures thirty-five ("five times sevenfold") and thirty-four, showing the dynamism at work. The functional division of the thirty-three varied. Like the Ugaritic lists, the figure is notional and formulaic rather than an accurate body-count. Prajāpati is numbered in the sequel to the passage above as the thirty-third member of the group, but is sometimes referred to as the thirty-fourth (Śatapatha Brāhmaṇa 5.1.2.13, 5.3.4.23; in vv. 12 and 22 in these passages he is described as "seventeen-fold"), implicitly encompassing all the others. P. Danielou noted that "[a]ll existing beings, subtle or gross, live within the three spheres of Agni, within the three worlds. The gods are the powers that rule these three worlds. There are therefore three kinds of gods, and the gods are said to be ruled by the number 3. This is why they are symbolically represented by multiples of the number 3. Their main epithet is the 'thirty' (*tridaśa*), though their number is often given as thirty-three or its multiples" (1964: 82). He also noted that the gods also numbered thirty-three in some Iranian thought. The *Bṛhaddevatā* states that the total number of the pantheon is 3,309 (BD 7.45, though the following verse 7.46 refers to the "thirty gods," on which

paired or grouped forms) in an entirely different cultural milieu, in three of the pantheon lists from Ugarit. Two of the three are in Ugaritic, and the other in Akkadian, and they may be presented synoptically as here.

	KTU 1.47 Ugaritic		KTU 1.118 Ugaritic		RS 20.24 Akkadian	English
1	il ṣpn					The gods of Saphon
	Ilib	1	ilib	1	dingir abi	The god of the ancestor
	Il		il		ilum^lum	El
	Dgn		dgn		^d dagan	Dagan
5	bʿl ṣpn		bʿl ṣpn		^d adad bel ḫuršan ḫazi	Baal of Saphon
	bʿlm		bʿlm	5	^d adad ii	Baal 2
	bʿlm		bʿlm		^d adad iii	Baal 3
	bʿlm		bʿlm		^d adad iv	Baal 4
	bʿlm		bʿlm		^d adad v	Baal 5
10	[b]ʿlm		bʿlm		^d adad vi	Baal 6
	[bʿl]m		bʿlm	10	^d adad vii	Baal 7
	[arṣ] wšmm		arṣ wšmm		^d IDIM ù IDIM	Underworld[9] and Heaven
	[kt̲r]t		kt̲rt		^d sasuratum	Kotharat
	[yrḫ]		yrḫ		^d sîn	Yarih
15	[ṣpn]		ṣpn		^d ḫuršan ḫazi	Saphon
	[kt̲r]	15	kt̲r	15	^d ea	Kothar
	[pdry]		pdry		^d ḫebat	Pidray
	[ʿt̲tr]		ʿt̲tr		^d aštabi	Athtar
	[ġrm w ʿmqt]		ġrm w [ʿmqt]		^d ḫuršanum u amutu[m]	Mountains and Valleys
20	[at̲rt]		[a]t̲rt		^d ašratum	Athirat

---

see n. 12, and it is possible that the syntax of vv. 45–46 envisaged the addition of all these deities, sc. 3,339). See Macdonell 1904:2:270. I wonder whether the fact that 3,306 divided by 33 = 100 (forgetting the decimal place .18 recurring) was regarded as significant in ancient India.

9. That this is the correct nuance, over against "earth," was made very clear in Noegel 2017.

	[ᶜnt]	20	ᶜnt	20	ᵈanatum	Anat
	[šp]š		špš		ᵈšamaš	Shapsh
	[a]rṣy		arṣy		ᵈallatum	Arṣiy
	[u]šḫry		ušḫry		ᵈišḫara	Ishhara
25	[ᶜ]ṯtrt		ᶜṯtrt		ᵈištar	Athtart
	il tᶜdr bᶜl	25	il tᶜdr bᶜl	25	ilânuᴹ tillat ᵈadad	the gods who help Baal
	ršp		r[š]p		ᵈnergal	Reshef
	ddmš		ddmš		ᵈdadmiš	Dadmish
	pḫr ilm		pḫr ilm		ᵈpuḫur ilâniᴹ	The assembly of the gods
30	ym		ym		ᵈtâmtum	Yam
	ut ḫt	30	ut ḫt	30	ᵈdug bur.zi.níg.na	Censer
	knr		knr		ᵈis kinarum	Kinnar (lyre)
	mlkm		mlkm		ᵈma.lik.meš	Kings
	šlm	33	šlm	33	ᵈsalimu	Shalem

The remarkable feature in the present group is the apparent arrangement of deities in sets, as recognized by del Olmo Lete[10]—though I have

---

10. Del Olmo Lete 2014: 59. See also Wyatt 1998 for my assessment, which differs in terms of the overall groupings (seven for his six: he omits the last group in the listing noted). The lines in the lists above are not original, but designed to assist analysis. There are other pantheon lists from Ugarit, *KTU* 1.102 (a list of fourteen chthonian deities followed by an equal number of hypostases of El and Baal/Hadd/Lim: cf. Pardee 2000: 1:520–31; Clemens 2001:1195–96, for a list of differing assessments); 1.123 (a list of male deities, Pardee 2000:1:691–706; Clemens 2001:1206–7, for a list of differing assessments); RS 26.142 (Clemens 2001:991–93); and 1992.2004 (Clemens 2001:1047: "more complete parallel to 26.142"); the latter two are both Akkadian. These have their own independent logical structures. On the general practice of enumerating gods in lists, see the perceptive remark of Hundley 2013:87 (of value beyond Mesopotamia, which was the cultural area of which he wrote):

> As a genre, lexical god-lists amass various aspects of deities, yet do so for different purposes. Rather than exalting any particular god, they often represent a scholarly exercise, serving as a more synthetic attempt to make sense of the "large more or less disordered and confused group" of deities. Nonetheless, rather than always assimilating all deities with a shared forename into a single divine form, (semi-) independent aspects are occasionally grouped together, demonstrating both their identity and difference.

KTU 1.47 and its parallels clearly constitute a "more synthetic attempt to make sense of . . . " the Ugaritian pantheon.

modified his classification—to preserve a "set" of thirty-three, while incorporating more, within a number of sub-sets:

il ṣpn (title of text)

Set 1: consisting of *ilib*, *il*, and *dgn*;

(3 gods, 1 + 2);

Set 2: *bʿl ṣpn*,
consisting of *bʿlm, bʿlm, bʿlm, bʿlm, bʿlm*, and *bʿlm*

(7 gods including *bʿl ṣpn*: 1 + 6);

Set 3: *arṣ w šmm*,
a merismic pair, containing *kṯrt, yrḫ, ṣpn, kṯr, pdry, ʿṯtr*

(7 chthonian-astral deities including *arṣ w šmm*; 1 + 6);

Set 4: *ġrm w ʿmqt*,
a further merismic pair, containing *aṯrt, ʿnt, špš, arṣy, ušḫry, ʿṯtrt*

(7 goddesses including *ġrm w ʿmqt*: 1 + 6);

Set 5: *il tʿḏr bʿl*
(lit. "the gods who assist Baal"), containing *ršp, ddmš*

(a pair/triad: 1 + 2);

Set 6: *pḫr ilm*,
containing *ym, ut ḥt, knr*

(a triad/tetrad: 1 + 3; and

Set 7: *mlkm* (taken as a plural form), typified by *šlm*

The precise constitution of some of these sets is uncertain, but it is surely significant that the numbers three and seven form a pattern, as though highlighting these particular integers within the larger whole.

Quite apart from general issues of how we square the number of divine names here with those occurring in other Ugaritic records, which through the course of history would have constantly fluctuated, we have the internal problem of how many deities the present list is intended to represent.[11] Do we take the binomial and merismic forms as indicating pairs of deities (so giving at least 35, but more if we unpack some of the plural categories), or do we take each pair in context as a unity (the 33 of our present computation, the number of *lines* in each list)? Some of the entries are inherently problematic. Numbers five to eleven are apparently seven hypostases of the storm-god (Akkadian Addu, Ugaritic Baʿlu [Baʿal], and Haddu, Hebrew Hadad),[12] and a further, unquantified group of assistants to Baʿal appears

---

11. See discussions in de Moor 1972 and del Olmo Lete 2014:60–66.

12. A set of "seven Adads" also appears in a text from Assur (KAR 142 RS iii 11–18, Schwemer 2001: 88):

ᵈAdad (iškur) ša Karkar^ki ša zunni (šèg) u [mīli (illu)], 'Adad of Karkar: he of rain and flood;'

as set 5. But only one god of this name features in Ugaritic literature and cult, Baʿal, although he has at least twenty-four titles in the extant poetic literature.[13] The thirteenth term, Kotharat, in Ugaritic ktrt, set 3, is usually found as a group of seven goddesses of gynaecological functions, as in KTU 1.24.40–50, but they are equated in the Akkadian text with the single goddess ᵈSasuratum.[14] That in itself may point the way this enquiry

---

ᵈAdad (iškur) ša Esagil gugal nārāti (gú.gal.i7.[meš]), 'Adad of Esagil, inspector of canals;'
ᵈAdad (iškur) ša Enamḫē ša nu[ḫši], 'Adad of Enamḫē, he of abundance;'
ᵈAdad (iškur) ša ᵘʳᵘZabban ša ar[urti], 'Adad of Zabban, he of the famine;'
ᵈAdad (iškur) ša Padaᵏⁱ ša ru[ṭubti], 'Adad of Pada, he of the dampness;'
ᵈAdad (iškur) ša Ḫalab ša be[r]qi, 'Adad of Aleppo, he of the lightning;'
ᵈAdad (iškur) ša Akusᵏⁱ ša ḫurb[āši], 'Adad of Akus, he of the frost.'

My thanks to Kenneth Cathcart for drawing this to my attention and assisting translation. In ll. 19–25 of the same text another group of seven is listed.

A further set of seven deities in Mesopotamia is known collectively as Šibittu, Sibittu, "the Seven." They are identified variously as the Pleiades, or a group of demons, offspring of Anu and the Earth. See Archi 2010 on the "dark gods" of the Hittite-Luwian tradition. Lambert (2013:147–48) cited seven-fold lists of Ištar's names and titles of Lamaštu, and eight titles of Nabu. The processional divine figures at Yazılıkaya are apparently arranged in a set of gods to the left and (an incomplete set of) goddesses to the right. The two processions arrive in front of Teššub and Hebat as the chief deities of the pantheon. Archi (2013:10) argued that the first gods in the left procession include seven Hurrian gods, with (some of) their consorts in the right procession:

1	Teššub/IM/U	Hebat
2	Tašmišu (Hittite Šuwaliyat)	—
3	Kumarbi/NISABA (= Dagan)	NIN.LÍL
4	É.A (Hayya)	Damkina (DAM.KI.NA)
5	Kušuh/30/EN.ZU (Sîn)	Nikkal (NIN.GAL)
6	Šimegi/UTU	Aya (A.A) (-Ekaldu)
7	Aštabi/ NIN.URTA	
(8	Nubadig.) . . .	

The exception here is Ea, fourth among the first seven. Nubadig is eighth of the gods in the continuing procession, whom Archi included in his set of seven Hurrian gods, having therefore to explain why Ea intrudes (and failing to do so). But since the procession continues, perhaps what we should note is the first seven figures, comparing this arrangement with the Ugaritic set of seven containing Saphon. Ea, whom the Hurrians called māti-ni (Hittite ḫattannas LUGAL-uš, Akkadian bēl ḫasīsi) "Lord of Wisdom" (cf. Kothar from Ugarit, identified in turn with Ea) is at the heart of the first seven. Notice too the epithet of the moon-god Kušuh: "Thirty!" This epithet must reflect the optimal period of a lunation, discussed below. It also appears in the Ugaritic Akkadian pantheon list RS 26.142.9, corresponding, as Arnaud showed, with yrḫ of the parallel KTU 1.148.29 (Arnaud 1994, followed by Schwemer 2001:522). See also the Vedic reference BD 7.45, noted in n. 8 above.

13. Wyatt 1992b. On Ugaritic divine epithets, see also Rahmouni 2008.

14. The seven Kotharat also correspond to a Hurrian heptad of birth-goddesses,

should go: that a larger number such as seven can denote one. Similarly, the twenty-ninth term, *pḫr ilm*, Akkadian $^{d}puḫur$ $ilâni^{m}$, denotes at least a considerable grouping of deities, if not the entire divine community, but seen as a unity, rather as the Viśvedevas are, particularly when given a grammatically singular form (*Viśvadeva*). So Śākalya's question to Yājñavalkya, "How many gods are there really?," remains an open question if addressed to the Ugaritic context.

I raise these issues to demonstrate the fluid nature of an ancient theological system, while considering that on one level the threefold document is indeed concerned to list precisely thirty-three divine personae, whose internal dynamism is recognized in the questions I have just raised, which would also have been raised however inchoately by the Ugaritian priests. The list is perhaps a kind of "upanishadic" and gnomic response to questions of this kind. But the thirty-three are as real in Ugaritian thought as are Yājñavalkya's thirty-three in Indian thought. And the curious formulation of *his* original 3,306, three hundred and three, and three thousand and three, may provide a clue to the other figure, another little game with three, as "thirty and three" (3,000 + 3; 300 + 3; 30 + 3; 3) in both contexts. And just to complicate matters, any pantheon would also be inherently dynamic in terms of historical development, since gods developed, split into multiples, coalesced, and died,[15] or shifted one way or the other along a divine-demonic axis. Given that "three" is a way of representing plurality, as in the Egyptian hieroglyph plural marker (|||), these sets may have been a way of representing various scales or "intensities" of plurality. A more intensive form, for instance, would be the multiplicative, as in 3 × 3, which gives us the classic Egyptian Ennead (nine also having a similar symbolic, all-inclusive function in Greek). The seven-headed dragon of the ancient Near Eastern world becomes the nine-headed Hydra in Greek thought.

The question to ask here is, why is the number 33 significant? In fact we can rightly ask why any number, including one, is significant in metaphysical discourse. A serious case can be made for each of the numbers up to twelve as representing essential parts of reality (or reality as a whole: we can think of Triads and Trinity, Tetrads and Quaternities, Pentads, the common Heptads of Mesopotamian theology, the Ogdoad, the Ennead, and so on), while higher numbers, thirty-three, a hundred, "three thousand, three hundred and six," even "ten thousand times ten thousand,"[16] and so on

---

the Hutena and Hutellura (*ḥdn ḥdlr*, in Hurrian texts *KTU* 1.42.32, 33; 1.60.14; 1.64.29; 1.135.11; bibliography in *DULAT* 382). The singular figure Sasuratum had seven assistants ("Wombs") whom Archi identified with the Kotharat (Archi 2013:19).

15. See Machinist 2011.

16. More modestly, Hittite tradition talks of the thousand gods (Telepinu, A I 19:

almost *ad infinitum*, appear in order to express some aspect of universality or totality, as though they really mean "beyond computation." Sometimes numbers are used to daze the mind, for all their apparent concern with exactitude, as in Indian computations of the Yugas and the Mahāyugas, or the "Great Year" (25,920 years) of ancient astronomy.[17] While it is of interest to ask how the ancients thought in this way, we must always allow for a "mystical," or at any rate poetic and aesthetic dimension—that is, not merely rational—to the thinking.

So, why thirty-three? We have no means of knowing with certainty. But we can speculate to some purpose. Perhaps we should begin with thirty. There are thirty letters in the "long" Ugaritic writing system. The "short" version, used in cuneiform documents from Beth-Shemesh and some other sites outside Ugarit, have twenty-two,[18] and formed the basis of the Phoenician and Hebrew systems.[19] The longer system, as well as giving two forms of *het* (ḥ, ḫ), contained phonemes for representing Hurrian sounds (ḏ, ẓ, ġ, s̀, and ṭ, and two additional alephs, each aleph having a vowel indicator, *a*, *i* or *u*, or *shewa*).[20] Cyrus Gordon proposed, following a suggestion of Kelley,[21] that the longer Ugaritic system, which had additional letters significantly added at the end of abecedaries, as clearly later additions, was the result of

---

Hoffner 1990:15).

17. See discussion of these related matters, with bibliography, in Wyatt 2001: 323–32. A Life of Brahmā and its associated *pralaya* (period of dissolution) lasted 622,080,000,000,000 years (ibid., 324).

18. Tablets from beyond Ugarit are *KTU* 4.766 (Tell Sukas, Syria), *4.767 (Tel Taanak, Israel), 5.24 (Tel Beth Shemesh, Israel), *6.1 (Nahal Tabor, Israel), *6.2, *6.67 (Tell Kamid el Loz, Lebanon), *6.68 (Hala Sultan Tekke, Cyprus), *6.70 (Sarepta, Lebanon), *6.71 (Tell Nebi Mend, Syria) and 6.104 (Tiryns, Greece). (* denotes those written in the "short" alphabet from Ugarit; as also are *KTU* 1.77, 4.31, 4.710, 5.7, 5.18, 5.22(?), 7.60: Tropper 2012:73, using different sigla.)

19. Dietrich and Loretz 1988 (summary 1999) argued that the early history of the cuneiform alphabet was complex, with a short version developed independently, and probably earlier than the long one (contrary to Gordon, cited below, n. 20); the latter, the main one in use in Ugarit, was influenced by second millennium forebears of the epigraphic South Arabian system, and subsequently further extended with the final three signs.

20. Gordon 1965:11–12: the last three letters (*i*, *u*, s̀) are additions to a 27-letter system ("appended to a preexisting alphabet ending in *t* like the familiar Hebrew ABC ..."). The five additional letters in the remaining set of 27 all coalesced with similar sounds in the shorter alphabets (ḫ > ḥ, ḏ > z, ġ > ʿ, ẓ > ṣ, ṭ > š), to produce the 22-letter Hebrew and Phoenician systems. Hebrew then distinguished š and ś (שׁ and שׂ), giving 23 letters. The 27-letter system was thus primary, not derivative, in his view, contrary to the assessment of Dietrich and Loretz (above, n. 19).

21. Kelley 1960.

linking the number of signs to the number of days in a lunar month.[22] The actual mean length of a (synodic) lunar month being 29.53059 days (29 days, 12 hours, 44 minutes, 2.8 seconds on current computations), thirty signs are required to cover it. We can discern the month functioning as a liturgical framework in the Ugaritic ritual calendar, with subdivision into weeks[23] (to which we shall come in due course). How Ugarit handled the epagomenal days, if they required to square the solar and lunar years of 354 and 365.25 days (as did the ancient Egyptians or Babylonians with greater or lesser success) is unknown, but the three outstanding letters may have found a use here. And the final three of thirty-three may have also served as an epitome, the essence, of the whole. Nor is the list a pure abstraction, or mere speculation, since apart from several abcedaries as scribal aids,[24] the Ugaritic ritual text *KTU* 1.148 is clearly modeled in part on the order of the pantheon as here listed in its sacrificial program.[25]

Thirty-three is also the sum of the bones in the human vertebral column, which normally consists of 33 vertebrae (made up of 24 presacral vertebrae: 7 cervical, 12 thoracic, and 5 lumbar, followed by the sacrum: 5 fused sacral vertebrae, and the coccyx: 4 fused coccygeal vertebrae, 24 + 5

---

22. Gordon 1970:194–95:

> In this, the oldest known form of our alphabet, all of the first twenty-nine letters have distinctive values so that none duplicates any other phonetically. Only the final thirtieth letter (ś) is phonetically superfluous, for it is interchangeable with the nineteenth (s). Thus the Ugaritic alphabet has 29 or 30 letters, corresponding to the days in a lunar month, which can number either 29 or 30 . . .

> The Ugaritic alphabet presupposes an earlier 27-letter alphabet from which the 22-letter Phoenician alphabet is derived. The five extra letters are original rather than added, because they appear in an order that cannot be explained graphically or phonetically as additions. The three final letters of the Ugaritic alphabet are additions to make it conform with the number of days (29/30) in a lunar month.

For a later treatment of the problem, see Bausani, 1978. He did not mention Gordon's work.

23. Del Olmo Lete 2014:18–21. Regarding the number of days in the month, he erred in supposing that *KTU* 1.148 has curtailed the pantheon from 33 to "28 or 29." The list is reduced to thirty, the minimum necessary to cover the month. One addition is Thirathiyu (*trty*, "Winey"), in l. 28. The missing ones are *ut ḫt* (Censer), Kinnaru (Lyre), and the final chthonian pair. *KTU* 1.41 has twenty-nine different deities or divine equivalents in the extant text, some of which are duplicated or even triplicated. Were there originally thirty distinct deities?

24. *KTU* 5.4, 5.5, 5.6, 5.8, 5.9, 5.12, 5.13, 5.14 (with syllabic names or phonetic values of signs), 5.16, 5.17, 5.19, 5.20, 5.21, 5.25, 5.31 and 5.32 (in various conditions of completeness, and in some cases, e.g. 5.9, mixed with other material. In addition, 5.2, 5.15, 5.24, 5.26 and 5.27 list letters in apparently random sequences.

25. Pardee 2000:779–806; del Olmo Lete 2014:102–10. For translation, see also Wyatt 2002:427–29

+ 4). Given the analogical use of the human form as a means of mapping the universe (particularly elaborately developed in Indian and Egyptian thought, but also found in Hebrew thought, and indeed probably occurring universally), and the common practice of conceptualizing the gods in human form, the number may here represent the pantheon as essentially a human organism, with which any anthropologist would happily concur. We may even surmise an awareness of the numerological link between the two alternative explanations as something perceived and appreciated by the ancients as a holistic synthesis.

While it is not at the center of the whole list—*that* would be number seventeen, Pidray—the central deity of the three sets of seven which dominate the list is Saphon, the deified sacred mountain, symbolically at the center of the Ugaritian, and indeed whole East Mediterranean, world.[26] This seems almost to be a further coded allusion to the idea that underlying the many gods, or perhaps rather at their heart, is one divine reality. It is also surely significant that though the name of the mountain (*ṣapūnu*) probably has no etymological link with *ṣāpan*, "hide,"[27] with a little bit of punning, playing on the forms of the two words which are linked with the toponym, *ṣpy*, "to spread," and *ṣpy*, "to look out,"[28] the sacred mountain may be understood by the discerning reader to lie hidden at the heart of the system. So an element of secrecy and mystery is sustained by these polysemic options.

The presence of sets of seven in the Ugaritic lists also reminds us that sevens abound in ancient cosmology, not least in both Ugaritic and Israelite-Judahite culture, where the week was an ancient institution. For all their awkwardness vis-à-vis a synodic month, months were for practical purposes divided into seven-day units. This is clear both in the extensive references to New Moons and Sabbaths in the Old Testament, and in the Ugaritic ritual texts, where the first, seventh, eighth and fifteenth days of the month were of particular ritual significance. E. Zerubbabel argued that the lunar calendar and the week of seven days developed entirely independently of one another, the latter deriving from early astronomical and astrological belief that there were seven planets (though they were considered to be stars; sc. Sun, Moon, Mercury, Venus, Mars, Jupiter, and Saturn). This is quite possible, given the awkwardness of attempting to reconcile seven-day units and lunations. But Zerubbabel also insisted that the resulting seven-day week was a purely cultural construct, an arbitrary system of time-division; this latter point was

26. See Wyatt 1995.

27. Koch 1993; Wyatt 1995; Healey 2007. For the "hidden" sense as the primary meaning of the name, see Grave 1980, 1982, cited in Wyatt 1995:213–14. For further remarks on *ṣpn*, see Schwemer 2001:513 n. 4174.

28. Wyatt 1995:230–31.

disputed by F. Halberg in a review of his book, on the ground that heptadian patterns also occur widely throughout nature.[29] Restricting ourselves to cultural aspects, the spatial organization of the world was widely seen in terms of seven, as with the seven gates of the underworld in Mesopotamian and Egyptian thought, and seven heavens in the former. A further contributory element to the symbolism of seven may have been musical, with reference to the seven intervals and seven notes of an octave, and Pythagoras, who travelled widely from Mesopotamia to Egypt, absorbing much older ideas, saw identities between numbers, the spatial world, and music.[30]

These considerations bring us back to the number seven as significant in theological enumeration, since we would expect there to be a congruence between the divine and natural worlds. Seven-day sequences occur throughout the Ugaritic ritual texts,[31] and evidently have significance as representing complete cycles in the literary texts.[32] (The same can be said

29. See Halberg 1985. See also the amusing mathematical puzzle of Gleizer n.d., dealing with life on the planet Heptadium, which has a seven-hour ("heptahour") day divided into forty-nine heptaminutes, which in turn comprise forty-nine heptaseconds. The Jewish week almost certainly predated the exile, before influence by Babylonian calendrical forms in the exilic period. The reasons for Sabbath-observance are celebration of creation in Exod 20:10-11, but in memory of slavery in Egypt in Deut 5:12-15. The former relates to the exilic creation account in Genesis 1, with its sabbatical cycle, but the latter reflects pre-exilic ideas, since although it belongs to the latest redaction of Deuteronomy, and obviously has a close relationship with the Decalogue of Exodus 20, it also reflects older ideas as evidenced in Deuteronomy 15, with its sabbatical year. New moons and Sabbaths were clearly part of Israelite and Judahite calendrical observance before the exile, as shown by such passages as 1 Sam 20:5, 18, 24; 1 Kgs 12:32; 2 Kgs 4:23, 11:5-9; Isa 1:13; Hos 2:13. And there is no reason to think that all the Pentateuchal references to it are late. For general treatment, see de Vaux 1961 (1957):468-83. His downplaying of the "Canaanite" aspect, implicitly including Ugaritic evidence (p. 478) perhaps overstates the case against such an original link. The significance of such systems in Ugaritic ritual indicates that the week is pre-Israelite. Quite independently of this temporal influence of lunations, a more deeply-rooted psychological foundation for the significance of seven is suggested by Miller 1956 and Sperling 1988, based on the human capacity for memorizing series.

30. See Wulstan 1968; James 1993:20-40. Isaac Newton famously concluded that there were seven colors in the visible light spectrum, because seven symbolized perfection. See "Visible spectrum," https://en.wikipedia.org/wiki/Visible_spectrum: "He chose seven colors out of a belief, derived from the ancient Greek sophists, of there being a connection between the colors, the musical notes, the known objects in the solar system, and the days of the week," adding indigo, which is not readily visible, to complete the "system."

31. See for example *KTU* 1.41.

32. See *KTU* 1.4 vi 24-35 (the building of Baal's temple); *KTU* 1.14-16 *passim*, with the application of seven diversified: the children or wives killed (however the "seven" element is construed); the seven-day march followed by the seven-day siege of Udum; the seven offspring of each gender born to Hurriya; and El's unsuccessful sevenfold appeal

of the biblical evidence.) We saw the three groups of seven in the Ugaritic pantheon lists. They invite the supposition that an older pantheon list of twenty-one deities lies behind the expanded list, and this in turn perhaps derivative from an even earlier seven.[33] We shall see just such a process of expansion in an Egyptian pantheon.

A different, literary, enumeration of the Ugaritian pantheon offers an alternative to the number thirty-three as the complement of the gods. It is mentioned only once, in the *Baal* Cycle,[34] where at the inauguration of his new temple Baal holds a sacrificial feast inviting the gods (*KTU* 1.4 vi 44–46):

44 ṣḥ aḫh bbhth	He invited his brothers into his house,
aryh 45 bqrb hklh	his kinsfolk into the midst of his palace;
ṣḥ 46 šbʿm bn aṯrt	he invited the seventy sons* of Athirat.
	* or: "children"

This is not as clear-cut as it appears. A strict arithmetical count must logically imply a pantheon of seventy-three members, the number seventy above, and in addition their putative father El, their mother Athirat, and Mot, who was deliberately omitted from the invitation to the feast (the wicked fairy factor!), and complains about the lack of courtesy, later in the narrative (*KTU* 1.5 i 22–25):

22 kl ṣḥn bʿl ʿm 23 aḫy	For Baal did not invite me with my brothers,
qran hd ʿm aryy	(nor) did Hadd summon me with my kinsfolk;
24 lḥmm ʿm aḫy lḥm	but he ate food with my brothers,
25 wšrp ʿm a*r[yy]³⁵ yn	and drank wine with my kinsfolk!

to the gods to heal Kirta; *KTU* 1.17 i 5–16: Danel's seven-day ritual performance in the temple; 1.17 ii 32–40: the birth of Aqhat; 1.17 v 3–4: Danel's reaction on the seventh day after Aqhat's birth. An eighth element sometimes brings the seven to a close, implicitly inaugurating a new heptadian sequence, as perhaps implied in *KTU* 1.12.

33. It is surely significant that the number is three times seven, both the prime numbers being keys in symbolic arithmetic. The supposition that this group of twenty-one deities stood alone in an earlier version of the pantheon list is supported by the fact that the rubric, *il ṣpn*, appearing in *KTU* 1.47.1, could be construed as those listed, who formally dwelt around Mount Saphon, which, as we see, lies symbolically at their heart, 1.47.[15] (restored from parallels).

34. But see *KTU* 1.12 ii 48–9, which refers to Baal's "seventy brothers ... eighty ... ," where the "eighty" is the *b* term in the numerical progression, balancing "seventy" as the *a* term; and *KTU* 1.15 iv 5, where Kirta summons his "seventy commanders ... eighty leaders ..."

35. Reading *a*r[yy]* in l. 25 for *aḫ[y]*, as read by *KTU*³, for example, in parallel, as in the previous text cited and the previous bicolon in this passage. See Wyatt 2002:119 n. 23. To interpret the text as it appears (thus *KTU*: *aḫy* ‖ *aryy*, *aḫy* ‖ *aḫy*), as simply a

It appears that Mot's brothers ... kinsfolk *were* invited, leaving poor Mot, excluded, to twiddle his thumbs. So the number seventy is clearly a symbolic rather than strictly computational number, no doubt playing on the symbolism of seven we have noted, multiplied by the similarly significant number ten.

Now this reference to the pantheon of the *Baal* cycle inevitably invites comparison with another famous seventy, the one occurring implicitly in Deut 32:8–9.[36]

běhanḥēl ʿelyôn gôyim	When The Most High dispersed the nations,
běhaprîdô běnê 'ādām	when he scattered the sons of Adam,
yaṣṣēb gěbulōt ʿammîm	he set up the boundaries of the peoples
lěmispar běnê šōr 'ēl	in accordance with the number of the sons of Bull El.
kî ḥēleq yhwh ʿammô	But the allotment of Yahweh was his kinsman,
yaʿăqōb ḥebel naḥălātô	Jacob the portion of his inheritance.

There are of course various explanations of this obscure text, though some are unnecessary complications by commentators ancient and modern. It seems to me that the similar passage from Ugarit clinches the matter as to who are being enumerated, the descendants of Jacob or the gods of the pantheon. It is surely the latter. Bull El (*ṯr il*) is a common title of El in the Ugaritic corpus, and Joosten's elegant solution to the problem of the reading in the fourth colon (the MT *běnê yisrā'ēl*, the LXX ἀγγέλων θεοῦ) renders further discussion superfluous on this score.

But a fresh translation still leaves us with exegetical problems. Where does Yahweh stand in this scenario? For many, he is one of the (seventy) "sons of Bull El," and therefore a subordinate deity.[37] This strikes me as a

---

poetic variation, is unconvincing. Alternatively, we should see chiasmus here, reading brothers ‖ kinsmen, kinsmen ‖ brothers, which requires correcting *aḥy* in l. 14 to *aryy*, and accepting a reading *aḥy* here in l. 25.

36. For my account of the passage, see Wyatt 2007a, 2007b. On whether the sons are those of Jacob or God, Stevens, between 1997: 139, and 2000: 412 n. 9, appears to have shifted from one position to the other. A good account was also given by Sanders 1996: 155–58 and Heiser 2001. For reading an allusion to Bull El, see Joosten 2007 and 2011: 100–2, reading *běnê šōr 'ēl* for MT *běnê yiśrā'ēl*; see also Wyatt and Wyatt 2013:436.

37. Thus, e.g., Eissfeldt 1956; Hammer 1986:316–18 (*Pisḳa* 311—presumably: the text is not entirely clear); Driver 1902:355–56 (citing *T. Ps-J.*) and remarking (356) that "[t]he idea will then be that the nations were allotted to the care of subordinate divine beings ... while Jehovah presided over Israel Himself. But the text yields a very suitable sense; *and there is no sufficient reason for preferring this reading*" (my emphasis); Eissfeldt 1956; Albertz 1994:271 n. 69; B. B. Schmidt 1995:86–87. M. S. Smith (2001: 48–49) envisaged a shift from Yahweh as subordinate to his identification with El. For

perverse understanding of the text. The relationship between the two gods, El and Yahweh, may be briefly summarized, though not, I hope, at risk of oversimplification. In many passages the two divine names are interchangeable (e.g. explicitly Gen 14:22; 16:13; Exod 6:2–3; implicitly Gen 32:31; 35:11–15; 49:25), indicating not just the equivalence, but the identification of the gods. The exodus is credited in Exodus 15 (but note v. 2cd!) to Yahweh, but in Num 23:22 and 24:8 to El:[38] the exodus narrative now effectively identifies them, though there may have been distinct strands to the prehistory of the tradition. In Hosea's polemics against the northern kingdom, 8:4–7 is a sustained attack on the bull-cult of Jeroboam, which I have explained as a reversion from Yahwism to an earlier "national" or perhaps local cult of El.[39] So Tur-Sinai's proposed correction of 8:6 from the acontextual *kî miyyiśrāʾēl* to *kî mi šôr ʾēl*, where the consonantal text is identical except for the ś, š shift, which is apparent only with a pointed text, is to be preferred as giving consistency to the passage, and reinforces Joosten's account of Deut 32:8.[40]

If Yahweh is not subordinate to El in the Deuteronomic passage, we must understand that El (= Yahweh) divides the number of the nations according to the number of the pantheon (seventy, the "sons of Bull El" in Israel corresponding to the sons of El's consort Athirat in Ugarit), but reserves Israel for himself, Yahweh (= El). There are thus seventy-one nations and seventy-one gods. This is a way of expressing the doctrine of election: Israel is supernumerary to the seventy nations. But as with the Ugaritic example, it leaves us with an anomaly, that the real number and the symbolic number are at variance. Mot no longer features, of course, and we may either infer that Asherah is present (seventy-two deities[41]) or that she too is now pensioned off, in which case Yahweh-El must be logically an androgynous parent (seventy-one deities representing the seventy nations

---

commentators supporting the "non-subordinationist" line adopted here, see Craigie 1976:378 (v. 9, "But . . ." asyndetive *kî*, or emphatic *kî*—n. 19); Mayes 1979:385; Christensen 1992:796 (implicitly); Sanders 1996:159 (implicitly); Tigay 1996:303. Wright observed that "[t]here is no possibility that Yahweh was simply one of the 'sons of the gods' (*sic*) to whom nations were allocated" (1996:300).

38. On the complexities of the tradition, see Wyatt 1978, 1979, 1992. See also Smith 2001:135–48, especially 146–48. On the more general matter of bull worship, see Wyatt and Wyatt 2013.

39. Wyatt and Wyatt 1995b.

40. Parallel to Joosten's account: Tur-Sinai 1964: i cols 31–33. See also Wyatt and Wyatt 2013: 436.

41. Cf. the seventy-two names of God in the Kabbalistic *Shemhamphorasch* (*šm hmpwrš*) formulation, based on the exegesis of Exod 14:19–21. See "Shem HaMephorash," http://en.wikipedia.org/wiki/Shemhamphorasch; Cornwell 1995.

and supernumerary Israel). The underlying seventy in both these examples appears to be a universal number, denoting all the gods. I suspect that as with the matter in the Ugaritic context, the ambiguity over the number is deliberate, inviting a sense of uncertainty, and the preserving an element of secrecy regarding Yahweh's true identity.

For a more restricted, specialized usage, let us come back to the storm-gods of the Ugaritic pantheon (set 2, and perhaps set 5 above), corresponding, we noted, to similar groups in Mesopotamian usage. These are perhaps the gods referred to in this passage from the Baal cycle:

6 wat qḥ 7 ʿrptk	As for you, take your clouds,
rḥk mdlk 8 mṭrk	your winds, your bolts, your rains,
ʿmk šbʿt 9 ġlmk	(take) with you your seven divine assistants,
ṯmn ḫnzrk	your eight boars . . .
(KTU 1.5 v 6–9)	

Here is an apparent dog's breakfast of subordinate deities! I previously took it that the numerical sequence n, n + 1, controls the idiom, and the seven is dominant here (7 + 8),[42] but in the light of the present discussion, I think the issue worth revisiting. The listed deities, clouds *et al.* are to be fitted in somehow, without the poet being concerned to specify precisely how. But notice how we have gone beyond the seven Baals of the pantheon lists (set 2). We now have Baal and his seven (yea, eight!) assistants. So, even forgetting the last colon as rhetorical, there are eight deities (Baal + seven), or with the eight, an Ennead. We might however expect there to be an even number of Baals, perhaps representing the winds of the cardinal points, and if eight, the intermediate points as well, perhaps with Baal himself as overlord. That there was a cosmological awareness of such an arrangement is clearly indicated in the ancient Babylonian world map, which shows that there were eight mountain-regions beyond the ocean, as confirmed by the accompanying text, and not seven as supposed in earlier discussions and representations.[43]

---

42. Wyatt 1987.

43. Horowitz 1998:20–40 (especially 30); Wyatt 2001:81–82.

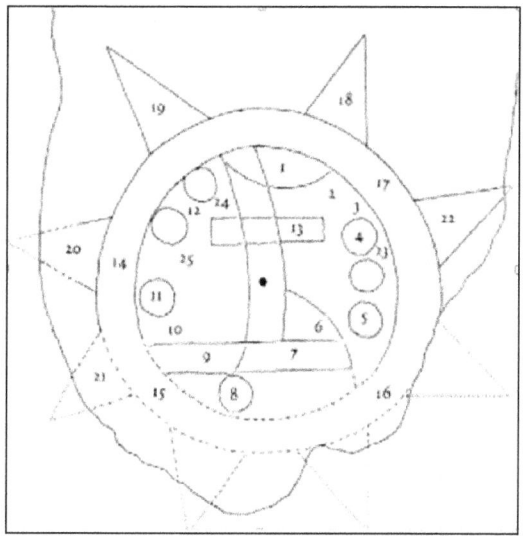

Fig. 1 The Babylonian map of the world (BM 92687)[44]

Such an implicitly spatial metaphor also evokes the image we noted above in examining the Ugaritic pantheon list, which places Saphon at the center of a spiritual system as though of a spatial system. We may reasonably ask the question, is there an intuitive process at work, which homes in on the center and on the eighth figure of a list, as a sort of revelatory progression, the final, ultimate power revealing itself only at the end of the intuitive process?

This issue of computation is comparable to another interesting biblical idiom, treating Yahweh and his accompanying spirits:

wĕnāḥāh ʿālāyw rûaḥ yhwh	And the spirit of Yahweh will rest on him,
rûaḥ ḥokmāh ûbînāh	the spirit of wisdom and understanding,
rûaḥ ʿēṣāh ûgĕbûrāh	the spirit of counsel and strength,
rûaḥ daʿat wĕyirʾat yhwh	the spirit of knowledge and fear of Yahweh.
(Isa 11:2)	

The perennial question here is, how many spirits are to be understood? Do we read the first colon as something distinct from Yahweh himself, then qualified by a set of six (or perhaps three) subordinate forms, or do we read it as seven spirits (or perhaps as four, each of the last three having two functions)? And if we take it as seven, does the first include Yahweh (distinct from "the spirit of Yahweh"), or make him an eighth? Or can this be compared to the sevenfold storm-deity galaxies of Assur and Ugarit, especially since

44. From Wyatt 2001:81.

the "spirits" (*rûaḥ*) may be the equivalent of "winds" (*rûaḥ*)? In comparison with these relatively straightforward computations, there remains a sense of uncertainty in the Isaianic passage, and we cannot seriously appeal to much later enumerations, such as the seven in Rev 1:4, 3:1, 4:5, 5:6, as "proof" of the heptadic sense of this passage, because they are interpretations of it, and indeed have their own arithmetical complications. The biblical passage also invites comparison with the seven spirits, the Amesha Spentas (*Aməša Spənta*), of Zoroastrian theology.[45] There are six of these spirits, manifestations of Ahura Mazda, making seven in all. Whether any direct relationship between the Hebrew and Avestan lists can be established (which might solve the problem with the Hebrew) depends entirely on dating, none of which can be determined with any confidence.

The pattern of obscurity we keep encountering in the passages we have examined is continued if we turn to the apparently strictly mathematical systems of Egypt.

Important higher numbers of theological interest in Egypt are eight and nine. Firstly let us consider the so-called Ogdoad from Hermopolis. We know that the number eight is significant here in view of the city's name Khemenu (Egyptian *ḥmnw*, Arabic *al-Ashmunein*, "Eight-Town," "Octoville").

Thoth (*dḥwty*) was the head of the divine system in Hermopolis. He was called the "self-caused" or "self-begotten,"[46] and had his theogonic tradition, like those of Ra, Atum, Amun, Ptah, and Khnum. His means of creating, like Ptah's, was through the spoken word, and given that Ptah was an artificer god, which made his "word" a redundancy, we may ask whether that Memphite trait was not in fact borrowed from Hermopolis, as were Nun and Naunet, incorporated from Hermopolis into the Memphite Ennead.

The Ogdoad was not a static, but a dynamic system, as can be seen in these passages, one Hermopolitan:

> I am One who became Two.
> I am Two who became Four.
> I am Four who became Eight.
> I am One who protects himself.
> —inscription on a coffin-lid of dynasty 21 (Pa-di-Amun)[47]

---

45. [*Vohu*] *Manah*, "[Good] Purpose," *Aša* [*Vahišta*], "[Best] Truth, Righteousness," *Xšaθra* [*Vairya*], "[Desirable] Dominion," [*Spənta*] *Armaiti*, "[Holy] Devotion," *Haurvatāt*, "Wholeness," *Amərətāt*, "Immortality."

46. Boylan 1922:119.

47. Maspero 1916:165, cited Piankoff 1957:12.

and one Theban:

> The Eight gods were thy first form,
> until thou didst complete them, being One.
> Mysterious is thy body among the Great Ones,
> concealing thyself as Amun at the head of the gods . . .
> —from a hymn to Amun.[48]

The first passage here counts eight gods, and the second passage nine (unless we insist that the principle at work is strictly "ogdonitarian," the eight being strictly hypostases of the one). The real problem here is whether the *original* theory in Hermopolis was based on 3 times 3, or on 2 times 4. These texts are in in favour of the latter assessment. The element of secrecy is particularly evident (if that is not an oxymoron) in the second excerpt, seeing the self-revelation alongside the self-veiling of Amun, whose name means "Hidden" (*imn*), the last deity of the Ogdoad, who became the chief god of Thebes. But secrecy permeates the entire system, as can be seen from the following considerations. Firstly, the Ogdoad contained a greater mystery: it was arguably an Ennead:

An Ogdoad at Hermopolis		An Ennead at Hermopolis	
		Thoth	
Nun	Naunet	Nun	Naunet
Huh	Hauhet	Huh	Hauhet
Kuk	Kauket	Kuk	Kauket
Amun	Amaunet	Amun	Amaunet

The eight point beyond themselves to a hidden "ninth," Thoth himself.[49] Secondly, if we consider the meaning of each constituent part, it is precisely the transcendence of human experience and the immediately real world that is represented, in personifications of the ineffable:

---

48. Gardiner 1905:30, cited Piankoff 1957:12.

49. This complex set, combined with Thoth, forms three threes, as it were the quintessence of plurality in a figure which nevertheless represents one. It corresponds in some ways to the number symbolism operating in the Christian Trinity, and to the Egyptian triads which preceded it. We should never underestimate the capacity of the ancient mind to see mystical significance in the most banal numeral quantities, and even more so when we consider the insights of ancient astronomy (to moderns largely astrology, of course) and the grand schemes that were elaborated.

Nun	Primordial Waters	Naunet
Huh	Infinitude	Hauhet
Kuk	Darkness	Kauket
Amun	Invisibility	Amaunet

Only the first pair correspond with any material reality. If the constituent, derivative parts are so mysterious, how much greater is the mystery of the overarching principle, Thoth himself, Hermes Trismegistos[50] as he became in Greek?

So a problem arises when we consider the god-group at Hermopolis. This looks like a classic Ennead, with a supreme deity and eight subordinate hypostases. But if so, why was the city called "Eight-town"? This supports the suspicion, raised by the fact that this local theology contributed something to late gnostic thought, in which an Ogdoad was the essential theological reality, that the ogdoadic principle was original, before further arithmetical games complicated it.

Among early commentators, Brugsch proposed that we have an original Ogdoad,[51] while Maspero[52] considered that they were linked with Thoth added to form an Ennead, modeled on the Ennead of Heliopolis (and thus derivative). But there is a third possibility, that the Ogdoad was originally a Pentad (including Thoth), with all five members androgynous: Maspero suggested that originally the "pantheon" of Hermopolis perhaps consisted of five deities, Thoth as supreme and the four deified cardinal points, since the chief priest of the Hermopolis temple was called "He who serves him that is Chief of Five."[53] Each cardinal deity was then doubled as male and female.

None of these issues can be resolved. The important and distinctive feature here is that we do not have a cosmogony at all in the sense of an explanation of the created world. Instead, it is a theogony: Thoth speaks, and thus produces four pairs of primordial deities. They are comparable to Nun, Shu and Tefnut, Geb and Nut, in the Heliopolitan tradition. However, as primordial deities, they are in effect the personification of cosmic principles, like many of the early principles in Hesiod's *Theogony*.

Even through the eight subordinate elements a "fourness" is evident. It is essentially a four which is doubled. The power of this structure in terms of

---

50. This title, a superlative superlativized, is susceptible only of an *enneadic* interpretation (3×3).

51. Brugsch 1887, cited (miscited!) Budge 1904:404.

52. Maspero 1889, cited Budge 1904:404.

53. Maspero 1889, cited Budge 1904:404.

theological potential is considerable. Four represents totality, on the Jungian principle of the quaternity, which we also see underlying the semantic rectangle, widely occurring in literary structures. Two represents duality, the simplest means of expressing potential, opposition, sequence, complementarity. Four doubles it, intensifying its power.

If we can draw any conclusion from this evidence, it is perhaps that a local tradition based on the number eight, if not on an older five, has subsequently been assimilated to the more widely prevalent nine-based system. It is worth noting, in support of this, that many Enneads, so-called, were actually of varying numbers of members. That is, the "Nine" (*psdt* [Gardiner *EG* 486, N9]) is imposed, as the ideal pattern, on systems to which it is manifestly secondary, rather as we saw above with the use of the numbers seven and seventy. In addition, we should note that whatever the final figure, the pairing is clearly paramount in the Hermopolitan system.

This is also the case in the Heliopolitan system. What seems to be afoot is a series of original binary pairings, evidently using sexual symbolism, since each is male and female. In any system, these are declared to be manifestations of a transcendent, unmanifest god. While we thus have One who may be analyzed as eight (much as the one god of Christianity is analyzed as three), the symbolism of three was early applied, thus making each system one + eight = nine.

This brings us to the other basic pattern, based on a symbolic number, in Egyptian thought, the widespread arrangement of deities in Enneads. I shall deal briefly with this immensely complex subject.

The Ennead of Heliopolis, the first to feature prominently in the religious history of Egypt, appeared in two forms, one superseding the other, probably in New Kingdom times. Their memberships were as follows:

Atum, Shu, Tefnut, Geb, Nut, Osiris, Isis, Seth, Nephthys

later:

Atum, Shu, Tefnut, Geb, Nut, Osiris, Isis, Horus, Nephthys

That the early version is formally related to the Hermopolitan system is clear if we arrange it in gender terms:

The early Ennead at Heliopolis	
Atum	
Shu	Tefnut
Geb	Nut

Osiris	Isis
Seth	Nephthys

Atum in this system was androgynous; all his divine offspring were paired off according to sex. Seth was later replaced by Horus. The same questions arise concerning the origin of the system, such as whether we have an original pentad, or whether the Ennead is unitary or pluralistic. As before, we cannot answer these questions, but may be confident that the potential symbolism of every option was entertained by the theologians.

An Ennead also featured in Memphis. Its most complete exposition is offered rather incompletely in the Shabaka Stone inscription, though we cannot be entirely certain of its constituent members, because it is not explicitly spelled out.[54] But all those featuring in the Heliopolitan Ennead appear, and it appears that Ptah has usurped it, carrying the generative process back a stage, and reversing the apparent system by making Atum a derivative power, stating that Ptah-Nun begot, and Ptah-Naunet bore him. Note that these two parents are Hermopolitan, though no other Hermopolitan deities feature, apart from Thoth who is mentioned independently in the text. If we wish to reconstruct the Memphite Ennead, it might possibly appear something like this:

The putative Ennead at Memphis	
Ptah	
Ptah-Nun	Ptah-Naunet
Atum	
Shu	Tefnut
Geb	Nut (?)
Osiris	Isis
Seth/Horus	Nephthys

But the result is an Ennead of twelve deities, or even thirteen if Thoth be included.[55] Seth appears in the narrative of his conflict with Horus, who

---

54. The poor condition of the inscription is usually attributed to the stela having subsequently been used as a millstone, with a central hole and radiating depressions. Thus the explanatory note by the exhibition the British Museum. A. Hawary has recently argued (2007, 2015) that the stone's condition belies this interpretation, and it is rather to be seen as having been adapted (or intended?) for use as a support for a column in a later building construction. For translations of the text, see Wilson 1969; Allen 1997; van den Dungen n.d.I. Hawary 2015 was not available to me.

55. Perhaps significantly, Amun is conspicuous by his absence from the Memphite system, though he may have appeared in missing text. Various other towns are

emerges triumphant, and eventually rules all Egypt. This reads like an apologia for Shabaka's accession to the throne. The overall theological and political function of the inscription, apart from legitimizing the rule of a Nubian Pharaoh in the preamble, is to claim Memphite hegemony over the Ennead of Heliopolis to the north and the Ogdoad (or Ennead) of Hermopolis to the south, as the city unites the Two Lands. And as with Hermopolis, the Ennead of Memphis lists manifestations of the ultimate deity, who remains hidden behind their number. Behind all Enneads, Ogdoads, and Pentads a unitary deity is veiled.

Enneads are of course plurals, triads squared, which brings us to this latter pattern. Triads are another common idiom for some kind of theological whole, the Christian form being at the tail-end of a long genealogy.[56] There are many examples from Egypt.

An example of a triad from Ugarit is the group of weather-goddesses, *ṭly, pdry*, and *arṣy*, two of whom appear in the "canonical" list above. They are listed at *KTU* 1.3 i 22-25 (adding <Arṣiyu> ?), iii 6-8, iv 50-52, v 41-43, 1.4 i 15-18, iv 55-57, (Arṣiyu to be added < . . . >), and vi 10 (adding <Arṣiyu>). In some instances they are identified as Baal's "perfect brides" (*klt knyt*): 1.3 i 26-27, 1.4 i 15, and in some they are said, unlike Baal, to have homes (sc. temples): 1.3 iv 50-52, v 41-43, 1.4 i 15-18, and iv 55-57. A representative instance, 1.3 iii 6-8, speaks of:

6 *yd pdry bt ar*	the desire of Pidrayu, daughter of Mist,
7 *ahbt ṭly bt rb*	the affection of Ṭaliyu, daughter of Gentle Rain,
dd arṣy 8 *bt yᶜbdr*	the love of Arṣiyu, daughter of Inundation.

The best account of this trio, who also appear in Greek tradition as Phaedra (Φαίδρα), Thalia (Θάλεια), and Erse (Ἔρση), is to see them as transparent personifications (sc. deifications) of the three sources of water, rain, dew and springs,[57] which appear in Danilu's curse of the land in *KTU* 1.19 i

---

mentioned in conjunction with Enneads ("the Ennead of Thebes" etc.) but their memberships are not listed. Perhaps like that of Memphis they were adaptations of those of Heliopolis and Hermopolis. "Greater" (PT 1655 etc.) and "Lesser" (PT 178) Enneads are also mentioned, and could apparently vary in number, as that of Memphis appears to have done, since the Abydos stela of Tuthmosis I lists seven members of "the great Ennead of gods dwelling in Abydos," namely: (1) Osiris Foremost of the Westerners, Lord of Abydos; (2) Khnum lord of Hirur, dwelling in Abydos; (3) Khnum lord of the cataract, dwelling in Abydos; (4) Horus Presider over Letopolis; (5) Harendotes (ḥr-nd-it.f: Horus protector-of-his-father); (6) Wepwawet of the south, and (7) Wepwawet of the north (Breasted 1906 [repr. 1988]: 2:39, §95). If the "Foremost of the Westerners" (ḫnty-imntyw) was still an independent deity (Andjeti?), the number would total eight.

56. Griffiths 1996.

57. *ar* = "mist": rather than "light," in keeping with the aqueous connections of

44–46, and its echo in 2 Samuel 1:21.[58] But though they form a natural triad, they really belong with Baal as hypostases, or manifestations of him, forming a tetrad. This is expressed in terms of their familial relationship to him: they are both his "daughters" and his "perfect brides" (*KTU* 1.3 i 23 [*bnt*], 1.3 i 26, 1.4 iv 54 etc. [*klt*]: there is no need to see a tension here), which makes them dependent on him, and inseparable from him.

There are many Egyptian triads. These are some representative examples. Each of the great theological traditions had a triad representing a divine family, parents and child; thus Abydos had Osiris, Isis, Horus (Harsiese: *ḥr-s3-3st*—Horus son of Isis, or Harpocrates: *ḥr-p3-ḫrd*—Horus the child); Heliopolis had Ra, Hathor, Horus (Horus the Elder or Great: *ḥr-wr*); Memphis had Ptah, Sekhmet, Nefertem; and Thebes had Amun, Mut, Khonsu. The primary function of these structures appears to have

---

Baal's other daughters. See DULAT 91. Or even "rain": the goddesses would then perfectly represent the three spheres of fertilizing water (rain, dew and springs) cursed in a different order by Danel in Text 1.19 I 44–45 (the passage can be read as a curse formulation—thus Wyatt 2002:296, text on the left here—or as a narrative account of the results of the curse, text on the right):

For seven years Baal shall fail,	But for seven years Baal failed,
for eight, the Charioteer of the clouds!	for eight, the Charioteer of the clouds!
(Let there be) no dew,	(There was) no dew,
no rain,	no rain,
no welling up of the deeps,	no welling up of the deeps,
no goodness of Baal's voice!	no goodness of Baal's voice!

These goddesses, who appear to be wives of Baal, are the antecedents of the Greek Graces. On the names, the forms may be compared as follows: Pidrayu: Phaedra or Pandrosos ("All-Dewy"); Taliyu: Thalia; Arṣiyu: Erse. See Astour 1969. Their meanings on this explanation are respectively "Fatty," "Dewy," and "Earthy." The last may however mean "Dewy:" Greek ἔρση, "dew"). "Inundation": so Wilfred Watson suggested: personal communication. This would explain it in the sense of "ground-water." The Wikipedia entry is interesting:

The name "Pandrosos" carries the meaning of "all dew" or "all bedewed" in the Greek language (drosos, dew). For this reason, Pandrosos is at times called the "Dew Goddess" and the three Kekropidai together are sometimes referred to as the "Dew Sisters."

Interestingly, the name "Herse" also holds connotations of dew in the Greek. This has led to speculation among scholars that originally there were only two Kekropidai and that Herse was a later addition to the myth, functioning essentially as a double of Pandrosos. The purpose of the creation of the character of Herse would have been to bring the number of Kekropidai up to three so as to conform to the common trope of three sisters in Greek mythology (in keeping with the *Three Fates*, the *Three Charites*, etc.) ("Pandrosus," https://en.wikipedia.org/wiki/Pandrosus).

This Wiki article would perhaps benefit from a link to the Ugaritic material.

58. *bl ṭl bl rbb bl šrʿ thmtm*: "no dew, no rain, no welling up of the deeps . . ." See Ginsberg 1938; discussed Wyatt 2001:292 (§11[29]), 2002:296 n. 203.

been as a statement of the king's divinity, because he was identified in his titulary or the rituals of his birth as the child of divine parents, implicitly identified with the son in these family groups.[59]

H. te Velde made some useful observations on Egyptian triads. He noted, for example, that

> [t]he triadic structure . . . was used in Egypt to answer the problem of divine plurality and unity. The triad restricts plurality and differentiates unity, as every plural number does. In Egypt the triad was an extremely suitable structure for connecting plurality and unity, because the number three was not only a numeral, but also signified the indefinite plural. This is apparent, for instance, in hieroglyphic writing: to express the plural, an ideogram may be repeated three times or three strokes placed after the signs indicating a noun.
>
> Thus the triad was a structure capable of transforming polytheism into tritheism or differentiated monotheism.[60]

While addressed to triadic structures, his observations may, *mutatis mutandis*, be applied to all the different numbers of deities we have encountered, in the sets which I have examined. None of them is simply a list of a pluralistic divine world. Each may be described as a numerological expression of a systematic theology in the different cultural contexts examined here.

The family triads noted above were merely one subset of all kinds of triads in Egypt. Morenz wrote of triads in the context of a discussion of "unity in plurality," citing a number of examples where three distinct deities functioned in a given context as a unity, even using singular forms of reference.[61] He called these "trinities."[62] Some he called "modalistic," such as Khepri—Ra—Atum of Heliopolis, a group in which the unifying figure speaks thus: "I am Khepri in the morning, R[a] at noon, Atum in the

---

59. Regarding the implicit divinity of the king, see Bell 1985 for the rationale of the temple of Luxor, dedicated to the cult of the royal ka (*k3*), and Leprohon 2013 for a catalogue of royal titularies.

60. Te Velde 1971:80. Considering the problems to be encountered in different forms of triad, he went on (p. 81) to observe that when a family was placed in the triadic structure, the concept of a differentiated monad could not subsist, and it remained a pluralistic totality and here I think he rather overstated his case, operating in a modern exclusivist mindset (rejecting ambiguity). Other useful discussions of Egyptian triads are Morenz 1973:142–46, 255–57; Griffiths 1996:11–113, 248–79; Wilkinson 2003:75–76 (all enumerations covered in 74–79; bibliography 246); Sales 2012.

61. Morenz 1973:145, 255.

62. Morenz 1973:142–43.

evening." A feature of such Egyptian triads or trinities which he seems not to have noticed is that they arguably point beyond themselves to a Hidden Fourth (the three and the "super-deity" who united and transcended them, as with Khepri—Ra—Atum, just cited), thus constituting a perfect Jungian quaternity. A quaternal nature is fairly obvious, for example, in the case of the triadic Amun-Ra—Ra-Harakhte—Ptah, appearing with Rameses II at Abu Simbel, marking a striking apotheosis of the king on the southern frontier of his empire. But the most striking feature of this example is that while in a quaternity the "fourth" is generally the elusive, ineffable feature to which the first three principles point, it *appears* in this instance to be working in reverse. Can it *really* be saying that Rameses is the sum of all the gods? Some apotheosis! An alternative and perhaps more probable view would have the king among the triad of living gods (with Amun-Ra and Ra-Harakhte), while the chthonian Ptah remained unspoken in the background.[63]

As a brief appendix to the mention of Egyptian triads, let us dwell briefly on the Christian Trinity, which Gwyn Griffiths concluded was ultimately inspired by the Egyptian formulations. Alan Watts represented the relationship between the persons in the Trinity in a striking diagram, with a triangle at whose apices are three circles, with a fourth at the centre. The apical circles represent the three persons, who may be perceived in the world, the cult and by introspection. They are "cognitively accessible." They remain distinct. In addition, each of them is related to the central circle, representing the ineffable and transcendent deity, who is beyond cognition. At the centre of the Trinity lies the hidden Fourth, a perfect example of Jung's quaternity theory.[64]

---

63. See the Wikipedia entry: "It is believed that the axis of the temple was positioned by the ancient Egyptian architects in such a way that on October 22 and February 22, the rays of the sun would penetrate the sanctuary and illuminate the sculptures on the back wall, except for the statue of Ptah, the god connected with the Underworld, who always remained in the dark "("Abu Simbel temples," https://en.wikipedia.org/wiki/Abu_Simbel_temples).

64. See Jung 1969:164–87. Jung's theory has had a bad press in recent discussion: see for example Noll 1994, in general, and Brabazon 2002 in particular, but it is not without a heuristic value. Of interest in this context is the following observation from the Jungian website:

One Trinity that was completed in the last century, with the bodily assumption of the Virgin Mary into heaven (defined as dogma in 1950 by Pope Pius XII), transformed the Christian Trinity into a Quaternity, and one that Jung believes was achieved by the overwhelming insistence of the Catholic masses (CW 9ii, 142) . . . the quaternity is the sine qua non of divine birth and consequently of the inner life of the trinity. Thus circle and quaternity on one side and the threefold rhythm on the other interpenetrate so that each is contained in the other . . . (CW 11 125). Jung believes that this was the most significant religious event since the reformation (quoted in EJ 321) ("On the Nature of Four—Jung's Quarternity, Mandalas, the Stone and the Self," http://www.

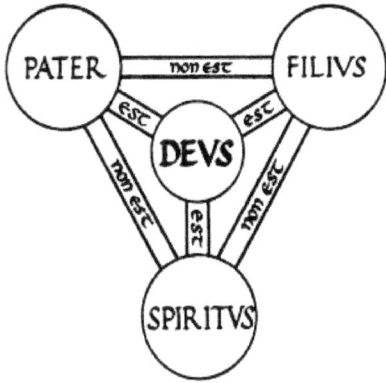

Fig. 2 The Structure of the Trinity[65]

What is the common factor in all the number-crunching we have surveyed so far? It is surely the drive for some kind of certainty in a world of uncertainty, an uncertainty compounded by the non-physicality and autonomy of the gods. Not only is the thought of inadvertently forgetting to welcome one of the gods to the sacrifice unbearable, but so is the fear that if one of their number withholds his or her name, then all the control which cultic precision enables a community to bring to bear on its security and well-being can be compromised or negated. This problem found perfect expression in Egypt in the myth of the secret name of Ra, when Isis tricked the sun god into revealing it to her so that she could heal him from the snakebite she had herself inflicted upon him.[66]

The other side of this coin, however, is that though priesthoods sought certainty, they nevertheless wished it to be veiled from the common people. Their inherently *secret* knowledge gave them rank and privilege.

We have lived for a long time in a cultural context where monotheism is the norm, and entirely part of our mental furniture, whether or not we actually believe in a deity. But it is worth asking what was the motivation for moving away from the polytheistic context in which it had its origins. For it is generally recognized that the ancient Israelite-Judahite god Yahweh had

---

redicecreations.com/article.php?id=1722).

This form of the quaternity should also be seen as a reversal, since the Virgin, the fourth, is the most accessible person in the group.

65. With acknowledgment to Watts 1953.

66. See Ritner 1997. He observed (p. 33) that "few texts illustrate so clearly the ritual significance of the personal name. Felt to be an intrinsic element and source of power, the name did not simply identify but defined an individual." This would apply equally to deities.

his origin in such a milieu. I do not think it was simply a retreat into a comfort-zone, away from all those uncertainties. For monotheism, wherever it occurred, always quickly developed its own mystique of hidden names and titles, and inaccessibility.

A final theme in our survey, which offers a pathway into monotheism, is the divine council, a trope common to most cultures in the ancient Near East, including ancient Israel and Judah.[67] Just as the numerical systems above may point beyond their plurality to a unitary principle, so the notion of a divine council is to be seen as representing a monarchical conception of the pantheon, on the cusp of monotheism.

The divine council rather nicely embodies the interesting insight of A. R. Johnson, now perhaps rather out of fashion, concerning the idea of corporate personality. This principle, which he applied initially to the biblical conception of human psychology,[68] informed Johnson's analysis of Yahweh and his relation to his subordinate spirits. He drew attention to Isa 31:3, which contrasts men (and horses, flesh) with God (spirit: *ruaḥ*). In considering the term *ruaḥ* in relation to Yahweh, that is, as a theological term, he cited H. Wheeler Robinson's assessment of 1 Kgs 22:19ff., which treats the lying spirit put in Micaiah's mouth by Yahweh, as the only instance of the *ruaḥ* of Yahweh being "*clearly* personalized."[69] He went on:

> In the light of the Israelite conception of man ... it would seem that this *ruaḥ*, as a member of Yahweh's heavenly Court [or "Household"!], should be thought of as an individualization within the corporate *ruaḥ* or "Spirit" of Yahweh's extended Personality; in other words, that we must be prepared to recognize for the Godhead just such fluidity of reference from the One to the Many or from the Many to the One as we have already noticed in the case of man.[70]

---

67. Israel: 1 Kgs 22:19–23; Judah: Isaiah 6. See Cross 1953, and for a recent treatment, see White 2014. In my view her criteria for recognizing the presence of the divine council were excessively restrictive.

68. Johnson 1961:1–12.

69. Wheeler Robinson 1928:9, in contrast to Volz 1910:2ff., both cited Johnson 1961:16 n. 1.

70. Johnson 1961:16. Wheeler Robinson's idea of corporate personality may seem somewhat dated nowadays, but still has some validity. See my observation with regard to Deut 32:8–9: "The language of divine sonship belongs in the context of royal ideology, and here the member of the community of Israel is an extension of the king's persona, which represents the nation, on a *pars pro toto* basis. The same royal metaphor for the nation is found in Hosea 11:1" (Wyatt 2007a:550 = 2010: 71).

This assessment shows rather well the fluidity between monotheism and polytheism, which is evident throughout much of the material we have been examining.

Oddly, the only area in which it probably does not generally hold true is ancient Israel-Judah, and here in one restricted context, the deuteronomic one, which however had an inordinate influence on the development of biblical theology. Two key passages express the new dimension of "palaeo-Protestantism." The first is Deut 6:4–14, which appears to demand a purely unitary view of divinity, though it may be more nuanced to say that this is an insistence upon monolatry, while on the cusp of monotheism:

> Listen, Israel! Yahweh is your god, Yahweh alone! (or: Listen, Israel! Yahweh your god, Yahweh is one!) . . . Do not follow other gods, from among the peoples around you.

This is perhaps to be seen against a background of local manifestations of Yahweh, which is suggested by the inscriptions from Kuntillet ʿAjrud and Khirbet el-Qom. These mention Yahweh of Shomron, presumably Samaria, and Yahweh Teman, either the site in Western Arabia, or at least a southern location. In that the divine name is here qualified with a specific location, it may be seen as threatened by a fragmentation, or perhaps what would be worse, an unconscious or uncritical identification of Yahweh with various local deities. The patriarchal narratives, locating theophanies of Yahweh at various shrines, Beer Sheba, Bethel, Shechem, open the door to such possibilities, as though these were different local *numina*.

The second passage, from Deut 30:11–14, deals with the matter of divine immediacy:

> Surely this instruction which I am giving you today is not too difficult for you or too far beyond you. It is not in the heavens, so that you have to say "who will go up for us to the heavens and get hold of it and allow us to hear it, so that we may observe it?" Nor is it over the sea, so that you have to say, "who will go across the sea for us and get hold of it and allow us to hear it, so that we may observe it?" On the contrary, the matter is very close to you, in your mouth and in your heart, to observe.

Deuteronomy, perhaps one of the earliest sectarian documents in history, dating from the cataclysmic events of the destruction of the Judahite state and its aftermath, firmly rejects theological fluidity and plurality in favour of singularity, as well as rejecting the idea of the innate *hiddenness* of religious truth, and declares it to be accessible, implicitly without mediating monarchical, priestly or hierarchical structures. With only one god, transparency is henceforth the order of the day! This is of course only one strand in the complex pentateuchal treatment of the national myth, being in strong tension with the quasi-divine presentation in the Exodus strand of Moses the king, who meets a god in the desert, ascends to the mountaintop, sees him face to face, and brings the Torah down from Heaven, like a new Hammurabi—or as A. Lenzi has it, an *apkallu*—maintaining all the while a measure of mystery.[71] Deuteronomy is also in tension with the divine council in Deutero-Isaiah, which also preserves the ancient mystery. It will also fall to the mystics and kabbalists of later times to reintroduce and reinforce the dimension of mystery which was thrown out by Deuteronomy with the polytheistic bathwater, eventually repluralizing God in the multitude of the angelic hosts bustling about his person.[72]

One final line of enquiry opens up from this discussion, concerning the narrative of the burning bush in Exodus 3. I proposed some years ago that the core material in the chapter (conventionally attributed to E) should be read in this order, verses 1, 4b, 6, 9, 10–12a, 20, 12b, thus:

> 1 wĕmōšeh hāyāh rōʿeh ʾet-ṣōʾn yitrô ḥōtĕnô kōhēn midyān wayyinhag ʾet-haṣṣōʾn ʾaḥar hammidbār wayyābōʾ ʾel-har ʾēl ... 4b wayyiqrāʾ ʾēlāyw ʾēl mittôk hāhār 6 wayyōmer ʾānōkî ʾēl ʾābîkā ... wayyastēr mōšeh pānāyw kî yārēʾ mēhabbîṭ ʾel 9 wĕʿattāh hinnēh ṣaʿăqat bĕnê yisrāʾēl bāʾāh ʾēlāy wĕgam-rāʾîtî ʾet-hallaḥaṣ ʾăšer miṣrayim lōḥĕṣîmʾōtām 10 wĕʿattāh lĕkāh wĕʾešlāḥăkā ʾel-parʿōh wĕhôṣēʾ ʾet-ʿammî bĕnê yisrāʾēl mimmiṣrāyim 11 wayyōmer mōšeh ʾel ʾēl mî ʾānōkî kî ʾēlēk ʾel-parʿōh wĕkî ʾōṣîʾ ʾet-bĕnê yisrāʾēl mimmiṣrāyim 12a wayyōmer kî-ʾehyeh ʿimmāk wĕzeh-lĕkā hāʾōt kî ʾānōkî šĕlaḥtîkā 20 wĕšālaḥtîkā ʾet-yādî wĕhikkētî ʾet-miṣrayim bĕkōl niplĕʾōtay ʾăšer ʾeʿĕśeh bĕqirbô wĕʾaḥărê-kēn yĕšallēḥ ʾetkem

---

71. See Lenzi 2007:362–73: he sees the presentation of Moses in Deut 34:10–12 as an "Israelite *apkallu*." The *apkallû* were seven in number (Reiner 1961), a quasi-divine heptad.

72. An entirely new approach to the whole matter of the existence of gods takes us into the realm of neuropsychology, which ought to be taken seriously if we really want to know why gods are imagined in the first place, and why various patterns of thinking concerning their nature, number and constitution arise. Julian Jaynes offered an interesting assessment of ancient gods when he observed that "the gods were organizations of the central nervous system" (Jaynes 1982:74). If a principle of revelation is rejected, on the grounds that it is unverifiable and unfalsifiable, then we are thrown back inevitably on the workings of the human mind (see citations at the head of this paper). Here the work of such scholars as Blank and his collaborators (Blank et al. 2014) becomes significant.

Should we read *bĕnê *šōr ʾēl* in these verses, and also in Exod 3:13 below, in accordance with the views of Tur-Sinai and Joosten (nn. 34, 38 above)?

12b *běhôṣî'ăkā 'et-hāʿām mimiṣrayim taʿabdûn 'et-'ēl ʿal hāhār hazzeh.*

1 Moses was tending the flock of Jethro, his father-in-law, priest of Midian. He led his flock to the far side of the wilderness and came to . . . the mountain of El. 4b And El called to him from the midst of the mountain. 6 "I am El your father," he said . . . At this Moses hid his face, afraid to look at El . . . [El said,] 9 "So now the cry of the sons of Israel has come to me, and I have also seen the way in which the Egyptians oppress them. 10 So come, I send you to Pharaoh to bring my people, the sons of Israel . . . out of Egypt." 11 Moses said to El, "Who am I, to go to Pharaoh and bring the sons of Israel out of Egypt?" 12a Then he said "I shall be with you, and this is the sign by which you shall know that it is I who have sent you: 20 I shall stretch out my hand and strike Egypt with all the wonders I am going to perform there. After this he will let you go. 12b After you have led the people out of Egypt you are to offer worship to El on this mountain."[73]

According to this reading, the narrative originally credited the exodus event to El, who now appears as the neutral *'ĕlōhîm* of MT. Crucially, vv. 13–15, conventionally seen as dealing with the "revelation" of the divine name[74] Yahweh, has no place in this original account, even though also commonly allocated to E. And this passage in turn may rightly be viewed with some suspicion. Here is the full text of Exod 3:13–15, Moses' question and the divine response:

13 *wayyōmer mōšeh 'el-hā'ĕlōhîm hinneh 'ānōkî bā' 'el-bĕnê yiśrā'ēl wĕ'āmartî lāhem 'ĕlōhê 'ăbôtêkem šĕlāḥanî 'ălêkem wĕ'āmĕrû-lî mah-šĕmô māh 'ōmar 'ălêhem:*

14 *wayyōmer 'ĕlōhîm 'el-mōšeh 'ehyeh 'ăšer 'ehyeh wayyōmer kōh tō'mar libĕnê yiśrā'ēl 'ehyeh šĕlāḥanî 'ălêkem:*

15 *wayyōmer ʿōd 'ĕlōhîm 'el-mōšeh kōh tō'mar 'el-bĕnê yiśrā'ēl yhwh 'ĕlōhê 'ăbôtêkem 'ĕlōhê 'abrāhām 'ĕlōhê yiṣḥāq wē'lōhê yaʿăqōb šĕlāḥanî 'ălêkem zeh šĕmî lĕʿōlām wĕzeh zikrî lĕdōr dōr:*

13 Then Moses said to God, "So I am to go to the Israelites and say to them, 'the god of your fathers has sent me to you.' They will say to me, 'What is his name?' What shall I say to them?"

---

73. For "sons of Israel" and "Israelites" in this excerpt and the next, perhaps read "sons of Bull El," as proposed above.

74. In general, see Huffmon 1999, with bibliography.

14 Then God said to Moses, "I am who I am." Then he said, "This is what you are to say to the Israelites, 'I am has sent me to you.'"

15 Then God also said to Moses, "This is what you are to say to the Israelites, 'Yahweh, the god of your fathers, the god of Abraham, the god of Isaac and the god of Jacob has sent me to you. This shall be my name forever, and this will be my memorial down the generations.'"

Not only is this passage in contradiction with the verses previously isolated, but it has its own inner contradictions, appears to be overloaded, and is evidently an amalgamation of a number of traditional strands. Brevard Childs observed that "the question remains a classic crux ... which has called forth dozens of solutions in countless articles ..."[75] Verse 14 offers two responses to Moses' question, first "I am who I am" and second "I am has sent me to you," while v. 15 gives a further three, first "Yahweh," second "the god of your fathers," and third "the god of Abraham, the god of Isaac and the god of Jacob." We are almost tempted to see a triad in this fifth answer!

This is not the place to deal at length with all the problems involved here, but we may draw our general discussion to a conclusion by focusing on v. 14a, 'ehyeh 'ăšer 'ehyeh. Is this a revelation, a self-disclosure by the deity to Moses? That is of course how it has been interpreted down the centuries, because such a view has always controlled both Jewish and Christian readings of the Hebrew Bible overall: we have here a religion of "historical revelation."

But there is another way to read the divine response 'ehyeh 'ăšer 'ehyeh, and that is as the deity's refusal to be drawn by such a loaded question.[76] By giving his name, Yahweh will put himself into the power of Moses. So he responds obliquely, hints at the name, teases Moses with a little ontological wordplay,[77] associating the tetragrammaton with the verb "to be," a juxtaposition which has been confusing theologians and misleading the philological community ever since. As the text has grown organically, possibly in an original writer's mind, but more probably with interpretative glosses progressively incorporated into it, the refusal to answer in 14a becomes in 14b a no-name for the deity; in 15a it is explained by the "real" name (Yahweh)

---

75. Childs 1974: 62. For the range of opinions, see pp. 60–70.

76. Contrast Exod 33:19, where Yahweh does reveal his name and his face to Moses. Cf. Rev 19:12.

77. Compare the formally "ontological" interpretation of the LXX: ἐγώ εἰμι Ο Ὤν. Further examples of a divine rejection of self-disclosure are Gen 32:29–30, Jacob at the Jabbok, and Judg 13:17–19, Manoah and the angel.

which has inspired the word-game, but which may not be pronounced; in 15b the "traditional" appellation "the god of your fathers" supplements it (and behind this there lurks a complex prehistory: it began life as an allusion to El![78]), and finally in 15c the tripartite patriarchal "theological genealogy" is used, summing up the national epic context of the climactic moment. The sequence is thus:

14a I am who I am
14b I am (has sent me to you)
15a YHWH
15b the god of your fathers (< El your father)
15c the god of Abraham, the god of Isaac and the god of Jacob

What do we have? A pentadic formulation in quasi-chiastic form, beginning with evasion, and then spelling it out progressively, culminating in a link with the ancient El cult, now presented, in 15b, as ancestral, and in 15c as a triadic or even trinitarian formula identifying the key ancestors.[79] Thus all the strands in the national theological tradition are woven together, with the unpronounceable "real name" hidden at its heart. The final formulation in 15d, "This shall be my name forever . . . ," appears to embrace the entire formula, not simply the tetragrammaton, thus preserving its peculiar mystery. My question concerning a triad in v. 15c is half serious. If the suggestion is plausible, does the entire divine response perhaps point to a heptad of gods? A very effective veil!

Such an idea is not entirely nonsensical. The revelation is taking place in the wilderness, and the deity is speaking from the burning bush. I suggested many years ago that what Moses saw was a vision of the temple menorah, which "burned but was not consumed."[80] The image is well-captured in Ernst Fuchs' 1957 painting, "Moses and the Burning Bush."

What is the most significant feature in all these arithmetical gymnastics? It is surely that correspondences were "felt" or intuited between the various aspects of the reality of human experience: time, with its days, weeks, months and lunar and solar years; space, with its planetary and stellar movements across the heavens; the rhythms of human psychology and physiology; in short, profound and extensive links between the divine,

---

78. Wyatt 1978.

79. Two formulations occur: "The God of Abraham, Isaac, and Jacob" (Exod 3:16; Acts 3:13) and "The God of Abraham, the god of Isaac, and the god of Jacob" (Exod 3:6; 3:15; note Gen 28:13; 31:42). It is noteworthy that Exod 3:15 uses the fuller, perhaps more "liturgical" version, but v. 16 the shorter one.

80. Wyatt 1986.

human and natural worlds, which determined every aspect of life and death. The culmination of this in an all-embracing "one," as with nascent monotheism, in no way interrupted or undermined this holistic world-view, but rather reinforced the holistic intuition, and as we see with the trope of the divine council and the growth of the angelic hosts, was still able to embrace and fulfil all the figures of plurality. And given that the arithmetical skills of the ancients were considerable, it is hard to believe that the fuzziness about actual numbers of deities in the various groups we have noted was not a deliberate ploy, in order to veil the true nature of divine identity from profane eyes. It cannot simply be dismissed as mathematical incompetence.

Some interesting supporting observations by other commentators may serve as a useful closure to my analysis. W. Brueggeman wrote: "Yahweh is hidden, free, and elusive, and refuses to be caught in any verbal formulation." (We might add: "or any mathematical formulation.") R. E. Friedman commented that "I am not sure that 'immanence and transcendence' are the right categories. It does not appear to me to be so much a matter of God's 'transcending' history as simply disappearing, becoming more and more hidden." And D. H. Aaron, citing these two, remarked that "One might even frame the history of a religion as a history of a belief system's management of ambiguity."[81] So much for certainty! It remains refreshingly elusive.

A NOTE ON THE STABILITY OF NUMBERS

Are odd numbers of deities in a pantheon inherently unstable? This suggests that pantheons of 3, 5, 7, 9, or any odd number (such as 33), are essentially dynamic; those with even numbers, 2, 4, 8, 10, 12, etc. will be stable and static.[82] Such a classification would make sense of some of our computations above.

The Ogdoad, for example, is essentially a formulation of how the world is, its basic, permanent properties. It is significant that all its members (apart from Amun who beyond Hermopolis goes his own way, and in other contexts as at Thebes becomes dynamic) are primordial, "intransitive" deities, and maintain an equilibrium. If Thoth is the sum of the eight parts, he participates

---

81. Brueggeman 1997:231; Friedman 1995:79; both cited Aaron 2001 (2002):10, 11 n. 16. Aaron passage, 16. For the kabbalistic seventy-two names of the one God ("Shemhamphorasch"), see "Shem HaMephorash," http://en.wikipedia.org/wiki/Shemhamphorasch and Cornwell 1995.

82. Marduk is assigned fifty names (*pul-ḫa-a-tu*: "Dreads", Lambert 2013, 57) in Enuma Eliš vi 121—vii 136. Is the list of names at the resolution of the conflict, being an even number, perhaps a sign of the stability of the world Marduk has now established? On the names and their general significance, see Lambert 2013:147–68; Litke 1998; Siri 2006.

in equilibrium. If he is supernumerary, a ninth member, he transforms the stable and static Ogdoad into an unstable and dynamic Ennead. With the uncertainties about actual numbers in the various groups above in mind, we can see how this principle appears to be applicable across the board.

Heptads may appear to pose a problem in such a scheme, and indeed show a tendency to move to ogdoads, as we have seen. But seven itself is almost a stable number in the temporal realm, since it brings closure to a self-contained week. However, in closing one week, it is also the springboard to the next, and its apparent resolution in an eighth day is in reality a new "one," the initiation of the new week. This ability of seven to fulfil two roles, at once dynamic and static, may account in part for the intuition that it is a perfect number.

One deity, that is one conceived monotheistically or at least practically so, as monolatrously, may be considered to be immune to these tensions. Yet single deities are perhaps the most dynamic of all by nature—if only on the ground that they concentrate in themselves the functions of an entire plural pantheon[83]—and in any case, their unicity is itself often unstable, as their hypostases or their subordinate associates, such as angels, multiply in direct proportion to their grandeur. This observation may have some explanatory value in an understanding why such systems tend to insistence on a form of orthodoxy (as Deut 6:4–14 cited above), and intolerance of dissent from a received "truth."

REFERENCES

Aaron, D. H. 2001 *Biblical Ambiguities. Metaphor, Semantics, and Divine Imagery*. Leiden: Brill, 2002 printing.

Albertz, R. 1994. *A History of Israelite Religion in the Old Testament Period*. 2 vols. Trans. J. Bowden. London: SCM.

Archi, A. 1973. "How a Pantheon Forms: The Cases of Hattian-Hittite Anatolia and Ebla of the 3rd Millennium." In *Religions-geschichtliche Beziehungen zwischen Kleinasien, Norsyrien und dem Alten Testament*, ed. B. Janowski et al., 1–18. OBO 129. Göttingen: Vandenhoeck & Ruprecht.

———. 2010. "The Heptad in Anatolia." In *Studia Anatolica in memoriam Erich Neu dicata, Hethitica XVI*, ed. R. Lebrun and J. de Vos, 21–34. Bibliothèque des Cahiers de l'Institut de Linguistique de Louvain 126. Leuven: Peeters.

---

83. A nice example of this is El (identified of course with Yahweh). Ugaritian El may be identified with Yariḫu, according to *KTU* 1.12.15–17, where the two handmaids are respectively ʾ*amt yrḫ* and ʾ*amt* ʾ *aṯrt*: we expect them to be the surrogate mothers of the couple El and Athirat, while his congener South Arabian El (with his own congeners ʿAmm and Wadd: see Jamme 1947; and Ryckmans 1947) is clearly a moon-god, and thus the thirty-day connection we have noted above (nn. 11, 21) implicitly contains within himself the "thirty" days of the month.

———. 2013. "The West Hurrian Pantheon and Its Background." In *Beyond Hatti: A Tribute to Gary Beckman*, ed. B. J. Collins and P. Michalowski, 1–21. Atlanta: Lockwood.

Arnaud, D. 1994. "Relecture de la liste sacrificielle RS 26.142." *SMEA* 34:107–9.

Astour, M. C. 1969. "La triade de deésses de fertilité à Ugarit et en Grèce." *Ugaritica* 6:9–23.

Bausani, A. 1978. "L'alfabeto come calendario arcaico." *OrAnt* 17:131–46.

Beckman, G. 1999. *Hittite Diplomatic Texts*. 2nd ed. SBLWAW 7. Atlanta: Society of Biblical Literature.

Bell, L. 1985. "Luxor Temple and the Cult of the Royal Ka." *JNES* 44:251–94.

Blank, O. et al. 2014. "Neurological and Robot-Controlled Induction of an Apparition." *Current Biology* 24:2681–86. doi: 10.1016/j.cub.2014.09.049.

Bodine, J. J. 2009. "The Shabaka Stone: An Introduction." *Studia Antiqua* 7:1–21.

Boylan, P. 1922. *Thoth, the Hermes of Egypt*. London: Oxford University Press.

Brabazon, M. 2002. "Carl Jung and the Trinitarian Self." *Quodlibet Journal* 4/2–3. http://www.quodlibet.net/articles/brabazon-jung.shtml.

Breasted, J. H. 1901. "The Philosophy of a Memphite Priest." *ZÄS* 39:458–79.

———. 1906–7. *Ancient Records of Egypt*. 5 vols. Chicago: Chicago University Press. Reprint, London: Histories and Mysteries of Man, 1988.

Brueggemann, W. 1997. *Theology of the Old Testament: Testimony, Dispute, Advocacy*. Minneapolis: Fortress.

Brugsch, H. K. 1887. *Religion und Mythologie der alten Aegypter: Nach den Denkmälern*. Leipzig: Hinrichs.

Budge, E. A. W. 1904. *The Gods of the Egyptians: or, Studies in Egyptian mythology*. 2 vols. Reprint, New York: Dover, 1969.

Burrow, T. 1973. "The Proto-Indoaryans." *JRAS* 2:123–40.

Childs, B. S. 1974. *The Book of Exodus: A Critical, Theological Commentary*. OTL. Philadelphia: Westminster.

Christensen, D. L. 1992. *Deuteronomy 21:10—34:12*. WBC 6b. Nashville: Nelson.

Clemens, D. M. 2001. *Sources for Ugaritic Ritual and Sacrifice*, vol. 1: *Ugaritic and Ugarit Akkadian Texts*. AOAT 284/1. Münster: Ugarit-Verlag.

Cornwell, J. A. 1995. "The Names of God." In *The Alpha and the Omega*. 3 vols. http://www.mazzaroth.com/Introduction/TheNamesOfGod.htm

Craigie, P. C. 1976. *The Book of Deuteronomy*. NICOT. London: Hodder & Stoughton.

Cross, F. M. 1953. "The Council of Yahweh in Second Isaiah." *JNES* 12:274–77.

Danielou, A. 1964. *Hindu Polytheism*. London: Routledge & Kegan Paul.

Dietrich, M., and O. Loretz. 1988. *Die Keilalphabete: Die phönizisch-kanaanäischen und altarabischen Alphabete in Ugarit*. ALASP 1. Münster: Ugarit-Verlag.

———. 1999. "The Ugaritic Script." In *Handbook of Ugaritic Studies*, edited by W. G. E. Watson and N. Wyatt, 81–90. HdO I 39. Leiden: Brill.

Driver, S. R. 1902. *Deuteronomy*. ICC. Edinburgh: T. & T. Clark.

Eaton, K. 2015. *Ancient Egyptian Temple Ritual. Performance, Pattern and Practice*. Routledge Studies in Egyptology 1. New York: Routledge.

Eissfeldt, O. 1956. "El and Yahweh." *JSS* 1:25–37.

Evans-Pritchard, E. 1987. *Theories of Primitive Religion*. Oxford: Oxford University Press.

Fisher, L. R. et al., eds. 1972–81. *Ras Shamra Parallels*. 3 vols. AnOr 49–51. Rome: Pontifical Biblical Institute.

Friedman, R. E. 1995. *The Disappearance of God: A Divine Mystery*. Boston: Little, Brown.
Gardiner, A. H. 1905. "Hymns to Amon from a Leiden Papyrus." *ZÄS* 42:12–42.
Ginsberg, H. L. 1938. "A Ugaritic Parallel to 2 Sam 1 21." *JBL* 57:209–13.
Gleizer, O. n.d. "Clock Arithmetic." http://www.math.ucla.edu/~radko/circles/lib/data/handout-394-490.pdf.
Gordon, C. H. 1965. *Ugaritic Textbook*. AnOr 38. Rome: Pontifical Biblical Institute.
———. 1970. "The Accidental Invention of the Phonemic Alphabet." *JNES* 29:193–97.
Grave, C. 1980. "The Etymology of Northwest Semitic ṣapanu." *UF* 12:221–29.
———. 1982 "Northwest Semitic ṣapanu in a Break-up of an Egyptian Stereotype Phrase in EA 147." *Or* 51:161–82.
Griffiths, J. G. 1996. *Triads and Trinity*. Cardiff: University of Wales Press.
Halberg, F. 1985. Review of Zerubbabel 1985. *Chronobiologica* 12:369–72.
Hammer, R. 1986. *Sifre. A Tannaitic Commentary on the Book of Deuteronomy*. New Haven: Yale University Press.
el Hawary, A. 2007. "New Findings about the Memphite Theology." In *Proceedings of the Ninth International Congress of Egyptologists*, ed. J. C. Guying and C. Cardin, 567–74. OLA 150. Leuven: Peeters.
———. 2015. *Wortschöpfung: die Memphitische Theologie und die Siegesstele des Pije—zwei Zeugen kultureller Repräsentation in der 25. Dynastie*. OBO 243. Göttingen: Vandenhoeck & Ruprecht.
Healey, J. F. 2007. "From ṣapānu/ṣapunu to Kasion. The Sacred History of a Mountain." In *"He Unfurrowed His Brow and Laughed": Essays in Honour of Professor Nicolas Wyatt*, ed. W. G. E. Watson, 141–51. AOAT 299. Münster: Ugarit-Verlag.
Heiser, M. 2001. "Deuteronomy 32:8 and the Sons of God." *BSac* 158:52–74.
Hoffner, H. 1990. *Hittite Myths*. 2nd ed. SBLWAW 2. Atlanta: Society of Biblical Literature. 1998.
Horowitz, W. 1998. *Babylonian Cosmic Geography*. MC 8. Winona Lake, IN: Eisenbrauns.
Huffmon, H. B. 1999. "Name." In *Dictionary of Deities and Demons in the Bible*, edited by K. van der Toorn et al., 610–12. 2nd ed. Leiden: Brill.
Hundley, M. B. 2013. "Here a God, There a God: An Examination of the Divine in Ancient Mesopotamia." *AoF* 40:68–107.
James, J. 1993. *The Music of the Spheres: Music, Science and the Natural Order of the Universe*. New York: Grove. [1995 printing cited].
Jamme, A. 1947. "Le panthéon sud-arabe préislamique, d'après les sources épigraphiques." *Le Muséon* 60:57–147.
Jaynes, J. 1982. *The Origin of Consciousness in the Breakdown of the Bicameral Mind*. Boston: Houghton Mifflin. Repr. of 1976.
Johnson, A. R. 1961. *The One and the Many in the Israelite Conception of God*. Cardiff: University of Wales Press.
Joosten, J. 2007. "A Note on the Text of Deuteronomy xxxii 8." *VT* 57:548–55.
———. 2011. "Deutéronome 32, 8–9 et les commencements de la religion d'Israël." In *Le monothéisme biblique: Evolution contexts et perspectives*, ed. E. Bons and Th. Legrand, 91–108. Lectio Divina 244. Paris: Cerf.
Jung, C. G. 1969. *Psychology and Religion: West and East*. Collected Works 11. 2nd ed. Princeton: Princeton University Press.

Kelley, D. H. 1960. "Calendar Animals and Deities." *Southwestern Journal of Anthropology* 16:317–37.

Koch, K. 1993. "Ḫazzi-Ṣafôn-Kasion: Die Geschichte eines Berges und seiner Gottheiten." In *Religionsgeschichtliche Beziehungen zwischen Kleinasien, Norsyrien und dem Alten Testament*, ed. B. Janowski et al., 171–223. OBO 129. Göttingen: Vandenhoeck & Ruprecht.

Lambert, W. G. 1975. "The Historical Development of the Mesopotamian Pantheon: A Study in Sophisticated Polytheism." In *Unity and Diversity: Essays in the History, Literature, and Religion of the Ancient Near East*, ed. H. Goedicke and J. J. M. Roberts, 191–200. Johns Hopkins Near Eastern Studies. Baltimore: Johns Hopkins University Press.

———. 2013. *Babylonian Creation Myths*. MC 16. Winona Lake, IN: Eisenbrauns.

Lenzi, A. 2008. *Secrecy and the Gods: Secret Knowledge in Ancient Mesopotamia and Biblical Israel*. SAAS 19. Helsinki: University of Helsinki.

Leprohon, R. J. 2013. *The Great Name: Ancient Egyptian Royal Titulary*. SBLWAW 33. Atlanta: Society of Biblical Literature.

Litke, R. L. 1998. *A Reconstruction of the Assyro-Babylonian God-Lists, AN: ^{d}A-nu-um and AN: Anu šá amēli*. Texts from the Babylonian Collection 3. New Haven: Yale Babylonian Collection.

Macdonell, A. A. 1904. *The Bṛhad-devatā Attributed to Śaunaka: A Summary of the Deities and Myths of the Rig-Veda*. 2 vols. Harvard Oriental Series 6. Cambridge: Harvard University Press.

Machinist, P. 2011. "How Gods Die, Biblically and Otherwise: A Problem of Cosmic Restructuring." In *Reconsidering the Concept of Revolutionary Monotheism*, ed. B. Pongratz-Leisten, 189–240. Winona Lake, IN: Eisenbrauns.

Maspero, G. 1889. *La Mythologie Égyptienne*. Paris: Leroux.

———. 1916. *La progression numérique dans l'Ennéade héliopolitaine*. Bibliothèque Egyptologique 8. Paris: Leroux.

Mayes, A. D. H. 1979. *Deuteronomy*. NCBC. London: Marshall, Morgan & Scott.

Miller, G. A. 1956. "The Magic Number Seven, Plus or Minus Two: Some Limits on Our Capacity for Processing Information." *Psychological Review* 63:81–97.

de Moor, J. C. 1972. "The Semitic Pantheon of Ugarit." *UF* 2:187–218.

Noegel, S. B. 2017. "God of Heaven and Sheol: The "Unearthing" of Creation." *HS* 58:119–44.

Noll, R. 1994. *The Jung Cult: Origins of a Charismatic Movement*. Princeton: Princeton University Press. Reprint, London: Collins Fontana, 1995.

Olivelle, P. 1998. *The Early Upanishads: Annotated Text and Translation*. New York: Oxford University Press.

del Olmo Lete, G. 2014. *Canaanite Religion according to the Liturgical Texts of Ugarit*. 2nd English ed. AOAT 408. Münster: Ugarit-Verlag.

Pardee, D. 2000. *Les Textes Rituels*. 2 vols. Ras Shamra-Ougarit 12. Paris: ERC.

Piankoff, A. 1957. *Egyptian Religious Texts and Representations*, vol. 3: Mythological Papyri. Bollingen Series 40.3. New York: Pantheon.

Porter, B. H., and S. D. Ricks. 1990. "Names in Antiquity: Old, New and Hidden." *By Study and Also By Faith: Essays in Honor of Hugh W. Nibley on the Occasion of His Eightieth Birthday, 27 March 1990*, ed. J. M. Lundquist and S. D. Ricks, 1:501–22. 2 vols. Salt Lake City: Deseret.

Radhakrishnan, S. 1953. *The Principal Upanisads*. London: Allen & Unwin.

Rahmouni, A. 2008. *Divine Epithets in the Ugaritic Alphabetic Texts*. HdO I 93. Leiden: Brill.

Reiner, E. 1961. "The Etiological Myth of the Seven Sages." *Or* 30: 1–11.

Ritner, R. K. 1997. "The Legend of Isis and the Name of Re (P. Turin 1993)." In *The Context of Scripture*. Vol. 1: *Canonical Compositions from the Biblical World*, edited by W. W. Hallo, 33–34. 3 vols. Leiden: Brill.

Robinson, H. W. 1928. *The Christian Experience of the Holy Spirit*. Library of Constructive Theology. London: Nisbet.

Ryckmans, G. 1947. "Les religions arabes préislamiques." In *Histoire Générale des Religions*, ed. M. Gorce and R. Mortier, 4:307–32. 4 vols. Paris: Quillet.

Sales, J. de C. 2012. "Divine Triads of Ancient Egypt." *Hathor* 1:115–35.

Sanders, P. 1996. *The Provenance of Deuteronomy 32*. OSt 37. Leiden: Brill.

Seri, A. 2006. "The Fifty Names of Marduk in Enūma eliš." *JAOS* 126:507–19.

Schmidt, B. B. 1995. "The Aniconic Tradition: On Reading Images and Viewing Texts." In *The Triumph of Elohim: From Yahwisms to Judaisms*, ed. D. Edelman, 75–105. Grand Rapids: Eerdmans.

Schmidt, W. 1912. *Der Ursprung der Gottesidee: eine historisch-kritische und positive Studie*. Münster: Aschendorff.

Schwemer, D. 2001. *Die Wettergottgestalten Mesopotamiens und Nordsyriens im Zeitalter der Keilschrift-kulturen*. Materialien und Studien nach den schriftlichen Quellen. Wiesbaden: Harrassowitz.

Smith, M. S. 2001. *The Origins of Biblical Monotheism: Israel's Polytheistic Background and the Ugaritic Texts*. Oxford: Oxford University Press.

Sperling, G. 1988. "The Magic Number Seven: Information Processing Then and Now." In *The Making of Cognitive Science: Essays in Honor of George A. Miller*, ed. W. Hirst, 71–80. Cambridge: Cambridge University Press.

Stevens, D. E. 1997. "Does Deuteronomy 32:8 Refer to 'Sons of God' or 'Sons of Israel'?" *BSac* 154:131–41.

———. 2000. "Daniel 10 and the Notion of Territorial Spirits." *BSac* 157:410–31.

Tigay, J. H. 1996. *Deuteronomy*. JPS Torah Commentary. Philadelphia: Jewish Publication Society.

Tropper, J. 2012. *Ugaritische Grammatik*. 2nd ed. AOAT 273.2. Münster: Ugarit-Verlag.

Tur-Sinai, H. 1964. "'ăbbîr, 'abbîr." In *Encyclopaedia Biblica of the Bialik Institute*, ed. E. L. Sukenik et al., 1:31–33. Jerusalem: Bialik Institute.

van den Dungen, W. n.d.I. "On the Shabaka Stone." http://www.maat.sofiatopia.org/shabaka.htm.

———. n.d.II. "The Memphis Theology." http://www.maat.sofiatopia.org/memphis.htm.

de Vaux, R. 1961. *Ancient Israel: Its Life and Institutions*. London: Darton, Longman & Todd.

Te Velde, H. 1971 "Some Remarks on the Structure of Egyptian Divine Triads." *JEA* 57:80–86.

Volz, P. 1910. *Der Geist Gottes und die verwandten Erscheinungen im Alten Testament und im anschliessenden Judentum*. Tübingen: Mohr/Siebeck.

Watts, A. W. 1953. *Myth and Ritual in Christianity*. London: Thames & Hudson.

White, E. 2014. *Yahweh's Council: Its Structure and Membership*. FAT 65. Tübingen: Mohr/Siebeck.

Wilkinson, R. H. 2003. *The Complete Gods and Goddesses of Ancient Egypt*. London: Thames & Hudson.

Wright, C. 1996. *Deuteronomy*. New International Biblical Commentary. Peabody, MA: Hendrickson.

Wulstan, D. 1968. "The Tuning of the Babylonian Harp." *Iraq* 30:215–28.

Wyatt, N. 1978. "The Problem of the 'God of the Fathers.'" *ZAW* 90:101–4. Reprinted in Wyatt 2005a:1–5.

———. 1979. "The Development of the Tradition in Exodus 3." *ZAW* 91:437–42. Reprinted in Wyatt 2005a:6–12.

———. 1986. "The Significance of the Burning Bush." *VT* 36: 361–65. Reprinted in Wyatt 2005a:13–17.

———. 1987. "Baal's Boars." *UF* 19: 391–98.

———. 1992a. "Of Calves and Kings: The Canaanite Dimension in Israelite Religion." *SJOT* 6:68–91. Reprinted in Wyatt 2005a:72–91.

———. 1992b. "The Titles of the Ugaritic Storm-god." *UF* 24:403–24. Reprinted in Wyatt 2007c:7–40.

———. 1995. "The Significance of Ṣpn in West Semitic Thought: A Contribution to the History of a Mythological Motif." In *Ugarit: Ein ostmediterranes Kulturzentrum im Alten Orient*, ed. M. Dietrich and O. Loretz, 213–37. ALASP 7. Münster: Ugarit-Verlag. Reprinted in Wyatt 2005a:102–24.

———. 1998. "Understanding Polytheism: Structure and Dynamic in a West Semitic Pantheon." *Journal of Higher Criticism* 5:24–63. Reprinted in Wyatt 2007c:47–84.

———. 1999. "Degrees of Divinity: Mythical and Ritual Aspects of West Semitic Kingship." *UF* 31:853–87. Reprinted in Wyatt 2005b:191–220.

———. 2001. *Space and Time in the Religious Life of the Ancient Near East*. BibSem 85. London: Bloomsbury.

———. 2002. *Religious Texts from Ugarit*. 2nd ed. BibSem 53. London: Continuum.

———. 2005a. *The Mythic Mind: Essays on Cosmology in Ugaritic and Old Testament Literature*. Bible World. London: Equinox.

———. 2005b. "There's Such Divinity Doth Hedge a King." In *Selected Essays of Nicolas Wyatt on Royal Ideology in Ugaritic and Old Testament Literature*. SOTS Monograph Series. London: Ashgate.

———. 2007a. The Seventy Sons of Athirat, the Nations of the World, Deuteronomy 32.6b, 8–9, and the Myth of Divine Election. In *Reflection and Refraction: Studies in Biblical Historiography in Honour of A. Graeme Auld*, ed. R. Rezetko et al., 547–56. VTSup 113. Leiden: Brill. Reprinted in Wyatt 2010:69–77.

———. 2007b. "Old Men or Progenitors? A Proposal to Emend the Text of Deuteronomy 32:7 and Proverbs 23:22." *Studi Epigraofici e Linguistici* 24:33–37. Reprinted in Wyatt 2010:78–82.

———. 2007c. *Word of Tree and Whisper of Stone, and Other Papers on Ugaritian Thought*. GUS 1. Piscataway NJ: Gorgias.

———. 2010. *The Archaeology of Myth: Papers on Old Testament Tradition*. Bible World. London: Equinox.

Wyatt, S., and N. Wyatt. 2013. "The Longue Durée in the Beef Business." In *Ritual, Religion and Reason: Studies in the Ancient World in Honour of Paolo Xella*, edited by O. Loretz et al., 417–50. AOAT 404. Münster: Ugarit-Verlag.

Zerubbabel, E. 1985. *The Seven Day Circle: The History and Meaning of the Week*. New York: Free Press. Reprinted, Chicago University Press.

6

To Be or Not To Be a Proverb

When Water Flows Beneath Straw (and Don't Think It Doesn't)

KATHERYN PFISTERER DARR

INTRODUCTION

DESPITE THE TENTH COMMANDMENT, Hebrew Bible (HB) scholars could covet the 17,000 plus Old Babylonian Akkadian inscribed tablets and fragments recovered from the site of the royal palace in Mari, the ancient kingdom of Mari's capital city.[1] Among other texts, the Mari archives have yielded over 2,000 letters, including some 1,600 from the reign of Zimri-Lim, the West Semitic Amorite king whose rule (*ca.* 1774–1760 BCE) ended when Hammurabi, King of Babylon, captured the city. Where in Tanak can we point to primary sources, place them within a tight chronological frame, confidently call their authors' names, and surmise some of their character traits? J. M. Sasson can say of Zimri-Lim, "[f]rom witty or proverbial statements attributed to him, we can determine that [his] sense of humor was more subtle than crude."[2]

---

1. J. M. Sasson, *From the Mari Archives: An Anthology of Old Babylonian Letters* (Winona Lake, IN: Eisenbrauns, 2015) 1, 4. See W. Heimpel's introductory chapter in *Letters to the King of Mari: A New Translation, with Historical Introduction, Notes, and Commentary* (Winona Lake, IN: Eisenbrauns, 2003) 3–36. "Mari" was also the name of the capital district. The three other districts were Terqa, Saggaratum, and the Habur Valley "to the southern margin of the Northern Plains" (Heimpel, *Letters to the King*, 7–13; quote on p. 8).

2. Sasson, *From the Mari Archives*, 7; see also Sasson, "The King and I: A Mari King

He describes letters from Ibal-pi-El, a "competent" but "vainglorious" *merḫum* (tribal troop leader) as "at once chatty and precise, with fine humor and irony."[3] Where in the HB are letters from "forceful," elite women whose names we know?[4] Zimri-Lim entrusts Queen Šiptu with "ritual duties that were normally not transferrable"; and Addu-duri, his aunt or mother, apparently reads omens "without consulting the professionals."[5] To be sure, analyzing correspondence from kings, royal family members, administrators, and others demands a critical eye.[6] Still, we can excuse scholars who, sans similar evidence, succumb to a twinge of envy.

Experts mine Mari's trove of tablets for clues to every aspect of its socio-cultural life, including its religious beliefs, practices, and personnel. The texts tell of gods and goddesses, priests and priestesses, temple sites, sacrifices, and other cultic rituals, diviners and modes of divination (especially extispicy), and an array of additional intermediaries between the divine and human spheres[7]—some "lay" dreamers and visionaries, but more often "prophets," whose labels, including *muḫḫûm* (m.)/*muḫḫûtum* (f.), from *maḫû*, "to go into a frenzy," and *āpilum* (m.)/*āpiltum* (f.), from *apālu*', "to answer," point to recognized, socio-religious roles.[8]

In this essay, a tribute to Dr. Simon B. Parker, my esteemed colleague and treasured friend for twenty-four years, I focus on three of the letters to Zimri-Lim that report prophetic activity:[9] one from Inib-šina, a high priest-

---

in Changing Perceptions," *JAOS* 118 (1998) 453–70; quotes on p. 456.

3. Sasson, *From the Mari Archives*, 139.

4. Ibid., 5.

5. J. M. Sasson, "The Posting of Letters with Divine Messages," in *Florilegium Marianum II: Recueil d'études à la mémoire de Maurice Birot* (ed. D. Charpin and J.-M. Durand; Mémoires de Nouvelles assyriologiques brèves et utilitaires 3; Paris: Société pour l'étude du Proche-Orient ancien, 1994) 299–316; quote on p. 304.

6. Sasson, *From the Mari Archives*, 7–8.

7. On prophets as intermediaries, see D. L. Petersen, "Defining Prophecy and Prophetic Literature," in *Prophecy in Its Ancient Near Eastern Context: Mesopotamian, Biblical, and Arabian Perspectives* (ed. M. Nissinen; SBLSymS 13; Atlanta: Society of Biblical Literature, 2000) 33–44; esp. pp. 37–39.

8. On the inadequacies of designating Mari's intermediaries as "prophets," see M. Nissinen, "Introduction," in *Prophets and Prophecy in the Ancient Near East* (SBLWAW 12; Atlanta: Society of Biblical Literature, 2003) 5–6.

9. See E. J. Hamori's study of fifty-two "prophetic letters" from Mari in "Gender and the Verification of Prophecy at Mari," *WO* 42 (2012) 1–22; esp. pp. 4–8.

ess and Zimri-Lim's (half-) sister (ARM 26 197);[10] one from Sammetar, then governor of Terqa (ARM 26 199); and another from Kanisan, son or servant of Kibri-Dagan (future governor of Terqa), whose dispatch (ARM 26 202) quotes from Kibri-Dagan's letter to him. These texts catch scholars' attention, in part, because the same adage, "beneath straw water flows" (*šapal* IN.NU.DA [=*tibnim*] *mû illakū*), appears in each, offering experts a prized opportunity to assess how these correspondents inform Zimri-Lim of what might be a single, oracular utterance.[11] Were they dutifully "conveying ... a fairly literal report of the original prophecies, or a mere summary [of same], or indeed a free adaptation according to their own sense of what needed to be said or could be said" to their king?[12] In his oft-cited article, Parker acknowledged that these tablets contribute "only indirect evidence" of the oracular utterance(s) they report.[13] But each provides "direct testimony" to what its author thought Zimri-Lim should know about the divine communiqué(s) and how best he should react.[14]

As a HB scholar, I could easily covet experts' mastery of all things Mariote. Parroting Amos 7:14, I aver that I am neither a Mari specialist, nor the daughter of a Mari specialist. Nevertheless, my research has long immersed me in paremiology, the study of proverbs and their usage worldwide.[15] Most scholars who identify "beneath straw water flows" as a proverb

---

10. Sasson identifies her as Zimri-Lim's "not likely uterine" sister (*From the Mari Archives*, 263).

11. In this essay, I use "proverb(s)," "adage(s)," and "saying(s)" interchangeably to refer to popular proverbs known and used by linguistic communities, or subgroups thereof (see N. R. Norrick, *How Proverbs Mean: Semantic Studies in English Proverbs* [Trends in Linguistics Studies and Monographs 27; Berlin: Mouton, 1985] 39–40).

12. S. B. Parker, "Official Attitudes toward Prophecy at Mari and in Israel," *VT* 43 (1993) 50–66; quote on p. 52.

13. Ibid. Durand suggests that for Mari's prophets, at least, "le discours est en quelque sort fixé ne varietur." Nevertheless, Parker states, "the interests of the writer of the letter are revealed even in the quo[t]ation of the oracle" ("Official Attitudes," 57). See J.-M. Durand, *Archives Épistolaires de Mari* [AEM] I/1, Archives Royales de Mari [ARM] (vol. 26; Paris: Éditions Recherche sur les Civilisations, 1988) 382. As K. van der Toorn acknowledges, "[i]n most, if not all, cases, the ipsissima verba of the prophet will probably elude us forever; the original voice has been modified through the intervention of scribes and informers, none of whom regarded verbal accuracy as an imperative in communicating the message to the king" ("From the Oral to the Written: The Case of Old Babylonian Prophecy," in *Writings and Speech in Israelite and Ancient Near Eastern Prophecy* [ed. E. Ben Zvi and M. H. Floyd; SBLSymS 10; Atlanta: Society of Biblical Literature, 2000] 219–34; esp. 228–33 [quote on p. 230]).

14. Parker, "Official Attitudes," 57.

15. P. Seitel defines proverb performance as "the strategic social use of metaphor ... the manifestation in traditional, artistic, and relatively short form of metaphorical reasoning, used in an interactional context to serve certain purposes" (P. Seitel,

neither explain why that label is apropos, nor address issues it raises.[16] In the following pages, I show how proverb studies illumine ancient adages and their use in (literary reports of) social interactions.

THREE EPISTOLARY REPORTS OF PROPHETIC ACTIVITY

We begin with Nissinen's translations of these three letters.
ARM 26 197 (from Inib-šina):[17]

Speak to my star:[18] Thus Inib-šina:

Some time ago, Šelebum, the *assinnu*,[19] delivered to me an oracle and I communicated it to you. Now, a *qammātum*[20] of Dagan of Terqa came and spoke to me. She said:

"Proverbs: A Social Use of Metaphor," in *The Wisdom of Many: Essays on the Proverb* [ed. W. Mieder and A. Dundes; New York: Garland, 1981] 122–39).

16. Experts who regard it as a proverb include: J. -M. Durand, AEM I/1, 405; J. F. Ross, "Prophecy in Hamath, Israel, and Mari," HTR 63 (1970) 1–28; C. R. Fontaine, *Smooth Words: Woman, Proverbs, and Performance in Biblical Wisdom* (JSOTSup 356; London: T. & T. Clark, 2002) 180–83; Nissinen, *Prophets and Prophecy*, 29 n. d; L. L. Grabbe, "Ancient Near Eastern Prophecy from an Anthropological Perspective," in Nissinen, *Prophecy in Its Ancient Near Eastern Context*, 27; and Hamori, "Gender and the Verification," 15 n. 25.

17. Durand identifies Inib-šina as the high priestess of Adad (J. -M. Durand, *Les documents épistolaires du palais de Mari* 3 [Littératures anciennes de Proche-Orient 18; Paris: Cerf, 2000] 402).

18. Zimri-Lim's daughters also used this term to address the king in their letters (Sasson, *From the Mari Archives*, 263).

19. Šelebum served the cult of the goddess Annunitum. Scholars variously translate *assinnu(m)* as "pederast" (Heimpel, *Letters to the King*, 559); "gynepathic transvestite" (Sasson, "Water beneath Straw: Adventures of a Prophetic Phrase in the Mari Archives," in *Solving Riddles and Untying Knots: Biblical, Epigraphic, and Semitic Studies in Honor of Jonas C. Greenfield* [ed. Z. Zevit et al.; Winona Lake, IN: Eisenbrauns, 1995] 599–608; quote on p. 604); and "cult singer" (H. B. Huffmon, "A Company of Prophets: Mari, Assyria, Israel," in Nissinen, *Prophecy in Its Ancient Near Eastern Context*, 47–70; p. 51). For Hamori, the "exact nature of the third-gender role of the *assinnu*" is less important than the fact that along with women, they belong to "the category of the 'not-men'" (Hamori, "Gender and the Verification," 3). See also M. Nissinen, *Homoeroticism in the Biblical World: A Historical Perspective* (trans. K. Stjerna; Minneapolis: Fortress, 1998) 28–36.

20. Moran rules out, but then allows, that *qammātum* is a personal name ("New Evidence from Mari on the History of Prophecy," in W. L. Moran, *The Most Magic Word: Essays on Babylonian and Biblical Literature* [ed. R. S. Hendel; CBQMS 35; Washington, DC: Catholic Biblical Association of America, 2002] 98–139; see pp. 136–37). Following Durand (ARM 26/1, 396), Sasson sees *qammātum* as West Semitic for *kezertum*, "a

"The peacemaking of the man of Ešn[unna] is false:[21] beneath straw water runs! I will gather him into the net that I knot.[22] I will destroy his city and I will ruin his wealth, which comes from time immemorial."

This is what she said to me. Now, protect yourself! Without consulting an oracle do not enter the city! I have heard people saying: "He is always distinguishing himself." Do not try to distinguish yourself!

ARM 26 199 (from Sammetar):[23]

Speak to my lord: Thus Sammetar, your servant:

Lupahum, prophet [*āpilum*] of Dagan, arrived here from Tuttul. The message that my lord entrusted him in Saggaratum: "To Dagan of Terqa entrust me!"—this message he transmitted and they answered him: "Wherever you go, joy will always find you! Battering ram and siegetower will be given to you, and they will travel by your side; they will be your companions." With this message they answered him in Tuttul.

On his arrival from Tuttul, I had him taken to Dir and he took my bolt to Diritum.[24] Previously, he had brought a *šernum* saying (to Diritum): "The *šernum* is of no use; it is waterlogged. Reinforce the *šernum*! Now he brought my bolt, and this was his message: "What if you (=Diritum) are negligent, trusting in the peacemaking of the man of Ešnunna? Your guard should be stronger than ever before!"

To me he spoke: "Wh[at] if the king, without consulting God, will engage himself with the man of [Eš]nunna! As before, when the Yamin[ite]s came to me and settled in Saggaratum, I was the one who

---

type of female votaries distinguished for their piled-up hairdo." But, he observes, terms for prophets and diviners in Mari usually "divide etymologically to 'seeing' or 'speaking', not 'standing', hence favoring *qabbātum*, 'spokeswoman'" (Sasson, "Water beneath Straw," 603, n. 10). In *From the Mari Archives* he notes the pairing of *qammātum* with *assinnum*, suggesting that the former may "refer to a woman with gender-neutral sensibility, the counterpart to an *assinnum*" (263 n. 83). Heimpel derives *qammātum* from *qamāmum*, which "designates hair standing up," and translates "shock-head," a female who "went into trances." "Unkempt" hair, he adds, was broadly attested among "religious devotees" (Heimpel, *Letters to the King*, 252 n. 3).

21. "The man of Ešnunna" is King Ibalpiel II, whose kingdom and capital city lay between the Tigris River and the Zagros mountains.

22. Or "he knots." Either translation is possible.

23. See J.-M. Durand, "La guerre ou la paix? Réflexions sur les implications politiques d'une prophétie," in *Leggo! Studies Presented to Frederick Mario Fales on the Occasion of His 65th Birthday* (ed. G. B. Lanfranchi et al.; Wiesbaden: Harrassowitz, 2012) 251–72.

24. The goddess Diritum's temple was in Dir (=Der), a city in the Mari district.

spoke to the king: 'Do not make a treaty with the Yaminites! I shall drive the shepherds of their clans away to Ḫubur[25] and the river will finish them off for you[.]' Now then, he should not pledge himself without consulting God." This is the message Lupahum spoke to me.

Afterwards, on the following [da]y, a *qammātum* of Dagan of T[erqa] came and spoke [to me]: "beneath straw water ru[ns]. They keep on send[ing to you] messages of friendship, they even send their gods [to you], but in their hearts they are planning something else. The king should not take an oath without consulting God."

She demanded a *laḫarûm*-garment and a nose-ring, and I ga[ve them to] her. Then she delivered her instructions in the temple of Belet-ekallim to the high pr[iestess In]ib-šina.[26]

The repo[rt of the words that] she spoke to me I have hereby sent to my lord. Let my lord consider the matter and act in accordance with his great majesty.[27]

ARM 26 202 (from Kanisan):

Speak to my lord: Thus Kanisan, your servant:

Kibri-D[agan], my father, [wrote to me] in Mari. [This is what] he wrote:

"[I heard] the words [that] were uttered [in the temple of Da]gan. Th]is is what [they] sp[oke to me]: 'Be[neath straw] water ru[ns]. The god of my lord has come! He has delivered his enemies in his hands.' Now, as before, the prophet [*muḫḫûm*] broke out into constant declamation."

This is what Kib[ri-Dag]an wrote [to me]. My lord [should not be negligent in] letting [ora]cles be delivered for his [own] goo[d …]

[break]

Let my lord not tarry, let him perform a sacrifice and let him go!

---

25. Possibly a play on the name of the Habur River; see Nissinen, *Prophets and Prophecy*, 32 n. g, citing D. Charpin, *Florilegium Marianum VI: Recueil d'études à la mémoire d'André Parrot* (Mémoires de Nouvelles assyriologiques brèves et utilitaires 7; Paris: Société pour l'étude du Proche-Orient ancien, 2002) 25 n. 149.

26. Nissinen's "then" suggests that Sammetar heard the *qammātum*'s oracle before Inib-šina. Sasson's "by the way" provides no clue about which correspondent heard it first (Sasson, "Water beneath Straw," 601).

27. Because lines 58–63 of Sammetar's letter turn to an unrelated matter, I do not address them in this essay.

TO BE OR NOT TO BE A PROVERB

Though the recurring presence of "beneath straw water flows" advanced his aims, Parker shows scant interest in the adage per se,[28] nowhere citing, for example, Marzal's analysis of this and other sayings in *Gleanings from the Wisdom of Mari*.[29] Nevertheless, he understands it to state "the *general truth* applicable here": "things are not what they seem on the surface."[30] For Moran, it is "clearly a proverb[;] and its meaning is that one cannot trust appearances, *like the flotsam lying so quietly on the surface while underneath flows the current*.[31] So too Marzal: "the *factual observation of experience*, and the *truth of the content* found in this utterance are features of a proverb."[32] Heimpel nowhere calls it a proverb in *Letters to the King of Mari*; but he too affirms the "*truth of its content*," noting, "[t]he image is of water whose surface is hidden under a cover of chaff, as happens in the time of winnowing," and adding, "the image of water beneath chaff was common."[33] But Sasson rejects the notion that our "prophetic phrase" is a warning that expresses, e.g., Marzal's "factual observation of experience":[34]

> Most scholars conjecture that … "beneath straw runs water" is a warning against trickery; something like "still waters run deep" is one of its possible meanings. But such an interpretation depends too much on Inibshina's own setting for it. In actuality, "*above running water there can only be moving straw*; and

---

28. Parker first describes the saying as "(quasi-)proverbial" ("Official Attitudes," 57). Elsewhere, he states that it "sounds like a proverbial saying" (ibid.) and twice calls it a "proverb" (ibid., 59).

29. A. Marzal, *Gleanings from the Wisdom of Mari* (Studia Pohl 11; Rome: Biblical Institute, 1976) 27–31. Because he worked from cuneiform copies in *Archives royales de Mari* 10: *La correspondance feminine* (ed. G. Dossin; Musée du Louvre, Department des Antiquités Orientales: Textes Cunéiformes 31; Paris: Geuthner, 1967), Marzal lacked access to Sammetar's and Kanisan's letters.

30. Parker, "Official Attitudes," 58 (emphasis mine).

31. W. L. Moran, "Akkadian Letters," in *ANET*, 632 n. 114. His observation suggests that "flotsam lying so quietly …" was a familiar sight.

32. Marzal, Gleanings from the Wisdom, 28; emphases mine.

33. Heimpel, *Letters to the King*, 255, 252 n. 4. Finet traces the image to brick making: when workers placed straw in pools of water and added clay to the mixture, the sight of floating straw fostered a false sense of security (A. Finet, "Citations littéraires dans la correspondance de Mari," *RA* 68 [1974] 35–47; p. 42). But "bassins" (basins) suggests standing, not flowing, water. See also Sasson, "Water beneath Straw," 606 n. 17.

34. In "Water beneath Straw," Sasson calls the phrase an "apothegmatic assertion," "aphorism," "adage," and "saying," but not a proverb.

the moving straw would cause the rush of the water to be more obvious to the beholder."[35]

Sasson accepts that the *qammātum*, to whom the phrase is twice attributed (ARM 26 197; ARM 26 199), included it in her oracle(s). He insists, however, that it "so baffled its hearers" that scribes took unusually meticulous care writing it.[36] Her "deceptively opaque phrase" could be an allegory, though "we elucidate [it] no better by assigning roles to straw or running water."[37] It might be a "riddle," which requires a correct solution.[38] But it also could be an "enigma, which, by implication, can never have enough levels of meaning."[39]

One could counter Sasson's claim that the saying is the same on each tablet because of its bewildering opacity: as part of Mari's proverbial stock, it was both familiar and resistant to change.[40] More perplexing is his notion that Zimri-Lim's correspondents (and the intermediaries whose oracles they report) would present the king with a baffling conundrum. Do they wish to leave him befuddled by the divine communiqué they convey? Or does our saying function, as (performed) proverbs so often do, to "sum up ['name'] a situation, pass judgment [on it], recommend a course of action, or serve as [a] secular past precedent[ ] to present action"?[41]

---

35. Ibid., 606–7. All three texts, Sasson notes, refer to "straw," not living "grass" or "reed," which remains stationary in flowing water (ibid., 607 n. 19). One can conceive of circumstances in which water flows (or is caused to flow) beneath stagnant straw. Nevertheless, I construe our adage as an erroneous assertion about how floating straw normally behaves in flowing water.

36. Ibid., 607.

37. Ibid.

38. Ibid.

39. Ibid. Sasson credits J.-M. Durand with suggesting "enigma" (ibid., 607 n. 20).

40. Shapin writes of a proverb's "mnemonic robustness," its "capacity . . . to seize the mind, to be easily remembered and retrieved, and to resist deformation as it circulates in the culture and over time . . . It is very important to say a proverb just right," he adds. "Modifying [it] at will, like summarizing or paraphrasing [its] message, would result in something which at once lacked the authority and the 'frame-breaking' character of the proper form: it's not done" (S. Shapin, "Proverbial Economies: How an Understanding of Some Linguistic and Social Features of Common Sense Can Throw Light on More Prestigious Bodies of Knowledge, Science for Example," *Social Studies of Science* 31 [October 2001] 731–69; quote on p. 738). Nevertheless, adages, conventional understandings of their themes, and the sorts of situations in which they often are cited can and do change over time; and variant forms of the same saying can co-exist within single linguistic groups.

41. See O. Arewa and A. Dundes, "Proverbs and the Ethnography of Speaking Folklore," *American Anthropology* 66/6 pt. 2 (1964) 70–85; quote on p. 71. Burke famously called proverbs "strategies for dealing with situations. In so far as situations are typical

TWO ANALYTICAL APPROACHES TO PROVERBS AND THEIR PERFORMANCE

Paremiologists respond to objections of the sort Sasson raises by: (1) identifying the theme of a saying per se;[42] (2) determining its theme's contextualized meaning within a particular interaction situation;[43] and (3) explaining how illogical/erroneous adages can express, nonetheless, "the shape truth takes in the world the proverb envisions."[44] Both Seitel's ethnographic, genre-powered approach and aspects of R. P. Honeck's most recent "Extended Conceptual Base Theory," "ECBT-2," speak to these issues.[45] For Seitel, a genre's "interpretive powers" arise from its capacity to identify and supply "a perspective on four conceptual spheres: categorization of texts, intertextual reference, performance in a social field, and 'form-shaping ideology'—a framework for creating and understanding kinds of speech."[46] Informed by the work of M. M. Bakhtin, W. Hanks, V. Propp,[47] and others, he constructs "a kind of literary interpretation" that:

> nurtur[es] creative understandings of verbal art ... that are culturally and historically specific yet have the richness of abstraction and allegory; that place a single work within the "community discourse history" from which it emerged; that attend to the creator and his or her work with a deep and complex critical gaze; and that provide a framework within which indigenous and outsider knowledge can engage in an always unfinished dialogue about form and significance. This system ... is based on

and recurrent in a given social structure, people develop names for them and strategies for handling them" ("Literature as Equipment for Living," in K. Burke, *The Philosophy of Literary Form: Studies in Symbolic Action* [3rd ed.; Berkeley: University of California Press, 1973] 293–304, esp. 296–97).

42. Seitel defines "theme" as "the significance ... produced by relationships between symbols present or implied in a text." A proverb's "abstract, culturally specific" theme remains "relatively constant" regardless of its context of usage (*Powers of Genre*, 31, 4).

43. Seitel defines "meaning" as "the result of relationships perceived between the utterance or work (in part or as a whole) and the context in which it is spoken or otherwise performed and received. A proverb's meaning changes with its context of performance and/or reception" (ibid., 4–5).

44. Ibid., 41.

45. R. P. Honeck, *A Proverb in Mind: The Cognitive Science of Proverbial Wit and Wisdom* (Mahwah, NJ: Erlbaum, 1997).

46. Seitel, *Powers of Genre*, 14.

47. M. M. Bakhtin, *Speech Genres and Other Late Essays* (ed. C. Emerson and M. Holquist; Austin: University of Texas Press, 1986); W. F. Hanks, *Language and Communicative Practices* (Boulder, CO: Westview, 1996); V. I. Propp, *Morphology of the Folktale* (2nd ed.; Austin: University of Texas Press, 1968).

the idea of genre as a specific, concrete, yet often changing body of texts, as a framework for creating and interpreting them, and as a "form-shaping ideology" through which both creator and critic enter into dialogue with the collective wisdom of a tradition.[48]

Seitel applies his etic, analytical tools to proverbs and performance practices among the Haya, an agricultural, cattle-owning, and fishing people who have lived in northwestern Tanzania for approximately two millennia.[49] His emic aim is to elucidate Haya performances of proverbs, folktales, and epics. But he also anticipates that his approach can illumine the verbal artistry of other peoples, societies, and cultures.[50] My analyses of proverb performances in Tanak support his optimism.

For Honeck, by contrast, cognitive science offers the "best prospect for revealing the secrets of the proverb."[51] The cognitive approach regards sayings as "*abstract entities* that can only be understood by a set of very general theoretical principles."[52] Construing and using sayings competently entails complex mental processes:

> ... however intelligence is conceived, either as a biological, societal, contextual, or information-processing phenomenon, ... the proverb is implicated at each of these levels ... proverb processing entails many mental activities that are typically discussed in conjunction with intelligence: analogy, induction, synthesis, pattern matching, mental flexibility, mental speed, mental transformations, an a storehouse of knowledge.[53]

Moreover, deploying adages effectively requires even more than these types of intelligence. "Creativity, talent, and social skills are involved as well," Honeck adds. "Especially the person who creates a proverb, but also those who use them appropriately, have performed a miniature form of art."[54]

To be sure, identifying the "cognitive foundations of proverb production, pragmatics, expertise, [and] emotion," as well as "the microcognitive aspects of proverb comprehension,"[55] remains an ongoing task. Neverthe-

48. Seitel, *Powers of Genre*, 3.
49. Ibid., 19–26.
50. Ibid, 4.
51. Honeck, *Proverb in Mind*, 1.
52. R. P. Honeck and J. G. Temple, "Proverbs and the Complete Mind," *Metaphor and Symbolic Activity* 11 (1996) 217–32; quote on p. 218.
53. Honeck, *Proverb in Mind*, 262.
54. Ibid., 263.
55. Ibid., 276.

less, aspects of his ECBT-2 enable readers better to grasp key issues in this essay.

I begin with Marzal's analysis of "under the straw water flows."[56] Next, I show how Seitel's genre-powered approach distinguishes between a proverb's theme and its potential, contextualized meanings in social settings. Turning to Honeck, I summarize how his cognitive theory explains the mental stages through which proverb audiences progress from a saying's "literal meaning model" (the adage itself) to its abstract ("figurative") theme.[57] (Here, my second disclaimer is in order, since I am neither a cognitive scientist, nor the daughter of a cognitive scientist; and I know little of the physiological intricacies of human brains.) Next, I show how each scholar's approach can respond to Sasson's claim that our inaccurate adage flummoxed its hearers. Finally, I analyze how our adage functions in each of its three epistolary contexts.

MARZAL AND THE PROVERB'S "INCOMMUNICABLE QUALITY"

In his Preface to *Gleanings from the Wisdom of Mari*, Marzal states that A. Taylor's classic, 1931 study, *The Proverb*,[58] so "excited [his] curiosity" that what began as a "modest" project—translating and supplying commentary for the tablets' "several proverbs"—grew into an exploration of how paremiology might enhance his work.[59] His analyses of these adages rely especially on G. B. Milner's definition of sayings as "quadripartite structures" and N. F. Barley's theory of how proverb audiences construct analogies between a saying's "internal relations" ("logical connections between the proverb's own elements") and its "external relations" ("those between the given term or image [in the saying itself] and [its] hidden term or answer" in a specific context situation).[60] His interdisciplinary approach is laudable; nevertheless, the analytical tools he uses show their age. Paremiology, like ancient

---

56. Marzal's translation in *Gleanings from the Wisdom*, 27–31.
57. Honeck, *Proverb in Mind*, 128–51.
58. A. Taylor, *The Proverb* (Cambridge: Harvard University Press, 1931).
59. Marzal intends his study to be "of interest not only to Assyriologists, but also paremiologists and some Biblical scholars" (*Gleanings from the Wisdom*, V).
60. Ibid., 10. See G. B. Milner, "What Is a Proverb?" *New Society* 332 (1969) 199–202; Milner, "Quadripartite Structures," *Proverbium* 14 (1969) 379–83; N. F. Barley, "A Structural Approach to the Proverb and Maxim with Special Reference to the Anglo-Saxon Corpus," *Proverbium* 20 (1972) 737–50.

Mariote and biblical studies, is an ever-growing field; and more recent advances equip us to exceed his achievements.

At the outset, Marzal cites Taylor's (in)famous remarks about the difficulty of defining "proverb": "The definition of a proverb is too difficult to repay the undertaking; and should we fortunately combine in a single definition all the essential elements and give each the proper emphasis, we should not even then have a touchstone. An incommunicable quality tells us that this sentence is proverbial and that one is not."[61] Many scholars have criticized Taylor's we-know-one-when-we-hear-it attitude. Gossen, for example, calls it "imprecise and ethnocentric," albeit "true in some respects."[62] Grzybek allows that it "seem[s] to be an evasion rather than a way out,"[63] while Briggs avers, "[t]his position uses an admission of defeat in justifying a remarkably powerful claim: that researchers can use a priori and intuitive criteria in the identification and analysis of proverbs."[64] Taylor's remarks might make sense for native proverb audiences, but a saying's "incommunicable quality" can whiz right over outsiders' heads!

Marzal shared Taylor's confidence, asserting his willingness to be "[g]uided by this 'incommunicable quality'" and to exercise his own "judgment to discover [it]."[65] But G. B. Milner rejected Taylor's "counsel of despair": "if there is something that 'tells us' what is, and what is not, proverbial," he insisted, "then we must continue to grapple with the problem until we are [able] to communicate what A. Taylor considers to be 'incommunicable.'" If one could show that "in widely different ages, languages and cultures, important statements tend to be cast in exactly the same mould," Milner reasoned, then "it [might] throw new light on the deep structure of the human mind."[66] His efforts convinced him that the saying's most significant characteristic is the "symmetrical structure of its form and content."[67]

---

61. Taylor, *The Proverb*, 3. He urged readers to "be content" to define the proverb as "a saying current among the folk" without defining "current" or "folk."

62. G. H. Gossen, "Chamula Tzotzil Proverbs: Neither Fish nor Fowl," in *Wise Words: Essays on the Proverb* (ed. W. Mieder; New York: Garland, 1994) 351–92; quote on p. 353.

63. P. Grzybek, "Foundations of Semiotic Proverb Study," in Mieder, *Wise Words*, 31–71; quote on p. 36.

64. C. L. Briggs, "The Pragmatics of Proverb Performances in New Mexican Spanish," *American Anthropologist* 87 (1985) 793–810; quote on p. 793.

65. Marzal, *Gleanings from the Wisdom*, 2, 14. He also relied on other criteria, including "the context, the style (universality of the statement; simplicity of diction; literary devices, such as alliteration, rhyme, rhythm, parallelism and contrast, metaphor) . . . [and] the content and function" (ibid., p. 15).

66. Milner, "What Is a Proverb?" 199.

67. Ibid., 200.

In terms of its formal structure, Milner postulates, the proverb consists of four quarters standing in "a balanced and structured relationship to one another." These quarters are "grouped" into two, "self-contained" halves—a "head," and a "tail."[68] Not all extant sayings exhibit quadripartite structures; some have been "eroded by the familiarity of usage," becoming "tripartite," "bipartite," or "unipartite."[69] Even so, the adage's "hidden," four-part structure remains perceptible at "the unconscious level of our minds."[70] Milner's structural definition has fared poorly among critics. "Even on a generous, general interpretation," Norrick observes, he "states only that many proverbs can be analyzed as quadripartite on the basis of their surface structures, others on the basis of their historical surface structures[,] and still others on the basis of some unconsciously perceived hidden (or deep?) structure. But this provides absolutely no basis for a structural proverb definition."[71]

In addition to describing the proverb's formal structure, Milner argues that a saying's "force and meaning" emerge from "the exact nature of the relationship" between its quarters.[72] To educe those relationships, he first allots plus (+) or minus (-) values to each quarter's significant word(s), depending on whether it is "good or bad, safe or dangerous, friendly or hostile, useful or useless, attractive or unattractive, agreeable or disagreeable."[73] He then assigns plus or minus values to the entire quarter, based on the value(s) of that word(s). The quarter's value determines its "value and function" within the entire saying.[74] If both quarters of a half are positive,[75] or both are

---

68. Ibid.

69. Ibid., 202. Dundes describes his thinking as "a 'survival' of English survival theory in which it is invariably assumed that the full, original form in the past has evolved or rather devolved through time suffering such ravages of attrition that only a fragment remains" (A. Dundes, "On the Structure of the Proverb," in *The Wisdom of Many: Essays on the Proverb* (ed. W. Mieder and A. Dundes; New York: Garland, 1981) 43–64; quote on p. 48. See also idem, "The Devolutionary Premise in Folklore Theory," *Journal of the Folklore Institute* 6 (1969) 5–19.

70. Milner, "Quadripartite Structures," 380. According to Dundes' own, structural definition, proverbs consist of at least one "topic" and one "comment." See A. Dundes, "On the Structure of the Proverb," *Proverbium* 25 (1975) 961–73.

71. Norrick, *How Proverbs Mean*, 54.

72. Milner, "What Is a Proverb?" 200.

73. Milner assumes that each significant word in a quarter has a plus value "until it becomes . . . impossible to continue treating it as such without making nonsense of the half in which it occurs (and therefore of the saying as a whole)" (ibid., 201).

74. Other words within a quarter might modify the value of that quarter and of its half; nonetheless, "the two quarters have independent values which modify each other, but [not] the quarters of the other half" (ibid., 200).

75. "New (+) brooms (+) sweep (+) clean (+) is an example of this type of proverb" (ibid.).

negative,[76] then the half is positive. If one quarter is negative and the other positive, however, the minus quarter dominates; and the half is negative.[77]

Critics observe that assigning plus and minus values to an adage's words, quarters, and halves is a subjective enterprise.[78] Dundes, for example, describes Milner's approach as "much too atomistic": "[His] error lies in trying to assign plus or minus values to each of the quarters as though the other three . . . were not present." Moreover, he never takes the next, essential step of considering how values assigned to a proverb's components can change depending on the situation in which it is uttered and the context to which the speaker applies it.[79] Identify an (isolated) adage's theme is the first task. But what of the two, heuristically distinguishable contexts in which it is quoted—the "vivid present" ("the immediate interactional setting" in which [it] is cited), and the "broader horizon against which the [proverb performance] takes place?"[80] Neglecting its broader horizon accords with his view that his criteria for assigning plus and minus values to proverb terms are valid even for adages from "very remote and exotic cultures." But he never explains how audiences are able to move from an adage's theme to its performance meaning.

Following Milner, Marzal allots values to our adage's quarters and halves—"under (-) the straw (+) [= negative head] water (-) flows" (+) [= negative tail]—and identifies its "internal logical connections": "open positive value of A may conceal hidden negative value of A."[81] Following Barley, he then correlates the saying's "given terms" ("under the [stationary] straw" and "water runs") with its "hidden terms" in Inib-šina's version of the oracle ("offers of reconciliation" and "treachery," respectively). Doing so supplies Milner's missing step. But because he has already assigned values to components of the proverb per se based on their "hidden" terms within her letter,

---

76. Milner's examples include "waste (-) not (-), want (-) not (-)." Both its head and tail are positive, because the minus values of their quarters cancel out each other (ibid.).

77. E.g., "sow (+) the wind (-) (and) reap (+) the storm (-)" (ibid.).

78. See Grzybek, "Foundations of Semiotic," 46–47; Norrick, *How Proverbs Mean*, 51–54.

79. Milner distinguishes, however, between the meaning of "rolling stones gather no moss" in England and in Scotland. For the former, "the allusion is to the desirable qualities of the moss found draped over stones in a peaceful brook." For the latter, it is "to a stone roller, which must not . . . remain idle for long, or it will gather unwanted moss . . ." The values assigned to the saying's quarters and halves turn on the referent for said "stone." Nevertheless, he ignores how the saying's contextualized meanings might change depending on the circumstances in which it is cited, either in Scotland, or in England (Milner, "What Is a Proverb?" 201; Milner, "Quadripartite Structures," 383).

80. Hanks, *Language and Communicative*, 142.

81. Marzal, *Gleanings from the Wisdom*, 29.

any distinction between the isolated saying's theme and its contextualized meaning collapses.[82]

The notion that our adage per se is "a warning against trickery" is inaccurate, since it expresses neither an *intrinsic* sense of "unexpected danger" and "deception," nor "the negative notion of hiding."[83]

To be sure, it can convey those meanings in certain contexts. In another social interaction, however, a person could cite it to inform an equally seasoned co-worker that their latest apprentice absorbs more instruction than his disinterested facial expression suggests. A physician could quote it to reassure anguished parents that their seemingly unresponsive child hears their comforting words. In short, whether our proverb's theme functions positively or negatively in its "vivid present" turns on the speaker's reason for applying it to a particular context.[84]

PROVERB THEMES AND CONTEXTUALIZED MEANINGS

Both Seitel and Honeck describe ways of identifying an (isolated) adage's theme and then discerning its potential, situation-specific meanings. Together, their approaches enhance our understanding of how proverb audiences progress from this first phase of understanding a proverb to the second. I begin with Seitel's early model for analyzing proverb performances, followed by his later, genre-powered system.

---

82. Marzal recognizes that the values he assigns to each of the proverb's components can seem arbitrary: "'Water', as applied to the agricultural society of Mesopotamia, should deserve a plus value; but in this proverb 'water' is considered in a context of danger and deception; therefore, a negative value should be assigned to it" (ibid.).

83. Sasson, "Water beneath Straw," 606.

84. Grzybek includes W. Mieder's list of potential, pragmatic proverb functions, including "warning, persuasion, admonition, reprimand, statement, characterization, explanation, description, justification, summarization, etc." ("Foundations of Semiotic," 38). "[I]t is well possible," Mieder explains, "that one and the same proverb takes completely different functions in different contexts of usage" (ibid., 38–39). See W. Mieder, "Träger und Gebauchsfunktion des Sprichworts," in *Sprichwort* (ed. L. Röhrich and W. Mieder; Stuttgart: Metzler, 1977) 78–82; quote on p. 81.

Seitel's Early and Later Approaches to Proverb Performance Analysis

C. R. Fontaine's *Traditional Sayings in the Old Testament* introduced many a biblical scholar to Seitel's early, etic model for proverb performance analysis.[85]

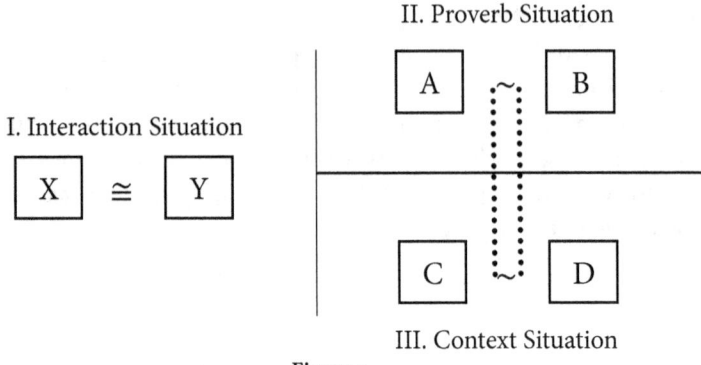

Figure 1

According to his model, a person (X) quotes an adage in an "Interaction Situation" (I), inviting addressees (Y) to view a specific "Context Situation" (III) through the metaphorical lens of the "Proverb Situation" (II). The symbol (≅) linking X and Y in the Interaction Situation represents the relationship between speaker and audience, including their respective ages, social statuses, genders, prior interactions (and possible future ones), and other factors (e.g., the significant presence or absence of onlookers). The symbol ~ signifies the relationships between terms (A and B) in the Proverb Situation, and between elements (C and D) in the Context Situation, while the broken, vertical lines connecting II and III in his model represent the (often analogous)[86] relationship the speaker posits between these two domains: (A:B::C:D).[87]

---

85. C. R. Fontaine, *Traditional Sayings in the Old Testament: A Contextual Study* (Bible and Literature Series 5; Sheffield: Almond, 1982) 57–63 and passim.

86. In some instances, the relationship between the Proverb and Context Situations is analogously opposite. For an example in the HB, see K. P. Darr, "Asking at Abel: A Wise Woman's Proverb Performance in 2 Samuel 20," in *From the Margins 1: Women of the Hebrew Bible and Their Afterlives* (The Bible in the Modern World 18; ed. P. S. Hawkins and L. C. Stahlberg; Sheffield: Sheffield Phoenix, 2009) 102–21. Audiences can choose either to accept or to reject the relationship proverb speakers posit between these two situations.

87. See Seitel, "Proverbs: A Social Use," 127. This version of his model appears in a reprint of this essay in *Folklore Genres* (ed. D. Ben-Amos; Austin: University of Texas Press, 1976) 129.

Seitel's early model does not appear in *The Powers of Genre* because its "Interaction Situation" cannot convey the breadth and complexity of that domain in his later, genre-powered approach. Following Hanks,[88] he expands his former Interaction Situation to embrace not only the "vivid present" of a proverb performance, but also "the broader horizon against which [that performance] takes place."[89] This broader horizon includes the wider "social historical context, a changing field of forces shaped by institutional practices, individual initiatives, and oppositions to them."[90] It further encompasses linguistic components, including genres. Generic utterances refer to "people, topics, and other utterances in the vivid present," Seitel explains, but they also refer to "people, topics, utterances, and genres in the broader horizon."[91] And with genres come socio-cultural assumptions and expectations. Before I testify at a legal trial in the U.S., for example, I must swear to tell "the truth, the whole truth, and nothing but the truth." Should I begin my testimony with "once upon a time," I am in trouble, since it evokes the generic interpretive framework for fairy tales; and fairy tales are fiction.

"Finalization" in Seitel's Genre-Powered System

"Finalization," the "sense of completion achieved in an artistic work," figured prominently in much of Bakhtin's thinking about genre; and it plays a vital role in Seitel's analytical approach, as well. Seitel defines this term as "the awareness by performer and audience that a work, or some part of it, is finished, complete":[92]

> Bakhtin observes that particular genres reach characteristic kinds of finalizations in the three dimensions of a literary work—composition, style, and theme. In this perspective, finalization is an artistic achievement by the collectivity of performers in a tradition, whose fertile, shared, enduring patterns assist creation and interpretation. Finalization is also an artistic achievement by individual performers who, if they are proficient, almost always transform shared patterns to create generic

---

88. Hanks, *Language and Communicative*, 142.

89. The vivid present is "dominant" for understanding how a saying is deployed: "Combining topic of conversation (the situation commented on by the proverb) with relationships among participants, [it] largely determines proverb selection and mode of use" (Seitel, *Powers of Genre*, 37).

90. Ibid., 5.

91. Ibid.

92. Ibid., 17.

artistic completion in seeming infinitely variable ways. And finalization is the achievement of engaged, informed audiences who cooperatively provide generically appropriate support for performances, which includes responding properly, supplying collateral understandings, and furnishing customary economic rewards.[93]

Seitel's diagram, "Nine ways of looking at a proverb: finalization in Haya proverb speaking," helps readers to visualize how sayings achieve thematic, stylistic, and compositional finalization at each of three levels: the saying itself ("local"); the adage speaker's complete utterance ("entire work"); and the performance "context" (in this essay, each letter in which our adage appears).[94] Bear in mind, however, that these three dimensions (and levels) operate in *concert with each other*. One can disentangle them for heuristic purposes, but they are inextricably interwoven in oral and written literature.

	A. Theme	B. Style	C. Composition
1. Local (proverb only)			
2. Proverb speaker's complete utterance			
3. Entire epistolary context			

Figure 2

Finalizations at the Local Level: Theme

For Seitel, proverbs achieve thematic finalization through contrasts between "paired, parallel, and opposing propositions."[95] The antithetical saying, "A wise child makes a glad father, but a foolish child is a mother's grief" (Prov 10:1), explicitly states both of its opposing propositions. But other adages express their themes through contrasts between an *explicit* proposition and an *implicit*, opposing one. The Haya proverb, "[The cow that] goes slowly drinks well," illustrates this second type of saying:

> The *theme* achieves completion at the *local level* . . . through an implied contrast between two cows. One cow goes slowly and arrives at a watering place after the others have finished

93. Ibid., 18.
94. Ibid., 38.
95. Ibid., 31.

drinking. By then, the mud they stirred up has settled, and so the cow drinks clear water. The . . . implied, contrasting cow goes quickly with the others and drinks muddy water. This contrast—between going slowly and drinking well and going quickly and drinking poorly—articulates the [proverb's] theme, even though the latter elements are unspoken. The theme attains finalization at this level when a listener supplies the needed contrast.[96]

Seitel identifies this saying's theme as "taking care." The Haya might quote it, he explains, "as part of brief advice and encouragement to a child who has brought a message from a neighbor but is in danger of garbling it in her haste to recite it. Here, as Burke (1957) points out, the proverb [names] the situation and urges a way to deal with it—Slow down! Be careful!"[97]

If Seitel's explanation of how audiences identify an adage's implicit, opposing proposition to determine its abstract theme sometimes seems elusive, Honeck's cognitive theory about how our minds arrive at the general ("figurative") meaning of a saying encountered "out of the blue" can prove useful:[98]

> If a stranger walks up to us . . . and says, *Not every oyster contains a pearl*, how do we respond? First, we build a *literal meaning model* . . . *the first phase of the overall proverb understanding process* . . . Because the utterance has no immediate referent and . . . is stated in a gnomic, nonpast tense way, *a problem recognition phase* results . . . We might . . . be tempted to think about [what the stranger has said], but we probably will need some motivation [to do so]. This is supplied by a *communication appraisal factor* that involves setting a criterion for deciding whether an utterance is worthy of further thought . . .

Together, the linguistic form of the proverb and the appraisal factor push the receiver off the literal level toward an ill-defined something else. . . . The linguistic form and basic communication modes seem to make the receiver say, "Something needs to be done with this utterance, but what? I do not know this person and why is he or she talking about oysters and pearls? . . . This is the beginning of deeper understanding . . . the receiver can use whatever clues are at hand to get the . . . now more preferred meaning. . . . the receiver's major clue is the utterance itself, . . . whatever literal meaning

---

96. Ibid., 38.

97. Ibid., citing K. Burke, "Literature as Equipment for Living," in *Philosophy of Literary Form* (rev. ed., abridged; New York: Vintage, 1957) 253–62.

98. Honeck, *Proverb in Mind*, 128–29.

model the receiver has developed for it . . . [he or she] has a hunch that the utterance is about itself, not [its literal meaning] model . . . per se, but what it might mean on another level. The ECBT now postulates that people follow an *ostension maximization principle*, which holds that a meaning should be developed that is general enough to instantiate anything that the literal meaning model could possibly be about, including itself . . . [99] Although the newer, preferred meaning should instantiate the literal model, it is also constrained by it. But it is not determined by it because new information must be gotten . . . that is outside the literal model. Getting this information [requires] inferences, associations, and elaboration in general. Most people already know . . . that oysters make pearls, and that pearls are valuable. That is part of the power of proverbs: They use familiar concepts to engender a more abstract meaning. Without supporting information . . . one would think that getting a . . . consensual meaning would be all but impossible. But language draws on built-in, schema-based logic. Some oysters contain pearls, some do not. What needs to be made salient is the positive value of pearls and the generic quality of oysters as a thing that makes something of value. This information can be synthesized in a new meaning: Not everything that makes valuable things does it all the time. This is the [proverb's] figurative meaning . . . [100]

How, using each scholar's approach, do we identify our adage's "abstract theme" (Seitel) or "figurative meaning" (Honeck)? For Seitel, the first task is discerning its "paired, parallel, and opposing propositions."[101] Its explicit proposition states that floating straw remains stationary as water flows beneath it. Its implicit, opposing proposition states that floating straw does not remain stationary as water flows beneath it.[102] The saying achieves thematic finalization when one supplies this implicit, opposing proposition.[103] For Honeck, encountering the proverb "out of the blue" engages its audience in a series of problem-solving, cognitive steps that begin with its literal meaning model and end with an understanding of its general,

---

99. Honeck borrows D. R. Hofstadter's concept of "strange loops" to explain how a proverb's "literal meaning model [helps to] build a figurative meaning model that acts, in turn, to instantiate the literal model" (ibid, 180–82; see D. R. Hofstadter, *Gödel, Escher, Bach: An Eternal Golden Braid* [New York: Basic Books, 1980]).

100. Honeck, *Proverb in Mind*, 128–30.

101. Seitel, *Powers of Genre*, 31.

102. See ibid., 43–44. Identifying our saying's implicit, opposing proposition requires "single negation"; Seitel's example requires "double negation": "A cow drinks well, going slowly and carefully, but the cow does *not* drink well, *not* going slowly and carefully" (ibid., 42).

103. Ibid., 38.

figurative meaning: things are not always as they seem. The proverb's figurative meaning model encompasses "beneath straw water flows" as an example of itself, and it can be applied to any context situation in which "more goes on than meets the eye."

Finalizations at the Local Level: Style and Composition

At the local level, our concise saying (only four forms) achieves stylistic finalization by means of two pairs of words that together express a complete thought: on one hand, *šapal* ("under, beneath"); IN.NU.DA (a logogram [=*tibnim*] meaning "straw"); on the other, *mû* ("water"); and *illakū* (a form of the verb *alāku*, "to go, come"). The proverb contains no *internal* tropes: each term conveys its conventional (so-called "literal") meaning.[104] It attains compositional finalization when its audience completes the task of supplying its implicit, opposing proposition and correctly identifies its theme. So long as one remains at the local (saying only) level, these thematic, stylistic, and compositional finalizations remain the same.

At this point, I offer my third, Amos-like admission: I am neither an hydrologist, nor the daughter of an hydrologist; and I cannot explicate with scientific precision circumstances under which floating straw might, or might not, remain stationary in flowing water. The saying's theme understandably strikes Sasson as illogical. How, then, might it "make sense?" To answer this question, we must look beyond the local level to determine how it achieves thematic, stylistic, and compositional finalization at the level of each of the oracles in which it appears.

THEMATIC, STYLISTIC, AND COMPOSITIONAL FINALIZATIONS AT THE LEVEL OF THE *QAMMĀTUM*'S ORACLE IN INIB-ŠINA'S LETTER

Content and Questions

We begin with Inib-šina's communiqué to Zimri-Lim, sans assumptions about which of our three letters contains the "original" oracle(s). Parker

---

104. The verb *alāku*, Sasson observes, "construes with water readily (see *CAD* A/1 310 sub g) but hardly ever metaphorically" ("Water beneath Straw," 606 n. 18). Nevertheless, "water flows" is scarcely more metaphorical than "water goes."

regards her version as most "authentic,"[105] but Sasson aptly counters, "it would be fruitless for us to search beyond this particular phrase for an 'original' among the three formulations."[106] "There is no 'original' to be had!"[107] Yet another observation is apropos as well: to my knowledge, we cannot identify which letter was composed and/or dispatched first, or the order in which they received Zimri-Lim's attention. Did the king construe a second letter in light of the first he heard, and a third's in light of the other two? Or did he attend especially to differences between, say, Inib-šina's and Sammetar's versions of the *qammātum*'s utterance?

Based solely on Inib-šina's account, we can say that Dagan of Terqa's *qammātum* embeds a saying in an oracle about the king of Ešnunna's deceptive peace initiatives. Though she purports to quote an authoritative source, she underscores its (and her own) authority by strategically inserting a bit of proverbial wisdom—believing, it seems, that the calculated citation of an apt adage enhances her chances of accomplishing what "ordinary" speech, even ordinary *divine* speech, might not.[108] The saying achieves thematic finalization within her complete utterance when Inib-šina: supplies its implicit, opposing proposition; identifies its theme; applies that theme metaphorically to the context situation (Ibalpiel II's duplicitous offer of a peace treaty) by correlating entities in the proverb situation with entities in that context[109] (floating, stagnant straw = Ibalpiel II's peace overtures; water flowing beneath it = their underlying deceitfulness); and grasps the analogy the *qammātum* posits between them.[110] It achieves stylistic final-

105. Parker, "Official Attitudes," 59.

106. Sasson, "Water Beneath Straw," 607. Though Parker allows that "the original prophecy" may have "come in different forms" ("Official Attitudes," 60), his statement that Sammetar may have "omitted the promises" (from the end of the oracle Inib-šina reports) presupposes that they were part of what he heard ("Official Attitudes," 59–60).

107. Sasson, "Posting of Letters," 306 n. 20.

108. Penfield defines "ordinary" speech as "speech acts [that] do not use proverbs but may express a similar notion or idea" (*Communicating with Quotes*, 14–15 n. 7). Because sayings convey "time-tested wisdom," Norrick observes, speakers "can draw on this authority. . . . Essentially the same effect [is] achieved by citing scripture, famous authors or recognized authorities in the relevant field. . . . the speaker adds authority and credibility to his utterance by identifying himself with traditional wisdom, beliefs and prejudices of the community at large . . . ." (Norrick, *How Proverbs Mean*, 28).

109. For a discussion of possible correlations between entities in the interaction, proverb, and context situations of proverb performances, see P. Seitel, "Saying Haya Sayings: Two Categories of Proverb Use," in *The Social Use of Metaphor: Essays on the Anthropology of Rhetoric* (ed. J. D. Sapir and J. C. Crocker; Philadelphia: University of Pennsylvania Press, 1977) 75–99.

110. Sasson's correlations between the adage's terms and elements in the context situation differ from mine. In his view, ". . . the aphorism reinforces *Ibalpiel's character*

ization within the entire oracle when its concise, out-of-context semantic content, which violates the "'usual' rules of conversation" (what have water and straw to do with political treaties?),[111] prompts her to construe it within its "generically [proverbially] favored" interpretive framework by applying its theme to the particular situation that is the "topic of discourse."[112] The saying per se lacks explicit, contextualizing elements, such as pronouns and other indexical terms, that could assist her in correlating its entities with entities in the context situation.[113] Nevertheless, its placement just after the intermediary's initial, straightforward assertion about the falsity of Ibalpiel II's peace initiative largely determines its compositional logic, that is, how Inib-šina arrives at its specific, performance meaning within the oracle. The *qammātum*'s divine communiqué ends with a triad of positive reinforcements: Dagan will capture Ibalpiel II in the net he knots, destroy his city, and plunder its long-held wealth. Since Ešnunna's fate is sealed, the king should eschew political entanglements with Dagan's foe.

At this point, we can see how our adage's explicit proposition expresses the "shape truth takes in the world [it] envisions."[114] Though its theme is neither logical nor true, these qualities are not requisite in the generically informed, interpretive worlds proverbs evoke. Seitel's example of another Haya saying, "one straw finishes the honey," further illustrates this type of compositional logic. It "describes a person using a single straw, dipping it again and again into honey and finishing the whole pot. One would not have thought it possible"; yet the proverb is "used to praise the value of perseverance."[115] Its implicit, opposing proposition, "one straw does not finish the honey" might be "expected and commonsensical," but in the context of usage Seitel describes, it is also "untrue":[116] "'One straw finishes the honey' [implies] and don't think it won't," just as "beneath straw water flows" implies "and don't think it doesn't."[117]

---

flaw. It has become, therefore, a moral indictment on which to justify the program of destruction Dagan is preparing for Eshnunna" ("Water beneath Straw," 605; emphasis mine). The initial accusation focuses on the falsity of his *peace overtures*, however, and not on his character per se.

111. Seitel, "Proverbs: A Social Use," 145.

112. Seitel, *Powers of Genre*, 31, 39.

113. Ibid. Sasson calls the *qammātum* in Inib-šina's letter "a fine punster," who engages in a "parosonantic play" on *šapal tibnim* in line 13 and forms of *šulputum* in line 17" ("Water Beneath Straw," 605).

114. Seitel, *Powers of Genre*, 41.

115. Ibid., 44.

116. Ibid., 44–45.

117. Ibid., 44.

Honeck's ECBT-2 offers a different explanation of how adages with nonsensical themes can "make sense" all the same. According to his "cognitive ideals hypothesis," an addition to his earlier ECBT, many proverbs state "an ideal, norm, or standard." "Societies and individuals judge that there are ideal, normative, or standard ways by which events should and do occur," Honeck explains. "Call these *generic ideals*." Generic ideals are "general and universal," but the adages that express them do so in "culturally or personally unique terms,"[118] that is, as "*specific ideals*, norms, and standards."[119] Such sayings "tell us what these ideals are, how to attain them, and what constitutes a deviation."[120] But other proverbs express *deviations* from specific ideals, norms, etc. "Not every oyster contains a pearl," for example, is the opposite of an ideal in which every oyster contains a pearl.[121] So also "great weights hang on small wires," since "[g]reat weights would normally be thought to hang on large, not small, wires."[122] People use ideal [norm, standard] deviant adages, he observes, to "comment critically on any situation that *does not conform to the [norm]*."[123]

Following Honeck, I view "beneath straw water flows" as a norm-deviant proverb. If "*above running water there can only be moving straw*," as Sasson insists, then it states a departure from the norm (floating straw goes where the water beneath it flows) and asks its audience to "consider the implications of [this unexpected] state of affairs."[124] What, in this context situation, does it mean that water flows beneath stationary straw? It means that while one would normally expect peace treaties to offer stability, security, and mutual cooperation, in this case, the opposite is true. In summary, we can neither deny our saying proverbial status because its explicit proposition is erroneous, nor assume that it inevitably befuddled its audiences.

If Sasson's "prophetic phrase" is a proverb, as I have argued, does its presence in (Inib-šina's version of) the *qammātum*'s utterance sum up a situation, pass judgment on it, and recommend a course of action? The answer to these questions is "yes." It both (a) *names* and (b) *judges* the situation to which it is applied metaphorically: (a) *the King of Ešnunna's peace overtures* are (b) *false* (and don't think they aren't). Moreover, because Dagan

118. Honeck, *Proverb in Mind*, 138.
119. Ibid., 137–38.
120. Ibid., 137.
121. Ibid., 138.
122. Ibid., 141.
123. Ibid., 142–43 (emphasis mine). Commenting need not be "critical" (negative), however, as my hypothetical examples of the seasoned co-worker and comforting physician show.
124. Ibid., 140.

promises to destroy Ibalpiel II, his kingdom, and its resources, Zimri-Lim need not fear reprisal when he (c) *obeys the deity by refusing Ešnunna's political alliance*. Note that Inib-šina's version of the *qammātum*'s oracle includes all of the information the king needs to understand it and to follow Dagan's instructions. Nevertheless, it does not convey everything the high priestess wishes to say.

THEMATIC, STYLISTIC, AND COMPOSITIONAL FINALIZATION AT THE LEVEL OF INIB-ŠINA'S LETTER

Content and Questions

Inib-šina begins the body of her letter by reminding her "star" that "some time ago," Šelebum, an *assinnu*, delivered an oracle that she reported to him.[125] Though she does not rehearse its content, she likely "expects the king to remember it and to [interpret] the oracle she goes on to report with the earlier one in mind." Perhaps, Parker opines, it "had a similar purport to the present one, if indeed it was not the same." In any event, "[t]he earlier warning and promise must have been proved right and are cited here as a forceful motivation [precedent] for taking the present oracle seriously."[126] Citing the past incident also underscores Inib-šina's value as a faithful, well-intentioned conveyor of divine communiqués to her king. Because she has dutifully relayed reliable oracles in the past, Zimri-Lim should take her letter to heart.

Now, she reports, Dagan of Terqa's *qammātum* has approached her, apparently of her own volition. Inib-šina does not specify the location or occasion of her oracle; and she does not call her by name (as she did Šelebum). Will the *qammātum*'s title and affiliation with a prominent deity's cult satisfy Zimri-Lim? After reporting the content of her utterance—an initial, situation specific accusation, followed by a proverb whose contextualized meaning confirms and underscores it—as well as Dagan's promises to destroy the perpetrator, Inib-šina adds her own, anxiety-riddled directives:

---

125. In ARM 26 213, Queen Šiptu informs Zimri-Lim that Šelebum, an *assinnu*, became ecstatic in the temple of Annunitum, warned the king of an impending rebellion, and urged him to take protective measures.

126. Parker, "Official Attitudes," 54.

the king must protect himself, order a confirming (or disconfirming) omen before entering the city,[127] and end his reported, risky behavior.[128]

How does our saying achieve thematic, stylistic, and compositional finalization at the level of Inib-šina's letter to her king? It attains thematic finalization when Zimri-Lim: supplies its implicit, opposing proposition; identifies its theme; metaphorically applies that theme to Ibalpiel II's false offers of peace by correlating terms in the proverb situation with elements in the context situation; discerns its performance-specific meaning; grasps the analogy that the *qammātum* posits between the proverb and context situations; and concurs that her (Dagan's) words (as Inib-šina reports them) apply to him. It achieves stylistic finalization when, in dialogue with these processes, the saying's concise style and out-of-context content prompt him to interpret it within its generic (proverbial) framework and to consider its meaning in light of Dagan's promises of military victory. Finally, it achieves compositional finalization when the logic of Inib-šina's entire, epistolary argument convinces him both to reject Ibalpiel II's peace treaty and to follow her directives for the sake of his personal safety.[129]

---

127. Sasson emphasizes the priority of divination over other means of consulting deities at Mari in *From the Mari Archives*, 271 n. 113, 272 n. 114; see also Sasson, "Water Beneath Straw," 599 n. 1. Van der Toorn suggests that entering the unspecified city (likely Mari) would have been "tantamount to entering the treaty" (K. van der Toorn, "From the Oral to the Written: The Case of Old Babylonian Prophecy," in *Writings and Speech in Israelite and Ancient Near Eastern Prophecy* [ed. E. Ben Zvi and M. H. Floyd; SBLSymS 10; Atlanta: Society of Biblical Literature, 2000] 219–34, quote on p. 231 n. 61).

128. The meaning of *ištanarrar* is uncertain. Following Sasson, Heimpel translates "scintillates" (*Letters to the King*, 251; see Sasson, "Posting of Letters," 306; Sasson, "Water beneath Straw," 604; idem, *From the Mari Archives*, 264 [where he offers "He is ceaselessly moving about by himself" as an alternative reading]). But the exact meaning of "scintillates" in this context eludes me. Heimpel also cites J. Cooper's private suggestion, "acts precipitously" (*Letters to the King*, 251 n. 232). One is tempted to translate "vacillates"—Zimri-Lim wavers between his options—but ARM 26 213 suggests otherwise. In that letter, Queen Šiptu reports Annunitum's order that the king surround himself with faithful servants and not go "by yourself." Does Inib-šina also aim to limit his physical mobility?

129. In fact, Zimri-Lim decided to accept "peace with Ešnunna," which was destroyed some four years later (Sasson, "Water Beneath Straw," 608).

THEMATIC, STYLISTIC, AND COMPOSITIONAL FINALIZATION AT THE LEVEL OF THE *QAMMĀTUM*'S ORACLE AS SAMMETAR REPORTS IT

Content and Questions

Sammetar's lengthy letter bristles with interpretive cruxes, including seeming inconsistencies, unspecified speakers and audiences (divine and human), and references to (for us, obscure) cultic objects. He surely assumes that Zimri-Lim can construe its contents, but experts struggle to fill the gaps. Has Lupahum, an *āpilum* of Dagan of Tuttul whom Zimri-Lim dispatched to "entrust me to Dagan of Terqa," returned with an oracle he received in Tuttul? If so, do Sammetar and the king already know why his destination changed, or simply take it in stride, or does Sammetar intend his thrice-repeated reference to Tuttul to raise suspicions about how the *āpilum* fulfilled his mission? Lupahum receives Dagan's promise of sweeping ("wherever you go") military victories, but over what foes? After he returns from Tuttul, do he and Sammetar take the latter's "bolt" to Diritum, or does Lupahum travel to Dir alone? Who warns whom to strengthen defenses slackened due to misplaced trust in Ešnunna's peace initiative, and in whose name is Zimri-Lim warned not to pledge himself without first consulting god? I cite several experts' answers to these questions,[130] but my primary aim is to demonstrate, to the extent his letter allows, how our adage achieves thematic, stylistic, and compositional finalization in (his account of) the *qammātum*'s oracle, and within the tablet as a whole.[131]

When Sammetar informs his lord that Lupahum brought his "bolt" to Diritum, he also cites a prior occasion, when the same *āpilum* took a defective *šernum* to the goddess demanding that she repair it. His reason(s) for recalling the earlier incident is not immediately apparent. Is he reporting it to Zimri-Lim for the first time, or does it serve some other purpose? Moreover, he does not say if Diritum fixed the faulty *šernum*. Does the king already know of the success or failure of Lupahum's prior mission? If it succeeded, is Sammetar reminding Zimri-Lim that Dagan's intermediary has been, and continues to be, an effective emissary? On whose authority did the *āpilum* command Diritum to restore the *šernum*? Heimpel questions

---

130. Sasson suggests that "visiting Tuttul," the site of another temple to Dagan, may have "fulfilled this requirement" (ibid., 602). Heimpel proposes that Lupahum went first to Terqa, but the god sent him to Tuttul for his response (Heimpel, *Letters to the King*, 254 n. 2).

131. My earlier observations about how our saying per se achieves finalizations in these three dimensions remain the same.

that a "cleric" would both "blame [her] for the malfunctioning of an instrument of divination" and give her a direct order. Perhaps, he opines, Lupahum actually voiced his complaint to one of her "female cleric[s]."[132]

After rehearsing the earlier incident, Sammetar reports the results of Lupahum's most recent trip to Dir. Scholars disagree about who utters and receives the ensuing lines. Are they the *āpilum*'s words to Diritum, or hers to him? Sasson opts for the former: "Whatever its symbolic value, the bolt seems to have had its effect on Lupahum, for we find him admonishing the goddess: 'You may count on a peace treaty with the lord of Eshnunna . . . and therefore have become negligent; however, your watchmen should be strengthened more than previously.'"[133] If he is correct, then either the *āpilum* himself dares to reprimand and command Diritum, or he relays a communiqué from some other deity. Sasson allows that Lupahum's words are "strikingly reminiscent of warnings that the gods repeatedly sent to Zimri-Lim." But, he suggests, Sammetar may have altered them for rhetorical purposes, intending that the *āpilum*'s speech "hit its target [the king] by bouncing off the goddess."[134] For Heimpel, the warning not to trust the Ešnunakeans is Dagan's message, which is written on the bolts (pl.) Lupahum brings to Diritum.[135] He rebukes, accuses, and instructs her, but he is only repeating Dagan's invective.[136]

These same identity issues arise in conjunction with the following speech, where the specter of a "binding oath" with Ešnunna reappears. Durand concludes that Lupahum speaks to the goddess.[137] Parker, by contrast, attributes the words to Diritum, who enjoins the king (via Lupahum) not to enter the alliance without "inquiring of the god."[138] For Sasson and Heimpel, Lupahum reports Dagan's words to Sammetar.[139] In any event, this speech also evokes an earlier incident, when Benjaminite tribes tried to gain a foothold in Saggaratum. Sasson sets the scene for that episode:

---

132. Heimpel, *Letters to the King*, 254 n. 1. Parker attributes these words to Diritum in "Official Attitudes," 54.

133. Sasson, "Water beneath Straw," 601.

134. Ibid., 602.

135. Heimpel, *Letters to the King*, 254 n. 2.

136. Ibid, 254 n. 1.

137. J.-M. Durand, "Textes Prophétiques," *Archives Épistolaires de Mari* I/1, Archives Royales de Mari XXVI (Paris: Editions Recherche sur les Civilisations, 1988) 421–22.

138. Parker, "Official Attitudes," 59.

139. Sasson, "Water beneath Straw," 601; Heimpel, *Letters to the King*, 253.

No sooner had Zimri-Lim come to rule Mari than he was forced to battle the Benjaminites, a cluster of tribes that moved in and out of Mari territory. The struggle became even more dangerous to the stability of the new king's throne, especially because Eshnunna, a major power to the south of Mari, was supporting the tribal leaders. Zimri-Lim did succeed in defeating the tribes and was now contemplating accepting the peace overtures of Ibalpiel II, king of Eshnunna.[140]

Against this backdrop, citing Zimri-Lim's prior military success also evokes thoughts of Ibalpiel II's past, anti-Mari machinations. Moreover, it reminds the king that at the time, the speaker instructed him not to enter a treaty with the Benjaminites. Now, essentially the same advice applies. The rest of this speech makes its (ultimately) divine origins clear, since no *āpilum* could claim to suppress the Benjaminites. Again, by whose authority does Lupahum speak?[141] Sasson senses something amiss in what Sammetar does not say. Where, he wonders, is:

> ... any clear indication that the *āpilum* was echoing words that reached him through a dream, vision, or trance ... in a long and complex letter that recalls multiple oracles, we miss unequivocal references to formulas such as "thus speaks the god such and such." Moreover, not once is there any allusion to sending validating objects, such as fringes and hair from the clairvoyant ... Dagan may well have had confidence in Lupahum and ... trusted him to speak for him at many forums; yet on a decision with so much at stake, Zimri-Lim was being left to rely on Lupahum's ex cathedra statements.[142]

For this reason, he submits, Sammetar seconds Dagan's warning by reporting a "complementary prognostication" he received from Dagan of Terqa's *qammātum* the following day: "Beneath straw water ru[ns]. They keep on send[ing to you] messages of friendship, they even send their gods [to you], but in their hearts they are planning something else. The king should not take an oath without consulting God."

---

140. Sasson, "Water beneath Straw," 602.

141. In Sasson's view, Lupahum speaks for Dagan (ibid., 603); Heimpel attributes his speech to Diritum (*Letters to the King*, 254 n. 3).

142. Sasson, "Water beneath Straw," 603.

THEMATIC, STYLISTIC, AND COMPOSITIONAL FINALIZATIONS AT THE LEVEL OF THE *QAMMĀTUM*'S ORACLE IN SAMMETAR'S LETTER

If we assume, for a moment, that Sammetar reports the *qammātum*'s oracle *verbatim*, could he make sense of it? The answer to this question depends, in good measure, on whether the adage was part of Mari's proverbial stock—an issue its presence on three tablets cannot resolve. If she (Dagan) has coined the expression, or if he has never heard it before, then Sammetar might conclude that she deliberately uses a "deceptively opaque phrase," as Sasson insists, initiating her communiqué with an erroneous statement about how stagnant straw behaves in flowing water. But if he knows it to be a (norm-deviant) saying, then he enters Honeck's "problem recognition phase" of proverb cognition.[143] Since she claims to speak Dagan's words, he likely decides that the phrase merits "further thought"—its significance must be greater/other than its "literal meaning model" suggests. He therefore uses all available clues, including the proverb, to arrive at its "more preferred meaning." The absence of a situation-specific statement (of the sort that launches Inib-šina's version of the *qammātum*'s oracle) could impede Sammetar's ability to correlate the saying with a particular context situation. Nonetheless, her examples of their (ostensibly) amiable overtures, followed by Dagan's assessment of their underlying intent, enhances his chances of discerning its contextualized meaning: "their" irenic activities are merely the (concealed) weapons they wield to pursue a treacherous goal. Both he and Zimri-Lim may already possess the additional information needed fully to reveal "their" identity, especially if the tactics she unmasks match Ešnunna's ongoing efforts. In my view, however, we should reject our momentary assumption about the oracle's authenticity and ask, instead, how Sammetar may have shaped it to suit his professional status and strategic goals. "His" *qammātum*, for example, insists that the king consult god before taking a binding oath. Inib-šina's similar demand appears *after* she reports (her version of) the intermediary's words. But Sammetar again places a warning *cum* command to Zimri-Lim in the mouth of a deity and his spokesperson. He does not issue direct orders to his lord!

If Zimri-Lim heard only Sammetar's version of the *qammātum*'s oracle, apart from its epistolary context, could he supply the saying's implicit, opposing proposition, identify its theme, determine its contextualized meaning by correlating terms in the proverb situation with her examples of "their" current, political activities, accept the analogy she posits between

---

143. Honeck, *Proverb in Mind*, 129.

them (such that writing messages and sending their gods, while concealing their actual intentions, is analogous to floating straw remaining stationary as water flows beneath it), surmise that the antagonists are, in fact, Ibalpiel II's emissaries, and take seriously Dagan's command not to take a binding oath without first consulting god? If so, then our saying achieves thematic finalization at the level of her entire oracle.[144] Stylistic features, including its out-of-context semantic content, lack of indexical (contextualizing) terms, and brevity play their part by prompting the king to undertake these tasks within the proverb's genre-specific, interpretive framework. Her entire utterance attains compositional finalization when all aspects of each of these dimensions—theme, style, and logic—work in concert to convince Zimri-Lim that Dagan's communiqué is "the shape truth takes in the world" her proverb (performance) "envisions" and he rejects Ibalpiel II's peace treaty.[145]

Sammetar has more to say about the *qammātum* whose oracle he conveys, including the payment she receives. I consider the effects of those lines in the following analysis of how her oracle achieves finalizations within his entire letter.

THEMATIC, STYLISTIC, AND COMPOSITIONAL FINALIZATION AT THE LEVEL OF SAMMETAR'S LETTER

Content and Questions

Sammetar begins the body of his letter by recalling that Zimri-Lim sent Dagan of Tuttul's *āpilum* to entrust him to Dagan of Terqa. Since the king initiated this mission, his official need not state its specific aim. Did Zimri-Lim seek the deity's word about a potential peace treaty with Ešnunna? Though we cannot answer this question with certainty, ensuing, explicit references to that issue make the supposition plausible.[146] He then reports a victory oracle Lupahum received in Tuttul. Sweeping ("wherever you go") and hyperbolic ("battering ram and siege tower . . . will travel, as companions, by your side"), it assures Zimri-Lim that Dagan will war against his

---

144. Though Sasson avers that scholars who identify our adage as a warning rely "too much on Inibshina's own setting for it," he writes of "the *qammātum*'s warning" in Sammetar's version of her oracle in "Water beneath Straw," 605.

145. Seitel, *Powers of Genre*, 41.

146. Van der Toorn affirms this possibility: "In a private communication to Sammêtar, the *āpilum* who transmitted the words of the prophets . . . intimates that the oracle of victory should be interpreted as *advice against the treaty*" ("From the Oral to the Written," 231; emphasis mine).

foes.[147] The appearance of this oracle so early in Sammetar's letter sets a positive tone. Does it further function to dispel his qualms about the possible consequences of refusing Ibalpiel II's offer?[148] If so, then this is just the first of many rhetorical strategies Sammetar employs to structure portions of his communiqué in ways most likely to influence Zimri-Lim. Indeed, I propose that his epistle both reveals and conceals the importance he places on the king's decision. Though he opposes the alliance, he couches his opinion in carefully wrought words in order to appear objective and show all due deference to his lord.

Sammetar's recall of Lupahum's earlier, likely successful trip to Diritum's temple inclines the king also to view favorably the results of his most recent time in Dir. While the speaker's and audience's identities are, for us, unclear, the following lines contain his letter's first explicit reference to the prospective peace treaty with Ešnunna—an admonition that weakened defenses occasioned by misplaced trust should be strengthened even more than before. Here, as noted, Sammetar places the warning in the mouth of Dagan's spokesperson (or Diritum). This speech is followed by a second, which also opposes taking a binding oath with Ibalpiel II. It too evokes an earlier incident (Ibalpiel II's support of the Benjaminites' attempted land grab in Saggaratum) before urging Zimri-Lim to consult god prior to forming an alliance. And again, these are not Sammetar's words—at least, not as he presents them.

Reporting an oracle he purportedly hears from a *qammātum* the next day allows Sammetar *explicitly* to add Dagan of Terqa's voice to the warnings against a treaty with Ešnunna his letter has relayed. Does he wish to fill the apparent void created when Lupahum returned from Zimri-Lim's mission with an oracle he received in *Tuttul*? Though her words do not explicitly identify Ešnunna's emissaries as the perpetrators of deception, his placement of her oracle on the heels of two earlier, negative references to Ibalpiel II's overtures invites that interpretation. In any case, his version of the *qammātum*'s pronouncement depends on its entire epistolary context far more than does Inib-šina's.

In summary, Sammetar appears to construct a subtle, complex, and sophisticated argument against entering an alliance with Ešnunna, encouraging, but nowhere instructing (in words he claims for himself) Zimri-Lim to reject Ibalpiel II's self-serving attempts to enlist Mari as an ally. To be

---

147. Sasson's translation in "Water beneath Straw," 602.

148. Parker suggests that Sammetar omits Dagan's promises of Ešnunna's destruction from Inib-šina's more authentic account of the *qammātum*'s oracle because he does not want Zimri-Lim to be "overconfident" (Parker, "Official Attitudes," 59). But the presence of a victory oracle early in his letter argues against this view.

sure, he also reports the economic reward/compensation the *qammātum* requests and receives—a garment and a nose ring.[149] For Sasson, this payment is "a sure sign that she feels her mission completed" (though, according to Sammetar, she resumes it the following day in the temple of Belet-ekallim).[150] Parker doubts that Sammetar was required to report disbursements of royal goods (though we cannot exclude that possibility). In his view, her requests "disclose major personal interests,"[151] so Sammetar takes the "exceptional" step of including "all circumstances that [might] be pertinent" to the king's assessment of her oracle.[152] Including them might raise a question in Zimri-Lim's mind about her motives. But it is equally likely that he includes their financial transaction in order to portray their interaction as dispassionately as possible.

Sammetar could add his personal assessment of the Ešnunna treaty option at this point.[153] After all, the rest of his letter addresses an entirely different matter; and he is not averse to stating his opinion, even when doing so means (respectfully) declining to act as his lord expects. If he knows that Zimri-Lim is favorably disposed toward Ibalpiel II's peace offer, however, he may think it unwise to express his view *directly*. Let members of the royal family chastise and issue orders to the king. Sammetar exerts his influence by means of more subtle strategies. Throughout the tablet, he has let others—divine and human—do the talking. Now, he commends the messages he has received and reported to the king's consideration, expressing confidence that Zimri-Lim will act in accord with his great ("royal") majesty.[154] Sasson reports that Sammetar died "a few months later," but not before inquiring about how "properly to welcome Eshnunna's delegation."

---

149. See Heimpel, "nose-rope" (*Letters to the King of Mari*, 254 n. 3); van der Toorn, "bracelet" ("From the Oral to the Written," 231).

150. Sasson, "Water beneath Straw," 603.

151. Parker, "Official Attitudes," 56.

152. Ibid., 52.

153. Koch notes the absence of the correspondents' opinions in portions of their letters that "quote" prophecies and the presence of same at the ends of their letters in "Die Briefe 'Profetischen' Inhalts aus Mari: Bemerkungen zu Gattung und Sitz im Leben," *Ugarit-Forschungen* 4 (1972) 53–77; esp. 72 n. 3.

154. Sasson, "Water beneath Straw," 601.

THEMATIC, STYLISTIC, AND COMPOSITIONAL FINALIZATIONS AT THE LEVEL OF THE ORACLE KANISAN QUOTES FROM KIBRI-DAGAN'S LETTER

Content and Questions

Kanisan's letter to Zimri-Lim is shorter than Sammetar's, but it too puzzles experts at points. His dispatch (sans four lines lost to breakage) ostensibly includes an excerpt from a letter he received from Kibri-Dagan, governor of Mari's Terqa district, and possibly his father (and Sammetar's son).

Together, the reference to Dagan's temple (likely in Terqa, whence Kibri-Dagan writes), our proverb's presence, and the deity's promise of military victory inclines modern (and ancient?) audiences to elucidate the terse oracle Kibri-Dagan relays by importing details from Sammetar and/or Inib-šina's letters.[155] Sasson states, for example, that Kanisan "cites his father's quotation of the *qammātum*'s iteration of Dagan's original words." In his view, all three (four) letters report versions of "one prophecy, delivered by a single divine messenger."[156] Yet Kibri-Dagan says nothing of a *qammātum*, or of a looming peace treaty with Ešnunna.[157] He only mentions a *muḫḫûm*, and the relationship between the oracle he transmits and the ecstatic's repeated "declamation" is uncertain.[158] For van der Toorn, by contrast, the *qammātum* plays a secondary role. Dagan's prophets at Terqa oppose a peace alliance with Ešnunna; and knowing that Zimri-Lim is inclined to accept it, they undergo "an outburst of frenzied activity."[159] Our saying, the "core" of their oracles, likely originated with the *muḫḫûm*, though the deity's other intermediaries augment it with promises of victory over Ešnunna's

---

155. Recall, however, that we do not know the order in which these three letters received Zimri-Lim's attention.

156. Sasson, "Water Beneath Straw," 600. So too Durand: "Il n'est pas impossible que *toutes* les citations de l'expression aient comme source le discours de la prêtresse-qammatum," though "le rapport entre la prophétie et le *muḫḫûm* (I. 15) ne soit pas clair" (*AEM* I/1, 405). In Parker's view, "[t]he *qammātum* and *muḫḫûm* cannot be equated, but both address "the same situation in the name of the same god with the same message" ("Official Attitudes," 58).

157. For these reasons, Heimpel concludes that the *muḫḫûm*'s and *qammātum*'s oracles are not "identical" and the former is unrelated to a potential Ešnunna alliance. In his view, "the image of water beneath chaff was common" (*Letters to the King*, 255).

158. For Sasson, Kibri-Dagan's reference to the *muḫḫûm* concerns "another incident altogether," though he allows that the source of the oracle he reports might have become "garbled" by this point ("Water Beneath Straw," 605 n. 15). Heimpel notes that the ecstatic could be either male or female (*Letters to the King*, 255 n. 246).

159. Van der Toorn, "From the Oral to the Written," 232.

ruler.¹⁶⁰ A *qammātum* may relay her oracle(s) to others (e.g., Inib-šina, Sammetar), embellishing it with "exegesis."¹⁶¹ But she neither acts "at her own initiative," nor proclaims an oracle she received directly from Dagan.¹⁶² Both experts' explanations cannot be equally correct. Yet each testifies to the challenges scholars of antiquity face when available evidence can be construed plausibly in more than one way.

I begin by identifying—to the degree Kibri-Dagan and Kanisan's letters allow—how our saying achieves thematic, stylistic, and compositional finalization at the level of the oracle Kibri-Dagan reports to his son. Unlike Inib-šina's version, this utterance has no initial, situation-specific statement. Like hers, however, it promises military victory. Like Sammetar's account, it begins with the proverb. But unlike his, the oracle includes no illustrative examples of the context situation to which the adage's theme is applied. Indeed, the only explicit clue to its contextualized meaning is the ensuing assurance of victory over Zimri-Lim's foes.

Earlier in this essay, I observed that our saying's theme need not express a sense of hazardous deception or a negative notion of hiding. In Inib-šina and Sammetar's letters, its contextualized meaning conveys both. Based solely on Kibri-Dagan's report, however, a different construal is possible: *some* situation seems settled, for good or ill, but Dagan is upending it, delivering Zimri-Lim's enemies into his hand. In this scenario, our saying might, or might not, *warn* its audience that things are not what they seem. It could, in fact, signal an unanticipated, positive outcome where none is expected. To be sure, this option can seem strained, especially to scholars primed by our adage's presence to apply Dagan's utterance to the context of Ibalpiel II's offer of a peace treaty. If we remove that situation-specific, hermeneutical lens from our eyes, however, we better perceive the proverb's performance potential in a variety of settings.

Were Zimri-Lim to hear only the brief oracle Kibri-Dagan transmits, sans awareness of its context of application, he might be more confused than enlightened. In van der Toorn's view, however, the king awaits such reports. Before concluding a peace treaty with Ešnunna, he dispatches multiple emissaries, including Lupahum, to "principal cult centers of his kingdom";¹⁶³ and he expects his officials to convey the results of their queries. Kanisan's letter is just one such response.

---

160. Ibid. But Kanisan's letter does not mention Ibalpiel II or Ešnunna.

161. Ibid.

162. Ibid., 231.

163. Van der Toorn, "From the Oral to the Written," 230. To my knowledge, however, we have no other epistolary evidence of responses to the king's query.

If either (or both) of Sammetar and Inib-šina's letters has already reached Zimri-Lim, then our proverb's appearance in Kibri-Dagan's missive reinforces what Zimri-Lim takes to be its context situation. After all, in their epistles, the saying speaks to Ešnunna's peace efforts. Yet even if Kanisan's report reaches him first, the king likely knows the typical *sorts of circumstances* to which our adage is applied. Proverbs sum up and judge context situations, but they also invite their audiences to perceive *this* circumstance as *that* type of circumstance. As Shapin observes, they are "resources for . . . making situations recognizable as situations of *a certain kind*."[164] If our saying is frequently deployed to name circumstances fraught with concealed dangers, then its presence alone signals to Zimri-Lim that the deity opposes entering a treaty with Ibalpiel II. The following promise of military success—which, van der Toorn reminds us, "is not the same as peace through alliance"—expressly states Dagan's decision to make war, not peace.[165] Our adage achieves thematic finalization within the entire oracular utterance when Kibri-Dagan, Kanisan, and Zimri-Lim supply its implicit, opposing proposition, identify its theme, apply that theme metaphorically to its (unstated, but tacit) context situation by correlating its terms with Ibalpiel II's seemingly irenic overtures (= floating, stationary straw) and his hidden, self-serving intentions (= water running beneath it), and recognize that Dagan opposes the king's preferred path to peace. Even the ensuing victory oracle is not good news to Zimri-Lim if he aspires to end hostilities between the two kingdoms by making peace, not war.

Our saying achieves stylistic finalization within Dagan's entire oracle by succinctly asserting a norm deviant statement.[166] For Sasson, the arrival of yet another (actually, two) reports containing the same "deceptively opaque phrase" leaves Zimri-Lim even more "perplexed" than before.[167] But if each man, including the king, knows it to be part of Mari's stock of sayings, then its presence prompts him to interpret it within a genre-appropriate framework in which verity is not a prerequisite. Its assertion is erroneous, but its proverbial status is not imperiled. The saying's "literal meaning model" alone does not convey what Dagan intends to say, though it constitutes an example of its abstract, or figurative meaning.[168] As Honeck

---

164. Shapin, "Proverbial Economies," 739 (emphasis mine).

165. Van der Toorn, "From the Oral to the Written," 230.

166. Sasson points appreciatively to another of the oracle's stylistic features: the "obvious play" between *mû illakū*, "water comes, goes [flows]" and the ensuing victory oracle's *illikma ilum*, "He came, my lord's god" (Water beneath Straw," 605 n. 15).

167. Ibid. Sasson assumes that the king has already heard the letters from Inib-šina and Sammetar by the time Kanisan's report arrives.

168. See above, n. 102.

explains, however, that model is only the beginning of the proverb cognition process.¹⁶⁹ Finally, our saying achieves compositional finalization within the intermediary's entire utterance when its audiences both grasp and take seriously Dagan's negative assessment of the prospective peace alliance and his promise to grant Zimri-Lim victory over his (should be) enemies.

Kanisan is not content to rest with the terse oracle Kibri-Dagan reports. After signaling its end ("This is what Kibri-Dagan wrote to me"), he—unlike Sammetar—*directly* offers his king advice about how best to proceed. Because the tablet is damaged, we cannot recapture the totality of his remarks. But the extant lines include a familiar warning.

THEMATIC, STYLISTIC, AND COMPOSITIONAL FINALIZATIONS AT THE LEVEL OF KANISAN'S LETTER TO ZIMRI-LIM

Content and Questions

After the customary identifications of addressee ("my lord") and dispatcher ("your servant Kanisan"), Kanisan turns to the letter from Kibri-Dagan. Does he quote from it *verbatim*? Has he omitted additional elements (e.g., Kibri-Dagan's initial and/or concluding statements) that might cause others to interpret his report differently? As is, the excerpt reads like a single link in a chain of communications (written, oral, or both) between insiders. Indeed, Kibri-Dagan might well be responding to a question like, "Have you heard the words uttered in Dagan's temple?" If so, such a query could constitute a routine attempt to stay abreast of affairs in one of a major deity's temples. More likely, however, it seeks specific information on a tacit topic. Does he omit the details scholars crave because repeating them to his intended audience(s) is either unnecessary, or ill-advised, or both?

Did Kibri-Dagan visit Dagan's temple in Terqa to carry out a directive from Zimri-Lim? Did he listen to the oracle he reports with an ear to its pertinence for the pending peace treaty with Ešnunna?¹⁷⁰ He mentions the *muḫḫûm* only *after* relaying that oracle's contents; and we cannot know if the ecstatic uttered any portion of the divine message he transmits to Kanisan. If he did not, however, then Kibri-Dagan's mention of his presence and recurring utterances is all the more curious.

---

169. See above.

170. In Parker's view, the original oracle (best preserved in Inib-šina's letter) was not so "vague"; either Kibri-Dagan or Kanisan has "reduced it to its mere essence" ("Official Attitudes," 58).

Inib-šina urges Zimri-Li not to enter the city without first seeking additional, divine guidance. Sammetar conveys much the same advice twice, albeit through the words of divine intermediaries. Kanisan speaks for himself, but he does not issue an order as such. Instead, he couches his counsel in terms suggestive of its *general* applicability: in this situation and all others in which the wellbeing of the king and his kingdom is at stake, he should not tire of ordering extispicies.

Kanisan has more to say, though we cannot recover it. His final, extant words urge Zimri-Lim not to delay: he must make his offerings and go! Does his communiqué achieve compositional (logical) finalization? Said differently, did it (perhaps in conjunction with the other three reports) convince Zimri-Lim further to pursue divine inquiries by other means? If so, then Kanisan's letter also achieves its goal—in part, at least—though Zimri-Lim was not dissuaded from entering an alliance with Ešnunna.

CONCLUSION

The prospect of entering a peace treaty with Ibalpiel II was no small matter in Mari. It spawned communications between the divine and human realms, as well as written reports from Zimri-Lim's officials. Even if our proverb were not present in Inib-šina and Sammetar's letters, experts could easily place them within the same orbit, since both cite the duplicity of Ešnunna's overtures, and each refers to Dagan of Terqa's *qammātum*. Sans our saying, would they as readily situate Kibri-Dagan and Kanisan's reports within that same context?

Unlike my late colleague and dear friend, Simon Parker, my primary interest in these letters lies in what I have argued is a popular proverb—more precisely, an ancient example of Honeck's norm deviant saying. Though the HB is my disciplinary home, my long-lived fascination with adages and their performance potential in social interaction situations has made these texts too tantalizing to resist. Against Sasson's insistence that this "prophetic phrase" baffled its audiences, I have demonstrated how two scholars' analytical approaches—one rooted in an ethnographer's etic instruments, and the other in a cognitive scientist's efforts to illumine our minds' problem-solving processes—equip us to understand how even illogical and factually inaccurate sayings can "make sense" of the context situations to which their themes are applied metaphorically. Once we grasp that key concept, both the presence and the functions of our proverb in each epistle become clear.

Dr. Lou Silberman was fond of telling his doctoral students at Vanderbilt University that people who cannot live with uncertainty should not go into biblical studies. The same advice surely applies to would-be Mari specialists, since the tablets from its royal archives routinely generate as many questions as answers. In analyzing each letter, I have occasionally indulged in speculation, knowing that Mari experts must do likewise and will adjudicate my conclusions. If this essay convinces them, and others, to consider how proverb studies might inform their research projects, I will count it a success.

7

The Birth Announcement
A Masoretic Note on Naming[1]

David Marcus

Although the Bible knows of some cases where fathers name children,[2] when a mother is described as having given birth to a child (וַתֵּלֶד בֵּן "she bore a son") it is she who names the child, not the father.[3] This rule is explicitly stated in a Masoretic note which also points out three notable exceptions, with Er (Gen 38:3), Gershom (Exod 2:22), and Beriah (1 Chr 7:23). In all three cases both ancient and modern scholars read differently and emend the text, but the Masoretic note cautions against any such change. According to the Masorah, despite the fact that in all three cases the

---

1. *Author's note*: The initial title of this paper is an homage to a distinguished colleague with whom I had the pleasure of working under his editorship on the Ugaritic translation project *Ugaritic Narrative Poetry* (ed. M. S. Smith and S. B. Parker; SBLWAW 9; Atlanta: Scholars, 1997). Simon was also the one who inspired this paper with his essay on "The Birth Announcement," in *Ascribe to the Lord: Biblical and Other Studies in Memory of Peter C. Craigie* (ed. L. Eslinger and G. Taylor; JSOTSup 67; Sheffield: JSOT Press, 1988) 133–49.

2. The leading examples are: Adam names his son Seth (Gen 5:3), who in turn names his son Enosh (Gen 4:26), Lemech names Noah, Abraham names both Ishmael (Gen 16:15) and Isaac (21:3), Isaac names Jacob (Gen 25:26), Jacob renames Benjamin (Gen 35:18), Judah names Perez and Zerah (Gen 38:29–30), and Joseph names Manasseh (Gen 41:51).

3. The latest article on this topic is by E. J. Bridge, "A Mother's Influence: Mothers Naming Children in the Hebrew Bible," *VT* 64 (2014) 389–400.

text says וַתֵּלֶד בֵּן "she bore a son," it was Judah who named Er, it was Moses who named Gershom, and Ephraim who named Beriah.

The Masoretic comment that outlines the rule with the three exceptions is given in a Mm note at 1 Chr 7:23.[4] The note reads:[5]

Throughout the Bible (the norm) is that (whenever it is written) "she gives birth" (then) "she names" (the child)	כל קריה ותלד ותקרא
apart from three cases where it is written "she gives birth" (then) "he names" (the child):	ב מ׳ג׳ ותלד ויקרא
Er, Gershom, (and) Beriah of Chronicles.	ער גרשום בריעה דדברי ימים
Their mnemonic is עגב	ע׳ג׳ב׳ סימ׳

The Masoretic note informs us that normally when a mother is described as having given birth[6] it is she who names the child, but that there are three exceptions to this rule: the cases of Er (Gen 38:3), Gershom (Exod 2:22), and Beriah (1 Chr 7:23).

In these three cases, despite the fact that it is stated that the mother gave birth (וַתֵּלֶד), nevertheless it is the father who names the child. To help remember these three occurrences, a mnemonic is provided consisting of the first letters of these three names Er, Gershom, and Beriah (עגב): the ע for Er (ער), the ג for Gershom (גרשם), and the ב for Beriah (בריעה).

An examination of birth narratives in the Bible shows that the Masoretic note is quite correct in its assertion that, where the text describes the mother as having given birth (וַתֵּלֶד), it is she who names the child. This naming is described nineteen times either with the formulation וַתִּקְרָא

---

4. In the Leningrad Codex, fol. 332r bottom left.

5. The note also appears in a much abbreviated form at Gen 38:3 on fol. 23v top left where it reads: ער . גרשם . בריעה ויקרא את שמו ג׳ "The phrase וַיִּקְרָא אֶת־שְׁמוֹ occurs three times, with Er (Gen 38:3), Gershom (Exod 2:22), (and) Beriah (1 Chr 7:23)."

6. In the version in the Rabbinic Bible (at Gen 38:3 and in the Mf) the note is expanded to include the word "she conceives" (ותהר). The note reads: כל ותהר ותלד ותקרא במ׳ג ויקר׳ עג״ב סי. But, whereas the combination ותהר ותלד applies to two of our three cases, that of Er (Gen 38:3), and of Beriah (1 Chr 7:23), it does not apply to the case of Gershom in Exod 2:22, where the text reads: ותלד בן ויקרא את שמו גרשם, without a mention of a preceding conception.

אֶת־שְׁמוֹ,[7] or without the definite article וַתִּקְרָא שְׁמוֹ.[8] Some of the prominent mothers that are described as having given birth (וַתֵּלֶד) and then naming their children are: Eve who names Seth (Gen 4:25),[9] Leah who names Reuben, Simeon, Naphtali, Issachar and Zebulun (Gen 29:32–33, 30:8, 30:18, 30:20), Rachel who names Joseph (Gen 30:24) and Ben Oni, prior to his being renamed Benjamin by Jacob (Gen 35:18), Manoah's wife who names Samson (Judg 13:24), Hannah who names Samuel (1 Sam 1:20), and Bathsheba who names Solomon (2 Sam 12:24).[10]

Clearly, as the Masoretic note indicates, the naming of a child by a mother (וַתִּקְרָא [אֶת] שְׁמוֹ) after she is described as having given birth (וַתֵּלֶד) is the norm in the Bible.

The three exceptions, noted by the Masorah, where the mother is said to have given birth (וַתֵּלֶד), but where the father names the child are: Er (Gen 38:3), Gershom (Exod 2:22), and Beriah (1 Chr 7:23). In all three cases some ancient and modern scholars read differently, or emend the text to וַתִּקְרָא "she called" to conform to the norm.

At Gen 38:3, Er is the only one of the three sons born to Judah's wife to be named by him. The text reads: וַתַּהַר וַתֵּלֶד בֵּן וַיִּקְרָא אֶת־שְׁמוֹ עֵר "she conceived and bore a son, and he named him Er."

The naming of the other two sons, Onan and Shelah whose births are described in the immediately following verses 4 and 5, are by Judah's wife.[11] The text of these verses read: וַתַּהַר עוֹד וַתֵּלֶד בֵּן וַתִּקְרָא אֶת־שְׁמוֹ אוֹנָן "she conceived again and bore a son, and she named him Onan," and וַתֹּסֶף עוֹד וַתֵּלֶד בֵּן וַתִּקְרָא אֶת־שְׁמוֹ שֵׁלָה "once again she conceived and bore a son, and she named him Shelah."

---

7. The phrase וַתִּקְרָא אֶת־שְׁמוֹ occurs ten times at Gen 4:25; 30:11; 30:13; 30:20; 30:24; 38:4; 38:5; Judg 13:24; 1 Sam 1:20; 2 Sam 12:24. The number is noted in Mp notes at Gen 30:13; 30:24; and the list is given in the Mm at Gen 30:24 (on fol. 18r), and at Judg 13:24 (on fol. 14v), see also Gérard E. Weil, *Massorah Gedolah* (Rome: Pontifical Biblical Press, 1971) §215.

8. The phrase וַתִּקְרָא שְׁמוֹ occurs nine times at Gen 19:37; 19:38; 29:32; 29:33; 30:8; 30:18; 35:18; Exod 2:10; 1 Chr 7:16. The number is listed in Mp notes at Gen 29:33; Exod 2:10; 1 Chr 7:16, and the list is given in C. D. Ginsburg, *The Massorah Compiled from Manuscripts, Alphabetically and Lexically Arranged* (1880–1905; repr., New York: Ktav, 1975) 2, ק, §264.

9. Seth curiously enough is also named by Adam in Gen 5:3.

10. There are two traditions regarding the naming of Solomon in this passage. In one it is Bathsheba who does the naming. This is the *qarê* (וַתִּקְרָא), and it is adopted by the LXX, Peshitta, and Targum. In another it is David who does the naming and this is the *katib* (ויקרא).

11. Judah's wife is unnamed in the text, though the Septuagint and Peshitta name her Bath-Shua; see A. Tal, *Biblia Hebraica Quinta: Genesis* (Stuttgart: Deutsche Bibelgesellschaft, 2016) 171.

Because of the closeness of these birth narratives, and because the last two namings have the regular feminine formula וַתִּקְרָא אֶת־שְׁמוֹ, a number of Hebrew mss,[12] and ancient versions including the Septuagint (καὶ ἐκάλεσεν),[13] Samaritan (ותקרא),[14] *Targum Neofiti* (וקרת), and *Targum Pseudo-Jonathan* (וקראת)[15] read here an underlying וַתִּקְרָא assimilating וַיִּקְרָא to וַתִּקְרָא of the following verses. Similarly, a number of modern commentators also argue for an original reading of וַתִּקְרָא.[16] The situation is summed up in the 2001 *Etz Hayim: Torah and Commentary*: "he named him: In some manuscripts, as well as in the Samaritan version and in an Aramaic translation, the reading here is 'she named'—that is, the mother named all three sons."[17]

At Exod 2:22, where Moses names Gershom, the text reads: וַתֵּלֶד בֵּן וַיִּקְרָא אֶת־שְׁמוֹ גֵּרְשֹׁם כִּי אָמַר גֵּר הָיִיתִי בְּאֶרֶץ נָכְרִיָּה׃ פ "she bore a son whom he named Gershom, for he said, 'I have been a stranger in a foreign land.'"

Here one fourteenth-century Hebrew ms. reads וַתִּקְרָא אֶת־שְׁמוֹ "she named him" instead of וַיִּקְרָא אֶת־שְׁמוֹ "he named him,"[18] and similarly, one ancient version, *Targum Neofiti* (וקרת) reads an underlying form וַתִּקְרָא for the Hebrew וַיִּקְרָא.

At 1 Chr 7:23, where Ephraim names Beriah, the text reads: וַתַּהַר וַתֵּלֶד בֵּן וַיִּקְרָא אֶת־שְׁמוֹ בְּרִיעָה כִּי בְרָעָה הָיְתָה בְּבֵיתוֹ "she conceived and bore a son, and he named him Beriah, because a calamity occurred in his house."

---

12. See C. D. Ginsburg, *Torah, Neviim, Ketuvim* (1908; repr. Jerusalem: Makor, 1970) ad loc., and Tal, *Biblia Hebraica Quinta: Genesis*, ad loc.

13. Though the Greek verb is indeterminate it most likely refers to its feminine antecedent, as the New English Translation of the Septuagint translates "and after she had conceived she bore a son and called his name Er"; see J. W. Wevers, *Notes on the Greek Text of Genesis* (SBLSCS 35; Atlanta: Society of Biblical Literature 1993) 632. Similarly, the Vulgate's reading *vocavitque* "called" must refer to Bath-Shua as the Douay-Rheims translation takes it: "and she conceived, and bore a son, and called his name Her."

14. A. Tal, *The Samaritan Pentateuch: Edited According to MS 6 (c) of the Shekhem Synagogue* (Tel Aviv: Tel Aviv University Press, 1994) 38.

15. The Targums may be accessed on line through the Comprehensive Aramaic Lexicon project http://cal1.cn.huc.edu/index.html.

16. C. Westermann, *Genesis 37–50* (Continental Commentaries; Minneapolis: Augsburg, 1986) 48, n 3a; Hamilton, *Victor P. Hamilton, The Book of Genesis Chapters 18–50* (NICOT; Grand Rapids: Eerdmans, 1995) 430 n. 5; J. A. Emerton, "Some Problems in Genesis xxxviii," *VT* 25 (1975) 339; and many early commentators such as J. Skinner, *A Critical and Exegetical Commentary on Genesis* (ICC; Edinburgh: T. & T. Clark, 1930) 451.

17. *Etz Hayim: Torah and Commentary* (ed. D. L. Lieber; New York: The Rabbinical Assembly, 2001) 233.

18. Ginsburg, *Torah, Neviim, Ketuvim*, ad loc.

Here some Hebrew mss[19] read וַתִּקְרָא, and various Targum mss,[20] and the Peshitta read וקרת, which reflects the underlying Hebrew feminine וַתִּקְרָא. Also one modern commentator [21] and the NJPS prefer the feminine reading.[22] Thus the NJPS translates "and she named him Beriah." All these ancient and modern commentators assimilate the feminine וַתִּקְרָא to the more usual וַיִּקְרָא form.

But the Masorah cautions against any such change, not only implicitly in its note at 1 Chr 7:23, but also explicitly by the fact that in some mss three passages are listed as *sebhirin* cases, that is, as passages whereby a different reading might seem to avoid a difficulty in the text, but the reader is warned not to adopt such a reading but to maintain the received text.[23] At these three references, of Gen 38:3, Exod 2:22, and 1 Chr 7:23, there are *sebhirin* notes that וַתִּקְרָא has been mistakenly suggested to be read instead of וַיִּקְרָא.[24] At all these passages Norzi (Minhat Shai) comments on the form וַיִּקְרָא: חד מן ג דסבירי ותקרא וקרי ויקרא that it is "one of three cases where it is thought (mistakenly) to read וַתִּקְרָא, but it is read וַיִּקְרָא."[25]

Thus, according to the Masorah, it was Judah who named his firstborn Er, it was Moses who named his first-born Gershom, and Ephraim who named his new son Beriah. This insight of the Masoretes is seemingly supported by the context of the passages under discussion.

---

19. See G. B. De Rossi, *Variae lectiones Veteris Testamenti librorum, ex immensa manuscriptorum editorumque codicum congerie haustae et ad Samaritanum textum, ad vetustissimas versiones, ad accuratiores sacrae criticae fontes ac leges examinatae* (vol. 4 of *Libri Psalmi, Proverbia, Job, Daniel, Ezras, Nehemias, Chronica seu Paralipomena, cum dissertatione praeliminaria de hujus collationis praestantia, utilitate, usu, et appendice additionum*; Parmae, 1784–88; repr. Amsterdam: Philo, 1969–70) 174.

20. See J. S. McIvor, *The Targum of Chronicles* (ArBib 19; Collegeville, MN: Liturgical, 1994) 74 n. q.

21. G. N. Knoppers, *1 Chronicles 1–9* (AB 12; New York: Doubleday, 2003) 456.

22. However, the 1917 JPS version translated "he named him."

23. *Sebhirin* notes are found scattered in various mss throughout Mp and Mm notes, and a number have been collected together in Ginsburg, *The Massorah*, 2, 62–33§§ ס, and S. Frensdorff, *The Massorah Magna* (1876; repr., New York: Ktav, 1968) 369–73.

24. See Ginsburg, *Torah, Neviim, Ketuvim*, at Gen 38:3, Exod 2:22, and 1 Chr 7:23.

25. For Gen 38:3 and Exod 2:22, see Z. Betser, *Minhat Shay on the Torah* (Jerusalem: World Union of Jewish Studies, 2005) 133, 161; and for 1 Chr 7:23, see his remarks at the back of most editions of *Miqra'ot Gedolot*. This Masoretic caution no doubt explains Weil's addition at all three of these references in his Mp notes in *BHS*, and in his transcription of the Masorah magna note in his *Massorah Gedolah* (§280) of the phrase דמטעֵ [דמטעין], that is, in these three cases where the text reads וַיִּקְרָא אֶת־שְׁמוֹ one is liable to make an error. And the error that one might make is reading the subject of this phrase as a feminine form (וַתִּקְרָא) as some versions and modern scholars do, rather than the masculine one in the text (וַיִּקְרָא).

In the most obvious of these cases, Moses, not Zipporah, named Gershom because of his own particular circumstances: כִּי אָמַר גֵּר הָיִיתִי בְּאֶרֶץ נָכְרִיָּה "for he said, 'I have been a stranger in a foreign land'" (Exod 2:22). Similarly, in the case of the naming of Beriah by Ephraim he, not his wife, named his son because of the tragic events in his life. Apparently Ephraim's other sons had been killed in an unsuccessful raid chasing cattle from the men of Gath (1 Chr 7:21), and Ephraim was forced to start a new family. Ephraim named the first born of that new family Beriah, a name which may mean something like "outstanding,"[26] but which in this context is given a folk etymology playing on the word רָעָה "calamity" or "misfortune."[27] Hence by taking the initial ב of the name as a preposition, בְּרִיעָה is taken to mean "in misfortune." This etymology clearly reflects the disaster that had occurred to his house, as the text relates וַיִּקְרָא אֶת־שְׁמוֹ בְּרִיעָה כִּי בְרָעָה הָיְתָה בְּבֵיתוֹ: "he named him Beriah because a calamity occurred in his house." Thus Ephraim, like Moses, named his son because of his particular circumstances. He named his son Beriah בְּרִיעָה "in misfortune" because of the calamity that had occurred to him.

Unlike these cases of Moses and Beriah, the naming of Er by Judah is not followed by any etiology, nor is it related to any particular circumstance that we know of. The name itself means "awake," "watchful," which is quite a positive one. However, just as with Beriah, though this is not stated in the text, there is an implied correspondence of the consonants of his name with the word רַע "evil," "calamity," which would represent a simple metathesis of עֵר to רַע. This supposition is all the more likely since the unspecified crime for which he was condemned by God (38:7) is termed a רַע (וַיְהִי עֵר בְּכוֹר יְהוּדָה רַע בְּעֵינֵי יְהוָה וַיְמִתֵהוּ יְהוָה) "But Er, Judah's first-born, was displeasing [רַע] to the Lord, and the Lord took his life"). The mention here that Er was Judah's first-born (בְּכוֹר יְהוּדָה) is significant. In all the three cases of naming that we have discussed the father names his first-born. Moses names Gershom his first born, Ephraim names Beriah, the first-born of his newly created family, and here Judah names Er, his first-born. While there are parallels to this naming procedure elsewhere in the Bible, as with Abraham, who names both Ishmael, his first-born of Hagar, and also Isaac his first-born of Sarah, and of Joseph who names his first-born Manasseh (41:51), there are also examples to the contrary as evidenced by Leah naming Reuben, Jacob's first-born, and Manoah's wife naming Samson, Manoah's

---

26. HALOT, 157. The name Beriah is found elsewhere, as a son of Asher (Gen 46:17; Num 26:44–45; 1 Chr 7:30–31), as a Benjaminite (1 Chr 8:13, 13:16), and as a Levite (1 Chr 23:10–11).

27. Another similar playful aetiological name in Chronicles is that of Yabez (יַעְבֵּץ) derived by metathesis from עֹצֶב "sorrow" (1 Chr 4:9).

first-born. So the Masoretic note is obviously not dealing with all first-born namings, only those where it is specifically stated that the mother gave birth (וַתֵּלֶד בֵּן). In these cases the mother always names the child apart from the three exceptional cases, highlighted in the Masoretic note, namely those of Er, Gershom, and Beriah.

8

1 Kings 13

A Story of Two Prophets United

HERBERT B. HUFFMON

FIRST KINGS 13 IS an extraordinary story. It includes devastating judgment, miraculous healing, reversals of role, internal prophetic deception, a tea party gone awry, animal behavior that is as strange as Balaam's talking ass, an old, "lying" prophet from Bethel who subsequently heaps praise on a man of God from Judah who had proven to be a wavering, somewhat gullible colleague, to whom the old Bethel prophet had conveyed God's judgment of an approaching death. Yet the Bethel prophet has the man of God from Judah buried in his own tomb, instructing his sons that he himself should be buried there with the man of God from Judah. They should set "my bones beside his bones" (v. 31).

This emphasis on contrasts helps account for the focus by many commentators on the theme of obedience to God, a theme that can otherwise be expressed as trusting your own experience, a theme that is clearly present in the story. This evidence as to divine revelation is underscored by the distinctive and repeated note in 1 Kings 13 that matters are conducted בדבר יהוה, "by the word of Yahweh." This dominating phrase in 1 Kings 13 is mentioned by the narrator (vv. 1, 2, 5, 9), assigned to the man of God (איש האלהים) from Judah (v. 17), and also assigned to the old prophet from Bethel (vv. 18, 32), the latter verse again in reference to the Judean man of God).[1] This

---

1. This phrase is rather distinctive of 1 Kings 13, with seven occurrences. Elsewhere the phrase occurs only five times in the MT, occurring once in connection with Samuel

repeated phrase is an indicator of the distinctiveness of 1 Kings 13 even in its present form with its citations of King Josiah and Samaria which go well beyond the assigned time period of the reign of Jeroboam. This phrase also contributes to what seems to be a somewhat different yet very important message in 1 Kings 13 that has only rarely been mentioned by commentators. The major focus of studies has been on other aspects of the story, especially the themes of prophetic obedience and/or conflict, by those analyzing this strange yet fascinating story.[2]

Perhaps the abundance of rhetorical fireworks in 1 Kings 13 has raised so much smoke that it is difficult to see the possibility of a different theme, Indeed, what initially drew my own attention to 1 Kings 13 was the peculiar situation of the man of God from Judah who successfully carried out the first, and presumably the major part of his commission, בדבר יהוה ("by the word of Yahweh"), initially culminating in his utterance of a divinely authorized oracle of judgment concerning the cult but who subsequently set aside

---

at Shiloh (1 Sam 3:21) and once in connection with another prophetic wonder story in which a member of the prophetic guild (1 Kgs 20:35) announces a forthcoming lion attack on a non-cooperative, disobedient member of that guild. The remaining occurrences (Jer 8:9; Ps 33:6; and 2 Chr 30:12) relate to rather different circumstances. The significance of this phrase was noted by B. Schmitz, *Prophetie und Königtum: Eine narratologisch-historische Methodologie entwickelt an den Königsbüchern* (FAT 60; Tübingen: Mohr/Siebeck, 2008) 154–55. Note also her comments on this phrase in 1 Kgs 20:35 and the linkage of that passage with both 1 Kings 13 and 1 Kings 22, pp. 345–48.

2. For an emphasis on prophetic conflict or the issue of "false" prophecy, note J. L. Crenshaw, *Prophetic Conflict* (BZAW 124; Berlin: de Gruyter, 1971); S. J. De Vries, *Prophet against Prophet: The Role of the Micaiah Narrative (1 Kings 22) in the Development of Early Prophetic Tradition* (Grand Rapids: Eerdmans, 1978); F.-L. Hossfeld and I. Meyer, *Prophet gegen Prophet: Eine Analyse der alttestamentlichen Texte zum Thema, Wahre und falsche Propheten* (BibB 9; Einsiedeln: Benziger, 1974); and G. Quell, *Wahre und falsche Propheten* (BFCT 46/1; Gütersloh: Bertelsmann, 1952). Another common approach, one which I followed previously (see Huffmon, "On Trusting Your Own Experience" [*Drew Gateway* 53/2 (1983) 1–5]), is to focus on the disobedience of the man of God who set aside his own direct word from God in favor of a subsequent override in an angelic revelation to someone else, in this case an old prophet living in Bethel. The emphasis on the issue of obedience is well illustrated by Werner K. Lemke's study ("The Way of Obedience: 1 Kings 13 and the Structure of the Deuteronomistic History," in *Magnalia Dei: The Mighty Acts of God. Essays on the Bible and Archaeology in Memory of G. Ernest Wright* [eds. F. M. Cross et al.; Garden City, NY: Doubleday, 1976] 301–26). Note also that David Marcus emphasizes "a number of fantastic situations, a considerable amount of ironies, many examples of ridicule and parody, and a variety of fine rhetorical features." He characterizes this story as a satire ("Elements of Ridicule and Parody in the Story of the Lying Prophet from Bethel," in *Proceedings of the Eleventh World Congress of Jewish Studies, Jerusalem June 22–29, 1993* [Jerusalem: World Union of Jewish Studies, 1994] 67–74, quotation from p. 68). See also his *From Balaam to Jonah: Anti-prophetic Satire in the Hebrew Bible* (BJS 301; Atlanta: Scholars, 1995) 65–91.

his own direct commission by God in favor of a counter, enticing revelation communicated by an old prophet from Bethel who cited the same attributive phrase (בדבר יהוה, v. 18). The man of God, in response, proceeded to abandon his own direct revelation from the Lord in favor of a rather different and more personally accommodating revelation concerning the mission of the man of God from Judah, a message in the tradition of a premature announcement of "mission accomplished." This failure of the man of God from Judah to follow his own revelation by substituting another's competing revelation, seemingly commendatory to him and simplifying the final segment of his mission, proved to lead to disaster. One could understand this new revelation from a senior colleague as perhaps being regarded by the man of God as a divine commendation for a job well done through his focused journey to Bethel and his condemnation of the Bethel cult being introduced by King Jeroboam. The new revelation, after all, excused him only from the concluding segment of his charge, i.e., to return to the nearby Judean territory by a different route, though still without the benefit of food or drink. He was to remain focused on his mission. Apart from that, he could take his time as there was no longer a schedule to keep. All he had to do was to complete a return to Judah without stopping for food or drink. The "divine" invitation to accept some hospitality, conveyed through the Bethel prophet, came at a time when the man of God's mission was virtually complete. All that remained was the apparently simple task of a return to Judah "by a different route." Judah itself was less than a day's walk from Bethel and hardly a challenging journey. The man of God presumably was already feeling more relaxed, having concluded his demanding mission of condemnation of the Bethel cult and having successfully dealt with King Jeroboam's tempting offer of hospitality, including a gift. The various elements that now actively involve the Bethel prophet in the story, however, also draw attention to an additional or alternative aspect of the story in 1 Kings 13, that of the unity of the prophetic traditions of Israel and Judah, with particular reference to an appropriate cult, as was suggested in a footnote by Werner Lemke in 1976.[3]

---

3. See Lemke, "The Way of Obedience," 325 n 102. Lemke, who focused on the theme of obedience, mentions this perspective as a feasible alternative understanding of 1 Kings 13, in that "[c]onceivably it [the joint burial, p. 317] may have been concerned thereby to underscore the religious unity of the prophetic movement in Israel which, while politically frequently divided, recognized no religious boundaries in the service of their common God." But Lemke does not develop this perspective, which I argue goes well beyond the joint burial, though that shared burial is a culmination. I have not found any citation of Lemke's intriguing comment, even in Barbara Schmitz's very comprehensive study of 1 Kings 13 (see n. 1) which cites Lemke's article several times. Karl Barth's famous exposition of 1 Kings 13 in his *Church Dogmatics*, vol. II,

The central characters in the story are the man of God from Judah (also twice identified as a נביא, including a reference assigned to the Bethel prophet himself, v. 18), and the old prophet from Bethel, who is consistently identified as a נביא (7x in 1 Kings 13). The two figures represent a unity that is reinforced by other elements in the story, as discussed below. Rather than understanding 1 Kings 13 as primarily focused on the important theme of obedience to divine revelation or as basically presenting another example of prophetic conflict,[4] this paper argues in favor of Werner Lemke's second choice, viz., the issue of the unity of the prophetic tradition in Israel and in Judah in regard to the setting aside of Bethel and the implied affirmation of the all-Israelite cult center in the recent Davidic acquisition of the centrally located Jerusalem and David's introduction there of the Ark. The subordination or even rejection of the Bethel cult is clear in 1 Kings 13. Having been condemned by the man of God from Judah and ignored by the old prophet residing in Bethel, what remains is the Jerusalem cultic center to which the Ark has been relocated. This option therefore implies the subordination of the Bethel cult, condemned by the man of God from Judah and ignored by the old prophet from Bethel, who himself subsequently affirmed the man of God from Judah as speaking truly in his condemnation of Jeroboam's establishment of the new Bethel cult as a national center for the northern kingdom. Although the Bethel cult was Yahwistic, it was in Jerusalem that the unifying shrine of the Ark was then located. Note the comment by Frank M. Cross:

> It is inconceivable that the national cult of Jeroboam was other than Yahwistic. Jeroboam and the tribes of the North seceded to the face of Solomonic innovations and remained the center

---

part 2: *The Doctrine of God* (ed. G. W. Bromiley and T. F. Torrance; Edinburgh: T. & T. Clark, 1957; German original, 1942), stating that "[T]he peculiar theme of the chapter is the manner in which the man of God and the (Bethel) prophet belong together, do not belong together, and eventually and finally do belong together; and how the same is true of Judah and Israel" (393). However, Barth's larger framework is the elect (Judah) and the rejected (Israel), which misses the point of the unity of the Bethel prophet with the man of God from Judah. The Bethel prophet tests the man of God from Judah and ultimately affirms him, and the man of God accepts the authenticity of the Bethel prophet's announcement of divine judgment. Without protest, but doubtless with dismay, the man of God quietly starts on his journey home with the use of the donkey provided by the Bethel prophet, only to be felled by a lion early on.

4. R. R. Wilson, *Prophecy and Society in Ancient Israel* (Philadelphia: Fortress, 1980) describes 1 Kings 13 as "a coherent but somewhat curious story . . . (that) [i]n its present form . . . cannot be earlier than the time of Josiah" (187); but he notes that "several tensions between this story and the account of Josiah's reform suggest that older traditions lie behind the present form of 1 Kings 13" (188). This paper pursues that "older" or, rather, that other tradition.

of League traditions. Jeroboam, desperate to consolidate his kingdom, wrenched from the Davidids and desirous of wooing his own people away from the shrine of the ark in Jerusalem and its pilgrimage festivals, would not have repudiated Yahweh and chosen a new god. Nor would he have flown in the face of fact and tradition by naming *another* god as the god who brought Israel up from Egypt.[5]

Cross followed up this observation with another comment very relevant to 1 Kings 13: "Apparently, Jeroboam's real sin was in establishing a rival to the central sanctuary in Jerusalem, not in the introduction of a foreign god or a pagan idol."[6]

Altogether, this perspective suggests that our peculiar story relates to the rivalry between the older Bethel sanctuary, with its patriarchal associations—Bethel being, after Jerusalem, the most frequently mentioned cultic center in the Hebrew Bible—and what David had established as the new cult center for all Israel by his introduction of the Ark into the formerly Jebusite city of Jerusalem, just across the tribal border in Judah, and close to Bethel. By setting up a shrine for the recovered and authenticated Ark (note 2 Sam 6:6-11), which prior to its capture had been domiciled in various Ephraimite cities—Gilgal, Bethel (Judg 20:26-28), and especially Shiloh[7]—David had established an all-Israel cultic location which was less than a day's walk south of Bethel.

The context of this story and its presentation of prophetic unity is appropriately associated with the time of Jeroboam I. In 1 Kgs 11:29-39 Jeroboam, an Ephraimite who had risen to a high status under Solomon, was designated by the prophet Ahijah of Shiloh as—at least potentially—another David, a king who could initiate an "enduring dynasty" (בית נאמן) for the ten northern tribes (v. 38), apparently with a wide range of royal choices (v. 37).[8] The expectations of Jeroboam cited by Ahijah in 1 Kings 11 reportedly were not ultimately met, as Ahijah is cited as subsequently rebuking Jeroboam and declaring a quick end to his dynasty in what seems to be

---

5. F. M. Cross, *Canaanite Myth and Hebrew Epic: Essays on the History of the Religion of Israel* (Cambridge: Harvard University Press, 1973) 74.

6. Cross, *Canaanite Myth*, 75.

7. Shiloh was also the home of the prophet Ahijah, the prophet whose role in God's designation of Jeroboam as king is discussed below.

8. An "enduring house (dynasty)" is promised through Samuel for the priest, Zadok (1 Sam 2:35), and through Nathan for King David (2 Sam 7:16), with the same phrase used regarding David by Abigail (1 Sam 25:28; see also Ps 89:38; Isa 55:3). The prophet Ahijah of Shiloh declares an "enduring house" for Jeroboam (1 Kgs 11:38; see also 1 Kgs 12:15), and his reference to Jeroboam as ruling "in all that you desire" (1 Kgs 11:37) seems open-ended. See the general discussion by Alfred Jepsen in *TDOT* 1:296-97.

a formulaic Deuteronomistic condemnation (1 Kgs 14:7–11).⁹ The stated reality is that Jeroboam ruled for 22 years, thus throughout the putative period of the primary portion of 1 Kings 13, outliving both King Rehoboam and his son, King Abijah, in Judah. Jeroboam was a serious figure to be dealt with during the alleged background period of 1 Kings 13. He was succeeded by his son, Nadab (1 Kgs 14:20), though Nadab was soon overthrown, bringing an early end to Jeroboam's dynasty.

In 1 Kings 13, however, King Jeroboam is a significant but ultimately a secondary figure. He was apparently seeking an alternative center to Jerusalem, using Bethel, which was a well-established cultic center with many associations with pre-monarchic Israel, including being one of the locations for the Ark of the Covenant (Judg 20:26–28). Bethel is also very close to Shiloh, a long-term host of the Ark. The primary figures are the man of God from Judah and the old prophet from Bethel who seem to serve as symbolic representatives for the Judean prophetic community and the Israelite prophetic community, respectively. Neither of these two figures is supportive of the Bethel cult, which raises the question of support for an alternative cultic site, though there is no specific mention of such an alternative. The man of God from Judah is first on the scene at the Bethel sanctuary, arriving on a mission of rebuke for King Jeroboam and the new Bethel cult (as viewed from a Deuteronomistic perspective in the present text). The man of God is sent there for the occasion of a special royal ceremony which the Bethel prophet apparently chose not to attend, though at least one of his sons was present (1 Kgs 13:11) and able to report concerning the special ceremony planned by Jeroboam.¹⁰ The mission of the man of God from Judah to Bethel is focused on the Bethel cult, but it also created an opportunity for prophetic interaction.

Representationally, the "man of God (from Judah)" is given that title 15x in 1 Kings 13, and his derivation from Judah is mentioned 5x. He is the only "man of God" provided with a tribal designation—and as a statement of affiliation he is also identified as a נביא by the Bethel prophet (v. 18) and in the narrative (v. 23). His primary title is echoed by that provided for the

9. See Cross, *Canaanite Myth*, 224–25.

10. Whether these sons were family or members of the prophetic guild (cf. 2 Kgs 2:2–3) is not clarified in 1 Kings 13 and is not relevant to the story. The absence of the Bethel prophet is important, however, and cannot be due to physical disability as stated in the retelling of this story in Josephus (*Ant.* 8.236), in that the story reports him as quite active in going to intercept the man of God after he has started on his return journey and then subsequently visiting the site of his death, with the lion still present, in order to retrieve the body for burial. For the curious treatment of 1 Kings 13 by Josephus, see the discussion by Christopher Begg, *Josephus' Account of the Early Divided Monarchy* (BETL 108; Leuven: Peeters, 1993) 41–63.

later wonder-working northern prophets, Elijah (7x) and Elisha (29x), who are rather less frequently identified as being a נביא in the MT (5x and 11x respectively).[11] The interconnections of the two prophets of 1 Kings 13 are reflected in the titles associated with them, as the Bethel prophet is identified exclusively as a נביא in 1 Kings 13,[12] and in addition is described as "old" (זקן), vv. 11 and 29, making him a senior colleague. The consistent title for the Bethel prophet has its analog in the prophets associated with David in Jerusalem, i.e., Nathan and Gad. Nathan is consistently identified as a נביא (14x) and Gad is identified as a נביא (1 Sam 22:5; 2 Sam 24:11) and also as a חזה, a visionary prophet (1 Chr 29:29), and as such in a special relationship with King David (1 Chr 21:9; 2 Chr 29:25). The titles that are used in 1 Kings 13 interconnect the two kingdoms, the man of God with northern prophetic figures and the Bethel prophet with prophetic figures in Judah under David.[13] The fluidity of titles in the biblical traditions about this period is also well illustrated by Shemiah, a contemporary of Jeroboam I. Shemiah, presumably from Judah given his connection with Rehoboam, is identified as a man of God in three texts (MT and LXX Vorlage): 1 Kgs 12:22//2 Chr 11:2 and 2 Kgdms 12:24y (LXX Vorlage) and as a נביא in 2 Chr 12:5, 15 (MT and LXX Vorlage). And Ahijah, the Shilonite, also identified as old (i.e., 60) in 3 Kgdms 12:24h, who announced Jeroboam's designation as king, is given the title נביא in 1 Kgs 11:29//3 Kgdms 11:29, as well as in 1 Kgs 14:2, 18, but the title "man of God" in 3 Kgdms 12:24.[14]

The setting of the story at Bethel in the early days of the reign of Jeroboam I is itself important for the issue of the matter of unity among the northern and southern prophetic circles. Bethel was a hallowed cultic site from the time of the patriarchs, and Jeroboam I had been designated by the prophet Ahijah of Shiloh as a king with the potential to be the founder of a

---

11. Note also that the Ephraimite Samuel is identified by the title "man of God" 4x (1 Sam 9:6–10), as well as by both נביא and (as archaic) ראה (1 Sam 9:9). In a northern context note also the "man of God" in 1 Sam 2:27 who speaks to Eli (at Shiloh) and the "man of God" mentioned in Judg 13:6.

12. Although his son(s) have a role in the story, and 2 Kgs 2:3 does refer to the presence of some "sons of the prophets" in Bethel in the Elijah–Elisha cycle, there is no indication that the son(s) mentioned in 1 Kings 13 are in a relationship other than family, though many scholars assume such a group relationship.

13. J. T. Walsh (*1 Kings* [Berit Olam; Collegeville, MN: Liturgical, 1996] 183), finds that "[t]he terms 'man of God' and 'prophet' are approximately synonymous" in 1 Kings 13. Their distribution, however, is striking.

14. In the LXX variant text in 3 Kgdms 12:24o, it is Shemiah, not Ahijah, who provides Jeroboam with ten pieces of a new garment.

lasting dynasty, a בית נאמן (1 Kgs 11:38) parallel to that of David's kingship,[15] a possibility that depended on Jeroboam's adherence to God's ways.

In the story as presented, the man of God from Judah announced the destruction and desecration of the Bethel altar by a future Judean king, specifically the much later Josiah (who is chronologically intrusive in 1 Kings 13), in keeping with his role as the new David,[16] presaged by the immediate sign of the altar breaking apart and the ashes spilling. This led to an attempted intervention by King Jeroboam who ordered the arrest of the man of God, but the king's commanding arm became paralyzed, the altar broke apart and the ashes were spilled. The king then set aside his command and sought help from the man of God, who could entreat God for healing. The man of God cooperated, entreating God, and the king's arm was restored to normal as the man of God continued to demonstrate his Elijah-Elisha style wonder-working. In return, the king acknowledged the power of the man of God and made the mitigating invitation for the man of God to come to the king's house for some hospitality as well as a gift. But the man of God responded negatively, invoking God's assignment to him of a special mission and asserting that even a royal invitation could not prompt him to disregard his divine commission:

> If you gave me half of your household I could not stay with you nor eat bread nor drink water in this place, because God commanded me, "by the word of Yahweh" (בדבר יהוה), saying, "You shall not eat bread nor shall you drink water, nor shall you return (to Judah) by the path by which you went." (v. 9)[17]

---

15. Regarding David, see 2 Sam 7:16 (also Ps 89:4-5, 37-38, and Abigail's affirmation in 2 Sam 25:28), and for a parallel commitment to the priestly line of Zadok see 1 Sam 2:35. Note the helpful summary of usage by Alfred Jepsen, *TDOT* 1:296-97.

16. See A. Laato, *Josiah and David Redivivus. The Historical Josiah and the Messianic Expectations of Exilic and Postexilic Times* (ConBOT 33; Stockholm: Almqvist & Wiksell, 1992).

17. Note the similarity with the instructions from Elisha to his "lad," Gehazi, regarding the apparent death of the divinely bestowed son of the great lady of Shunem, who had rushed to seek out Elijah at Mount Carmel, aided by an attendant and a donkey (2 Kgs 4:24). Elisha responds by sending Gehazi on ahead to Shunem from Mount Carmel with Elisha's staff while Elisha and the great lady follow at a donkey's pace. Gehazi was instructed to hurry to Shunem: "if you come across anyone, do not greet him, and if anyone greets you, do not answer him" (2 Kgs 4:29)." This instruction is even more restrictive than the instruction to the man of God from Judah, and the distance from the Mount Carmel area to Shunem is much greater than the distance between Bethel and the land of Judah, though a specific starting point for the journey of the man of God from Judah is not mentioned. The situation in each case is the story of an urgent mission, not allowing any distractions. In the case of the man of God from Judah, the return by a different route also fits with the sense of a secret mission: go,

Subsequently, in the encounter of the man of God from Judah with the old prophet from Bethel, after the man of God had started on his final and easiest part of his task—to return to Judah by a different route—he receives another offer of hospitality. This second offer has additional elements. The one who makes the offer is an old man (1 Kgs 13:11, 25, 29) who came on a donkey, not yet further identified to the man of God whom he has sought out. And when an offer of hospitality was turned down again by the man of God, citing virtually the same divine command as before, the old man reinforces his invitation by identifying himself—"I also am a prophet like you" (גם אני נביא כמוך, v. 18), i.e., a fellow prophet as well as a senior colleague. He then invokes a divine command mediated to the old prophet by an "angelic messenger" (v. 18), to the effect that the old prophet should "bring him back with you to your house and let him eat bread and drink water." At this point the narrator adds a comment, "He (the old prophet) deceived him."[18] The so-called "deception," however, is very important because it allows the possibility of a further confirmation of the authenticity of the man of God from Judah and his message. If the man of God had continued to follow his commission and just proceeded on his way, we would not have a story. The deviation by the man of God from his mission provides for the possibility of a reinforcing divine judgment that could further authenticate the mission of the man of God—a second opinion, as is a common feature of the divination process. Something beyond a dismissal of the offer by the man of God is necessary in order to develop the bond between the Bethel prophet and the man of God from Judah and to solidify their setting aside of the Bethel cult through further confirmation of the authenticity of the message delivered by the man of God. Clearly, divine judgment should follow if the man of God deviates from his commission, and such judgment would confirm his mission as genuine. In the present text there was initially an immediate demonstration of divine rejection of the Bethel cult (v. 5), but the more important issue is the long-term future of the Bethel cult. The only way to clearly certify the authenticity of the announced future development

---

do what you have been assigned to do, and return by a different route to preserve the secrecy of your mission (like World War II commando raids). Note also the promise of non-disturbance of the local communities and no deviation from "the king's highway as the Israelites pass through Edom on their journey from Kadesh to the land of Canaan (Num 20:16–19).

18. The term used, כחש (pi), means "deny, delude, dissemble." K.-D. Schunck cites "prophets who consciously conceal their intentions from others by deceptive words or actions," referring specifically to 1 Kgs 13:18 (*TDOT* 7:133–34). Compare the initial deception of the kings by Michaiah ben Imlah (1 Kgs 22:14–23), in a context of seeking a second opinion, and Elisha's deception of King Hazael (2 Kgs 8:7–10). Deception can be part of a truth-seeking process.

is to reinforce the authenticity of the man of God from Judah as truly carrying out a divine commission. An uninterrupted, safe return to Judah would provide no additional confirmation of his announcement, but punishment (even death) of him for abandoning his explicit commission would clearly provide authentication of the commission and therewith the message regarding Bethel. An immediate parallel from the tales of wonder-working prophets is the story of a rejection by one member of the prophetic guild of a request from another member, leading to his death from a lion attack, which authenticated the attempt by the requesting member of the prophetic guild to deceive the Israelite king (1 Kgs 20:35–43).[19] Clearly, the story in 1 Kings 13 cannot end with yet another refusal of hospitality by the man of God.

As the story in 1 Kings 13 has unfolded so far, the man of God from Judah began by following the word of the Lord (v. 1), providing a sign (vv. 3–5), reversing the paralyzed arm of King Jeroboam (v. 6), and successfully rejecting the king's offer of generous hospitality (vv. 7–9). He then started on his return journey to Judah, using a different route (v. 10). At this point the other main character in the story, the old prophet from Bethel, enters the picture-e. The Bethel prophet had, significantly, absented himself from the temple ceremony, though his son(s) were present and reported to him what had happened. The Bethel prophet then inquired of his sons as to the route that the man of God had taken on his way back to Judah, and had his sons saddle the donkey for him. He managed to catch up with the man of God from Judah who was enjoying a rest stop and he was able to persuade the man of God to come home with him to join with him for some food and drink (vv. 14b–15), even though the man of God had initially invoked his commission and rejected the offer of hospitality (vv. 16–17). In response, the Bethel prophet had then identified himself as a prophet and granted the man of God full recognition as a fellow prophet, using the title נביא, as noted. At this point the dynamics of the story shift, as the old Bethel prophet follows his egalitarian comment with a mediated revelation through a messenger (מלאך) who spoke בדבר יהוה—"by the word of Yahweh" (v. 18), thus not a direct revelation from God but yet a revelation that ostensibly claimed to override the commission that the man of God had twice already firmly upheld (vv. 10, 18). Yet on the third opportunity to affirm his commission,

---

19. Concerning the danger of lions in the Assyrian province of Samaria, see 2 Kgs 17:25–26. Lions were also a danger to people and stock animals in the areas outside the gates of Ashurbanipal's capital in Assyria; see E. Weissert, "Royal Hunt and Royal Triumph in a Prism Fragment of Ashurbanipal (82-5-22, 2 and parallels)," in *Assyria 1995* (ed. S. Parpola and R. M. Whiting; Helsinki: The Neo-Assyrian Text Corpus Project, 1997) 339–58, esp. 342–43.

the man of God stepped aside from his instructions. This act of disobedience, however, made it possible to have another, virtually immediate confirmation of his mission due to divine wrath for such disobedience. The actions of a future king, viz. Josiah (v. 2), would come centuries later than the presented time of Jeroboam, when the issue of the new role of the Bethel cult vis-à-vis Jerusalem (with the shrine of the Ark) was more pressing.

After the collegial sharing of food and drink by the man of God and his senior colleague was nicely underway, the old prophet pronounces God's direct judgment on the man of God for abandoning his commission, announcing that the man of God would not return to life with his family, even as a corpse. Nevertheless, the Bethel prophet sends the man of God on his way with the added convenience of a donkey, suggesting that the precise divine instructions to the man of God, having been violated, were no longer an issue. What does remain is the divine pronouncement by the old Bethel prophet that the man of God's body, upon his death, would not be buried in his family tomb (v. 22).

First Kings 13 is in keeping with the prophetic legend of 1 Kgs 20:35–36, already cited, in which a member of the prophetic guild had refused an order given specifically "by the word of Yahweh" (בדבר יהוה), and was advised that because of this disobedience, "upon leaving me a lion will kill you." I Kgs 20:35–36 and 1 Kings 13 share the affirmation in prophetic tradition that the message is more important than the messenger. Those who assist in the confirmation of the message, even through their death by (heaven sent) lions, are important figures. In 1 Kings 13 the old prophet is not the victor is some sort of prophetic competition,[20] but the survivor who ultimately ends up honoring his colleague, the man of God from Judah who spoke the truth about Bethel.

At this stage in our story, however, the man of God had made little progress on his return trip back to Judah when a lion came across him as he was proceeding along the path with the donkey and the lion killed him (v. 24).[21] To emphasize the special character of this death, the story advises that the lion, having killed the man of God, merely stood beside the body, not eating of the kill, and, for that matter leaving the apparently "stunned" donkey basically untouched. Both the lion and the donkey, as it were, serve as silent sentinels awaiting further developments.[22] Passersby observe this

---

20. Contrary to the statement by Schmitz, *Prophetie und Königtum*, 152–53, who identifies the Bethel prophet as the "'Sieger' aus der Auseinandersetzung" of the two prophets.

21. Note the reference in 2 Kgs 17:24–25 to God sending lions against the peoples resettled by the Assyrians in Samaria, punishing them for not worshipping the Lord.

22. For a remarkable representation of this scene in a woodcut by Doré, showing

strange phenomenon and report their discovery to people in Bethel, and word reaches the Bethel prophet.

The story has moved beyond the issue of "obedience" or "trusting your own experience," and even the issue of the authentication of the man of God from Judah, and focuses on the bond between the man of God from Judah and the old prophet from Bethel, i.e., their testimony to the unity of the prophetic traditions in both Israel, the northern kingdom, and Judah, the southern kingdom, together with the downgrading of Bethel as a religious center. This meant, by implication, the acceptance of Jerusalem, with the shrine of the Ark, as the true religious center.

With the recovery of the body of the man of God from Judah who had been killed by a lion, the authenticity of the man of God as having been sent by God on a mission, which he mistakenly aborted during the final segment of his task, has been confirmed. God had sent him.

The man of God from Judah was denied burial in the family tomb, but the Bethel prophet was determined to honor the man of God from Judah and his mission. The question of what to do with the body of the man of God was quickly resolved. The Bethel prophet had the body buried in the tomb that had been prepared for the Bethel prophet himself, with appropriate lamentation, as the Bethel prophet poignantly declared "Alas, my brother" (v. 30), emphasizing the close bond between the two of them. The old prophet then instructed his sons:

> Upon my death you are to bury me in the tomb in which the man of God is buried. Beside his bones place my bones. For surely the word which he pronounced by the word of Yahweh (בדבר יהוה) concerning the altar which is in Bethel and concerning the cult places in the cities of Samaria shall come to pass. (vv. 31-32)

These verses, even with the clear presence of later redaction by the reference to Samaria, give a clear ending to the story. The old prophet from Bethel and the man of God from Judah are united in their disregard for the Bethel cult established by Jeroboam and, by implication, the affirmation of Jerusalem, presumably especially for the presence there of the Ark, the ancient symbol of divine presence that was so closely associated with the area of Ephraim.

This final sharing fits together with the Bethel prophet's failure to attend the inaugural ceremony led by King Jeroboam I at the Bethel temple.

---

the Bethel prophet approaching, with a donkey and the lion majestically keeping watch, see W. Brueggemann, *1 & 2 Kings* (SHBC; Mason, GA: Smyth & Helwys, 2000) 174, though it omits the donkey that had been supplied earlier to the man of God.

It also fits with the reference in Jer 41:4–5 to the pilgrimage group of eighty mourning men from Shechem, Shiloh and Samaria who are on their way to Jerusalem, after the fall of the city to the Babylonians, bringing offerings and frankincense for the Beyt-Yahweh, not specifying the Ark. In the area of the northern kingdom there must have been many who had a special attachment to the Jerusalem temple, the location of the Ark of the Covenant and a sanctuary that was built during a period of Israelite unity under David and Solomon.[23] There must have been many persons in the northern kingdom who held Jerusalem in high regard, even before the time of Josiah. For example, note that the Rechabites, whose acknowledged founder, Jehonadab, was active in the north in the time of Jehu (2 Kings 10), are mentioned as a group in the time of Jeremiah (Jeremiah 35) that had taken refuge in Jerusalem during a time of Neo-Babylonian threats to the kingdom of Judah.

In summary, the old prophet from Bethel and the man of God from Judah apparently shared a compelling allegiance to the Israelite deity, Yahweh, a lack of enthusiasm for the Bethel cult, a recognition of each other as true messengers of Yahweh, and even a burial place. Their commitment to Yahweh transcended the territorial boundaries among the Israelite people. This motif is also fully in keeping with what Cross describes as the "First Edition" of the Deuteronomistic history.[24] In 2 Kgs 23:17–18, following Josiah's reported destruction of the Bethel altar and shrine, there is a reference to a marker on a nearby tomb:

> He (Josiah) said, "What is that marker that I see," and the men of the city told him, "It is the tomb of the man of God who came from Judah and announced these things that you have done regarding the Bethel altar. He (Josiah) said, "Let him rest. No one should disturb his bones." So they did not disturb his bones (that were there) with the bones of the prophet who came from Samaria. (2 Kgs 23:17–18)

The man of God from Judah and the old prophet from Bethel were joined together in life, in knowing the importance of adhering to God's words, and ultimately in death, giving joint if indirect testimony to Israel's unifying shrine in Jerusalem, the home of the Ark in their own presumed time and for many centuries following.

---

23. Patrick D. Miller in his commentary on Jeremiah observes that for these mourners "[t]heir journey from the north attests to the significance of Jerusalem as a center of worship for all Israel. That may be a testimony to the attraction of the Temple from its earliest days, or it may reflect the impact of Josiah's reform" (*NIB* 6:859). Of course, such motivations are not mutually exclusive.

24. See Cross, *Canaanite Myth*, 278–85; note esp. 284, though the subtle story of 1 Kings 13 may to some extent be independent of the Deuteronomistic History.

Various lines of evidence in 1 Kings 13 suggest a reinforced and compelling affirmation by the man of God from Judah and the old prophet from Bethel, representing a unified prophetic community, north and south. They were joined together in the affirmation of Yahweh and, apparently, of Jerusalem as the cultic center of the united monarchy, established in the previously "neutral" territory of a formerly Jebusite city that became Israelite only in the time of David. To an important extent for the two prophets of 1 Kings 13, Bethel was not a unifying center. That was the role of Jerusalem, sheltering the long enduring Israelite symbol of the Ark, which transcended the division into the two kingdoms.

— 9 —

"Enthroned upon Donkeys"

The Entry of Divine Jesus into Jerusalem according to Matthew[1]

BERNARD F. BATTO

AT FIRST BLUSH IT might seem inconceivable that concepts and motifs in vogue at ancient Ugarit in the fourteenth century BCE. could survive in the region of Syria nearly a millennium and a half, and eventually find their way into the fabric of the New Testament toward the end of the first century CE, especially given the profound cultural paradigm shifts that transformed the Levant, initially from an ancient Near Eastern worldview to a radically different Hellenistic cultural world following upon the conquests of Alexander the Great in the late fourth century BCE and still later to full-blown Greco-Romanization under Roman rule. Yet some traditions and cultural motifs did persist at various Syrian sites, notably Palmyra, Dura-Europos, and Hatra. Art from such sites reveal a certain resistance to the classical culture that swept across the eastern Mediterranean.[2] The burden of this paper is to demonstrate the survival of one specific ancient

---

1. *Author's note*: It is an honor to dedicate this article to Simon B. Parker, who as a senior graduate student at The Johns Hopkins University and later as a mentor to me as a beginning scholar in the Pacific Northwest region of the SBL offered guidance more than once that spared me from potentially embarrassing errors in my publications.

2. F. Millar, "Narrative and Identity in Mosaics from the Late Roman Near East: Pagan, Jewish, and Christian," in *The Sculptural Environment of the Roman Near East: Reflections on Culture, Ideology, and Power* (ed. Y. Z. Eliav et al.; Interdisciplinary Studies in Ancient Culture and Religion 9; Leuven: Peeters, 2008) 225–56, esp. 226–27.

Near Eastern trope, namely, that deities were thought appropriately to be mounted upon a symbolic animal or fantastic creature particularly when moving to or from their cult centers, and that the evangelist Matthew appropriated this trope for the scene of Jesus entering Jerusalem on the back of two donkeys so as to depict Jesus as truly *Immanu-el* ("God-with-us").

THE MOTIF OF DEITIES MOUNTED UPON A SYMBOLIC ANIMAL

The ancient Near Eastern motif of deities associated with, or mounted upon, a symbolic animal or fantastic creature hardly needs any introduction. It is well attested in iconography and the literature of Mesopotamia and the Levant, from the middle of the third millennium BCE to the middle of the first millennium BCE Moreover, each deity could be identified by the specific animal or fantastical creature upon which he or she was mounted or rode, usually standing. In Canaan and Syria, El, the head of the Canaanite pantheon, is normally shown sitting upon a cherub throne.[3] The storm god Haddu (Hadad, Adad, Baal) was typically depicted as standing upon the back of a young, i.e., vigorous, bull.[4] In Mesopotamia the goddess Ishtar is normally pictured as standing upon a lion or seated upon a lion throne.[5] Likewise, Ninurta is depicted as standing upon a fire-breathing, winged lion.[6] And in Babylonian iconography the god Marduk—alternatively, Marduk's son Nabu—stands astride a *mušḫuššu*-dragon.[7] Similarly, for the other gods. At

---

3. See *ANEP* #493, where only the legs of the cherubs are depicted. See also *ANEP* ##456 + 458 with King Ahiram seated upon a cherub throne, in imitation of the chief deity; also #332. Compare also a carved ivory box from Megiddo with sphinxes and lions (*ANEP* #128).

4. *ANEP* ##500, 501; cf. ##531, 534, 537.

5. ANEP ##522, 525, 526. See also a drawing of a wall panel at Mari palace of the investiture of Zimrilim by Ishtar, with one foot upon a crouching lion; see B. F. Batto, "The Divine Sovereign: The Image of God in the Priestly Creation Story," in *David and Zion: Biblical Studies in Honor of J. J. M. Roberts* (ed. B. F. Batto and K. L. Roberts; Winona Lake, IN: Eisenbrauns, 2004) 143–86, esp. 159, Fig. 13; reprinted in B. F. Batto, *In the Beginning: Essays on Creation Motifs in the Ancient Near East and the Bible* (Siphrut 9; Winona Lake, IN: Eisenbrauns, 2013) 110, fig. 13.

6. Standing upon a composite lion-like creature, the god Ninurta(?) attacks Anzu(?); see Fig. 15, in Batto, *In the Beginning*, 33.

7. *ANEP* #523. For a convenient synthesis of the history of this "furious snake" in Mesopotamian literature and art, see W. G. Lambert, *Babylonian Creation Myths* (Mesopotamian Civilizations 16; Winona Lake, IN: Eisenbrauns, 2013) 232–36; F. A. M. Wiggermann, *Mesopotamian Protective Spirits: The Ritual Texts* (Cuneiform Monographs 1; Groningen: Styx, 1992) 168–69, and 186 with corresponding figures 3a–d on p. 188.

Maltaya a whole procession of deities is depicted, each standing upon his or her symbolic animal or fantastical mount, or sometimes standing upon two such mounts, including horses.[8] In this connection, it is worth mentioning an Assyrian inspired solar cult was once practiced within the temple in Jerusalem; as one of Josiah's reforms, "he removed the horses dedicated to the sun ... and he burned the chariots of the sun with fire" (2 Kgs 23:11). This corresponds to depictions of processions from other sites in which the sun god rides in a horse-drawn chariot, or sometimes actually sits on a horse.[9]

Such depictions are less common in literary texts, being more implicit than explicit. At Ugarit, for instance, the head of the pantheon is commonly referred to by his title Bull El, while Baal (Haddu) is not infrequently likened to a young bull or bull calf. But Ugaritic texts do not inform us, however, specifically that these deities were enthroned upon cherubs or mounted on a young bull, respectively, as depicted in surviving iconographic representations. Indeed, the lone literary attestation from Ugarit to a deity riding an animal concerns El's consort, Athirat-of-the-Sea, when she mounts a donkey to go before El in his mountain sanctuary to intercede for Baal, that Baal be granted his own "house" (palace). Athirat is accompanied by her servant Qudsh wa-Amrar, with the gods Baal and Anat preceding them, as if in a mini-procession. The scene opens with Athirat commanding her servant to prepare her mount for the journey:

> "[Hear, O Qudsh] wa-Amr[ar]
> [O Fisher of Lady] Athirat of the Sea:
> [Tie the donkey], bind the mule;
> Se[t ropes of] silver,
> [Bridles] of gold;
> Prepare the ropes of [my] ass."
> Qud<sh> wa-Amrar complies.
> He ties the donkey, binds the mule;
> He sets ropes of silver,
> Bridles of Gold;
> He prepares her ass.
> Qudsh wa-Amrar clasps,

---

8. *ANEP* #537; cf. #538 in which Assyrian soldiers carry away statues of the gods of a captured city.

9. See E. J. Stendebach, "סוס *sûs*," *TDOT* 10:178–87, esp. 185; J. R. Bram, "Sun," in *Encyclopedia of Religion* (ed. L. Jones, M. Eliade, and C. J. Adams; 2nd ed., Detroit: Macmillan Reference, 2005) 8834–44; and J. G. Taylor, *Yahweh and the Sun: Biblical and Archeological Evidence for Sun Worship in Ancient Israel* (JSOTSup 111; Sheffield: JSOT Press, 1994).

> Sets Athirat on the back of a donkey,
> On the beautiful back of a mule,
> Qudsh starts to burn,
> Amrar, like a star.
> Ahead Adolescent Anat goes,
> While Baal departs for the summit of Sapan.
> Now she heads out
> For El at the springs of the Rivers,
> Amid the streams of the Deeps.
> She comes to the mountain of El and enters
> The tent of the King, the Father of Years.
> At the feet of El she bows down and falls,
> Prostrates herself and honors him.[10]

This scene seems atypical of other mounted deities in Canaanite literature. Why does Athirat travel on a donkey? Because she is going before the king of the gods to plead Baal's case for a palace of his own, one may speculate that Athirat deliberately assumes a posture of deference and humility before the divine king in hopes of increasing her odds of success. If so, then the conceit of riding upon a donkey to express humbleness is much older than Zechariah 9 and Matthew 21, to be discussed below.[11]

This scene with Athirat is also reminiscent of other situations in which one deity goes to visit another deity, often depicted as being carried in ritual procession from one temple or sanctuary to another, located perhaps even in another city. Deities may also be inducted into their own temple transported on the backs of animals, or by cart, or carried by humans. One is also reminded of comparable biblical depictions, e.g., of King David ushering into Jerusalem in an ox-drawn cart "the Ark of God," upon which the invisible deity was believed to be seated (2 Sam 6), and still later, of the priests carrying the ark into Solomon's newly dedicated temple, whereupon "the cloud, the glory of the Lord filled the house of the Lord" (1 Kgs 8:11).

---

10. "The Baal Cycle," translated by M. S. Smith, in *UNP*, 126–27.

11. There is no certainty that riding a donkey here represents humbleness, since asses were ubiquitous both as mounts and as beasts of burden and were commonly owned by simple folk and by wealthy folk. At least in the time of David, however, it appears that the mule (*pĕrĕd*), rather than ass or donkey, was the customary royal mount; see 2 Sam 13:29, 18:9; 1 Kgs 10:25.

BIBLICAL ADAPTATIONS OF THE MOTIF

Patently, the Israelites adapted the motif of a god mounted upon a symbolic animal to serve their own national deity. According to the Priestly tradition, Moses constructed the ark after a heavenly prototype, according to which the ark was topped by two cherubs with their outstretched wings forming a canopy over the mercy seat of the (invisible) deity between them (Exod 25:18–22; 37:7–9). When Solomon built the temple in Jerusalem to house the ark within the holy of holies, he decorated the walls and doors with "carved figures of cherubim and palm trees and flowers," in addition to lions, oxen, and other symbols of divine presence (1 Kgs 6:29–35; 7:29, 36). Into this richly ornate sanctuary Solomon introduced the art of the covenant of "the Lord of hosts who sits enthroned on the cherubim" (2 Sam 6:2; cf. Pr Azar 1:32 [Dan 3:55]). Indeed, one of the common ways to address Israel's God was as "Thou who art enthroned upon the cherubim" (Ps 80:1; Isa 37:16; 1 Sam 4:4) and "He sits enthroned upon the cherubim" (Ps 99:1).

Cherubs had long been a part of the ancient Near Eastern worldview. In the Canaanite culture at Ugarit, the chief god El characteristically is depicted as sitting upon a throne supported by two cherubs.[12] Israelite religious practice was steeped in such cultural syncretism. On the one hand, the Israelites ascribed to their national deity Yahweh many of the characteristics of El as the king of the gods and head of the Canaanite pantheon. On the other hand, there was also a tendency to ascribe to Yahweh various characteristics of the storm god Baal.

Likely because of the assimilation of Yahweh primarily to El, the Israelites mostly settled upon cherubs as the proper mount for their deity, as noted above. Nevertheless, there were competing traditions. A competing tradition, however, attempted to make a young bull the appropriate mount for Israel's god. When Jeroboam I split the northern tribes of Israel off from the kingdom of Judah after the death of Solomon, he placed "calves," i.e., young bulls in their prime, in the royal sanctuaries at Dan and Bethel—and presumably also in his capital city of Shechem—as visible symbols that the invisible God of Israel was present in the northern royal sanctuaries just as surely as in the Davidic royal city of Jerusalem (1 Kgs 12:25–33).[13] Similarly, at Sinai when Aaron and the Israelites made the "golden calf," undoubtedly

---

12. See note 2, above.

13. The incident is fraught with historical, literary, and theological complexities; for a survey of opinions see J. R. Spencer, "Golden Calf," in *ABD* 2:1065–69; N. Wyatt, "Calf," in *DDD* 344–48. For understanding Jeroboam's calf as a pedestal for Yahweh, see O. Eissfeldt, "Lade und Stierbild," *ZAW* 58 (1940–41) 190–215; B. W. Anderson, *Understanding the Old Testament* (4th ed.; Englewood Cliffs, NJ: Prentice-Hall, 1986) 259–61.

their intention was to craft a mount for the invisible Yahweh, as Aaron proclaims, "Here is your God (!) who brought you out of Egypt" (Exod 32:8).[14] This attempt to associate the God of Israel with a young, vigorous bull is roundly condemned in the Hebrew Bible (Hos 8:5–6; 10:5; Amos 7:13), undoubtedly because the Bible was transmitted to us through Judean hands. These Southern Kingdom transmitters invariably castigated every vestige of the "bull" tradition because of its association with the Northern Israelite kings' attempt to claim legitimacy and divine approval for their secession from the Davidic Kingdom centered in Jerusalem. The rival (Davidic/Solomonic) tradition of having Yahweh mounted upon cherubs suffered no comparable condemnation at the hands of the ultimate transmitters of the Bible. Indeed, the tradition of cherubs was embraced as the most appropriate mount for Israel's God.

In Ezekiel the "four living creatures" that bear up the deity are eventually identified as cherubs (Ezek 10:1). But Ezekiel's cherubs are different in that there are four of them, and not just two as elsewhere in the Hebrew Bible. They also differ in the manner of their form, being composite beings. Mostly humanoid in form, they each have the feet of a bull and four wings, however. Moreover, each creature has four "faces" or heads (human, lion, ox, and eagle), one looking in each direction (forward, right, left, and rearward). Together they form an omni-directional chariot-like throne for the indescribable deity seated above them (Ezekiel 1). Such deity-supporting creatures are also known from other ancient Near Eastern contexts,[15] so it is not surprising that they make their appearance in the biblical tradition.

Poetically, Yahweh could be portrayed as riding upon cherubs or as flying upon the wings of the wind:

> He bowed the heavens, and came down;
> thick darkness was under his feet.
> He rode on a cherub, and flew;
> he came swiftly upon the wings of the wind. (Ps 18:9–10)

2 Sam 22:10–11 is almost identical, except that the last colon reads, "he was seen upon the wings of the wind." Note also the similar imagery of Ps 104:3:

---

14. Hebrew grammar allows either a singular or plural reading here ("God" or "gods"). Later (Judean) writers patently read a plural here, undoubtedly as a polemic against the actions of Jeroboam I in placing "bulls" in his royal sanctuaries, in opposition to the cherubs that Solomon established in his royal sanctuary, the Jerusalem temple; see J. Gray, *I & II Kings: A Commentary* (2nd ed.; OTL; Philadelphia: Westminster, 1970) 316.

15. See *ANEP* ##644–649. Batto, "The Image of God," 143–86, esp. 174–79.

> You make the clouds your chariot,
> you ride on the wings of the wind. (Ps 104:3)

Yahweh could also be imagined as furiously driving a horse-drawn chariot as he lashes out against human and cosmic enemies, as in Hab 3: 8, 15:[16]

> Was your wrath against River, O Lord?
> Or your anger against River,
> Or our rage against Sea,
> When you drove your horses,
> Your chariots to victory? (Hab 3:8)

> You trampled Sea with your horses,
> Churning the mighty waters. (Hab 3:15)

The point is that in biblical tradition the deity can—and apparently does—employ a variety of different conveyances when making an appearance, with some form of a symbolic animal being the more common conceit.

FIRST-CENTURY CE VESTIGES OF THE MOTIF

With the conquests of Alexander the Great in the later fourth century BCE and the concomitant attempt to impose the Hellenic culture upon the population, much of the older ancient Near Eastern cultural views disappeared from the eastern Mediterranean. Nevertheless, despite a determined policy among the elites of Hellenization and assimilation to the politically dominant culture, there was little percolation "down to the mass of the population, who remained faithful to the old Aramaic idiom."[17] Many aspects survived in diminished form all the way into the Greco-Roman world of the New Testament. This was especially true in Syria, where scholars postulated that the Gospel of Matthew likely was written (Antioch).

Much of the physical evidence for first century CE pagan worship is now lost to us, in no small part because of the concerted efforts of Christians in the fourth and fifth centuries CE to obliterate the remaining vestiges of pagan beliefs and religious practice. The emperors Constantine the Great

---

16. "The background is the Ugaritic myth, in which the 'rider of the clouds' Baʻal measures himself against the sea god Yamm," Stendebach, *TDOT* 10:185–86, following F. Horst, *Die zwölf Kleinen Propheten: Hosea bis Micha* (2nd ed.; HAT 14; Tübingen: Mohr/Siebeck, 1954) 171–72.

17. G. Degeorge, *Dasmascus* (Paris: Flammarion, 2004) 23.

and Theodosius I set about systematically to remove statues of pagan gods from the empire. Likewise, Christian apologists lauded the destruction of pagan statuary from Egypt to Syro-Palestine to Constantinople.[18] There is little point in mentioning as well the renewed destruction of ancient pre-Muslim religious monuments in recent years at the hands of Al-Qaida and ISIL fanatics, for example, the leveling of the small temple of Bel at Palmyra. Given this history, it is a wonder that any remains at all have survived until the present.

Among the ruins of the temple of Bel at Palmyra is a well known relief on the crossbar of the peristyle of the entrance of Bel's cella depicting a procession by which the goddess Allat is brought into Palmyra.[19] The relief features prominently a donkey and a camel, with veiled women preceding and following, as well as various men standing about with one arm raised in apparent greeting. The donkey, with a trailing bridle, leads the procession, whether by its own volition or directed by an unseen divine hand. The camel follows, but led by a human guide. The camel carries upon its back what appears to be a *qobba*, a portable shrine used by the Arabs to transport betyls or other sacred objects. The relief is incomplete, with both ends broken off, and one indistinct figure or more ill preserved.[20]

The interpretation of the scene is much debated.[21] Comparing a fragmentary relief from Dura-Europos in which the god Arsu (?) appears to lead a camel, Susan Downey posits that the figure leading the camel in the Bel relief likely is to be identified as Arsu also.[22] Lucinda Dirven argues, however, on the basis of a fragmentary relief recently discovered in the temple of Allat at Palmyra which partially replicates the temple of Bel relief, that the depicted event is to be identified as the arrival of the goddess Allat in Palmyra.[23] The Allat temple relief is worked on both sides; the reverse

18. F. R. Trombley, "The Destruction of Pagan Statuary and Christianization (Fourth–Sixth Century C.E.)," in *The Sculptural Environment*, 143–64, esp. 148–55; D. Frankfurter, "The Vitality of Egyptian Images in Late Antiquity: Christian Memory and Response," in ibid., 659–78, esp. 664–66, 674–75.

19. Allat, whose name means "goddess," was the principal female deity of the first century nomadic Arabs of Palmyra. Elsewhere Allat is identified with both the Semitic goddess Atargatis and the Greek goddess Athena.

20. The relief was published by H. Seyrig, in *Le Temple de Bêl à Palmyre* (2 vols.; Institute Français d'Archéologie de Beyrouth; Bibliothèque archéologique et historique 83; Paris: Geuthner, 1975) 1:88–89. With plate 42,1; a drawing is found in vol. 2, fig. 91.

21. See the discussion by S. B. Downey, "The Role of Sculpture in Worship at the Temples of Dura-Europos," in *The Sculptural Environment*, 413–35, esp. 421–24.

22. Ibid.

23. L. Dirven, "The Arrival of the Goddess Allat in Palmyra," *Mesopotamia* 33 (1998) 297–307; Dirven, *The Palmyrenes of Dura-Europos: A Study of Religious Interaction in*

side preserves the tail end of wagon or cart that likely depicted the transport of the cult statue of the goddess for installation in her temple at its inauguration.[24] Other interpreters suggest that regular processions (perhaps annual) of divine effigies transpired between the temples of Bel and Allat at Palmyra, though this remains speculative.[25] The Bel temple relief can be dated to approximately 80 CE. The Allat temple relief is perhaps a century older or more. The younger relief appears to be copied from the older one, a case of deliberate archaizing which suggests a conscious and deliberate attempt at preserving religious practices from the past. Indeed, Dirven argues that these and similar reliefs may ultimately connect Bel (Baalshamin) and Allat (Atargatis) to cultic and religious traditions going all the way back to the Nabu-Bel versus Tiamat myth.[26]

Allat is frequently depicted with a lion, sometimes two lions. But rather than being Allat's vehicle or mode of transport, the lion(s) may have served as guardian(s) of the goddess and her sanctuary. Although the original cult statue of Allat from her temple has not survived, there exist a couple of replicas which suggest what it must have looked like. One of replicas depicts a goddess standing between two lions. Although the top half of the figure is broken away, an Aramaic inscription carved into the base of the relief reads 'lt, leaving no doubt that Allat is the figure depicted.[27]

The evidence, thus, is insufficient to decide precisely what event is being depicted in the Bel Temple relief, nor which deity is being honored in the procession. What seems clear, however, is that a divine figure is being enthusiastically received by the throng via an elaborate procession and that great honor is being bestowed upon the arriving divine figure.

Processions, of course, are nothing new. The tradition of deities traveling about or being carried from temple to temple and from city to city in cultic processions is a universal phenomenon.[28] Looking specifically back to Babylon from where various aspects of the cult of Bel at Palmyra derived, one need only recall the Akitu festival and the famous processional way at Babylon.

Roman Syria (Religions in the Graeco-Roman World 138; Leiden: Brill, 1999).

24. M. Gawlikowski, "The Statues of the Sanctuary of Allat in Palmyra," in *The Sculptural Environment*, 397–411, esp. 405–8.

25. T. Kaizer, *The Religious Life of Palmyra: A Study of the Social Patterns of Worship in the Roman Period* (Oriens et Occidens 4; Stuttgart: Steiner, 2002) 200–203.

26. L. Dirven, "The Exaltation of Nabû: A Revision of the Relief depicting the Battle against Tiamat from the Temple of Bel in Palmyra," *WO* 28 (1997) 96–116.

27. Gawlikowski, "The Statues of the Sanctuary," 404–5, with figs. 5 and 6.

28. On processions in general, see P. B. Duff, "Processions," in *ABD* 5:469–73; R. L. Grimes, "Procession," in *Encyclopedia of Religion*, 7416–18.

Kevin Butcher describes the situation in Roman Syria thus: "Each deity had feast days, and the major cults had grand public processions . . . that helped validate the social order and identity of the community . . . In processions the deity rode around in a portable shrine, carried on the shoulders of bearers or propelled on wheels like a juggernaut. Civic coins provide us with a selection of divine modes of transport (figs. 81.2, 155.2) . . . The effect of carrying these images around cities must have been very much like the processions in religious ceremonies today. There were also organized processions to temples, especially if the sanctuary was located in the countryside."[29] Moreover, it was considered a great honor to be one of the bearers of the divine effigy, apparently; "at Seleucia the privilege of bearing the symbol of Zeus Keraunios ("of the thunderbolt") went to two elected *keraunophors*, 'bearers of the thunderbolt.'"[30]

The importance of Palmyra as representative of the whole region cannot be underestimated. Being an oasis city in a desert region, Palmyra was a major destination for caravan merchants coming from south, north, east, and west. There not only were various merchandises exchanged but also ideas, resulting in the dissemination of cultural views and religious practices from far and near. The direction of the flow of ideas cannot always be determined, however.

JESUS' ENTRANCE A DIVINE ARRIVAL ACCORDING TO MATTHEW

Remote as the possibility may have seemed initially, such cultural tropes apparently do provide a back story for the evangelist Matthew's narrative about Jesus' entrance into Jerusalem. According to the Gospel of Matthew (21:1–11), Jesus entered Jerusalem mounted on two animals, an ass and a colt, thereby fulfilling the ancient prophecy of Zech 9:9. By contrast, the other gospels depict Jesus as entering the city riding on a single animal, a colt (Mark 11:2–6; Luke 19:30–36; John 12:14–15). Assuming that the latter group represents the original—and historically more accurate—tradition, how should one account for the discrepancy in Matthew's presentation? Several proposals have been proffered, nearly all revolving around Matthew's citation of the prophecy of Zech 9:9, which in Matthew's reading seemingly necessitates that Jesus mounts two different animals. (John also cites Zech 9:9, but in a very different form, and assumes but a single animal is involved.)

29. K. Butcher, *Roman Syria and the Near East* (Los Angeles: Getty, 2003) 348.
30. Ibid.

Matthew's citation of Zech 9:9 does not conform completely either to the Hebrew MT text or to the Greek LXX version. Elsewhere, when Matthew cites the Hebrew Scriptures, it can be shown that as a rule he follows the LXX. That makes his deviation in this case all the more puzzling.

Zechariah 9:9	Matthew 21:5
Χαῖρε σφόδρα, θύγατερ Σιων· κήρυσσε, θύγατερ Ιερουσαλημ· ἰδοὺ ὁ βασιλεύς σου ἔρχεταί σοι, δίκαιος καὶ σῴζων αὐτός, πραῢς καὶ ἐπιβεβηκὼς ἐπὶ ὑποζύγιον καὶ πῶλον νέον.	Εἴπατε τῇ θυγατρὶ Σιών· ἰδοὺ ὁ βασιλεύς σου ἔρχεταί σοι πραῢς καὶ ἐπιβεβηκὼς ἐπὶ ὄνον καὶ ἐπὶ πῶλον υἱὸν ὑποζυγίου.
Rejoice greatly, O daughter of Zion! Shout aloud, O daughter of Jerusalem! Behold, your King comes to you; triumphant and victorious is he, humble and riding on a draught animal, on a young donkey.	Say to the daughter of Zion, Behold, your King comes to you, humble and riding on a ass and on an ass, the colt of a draught animal.

Patently, Matthew departs from the LXX text of Zech 9:9 in major ways. First, he replaces the double exhortation to the "daughter of Zion/Jerusalem" to rejoice and celebrate with an announcement formula, "Say to the daughter of Zion," a formula taken from a related text of Isa 62:11. One might suppose that Matthew was quoting from memory and has confused the two texts, especially because they are partially overlapping in content. But given the manner in which Matthew has altered the text of Zechariah in other respects to suit his own theological agenda, one may postulate, better, that Matthew has deliberately substituted the Isaiah text to prepare the reader for the tumult in the city caused by Jesus' arrival. Mathew has transformed it into a summons for the people to assemble to celebrate the arrival of the long awaited divine messianic king.

Second, by omitting the phrase "triumphant and victorious is he," Matthew emphasizes the humble, peaceful demeanor of this King who is arriving. This surely is a conscious attempt to put a different face on Jesus as the fulfillment of the prophecy, exactly in keeping with the unique way in which the Matthean Jesus characterizes himself (πραῢς εἰμι καὶ ταπεινὸς τῇ καρδίᾳ "I am humble and lowly of heart") and offers himself as the model that his disciples should imitate (Matt 11:29).[31] (Is it possible, further, that

---

31. Misguided are attempts to downplay Jesus' humbleness here by stressing that, in contrast to Zechariah's use of Hebrew ʿōnî "lowly," Matthew employs the LXX translation πραῢς "gentle," thereby emphasizing the *peaceful* character of Jesus' entry; so D. R. Hare, *Matthew* (Interpretation; Louisville: Westminster John Knox, 1993) 238.

Matthew also contains a faint echo of Athirat of the Sea humbling herself by appearing before the king of the gods riding on a donkey?)

Third and most obvious, Matthew has Jesus enter the city mounted on two animals, rather than one as in Zech 9:9. Numerous explanations have been proffered to account for this discrepancy, e.g., that Matthew was citing from a faulty memory or that Matthew used a Greek text with a different Vorlage. The most common explanation, however, is that Matthew simply misunderstood the poetic nature of the text, misreading the copulative (Greek καὶ = Hebrew -וְ) as a true grammatical copulative, rather than as an emphatic element ("even," "indeed") whose function in the poetic technique of parallelism is to link closely the second member of a poetic couplet to the preceding member.[32] Because Matthew read the copulative "literally," he understood the text to imply that two animals were involved, when in fact the prophet intended but a single animal.

That the evangelist did not understand the intended parallelism of the prophetic text seems highly unlikely, however. Already in this verse alone Matthew has twice felt free to omit one of the two members of parallel cola: "daughter Zion" // "daughter Jerusalem"; "triumphant and victorious" // "humble and riding on a draught animal." Clearly Matthew understood Hebrew poetic parallelism. Accordingly, an explanation must be sought elsewhere.

I suggest that Matthew deliberately chose to ignore the poetic parallelism involved and instead to read the text *literally* as speaking of *two* animals because it advanced his larger thesis of presenting Jesus as Immanuel, "God with us."

JESUS AS IMMANUEL, "GOD WITH US"

A major aspect of Matthew's Christology is that Jesus is literally Immanuel, "God with us." Matthew prefaces his gospel of "Jesus Christ" (or "Jesus Messiah") (1:1, 18; cf. 1:16) with a birth story that leaves no doubt that Jesus is more than a mere human. Jesus' conception is of divine origin. Speaking of Mary's pregnancy, the angel of the Lord informs Joseph, "that which is conceived in her is of the Holy Spirit" (1:20), thereby fulfilling the prophecy:

Similarly, Alfred Plummer's contention (*An Exegetical Commentary on the Gospel according to S. Matthew* [New York: Scribner, 1910] 285) that "we are not to regard Christ's riding on an ass as a special act of humility" cannot be sustained in view of Matthew's adroit manipulation of this verse.

32. For a discussion of parallelism in ancient Near Eastern literature, and in Ugaritic literature in specific, see S. B. Parker, *The Pre-Biblical Narrative Tradition* (SBLRBS 24; Atlanta: Scholars, 1989) 7–17.

"'Behold a virgin shall conceive and bear a son, and his name shall be called Immanu-el,' which means God-with-us" (1:23). The evangelist notes that in conformity with the angel's instructions, Joseph did take Mary as his wife but adds emphatically that "he did not know her until she had borne a son" (1:25), thereby reaffirming the divine origin of the child. Here, as elsewhere, the evangelist is careful to say that with respect to Jesus nothing happens by chance; everything is accomplished by divine providence.

Similarly, Matthew deliberately alters the ending of his Gospel from that of the received tradition so as to maintain his Christology of Jesus being Immanu-el, "God with us." Both in Synoptic tradition and in the Johannine tradition the risen Jesus ascends to the father, leaving the disciples alone to cope without him, albeit with the aid of the Holy Spirit whom Jesus imparts to them for guidance. Matthew knows this tradition well. Following especially his Markan guide, Matthew even has the disciples go to "the mountain" in Galilee, just as they were directed (Mark 16:7; cf. 14:28). But instead of ascending into the heavens (Luke 24:50–51; Acts 1:9–11; cf. John 1:17), the Matthean Jesus does not ascend into the heavens. Instead, Jesus transfers his own authority to his disciples and commissions them to go make disciples of all peoples. But he does not then leave. Rather, he explicitly declares, "I am with you always, to the end of the age" (Matt 28:20). In short, Matthew's "good news" is that Jesus Christ will continue on forever as Immanu-el, "God with us."

In scene after scene throughout the gospel the evangelist affirms the divinity of Jesus, continually reminding the reader that Jesus is the Son of God. One may note especially the following: (1) At the baptism by John a voice from heaven announces "This is my Son, the Beloved, with whom I am well pleased" (1:17). (2) At the temptation, the devil repeatedly tests Jesus, "If you are the Son of God . . . " (4:1–11). (3) When Jesus expels the demons from the Gadarene demoniacs, they exclaim, "What have you to do with us, Son of God? Have you come here to torment us before the time? (8:29). (4) In speaking of God as his Father, Jesus proclaims, "All things have been handed over to me by my Father, and no one knows the Son except the Father, and no one know the Father except the Son and anyone to whom the Son chooses to reveal him" (11:27). (5) On the occasion of Jesus walking on the water, his disciples in the boat "worshipped him, saying, 'Truly you are the Son of God'" (14:32).[33] (6) At Caesarea Philippi, when Peter

---

33. One should compare the similar episode in which Jesus stills the storming sea (8:23–27). Although there is no statement about Jesus being the Son of God, clearly Matthew intends the reader to understand this scene as epiphanic of Jesus' divinity. The power to still the sea belongs to the deity alone; see B. F. Batto, *Slaying the Dragon: Mythmaking in the Biblical Tradition* (Louisville: Westminster John Knox, 1992)

answers Jesus' question about his identity, Peter says, "You are the Christ, the Son of the living God." The Matthean Jesus—in stark contrast to the Markan Jesus—affirms the correctness of Peter's response with the statement, "Blessed are you, Simon son of Jonah! For flesh and blood has not revealed this to you, but my Father in heaven" (16:15–17, cf. Mark 8:27–29). (7) Divine revelation of Jesus' true identity is also given at the transfiguration, as the voice from the overshadowing cloud announces, "This is my son, the Beloved; with him I am well please; listen to him!" The response of the disciples is correctly one of awe and worship: "When the disciples heard this, they fell with their faces to the ground, and were overcome with fear" (17:5–6). (8) When Jesus challenges the Pharisees regarding the paternity of the Messiah, whose son is he, they answer "David's." Jesus reminds them that David in Ps 110:1 addresses the (forthcoming) Messiah as "Lord," so "if David thus calls [the Messiah] Lord, can he be his son?" Because a father never addresses his son as Lord, the obvious answer to the question of whose son is he must be: God's—the truth of which the reader has been informed multiple times already. (9) During the trial before Caiaphas, the high priest asks Jesus to declare under oath whether he is "the Messiah, the Son of God" (26:57–67). The violent reaction of the high priest and the whole council leaves no doubt that Jesus' oblique response is to be understood in the affirmative. (10) Finally, the terrified centurion and those with him, witnessing the earthquake and the tumultuous events accompanying the death of Jesus, bear witness to the true identity of Jesus: "Truly this man was God's Son!" (27:54).

Patently, Matthew is at pains to convey Jesus' true identity as God-with-us, the Son of God, somewhat analogous to the way in which the Johannine Jesus is the Word-made-flesh, but in Matthew without any hint of pre-existence. It appears that Matthew's concern to underscore the divinity of Jesus has profoundly shaped the evangelist's story about Jesus' entry into Jerusalem.

The Hebrew text of Zech 9:9 has *rōkēb*, a verb which can have reference either to the act of riding in the sense of "sitting astride" a horse, or to the posture of mounted upon or standing upright, as for example, in a chariot.[34] This ambiguity seems to figure into Matthew's understanding of Zech 9:9, when compared with other New Testament authors' citation of this prophetic passage.

181–85. It is therefore with no little irony that the disciples ask in amazement, "What sort of *man* is this, that even the winds and the sea obey him?"

34. See √RKB in BDB.

Mark—and similarly John—employs the verb καθίζω "to ride/mount." (Luke 19:35 uses a different verb: ἐπιβιβάζω "to mount/sit or to cause to mount/sit upon.") With but a single animal involved, Mark, Luke, and John all understand Jesus to have mounted the animal by sitting upon it, that is, in the usual manner of sitting astride its back. Matthew (21:7), however, alters Mark's (11:7) straightforward wording "and he sat on/mounted it" (καθίζω) by strengthening the verb and making it plural: "and they made [him] mount/sit upon" (ἐπικαθίζω) and changing the preposition from ἐπι "on" to επάνω "over/above."[35] Thus, Mark's simple reading, "and [Jesus] sat on it," became in Matthew's description something more like "and *they* make [Jesus] mount up upon *them* [i.e., the two animals]." It appears that Matthew felt the inadequacy of Mark's language for describing Jesus' action of being mounted upon *two* animals. It is unclear whether Matthew intends the reader to understand Jesus as somehow seated on both animals, i.e., riding straddled across both animals simultaneously. An older proposal—namely, that Jesus rode first one animal, dismounted, and subsequently mounted the second animal—seems entirely ruled out by Matthew's own language. More likely, Matthew did not intend to clarify the precise manner of how Jesus physically accomplished the task of mounting both animals; he merely wished to suggest to the reader that Jesus was mounted above the donkeys in a manner reminiscent of a deity mounted above his symbolic mount, much like Yahweh mounted above the cherubs. In Jesus' case, however, the mounts have a further symbolic connotation, namely, the humbleness of the rider.

CONCLUSION

Given Matthew's goal of presenting Jesus as Immanuel, one cannot but conclude that Matthew consciously cloaks Jesus in imagery of the deity drawn from the Hebrew Scriptures, and particularly the image of God as a deity who comes among his people seated or mounted upon cherubs. Nevertheless, Matthew seems to have adapted the imagery of a divine arrival to the cultural conventions of his 1st century audience in Syria where, to judge from our sparse evidence from Palmyra and neighboring sites, people were more accustoming to thinking of arriving divinities being transported in wheeled vehicles, or borne by camel, or riding upon a horse or a donkey. Zech 9:9 proved providential for Matthew. Through it Matthew was able to retain the Israelite tradition of the deity being borne by two symbolic creatures, while also maintaining the thrust of Zechariah that the Messiah

---

35. Plummer, *Matthew*, 286; Lowe & Nida I.17.15.

would be a humble royal figure riding upon lowly donkeys—and perhaps echoing a long standing tradition of the region as well. Yet while Jesus enters as a humble king, the crowd recognizes the significance of the one arriving. Much like the Palmyrenes welcoming the goddess Allat into their city and celebrating the arrival of their god, so in Matthew's telling of the event, the Jerusalemites enthusiastically welcome Jesus into their holy city, acclaiming him as the expected divine Messiah who has come at long last. He is truly *God-with-us,* which the crowds, at least for a time, authentically acknowledge and celebrate.

— 10 —

Narrative-Ancestry-Dot-Com

*The Gettysburg Address,
Descendant of the Book of Jonah*

TIM KOCH

"What has been will be again, what has been done will be done again;
there is nothing new under the sun."

—QOH 1:9, NIV

FOREWORD: NARRATIVE AND ANCESTRY

I SUBSCRIBE TO THE popular genealogical site, Ancestry.com®. Along the way, I have learned fascinating things about my ancestors including that I am descended from the (in)famous Captain Morgan (Welsh pirate of rum fame), that the strand of family that everyone thought was Irish (based on the name "Shirey") is in fact German (originally "Scheurer"), and that I have a goodly dollop of Swiss in me, going back at least six centuries.

One way to apply this information regarding my ancestry is predictive: How Teutonic should my features be? Do I have a love of the sea in me? What about any bardic tendencies? Am I a natural-born yodeler? (The answers, respectively, are Somewhat, No, Scarcely, and TBD.) A more fruitful approach is to begin with my own life and utilize the hints, traces, seeds, or strains from that (admittedly incomplete) repository of my past to help me better understand the person-in-context that I am today.

Simon B. Parker was figuratively enrolled in a similar enterprise that I would label "NarrativeAncestry.com." That is, Parker researched the historic and linguistic ancestors of Ancient Israel, in order to gain insights into the literature and history of Ancient Israel, specifically regarding how the Hebrew Scriptures came to be the texts-in-context that they became. Both his study of Ugaritic narrative poetry in *The Pre-Biblical Narrative Tradition*[1] and his work on Northwest Semitic inscriptions in *Stories in Scripture and Inscriptions*[2] exemplify the ways in which ancestral narrative repositories can illuminate, vivify, and offer new perspectives on later narratives and stories subsequently performed by their linguistic descendants.[3]

The present study recognizes nineteenth-century United States President Abraham Lincoln as a literary inheritor of the King James Version of the Bible. Lincoln's own story of America, as put forward in his Gettysburg Address, is both a beneficiary and an extension of this ancestral repository. One prophetic work in particular, the book of Jonah, is plumbed for its ability to illuminate and contribute to a more comprehensive understanding of Lincoln's Address. Just as a family tree reads both forwards and backwards in time, a deeper understanding of the descendant (the Gettysburg Address) may in turn reveal aspects of the ancestor (Jonah) heretofore unknown or unsuspected.

INTRODUCTION: ART AND TRANSFORMATION

Emily Dickinson, in one of her occasional prose passages, proclaimed: "If I read a book and it makes my whole body so cold no fire can ever warm me, I know that is poetry. If I feel as if the top of my head were taken off, I know that is poetry. These are the only ways I know it. Is there any other way?"[4]

---

1. S. B. Parker, *The Pre-Biblical Narrative Tradition: Essays on the Ugaritic Poems Keret and Aqhat* (SBLRBS 24; Atlanta: Scholars, 1989).

2. S. B. Parker, *Stories in Scripture and Inscriptions: Comparative Studies on Narratives in Northwest Semitic Inscriptions and the Hebrew Bible* (New York: Oxford University Press, 1997).

3. Just as families are often depicted in "trees," so too are languages. Ugaritic and Ancient Hebrew are both members of the family of Northwest Semitic languages, with the Ugaritic language sitting in the tree as a sibling to Canaanite, from which Ancient Hebrew is a direct descendant; thus, Ugaritic perches as the linguistic equivalent of an aunt or an uncle to Hebrew. See, among many others, A. D. Rubin, "The Subgrouping of the Semitic Languages," *Language and Linguistics Compass* 2/1 (2008) 84, fig. 1.

4. M. D. Bianchi, *The Life and Letters of Emily Dickinson* (New York: Biblo & Tannen, 1924) 276.

This transformative power would have been no less palpable for those gathered on November 19, 1863, to dedicate the Soldiers' National Cemetery in Gettysburg, Pennsylvania. Nor, indeed, could the ancient, post-exilic reader scarcely avoid this same turning of everything upside-down[5] upon encountering the book of Jonah.

Hans-Georg Gadamer, in his work, *Truth and Method*, discusses transformation as it relates to defining the nature of art and its impact upon those who encounter it:

> Transformation is not alteration, even an alteration that is far-reaching. Alteration always means that what is altered also remains the same and is maintained . . . But transformation means that something is suddenly and as a whole something else, that this other transformed thing that it has become is its true being, in comparison with which its earlier being is nil . . .[6]

Gadamer's prose offers a philosophical description of what Emily Dickinson means when she wrote that poetry feels physically as if the top of her head were taken off—the transformation is not simply a modification: it is a revelation, dramatically revolutionizing the perceptions of the one transformed, from that point onward.

The transformation that is a re-formation of a situation's entire meaning is spoken of in numerous disciplines and in diverse ways: as an epiphany, as that "a-ha!" experience, as a "world turned suddenly upside-down." It is a meta-level change that Gadamer identifies as transformation, that Dickinson describes in her experience of poetry, and what nurse theorist Rosemarie Rizzo Parse refers to when she writes of "the all-at-once transfiguring of an unfamiliar perspective to the familiar, as others, ideas, objects, and situations are viewed in a new light."[7]

Connections and parallels between Lincoln's speech and the book of Jonah hold significant heuristic value. Unlike the Gettysburg Address, of course, one does not know with any degree of certainty the date or the occasion for the writing of the book of Jonah. Yet, the absence of concrete references does not mean that a document is not addressing some very specific, historical contingency in the lives of its readers or hearers. Proverbs, for example, are certainly more generic and less time-tied than either Lincoln's

---

5. Much like Jonah's prophecy to the Ninevites that, within 40 days, they would be *nehpāket*: turned/overturned/flipped over/transformed (cf. BDB). Jonah 3:4.

6. H.-G. Gadamer, *Truth and Method* (2nd rev. ed.; trans. J. Weinsheimer and D. G. Marshall; New York: Crossroad, 1989) 110–11.

7. R. R. Parse, *The Human Becoming School of Thought: A Perspective for Nurses and Other Health Professionals* (Thousand Oaks, CA: Sage, 1998) 35.

speech or the book of Jonah. As Kenneth Burke's insightful definition reveals, "Proverbs are *strategies* for dealing with *situations*."[8] Thus an argument that the absence of historical referents somehow implies an absence of a specific context cannot be sustained.

Both the book of Jonah and Lincoln's speech are short documents, easily perused in a few minutes. Both build in, for their audience/readership, safe distance for contemplation: one begins with "Four score and seven years ago," the other with the equally "biblical-sounding" and standard narrative opening, "Now it came to pass . . . ." Both use genres familiar to their audiences (funeral oratory in one, prophetic narrative and disputational folktale in the other[9]), and both employ vivid, BIG imagery, freely using the adjective "great" (Lincoln speaks of "a great civil war" and the "great task remaining before us"; the book of Jonah contains near one score uses of the word *gādôl* [Hebrew for "big, great, large"]). Most importantly, both utilize their people's historical traditions in order to paint a picture, not of some *new* thing being initiated, but of something *bigger*, of a history that in fact extends further back than they were cognizant of, a story of how things have *actually* been since the very beginning. Yet, all the while, neither document purports that reciting a history is its goal: one is a dedication of a cemetery, and the other, a story about a pre-exilic prophet from the Northern Kingdom.

THE LITERARY INHERITANCE OF THE BOOK OF JONAH

Beginning at the End of the Book of Jonah

At the end of the book of Jonah, the prophet (and, by extension, the reader) is challenged with the following question:

---

8. K. Burke, *The Philosophy of Literary Form: Studies in Symbolic Action* (2nd ed.; Baton Rouge: Louisiana State University Press, 1967) 296 (emphasis original). A useful study of how proverbs function historically in prophetic literature is found in K. P. Darr, *Isaiah's Vision and the Family of God* (Literary Currents in Biblical Interpretation; Louisville: Westminster John Knox, 1994), esp. 205-27.

9. For a discussion on the astounding structural similarities between a type of African folktales that ethnographer Roger D. Abrahams has labeled "Stories to Discuss and Even Argue About," see T. R. Koch, "The Book of Jonah and a Reframing of Israelite Theology: A Reader-Response Approach" (Ph.D. diss., Boston University Graduate School of Arts and Sciences, 2003) 55-59, 172-73, 200-203, 239-40, discussing R. D. Abrahams, *African Folktales: Traditional Stories of the Black World* (New York: Pantheon, 1983) 107-52.

Yahweh said, "You, you are heartsick over the *qīqāyôn*,[10] for which you neither labored not grew it Great . . . something that came into being as a child of the night and as a child of the night perished. So I, should I not be heartsick over Nineveh, the Great City, in which there is a human population in excess of twelve-times-ten-thousand—that does not know its right hand from its left—plus many animals?!!"[11]

How does the ancient reader respond to this question? Given that the question is put to Jonah, the reader, with historical distance, has sufficient room to maneuver intellectually, by speculating on how *Jonah* would (and ought to) respond to Yahweh. The ancient reader recognizes—even if Jonah does not—that Yahweh's intrinsic graciousness and mercy have not only preserved the mariners' and the Ninevites' lives (not to mention the *qīqāyôn*), but are the very reason that Jonah is alive as well. Thus, for the reader, it is clear: Jonah should get down on his knees in thankfulness that Yahweh-God is so profligate in showing compassion, and that the Creator God Who indeed made everything and everyone that exists takes such a proprietary interest in *all* of creation.

The Pocket-Picking that Occurred in the Book of Jonah

At first glance, the conclusion by the ancient reader that Jonah should be thankful is not particularly startling nor jarring to present-day (and especially Christian) sensibilities at all—the graciousness of God freely extended to Jew and non-Jew alike is integral to many (though not all) Jews' and Christians' expressions of faith. Yet it is worth exploring how dependent the ancient reader's conclusion about God's graciousness is upon the story that she or he has just read. To wit, *prior to reading the book of Jonah*, would an ancient reader have affirmed that YHWH, the God of Israel should be (or, historically, should have been) "heartsick over Nineveh, the Great City," so heavily populated by humans and animals?

---

10. The decision to leave the plant untranslated is two-fold: first, the word *qīqāyôn* is a *hapax legomenon*, unique to the book, and any determination of what it refers to (mustard plant, gourd, ivy, or palm) is conjectural; second, the contrast being drawn is between care for the *qīqāyôn* and care for *Nineveh*, and keeping the plant untranslated preserves the similarity of cadence between the two objects of concern.

11. This section of the book of Jonah is the author's own translation from the Hebrew.

One can fairly assume that a reader living in post-exilic Judah was only too well aware that the Assyrians were ruthless, cruel, vicious—a people of violence and bloodshed. The reader would have been taught of the Assyrians' responsibility for the destruction of the northern kingdom of Israel and would have, were it not for Yahweh's miraculous intervention, taken down Judah and Jerusalem as well.[12] Additionally, prior to reading the book of Jonah, the reader's awareness of prophecy regarding Nineveh—"City of Bloodshed"—might have derived primarily from the book of Nahum in which the utter destruction of those people (and presumably their livestock) is prophesied and even celebrated.

In Nahum, there is no sense that anyone, least of all Yahweh, would pause to be "heartsick" over these violent, blood-thirsty people. Thus, the reader's conviction after reading the book of Jonah that *of course* Yahweh-God should and would be heartsick over, feel compassion toward, and treat mercifully (at least for a time) the people and animals of Nineveh represents nothing less than a truly revolutionary transformation of perspective.

What has happened? Without any explicit realization, by the time the reader engages the question at the end of the book of Jonah, the reader has already taken as given that Yahweh has an independent relationship with the Ninevites, apart from that with Israel. In order to "discuss and even debate"[13] the question that closes the book of Jonah, the reader must have already granted the premise that Yahweh might well care independently about the welfare of a people *other* than Israel.

Yet nowhere in the text of Jonah is this premise made explicit; it is simply posited. This technique of getting an audience (or readership) to focus on a particular question for the purpose of discussion and debate, as a means to gain an unwitting agreement to another or greater premise—what historian Garry Wills refers to as a bold act of "open-air sleight of hand" and "an intellectual pickpocket"[14]—is comically and artfully exemplified in the 1982 movie, *Victor/Victoria*. In this film, an out-of-work singer named Victoria Grant (portrayed by Julie Andrews) is talked into posing as a female impersonator by her new-found friend Carroll "Toddy" Todd (played by Robert Preston). The way Toddy suggests for getting people to believe that she, Victoria, is actually a man is to claim that the *man* she is pretending to be is a Polish count. Consider the following movie dialogue:

---

12. The biblical account of the deliverance of Judah from the Assyrians is found in Isaiah 36–37.

13. See n.9, above, discussing Abrahams, *African Folktales*, and the genre of "Stories to Discuss and Even Argue About."

14. G. Wills, *Lincoln at Gettysburg: The Words That Remade America* (New York: Simon & Schuster, 1992) 38.

CT: What's wrong?

VG: What's wrong?! What's right!? A woman ... pretending to be a man ... pretending to be a woman?!

CT: Ridiculous!

VG: It's, it's *preposterous*!

CT: In fact, it's so preposterous no one would ever believe it.

VG: And yet you expect them to believe Count ... what's his name?

CT: Grazinsky

VG: ... Grazinsky—gay ... Polish ... female impersonator.

CT: Darling, all anyone has to believe is that you're a man.

VG: Well?!

CT: To convince an audience that an illusion is real, the magician creates a plausible diversion. Count Grazinsky is our plausible diversion!

VG: Toddy, no audience is that gullible; they'll *know* he's a phony!

CT: Right!

VG: Well?

CT: They'll know *he's* a phony![15]

Once audiences begin discussing and even debating whether or not the female impersonator is *actual* Polish aristocracy—feeling rather proud of themselves for seeing through Victor Grazinsky's affectation—they have already bought into the belief that they are talking about a *man*!

Just so, once the reader is engaged in pondering whether or not Yahweh should take pity upon the (at least temporarily) repentant Ninevites, he or she has *already* accepted the premise that it is not only conceivable but also consonant with Yahweh's character to take an active interest in the lives of people (and animals) who are *not* Israelite, and to be interested in them for their own sake. That is, once the reader actively engages the question at the end of the book of Jonah, the transformation of his or her reading of Israel's history has already come to pass—whether he or she realized it or not.

How This Happens in the Book of Jonah

Prior to reading the book of Jonah, our ancient reader can be assumed to have held what might be termed a dispensationalist view of history.[16] That

---

15. B. Edwards, prod., *Victor/Victoria* (dir. and screenwriter, B. Edwards; Los Angeles: MGM/Perrford/Ladbroke Entertainments, 1982).

16. This is not to be confused with a thoroughly developed theology of

is, the reader was informed by the view of history as put forward by the Priestly redactors of the Torah, a history framed by genealogies and progressive covenants that led the God who created the heavens and the earth ultimately to concern Himself with Israel (and Israel alone). This history can be conceived of as a series of filters, by which YHWH-God "begins" with all of creation; then, from among those who survive the Flood, God chooses Abraham and his descendants; from among these, YHWH "becomes the God" of and for those Hebrew who come up from slavery in Egypt to take possession of the land of Canaan. In this schema, the most important of these covenants becomes the last, for it is the most definitive, most restrictive, most specific. By positing the equivalence of the God of Creation with the God that chooses Israel, the Priestly history affirms that YHWH is not merely a tribal god among others, but is in fact the *one and only God*, the God who is supreme over all creation, all events, all places, and all times, and *who has selected Israel as His own*.

The reader of the book of Jonah utilizes this same equivalence—but with the current running in the opposite direction. The reader encounters a pre-exilic prophet, one that ironically quotes the affirmation of God's compassionate character recorded in the book of Exodus. This is a prophet who, on a ship about to break up in the midst of a terrible storm at the outset of the story identifies himself to the mariners as a "Hebrew"—yet instead of giving this self-identification apposite to "the God of Abraham, Isaac, and Jacob," identifies himself, saying "I am a Hebrew; and I fear the Lord, the God of heaven, which hath made the sea and the dry land" (Jonah 1:9, KJV). This is a prophet who is thrown into the arms of a God lifted almost directly from the time of Noah.[17] Through encountering Jonah, the ancient reader finds his or her own reading of Israel's *most* important covenant pushed back and back in time.

The Torah explains how the God of all creation, the God of Noah, becomes the God of Abraham, Isaac, and Jacob, and hence the God of Israel. Yet in the book of Jonah—perhaps for the first time—our ancient reader of biblical texts is offered this assertion in reverse form: the God of the Hebrews, the God of Israel, has always *been* the God of Noah, the God of all creation! The mythic origin of Israel's history is found not in the covenant at Sinai nor even in the covenant with Abraham. The *Ur*-Covenant is the one made with Noah, and therefore with all subsequent humanity . . . plus many animals besides. Suddenly, the very God who seems to have winnowed out

---

dispensationalism (or, even, "progressive dispensationalism"), as espoused by certain evangelical Christian theologians.

17. To review a thorough listing of Noachic "sampling" scattered throughout the book of Jonah, see Koch, *Book of Jonah*, 283–91.

entire peoples and nations and tribes and families in choosing Israel as His own is presented anew as the God who has always and all along been the compassionate, merciful God of Israel (yes), yet also of the Edomites, Ishmaelites, Canaanites—in short, the God of everything and everyone, including, of course, the Ninevites. Having entered into the belly of this scant, 48-verse story, the reader finds him or herself spat out with a *new* history, a story of a people and their God that, like the Ninevites, has been utterly turned upside-down.[18]

LINCOLN AS INHERITOR

Religious historian Brian C. Wilson, in his study, "KJV in the USA: The Impact of the King James Bible in the USA," discusses the Authorized Version's "exceptional influence on the development of American political rhetoric and American literature in the 19th century."[19] Wilson specifically reports, "Raised on a 1799 SPCK [Society for Promoting Christian Knowledge] printing of the King James Bible, Abraham Lincoln imbibed the language and style of the Authorized Version from boyhood and he developed a remarkable ability to cite passages of Scripture at length. As a young man, Lincoln also learned to incorporate creatively these elements into his writing. . . ."[20] American literary scholar Roy P. Basler, observes of Lincoln's use of rhetoric that "Hebrew literature through the King James Bible probably provided the literary examples which Lincoln knew best; and to his fondness for biblical phraseology we may trace at least a part of his mastery of the technique."[21]

In his study, *The Almost Chosen People: A Study of the Religion of Abraham Lincoln*, historian William J. Wolf asserts that "Lincoln's knowledge of the Bible was so thorough that his political opponents found themselves on dangerous ground when they quoted it against him."[22] More specifically, Lincoln saw "the nation's history as in a continuity of purpose with the acts of God as interpreted by the biblical prophets."[23] In a speech Lincoln gave in

18. Jonah's prophecy to the Ninevites, as discussed in n. 6 above.

19. B. C. Wilson, "KJV in the USA: The Impact of the King James Bible in the USA," *Comparative Religion Publications*. Paper 2 (2011) 6. http://scholarworks.wmich.edu/religion_pubs/2.

20. Wilson, "KJV in the USA," 6.

21. R. P. Basler, "Abraham Lincoln's Rhetoric," *American Literature* 11/2 (1939) 167–82.

22. W. J. Wolf, *The Almost Chosen People: A Study of the Religion of Abraham Lincoln* (Garden City, NY: Doubleday, 1959) 132.

23. Wolf, *Almost Chosen People*, 59.

Lewiston, Illinois, in 1858, he described the Declaration of Independence as explicitly reflecting God's eternal design for everyone: "This was their [the Founding Fathers'] lofty, and wise, and noble understanding of the justice of the Creator to His creatures. Yes, gentlemen, to *all* His creatures, to the whole great family of man."[24] One can almost hear the author of the book of Jonah intoning to an ancient audience, "Yes, indeed the justice of the Creator extends to *all* His creatures, to the whole great family of man (and all animals, besides)."

LINCOLN'S SPEECH AT GETTYSBURG

The Pocket-Picking that Occurred

Garry Wills' Pulitzer Prize winning study of Abraham Lincoln's most famous speech indicates the power of 272 words to bring about transformation: it is entitled *Lincoln at Gettysburg: The Words That Remade America*.[25] Wills' thesis is that Lincoln's words effected a reframing of how Americans ever since 1863 have construed their nation's historic origins. Wills asserts that Lincoln accomplished this through a brilliant and polished speech that successfully creates new categories, *derived from the nation's own past*, that lead the audience (and those of us who have come after) to interpret the events of that battle and the entire Civil War with the rubric of this irrevocably reframed history:

> Both North and South strove to win the battle for interpreting Gettysburg as soon as the physical battle had ended. Lincoln is after even larger game—he means to "win" the whole Civil War in ideological terms as well as military ones. And he will succeed: the Civil War is, to most Americans, *what Lincoln wanted it to mean*. Words had to complete the work of the guns.[26]

The impact of that speech reverberates even to the present day.

Lincoln begins building this new framework at the very start of his speech, when he declares, "Four score and seven years ago." By using this seemingly benign, biblical-sounding way of naming a date for America's beginnings—instead of more baldly stating, "In 1776"—Lincoln invites his audience to cast their minds backward into America's mythic, even *sacred* origins. By inviting those present to consider their "hallowed past," Lincoln

---

24. Wolf, *Almost Chosen People*, 96 (emphasis original).
25. Wills, *Lincoln*.
26. Wills, *Lincoln*, 37–38 (emphasis added).

makes it possible for them to transcend the actual (recent) events that have brought them to this cemetery, to step outside of this tragic moment of indescribable carnage just long enough to consider (from a "safer distance") the conception and birth of the United States of America.

So what has been reframed? After all, the United States celebrates the Fourth of July as a national holiday, annually marking its country's birthday. So, other than being an interesting turn-of-phrase, what is the significance of Lincoln's opening words? The importance of "Four score and seven years ago" is this: before his audience has even fully tuned into his speech, Lincoln sneaks in a different date for the origin of the American nation than the one in use *by the people of his day*—that of the ratification of the Constitution! It is not so much that the country had ever been in the habit of celebrating "Constitution Signing Day" (it was not) but that most Americans in the mid-eighteenth century regarded the Constitution as the *Ur*-Covenant of the United *States*. The country's origin had theretofore been thought of as a compact made between and among separate and distinct states, bound together by signatures on an agreed-upon document.

The difference between seeing, on one hand, the origins of the United States as issuing from a contractual agreement among separate parties (an agreement that presumably can be vitiated, renegotiated, and/or dissolved) and, on the other hand, believing that "in the beginning" there was created "a new nation, conceived in Liberty, and dedicated to the proposition that all men are created equal"—this difference is, so to speak, all the difference in the world. In the latter case, the United States *begins* its existence as an organic unity—a nation that has been born—springing from the transcendent state of Liberty and christened by the likewise transcendent principle of equality. In this framework, the very idea of individual states trying to secede from this one nation becomes akin to the idea of a hand, an ear, or an eye seeking to secede from its body.[27]

Wills further demonstrates Lincoln's mastery at utilizing what was, to his 1863 contemporaries, the familiar genre of "funeral oratory," all presented with beguilingly simple, vivid language—much of it with a biblical

---

27. See Paul's words in the New Testament employing this imagery (1 Corinthians 12). Of course, as Wills points out, Lincoln's speech did not eradicate those who maintain what are commonly called the "states' rights school of constitutional interpretation." What this fact demonstrates is that *decentering* rather than *erasing* has taken place in the presence of a new text and/or new ideas. Yet, as Wills wryly observes, "Edwin Meese and other 'original intent' conservatives . . . want to go back before the Civil War amendments (particularly the Fourteenth) to the original founders. Their job would be comparatively easy if they did not have to work around the values created by the Gettysburg Address. Its deceptively simple-sounding phrases appeal to American . . ." Wills, *Lincoln*, 39; see also 129–33.

or religious ring to it—all in the service of reframing his country's history. In this way, Lincoln is able, astonishingly, to offer his audience an historical distance from the almost unimaginable bloodshed and misery of that past summer, through *not* referring to the specifics of the war. Wills writes:

> Despite verbal gestures to "that" battle and the men who died "here," there are no particulars mentioned by Lincoln—no names of men or sites or units, or even of sides (the Southerners are part of the "experiment," not foes mentioned in anger or rebuke) . . . Lincoln eschews all local emphasis. His speech hovers far above the carnage. He lifts the battle to a level of abstraction that purges it of grosser matter—even "earth" is mentioned as the things from which the tested form of government shall not perish . . . The nightmare realities have been etherealized in the crucible of his language.

Wills goes on:

> But that was just the beginning of this complex transformation. Lincoln did for the whole Civil War what he accomplished for the single battlefield. He has prescinded from messy squabbles over constitutionality, sectionalism, property, states. Slavery is not mentioned, any more than Gettysburg is. The discussion is driven back and back, beyond the historical particulars, to great ideals that are made to grapple naked in an airy battle of the mind. Lincoln derives a new, a transcendent significance from this bloody episode.[28]

It is astounding how this short speech, lasting perhaps three minutes, could so dramatically, so thoroughly reshape how Americans from that point forward have come to think about our history. Truly, as Wills concludes, "Lincoln has revolutionized the Revolution, giving people a new past to live with that would change their future indefinitely."[29]

TRACING NARRATIVE LINEAGE

Dutch philosopher of history Johan Huizinga asserted, "*History is the intellectual form in which a civilization renders account to itself of its past.*"[30] In

---

28. Wills, *Lincoln*, 37.
29. Wills, *Lincoln*, 38.
30. J. Huizinga, "A Definition of the Concept of History," in *Philosophy & History: Essays Presented to Ernst Cassirer* (ed. R. Klibansky and H. J. Paton; New York: Harper & Row, 1963) 9, emphasis original.

Huizinga's sense, both the book of Jonah and Lincoln at Gettysburg conscripted their audiences into the process of history-*making*. Lincoln rendered to the American people an intelligible, if poetic, accounting of their collective past. Crucially, Lincoln accomplished this not by saying that the past was *wrong* (such as William Lloyd Garrison did in publicly burning a copy of the Constitution), but, rather, by *extending* America's past, back and back to a point before the composition and ratification of the United States Constitution, back to the Declaration of Independence.

So, too, the book of Jonah put a new, larger frame around Israel's history, Israel's understanding of what it means to be "Hebrew." In so doing, the book of Jonah invited the post-exilic people into a new, larger story about themselves and their place in history—again by extending their history with God back and back, beyond Sinai, before Abraham, and to the very time of Noah.

In both cases, rhetorical magicians selectively draw upon their people's own traditions, genres, and sensibilities, and play masterfully upon their audiences' unconscious yet visceral needs to understand who they are in the context of their own national histories. With the same narrative life-blood flowing through both the book of Jonah and Lincoln's Gettysburg Address, the audiences walk away thinking that they merely have been engaged by a short, image-filled story, while all the time their pockets were being filled with nothing less than a prophetic reshaping of their histories.

— 11 —

A Song of Love
Isaiah 5:1–7[1]

F. W. DOBBS-ALLSOPP

IN EZEK 33:30–33 YAHWEH likens the prophet to a literal singer of "love songs" (*šîr ʿăgābîm*),[2] a skilled musician (*mēṭîb naggēn*, lit. "one who plays pleasantly") with a "beautiful voice" (*yĕpê qôl*) performing before a live audience, whose (good, pretty, cf. Ps 45:2) words are heard but not acted on. The Song of Songs, of course, offers the Bible's most obvious examples of

---

1. *Author's note*: Abbreviated versions of this essay were presented orally on several occasions, including as "Reading Biblical Poetry: Isaiah's Love Song (Isa 5:1–7)" (a public lecture at Princeton Theological Seminary, 15 March 2016) and as "Isaiah's Love Song: A Reading of Isa 5:1–7" (the J. J. M. Roberts Annual Lecture in Old Testament Studies at the Christian Scholar's Conference, Lipscomb University, 9 June 2016). I am grateful to the organizers of these events for their invitations to participate and to the participants for their observations and criticisms, which have greatly enhanced my reading. This shorter essay will appear as "Isaiah's Love Song: A Reading of Isa 5:1–7" in *Close Readings: Biblical Poetry and the Task of Interpretation* (eds. J. B. Couey and E. T. James; Cambridge: Cambridge University Press, forthcoming). It is a pleasure to offer this longer, fully philologically hopped version of my reading of Isa 5:1–7 in memory of Simon Parker, a fellow Hopkins alum and good friend and colleague who is much missed. Rest in peace, Simon.

2. The reading of M is supported by all the versions, though none of them understand *ʿăgābîm*—S does not even try but simply renders *zmyrt'* "song." Many suggest emending M to read *kĕšar ʿăgābîm* "like a singer of love (songs)" (e.g., *BHS*; *HALOT*, 1482) or something analogous (cf. W. Zimmerli, *Ezekiel 2* [trans. J. D. Martin; Hermeneia; Philadelphia: Fortress, 1983] 197). However the textual difficulties are resolved, the informing image of the prophet as a singer of love songs is at least clear.

what such love poetry was like. But Isa 5:1–7 remains of interest for a variety of reasons. If genuine to Isaiah of Jerusalem,[3] it provides relatively early evidence (ca. eighth century) for the knowledge of love poetry in Judah (e.g., roughly contemporary with the Akkadian "Love Lyrics of Nabû and Tašmetu," IM 3233 = TIM 9 54 = SAA 3 14[4]). It also evidences in scope, the same relatively brief scale that typifies most love poems from the ancient East.[5] And this Isaianic lampoon seems to trade on the very same awareness of the allure of the lyrical that informs the Ezekiel passage. In the close (and slow) reading of Isa 5:1–7 that follows I track the lyricism of Isaiah's lampoon, situating it against the backdrop of ancient love poetry generally and

---

3. With many, I see little reason to deny the song's association with Isaiah of Jerusalem (e.g., H. G. M. Williamson, *Isaiah 1–27* [ICC; London: T. & T. Clark, 2006] 1:330–31; J. J. M. Roberts, *First Isaiah* [Hermeneia; Minneapolis: Fortress, 2015] 3–4). Further, I assume scribal mediation of various kinds in the process of writing the poem down and ultimately including it in a larger scroll collecting prophecies, oracles and other textual bits editorially related to Isaiah of Jerusalem (for a helpful working conceptualization of the production of prophetic scrolls in ancient Israel and Judah, see K. van der Toorn, *Scribal Culture and the Making of the Hebrew Bible* [Cambridge: Harvard University, 2007] esp. ch. 7). I mostly abstain from a discussion of how Isa 5:1–7 interacts within its larger literary context(s), though this would surely be a relevant line of inquiry to a fuller appreciation of this song as it has been preserved textually. However, as H. G. Williamson notices, for example, the song "is clearly to some extent a self-contained unit" (*Isaiah 1–27*, 1:324)—note how extra spacing is used to separate the song from what precedes and follows it in Aleppo, B19a, and 1QIsa^a. This, then, along with an understanding of how prophetic verbal art normally would have been written down and collected, mostly belatedly, provides warrant for attending, at least in the first instance, to the song itself, which is my principal concern in the body of this paper.

4. See A. Livingstone, *Court Poetry and Literary Miscellanea* (SAA 3; Helsinki: Helsinki University Press, 1989) 35–37; M. Nissinen, "Love Lyrics of Nabû and Tašmetu: An Assyrian Song of Songs?," in *"Und Mose schrieb dieses Lied auf": Studien zum Alten Testament und zum Alten Orient* (eds. M. Dietrich and I. Kottsieper; AOAT 250; Münster: Ugarit-Verlag, 1998) 585–634. http://oracc.museum.upenn.edu/saao/saao3/P223388/. Hand-drawing: http://oracc.museum.upenn.edu/cdli/P223388/image.

5. Some Egyptian love songs are even written on an ostracon (e.g., Gardiner, 304) and most are enacted very much on the same realtively brief scale as is the Bible's non-narrative verse more generally, including what scholars have posited as independent poems in the Song (e.g., 2:8–17; 3:1–5; 4:1–7; 5:2—6:3). Similarly, much of the Sumero-Akkadian tradition of "erotic-lyric" poetry also is enacted on a mostly smaller scale. "The outstanding feature" of the Sumerian balbale-songs, for example, which comprise a prominent portion of the preserved Dumuzi-Inanna love songs, writes Y. Sefati, "is their brevity," with most not exceeding "30–40 lines on the average" (*Love Songs in Sumerian Literature: Critical Edition of the Dumuzi-Inanna songs* [Ramat Gan: Bar-Ilan, 1998] 28). The smaller corpus of Akkadian love poetry holds to a relatively small scale. Even the Neo-Assyrian "Love Lyrics of Nabû and Tašmetu" only comprises the obverse and reverse of but a single tablet, some 56 lines in total.

following its logic of love through to its prophetic end—justice (*mišpāṭ*) and righteousness (*ṣĕdāqâ*).[6]

The genre of the poem has been much debated[7] but there can be little doubt that it was intended and heard as a riff on a love song, literally a *šîrat dôdîm* "a song of love" (after G[AS]).[8] Even if M's *šîrat dôdî* lit. "a song of my beloved" is retained in v. 1 (so most of the versions and many commentators),[9] the phrase's allusive gesture to a love song proper (e.g., *šîrat dôday* "(my) love song" or *šîrat dôdîm* "love song"; cf. *šîr yĕdîdōt* "love song," Ps 45:1; *tšr. l. dd. aliyn b'l* "she [Anat] sings about the love of Mightiest Baal," *CTU* 1.3.III.5–6) is patent. Why else, for example, reference Yahweh (even if only belatedly and obliquely) as *yĕdîdî* "my love" (and *dôdî* "my beloved" in M)? Nowhere else in the Hebrew Bible is Yahweh so designated (hence the commentary tradition is at pains to emphasize the nonerotic capacity of the terminology).[10] The love song conceit is sustained through to the end of the little poem—*šaʿăšûʿāyw* "his delight" (v. 7) is language of intimacy (esp. Jer 31:20; Prov 8:30–31; cf. Isa 11:8, 66:12; Ps 94:19, 119:47 [*š-ʿ-ʿ* /

---

6. See Appendix for my construal of the text of Isa 5:1–7 with textual notes and a working translation.

7. See esp. J. T. Willis, "The Genre of Isa 5:1–7," *JBL* 96 (1977) 337–62; and more recently, the review of Williamson, *Isaiah 1–27*, 1:327–28.

8. The rendering of *šîr yĕdîdōt* "love song" in G at Ps 45:1 (LXX Ps 44:1), ᾠδὴ ὑπὲρ τοῦ ἀγαπητοῦ 'a song for the beloved,' suggests that G[AS] in Isa 5:1, ᾆσμα τοῦ ἀγαπητοῦ 'a song of the beloved,' could reflect the very material reading long posited by R. Lowth as a conjectural emendation, *šîrat dôdîm* (*Isaiah. A New Translation: with a Preliminary Dissertation* [London: Nichols, 1778]; reprinted in *Robert Lowth (1710–1787): The Major Works* [8 vols.; London: Routledge, 1995] 2:55–56). M, 1QIsa[a], and all the versions except G[AS] preserve a different material reading, *šyrt dwdy*, which most construe after M, *šîrat dôdî* lit. "a song of my beloved" (e.g., J. A. Emerton, "The Translation of Isaiah 5, 1," in *The Scriptures and the Scrolls: Studies in Honor of A. S. van der Woude on the Occasion of His 65th Birthday* [eds. F. García Martínez et al.; VTSup 49; Leiden: Brill, 1992] 18–30; Williamson, *Isaiah 1–27*, 1:317–18). Others advocate vocalizing *dwdy* as *dôday* "my love," resulting in an explicit reference to a love song: *šîrat dôday* "(my) love song" (e.g., Roberts, *First Isaiah*, 70, n. b; cf. J. Blenkinsopp, *Isaiah 1–39* [AB; New York: Doubleday, 2000] 205, 206, 207). But the addition of the possessive suffix in M (and the other witnesses) looks suspiciously like a explicating gloss to clarify whose love song is being sung, namely, the lover's/farmer's and not the singer's.

9. See Williamson, *Isaiah 1–27*, 1:317–18 (with summary of previous scholarship).

10. So already Aq (πατραδέλφου μου) and Jerome (*patruelis mei*). As will become clear below, however, the erotic was certainty a vernacular used in antiquity to give expression to the divine-human relationship (e.g., sacred marriage texts in Sumerian, the marriage metaphor in biblical prophecy).

'-*h-b*]; *ḥāpēṣ* in Gen 34:19) that gestures back to the song's opening vocabulary of love.[11] Indeed, once Yahweh is implicated as the lover in v. 7 (of Isaiah, cf. *yādîd* in Deut 33:12; Jer 11:15; Pss 60:7; 108:7; 127:2; and of the vineyard) the song (retrospectively) taps into the kind of ideology prominently promoted in the rituals and poetry of divine love best exemplified from ancient Mesopotamia (especially as reflected in the Akkadian sources from the eighth through the second century BCE),[12] namely, to symbolize "an intimate connection between the divine and human worlds and ... to secure divine blessings—not only for the king but also for the people."[13] The chief upshot of Isaiah's little allegory,[14] after all, is to reveal just how out of sorts the divine–human relationship is, *miśpāḥ* and *ṣĕʿāqâ* instead of *mišpāṭ* and *ṣĕdāqâ* (v. 7). Unlike in Egypt or in the Bible's Song of Songs, most of the erotic-lyric tradition in Mesopotamia gets projected mythologically. Ironically, perhaps the Song of Song's best known mode of reception, the allegorical, reads the Song back towards the mythological.[15] But in the Bible

---

11. The repetition of the words *kerem* and *wayqaw* and the root *n-ṭ-ʿ* in v. 7 also draw the auditor's attention back to the poem's opening stanza. On the perseverance of the love song conceit throughout the poem, see especially Roberts' brief comments in his *First Isaiah* (70–74).

12. For a convenient review of these sources, see M. Nissinen, "Akkadian Rituals and Poetry of Divine Love," in *Mythology and Mythologies: Methodological Approaches to Intercultural Influences* (ed. R. M. Whiting; Melammu Symposia 2; Helsinki: Neo-Assyrian Text Corpus Project, 2001) 93–136.

13. M. Nissinen, "Song of Songs and Sacred Marriage," in *Sacred Marriages: The Divine-Human Sexual Metaphor from Sumer to Early Christianity* (eds. M. Nissinen and R. Uro; Winona Lake, IN: Eisenbrauns, 2008) 202 Nissinen is summing here J. S. Cooper's understanding of the central ideology of Sumerian sacred marriage texts, but he believes this holds more generally for the first millenium Akkadian sources that are his own principal concern, Nissinen, "Akkadian Rituals and Poetry," 127–29.

14. "Little" both in reference to the relative brevity of Isa 5:1–7 and the limited nature of its allegory, i.e., on my read (see below) there is little evidence in the poem itself to support the kind of full-scale allegorical mapping of the song that is sometimes found in the secondary literature (cf. Williamson, *Isaiah 1–27*, 1:328).

15. M. Nissinen has rightly problematized the rigid distinction between scared and secular love songs in antiquity ("Akkadian Rituals and Poetry," 125–27; cf. J. G. Westenholtz, "Love Lyrics from the Ancient Near East," in *Civilizations of the Ancient Near East* (4 vols.; ed. J. M. Sasson; New York: Scribner, 1995) 4:2471–72)—indeed, the secular as such is a distinctly modern construction and can only be applied to antiquity heuristically and anachronistically. The same language and imagery of love may be voiced by god or human. Nevertheless, it remains unclear whether the Song itself was ever read mythologically in antiquity (prior to the Hellenistic period). Certainly the earliest line of interpretation, the addition of the incip *šîr haššîrîm 'ăšer lišlōmōh* lit. "the song of songs of/to/for Solomon" (Song 1:1), is pointedly nonmythological and nothing in the Song requires a mythological staging. This contrasts quite markedly with other allegories in the Bible, such as Isa 5:1–7, where the allegory itself is made explicit, viz. "the

that dimension of the erotic-lyric tradition is most obviously manifested in prophetic compositions like Hosea 2, where the divine-human relationship is imagined through the marriage metaphor, or, as I want to suggest, in a poem like Isa 5:1-7—though here marriage is nowhere in view (as is also true of the Song). Of course Isaiah's performance is anything but that of a straightforward love song (divine or otherwise). He ultimately bends the genre to suit his prophetic critique—genre's are rarely pure or univocal. In fact, such swerves away from the love song's animating centers of focus are known in other traditions as, for example, in the so-called jealousy poems from Mesopotamia.[16]

The poem itself is shaped in a traditional ring structure. The opening (vv. 1-2) and closing (v. 7) sets of lines reference the beloved/farmer in the third person and envelop the two internal stanzas (vv. 3-4, 5-6), each of which begins with *wĕ'attâ* "and now" and is voiced in the first person of the beloved farmer (in M).[17] The major rhythmic contours of these sections get marked (among other ways) by variation in line length.[18] At the seams of the song's several sections, in particular, shifts back and forth between subtly longer and shorter sets of lines may be observed. The opening description of the lover's vineyard (vv. 1-2) is conducted in short lines, mostly comprised of six or seven syllables—the succession of *way'azzĕqēhû waysaqqĕlēhû* in v. 2 at ten syllables being the only overly long line in the section.[19] The call for judgement (vv. 3-4) begins with a couplet composed of two noticeably longer lines, containing fourteen and nine syllables respectively—the contrast (with what precedes) making the longer lines all the more striking. The next juncture, the announcement of de-cultivation beginning at v. 5 also opens with long lines (syllables: nine, nine, twelve, eleven). And the poem's

---

vineyard of Yahweh Sabaoth *is* the house of Israel" (Isa 5:7).

16. See W. G. Lambert, "Divine Love Lyrics from Babylon," *JSS* 4 (1959) 1-15; "The Problem of the Love Lyrics," in *Unity and Diversity: Essays in the History, Literature, and Religion of the Ancient Near East* (eds. H. Goedicke and J. J. M. Roberts; Baltimore: Johns Hopkins University Press, 1975) 98-135; G. Leick, *Sex and Eroticism in Mesopotamian Literature* (New York: Routledge 1994) 239-46; Nissinen, "Akkadian Rituals and Poetry," 123-25; A. R. George, "A Field Full of Salt," in *Babylonian Literary Texts in the Schøyen Collection* (CUSAS 10; Bathesda, MD: CDL, 2009) 60-66, pl. 27-30 (MS 3285).

17. G and T use first person forms throughout vv. 2 and 7 (S and V follow suit in v. 7), assimilating to the voice used in the middle sections of the song (vv. 3-6), and thus destroying the inclusio so evident in M.

18. H. Wildberger makes essentially the same point, though his structural analysis and division of lines differ from my own and he uses the vocabulary of "meter" and measures by the number of stresses (*Isaiah 1-12* [trans. T. H. Trapp; Continental Commentaries; Minneapolis: Fortress, 1991] 179).

19. The length anomaly is partially set off by the line only having two major stresses.

final movement (v. 7), where the meaning of the little allegory is revealed, is composed in longer lines (syllables: eleven, ten, ten, nine). Here, too, the contrast with an immediately preceding run of shorter lines (v. 6) stages and thus underscores the final shift to longer lines. The whole coheres around a central focus on the *kerem* "vineyard" (its upkeep and destruction), the prototypical site of love in ancient Mediterranean love poetry. The term *kerem* itself is repeated six times in the short song (vv. 1 [2x], 3, 4, 5, 7) and joins other word repetitions (e.g., *q-w-h* "to wait, hope," vv. 2, 4, 7; *'-ś-h* "to do, make," vv. 2 [2x], 4 [4x], 5) and chains of sound plays (e.g., end-rhyme: *'ănābîm // bĕ'ušîm*, vv. 2, 4; internal rhyme: *mišpāṭ // miśpāḥ* and *ṣĕdāqâ // ṣĕ'āqâ*, v. 7) to stitch the poem together as a single whole. The most conspicuous of these chains involves the conjunctive *waw*, which heads fifteen of the poem's twenty-nine lines (and appears twenty-four times in total).

I

The opening couplet would appear to be intentionally ambiguous, even misleading.[20] The first line, *'āšîrâ nnā' lîdîdî*, on its own may be heard straightforwardly as articulating the intent to sing a song to or about the singer's lover. A most traditional opening to a song (e.g., *'āšîrâ la-yhwh*, Exod 15:1; *ăzammēr la-yhwh*, Judg 5:3; *a[š]r nkl wib*, CTU 1.24.1; *ur-ša-nam re-e-a a-za-am-mur-ma*, BM 47507, l. 40 [= KAR 158 i7]). The second line provides the object of the singing, namely, "a love song about his vineyard." In itself such denominations are not uncommon either, e.g., *'ĕlōhîm šîr ḥādāš 'āšîrâ lāk* "O God, a new song I will sing to you" (Ps 144:9); *wa'ănî 'āšîr 'uzzekā* "and I will sing (of) your might" (Ps 59:17); *idmr šm* "let me sing the name" (RIH 98/02.2); *tšr. l. dd. aliyn b'l* "she [Anat] sings about the love of Mightiest Baal" (CTU 1.3.III.5–6; cf. 1.101.16–18). There are even lines that include both direct and prepositional objects (e.g., *šîrû la-yhwh šîr ḥādāš*, Ps 96:1) as well as syntactic elaborations that carry over to a second line (e.g., *'êk nāšîr 'et-šîr-yhwh / 'al 'admat nĕkār*, Ps 137:4; cf. Ps 98:1). The misdirection comes in the specification of the love song that is to be sung as that about a vineyard belonging to the singer's beloved. That is, the initial impression of a singer singing to his lover requires immediate revision in light of the syntactic elaboration in the second line of the couplet. The love song sung is now at some remove. It is about another lover and his beloved, or in terms

---

20. Esp. G. R. Williams, "Frustrated Expectations in Isaiah v 1–7: A Literary Interpretation," VT 35 (1985) 459–65.

of the allegory, about a farmer (who is not Isaiah) and his vineyard (M's *šîrat dôdî* lit. "a song of my beloved" ramifies this redirection).[21]

Also to be emphasized is Isaiah's explicit naming of the song a "love song," *šîrat dôdîm* (with G[AS]), and the use of the vocabulary of love in these initial lines. The former perhaps comes most conspicuously into view in contrast to the more allusive reading of M (and the other versions; also compatible with 1QIsa[a]), *šîrat dôdî* lit. "a song of my beloved," a song, that is, that need not be a literal love song—singing, of course, would have accompanied work in the vineyards, especially during the harvest (e.g., Judg 21:20–21; Isa 16:10; Jer 48:3; Amos 5:17; cf. Isa 27:2).[22] Such an insistent designation is troubled almost immediately by the additional specification, *lĕkarmô* "for/about his vineyard," since normally lovers (human or divine) are serenaded in ancient love songs and not their vineyards (or other landscapes, cf. Isa 27:2). Indeed, part of the poem's initial ambiguity is precisely the misfit between its denomination as a love song and its content—especially in the body of the poem (vv. 2–6) which features the cultivation and destruction of a literal vineyard.

The use of *dôdîm* "love" (or *dôd* in M) and *kerem* "vineyard" intentionally employs the vocabulary of love (cf. "Let us go early to the vineyards [*kĕrāmîm*]/ ... there I will give my love [*dōday*] to you," Song 7:13).[23] And the song's second couplet, *kerem hāyâ lîdîdî / bĕqeren ben-šāmen* "a vineyard belonged to my lover/ on a fertile spur," continues in the traditional vernacular of love, as is made clear by the line from Song 8:11, *kerem hāyâ lišlōmōh bĕbaʿal ḥāmôn* "a vineyard belonged to Solomon in Baal-Hamon" (cf. 1 Kgs 21:1). But in borrowing this image from the traditional repertoire of love poetry the prophet is also fixing on the primary focus of his (love) song, the vineyard. The term *kerem* itself in the space of two lines is repeated twice, at the end of the second line and then again immediately at the beginning of the third. This manner of repetition and placement effectively slows the movement of the poem for auditory fixation and emphasis. The vineyard (and garden, BH *gan*) is one of the the premiere settings for love in

---

21. The misdirection remains regardless of whether *šîrat dôdî* (M) or *šîrat dôdîm* (G[AS]) is read, though in this light the former (if not simply a good variant) may be viewed as an explicating gloss that makes explicit whose love song is being referenced, i.e., the lover's/farmer's and not the singer's. On such glosses from a traditional text-critical perspective, see P. K. McCarter, *Text Criticism: Recovering the Text of the Hebrew Bible* (GBS; Philadelphia: Fortress, 1986) 34–35, 36.

22. Cf. C. E. Walsh, *The Fruit of the Vine: Viticulture in Ancient Israel* (HSM 60; Winona Lake, IN: Eisenbrauns, 2000) 181–86.

23. Cf. Williams, "Frustrated Expectations," 360.

ancient Mediterranean love songs.[24] And on occasion in the Song of Songs, for example, the vineyard may even be metaphorized such as to implicate a reference to the beloved girl herself or her sexuality. For example, this happens most prominently toward the beginning of the Song where the girl, commenting on her sun-darkened skin, explains that her brothers (out of anger) set her as the "keeper (*nōṭērâ*) of the vineyards (*hakkĕrāmîm*)," but, she says teasingly, "my own vineyard (*karmî šellî*) I have not kept (*lōʾ nāṭārtî*)" (Song 1:6; cf. 2:15). Commentators on Isaiah's love song habitually ascribe such metaphorization to the several mentions of the vineyard there,[25] failing to appreciate that this figurative usage is not a part of the word's basic semantics but is everywhere created by local poetic artifice. So in Song 1:6 the identity of vineyard and girl is created as an implication of the girl's language game as she (or the poet through her voice) plays on her real world task of tending the vineyards (viz. we are not to imagine she had her own personal vineyard; note the disjunctive word order and the extra emphasis on "my," *šellî*) and the fact that the vineyard (in the Song at any rate) was a primary site for a romantic tryst.[26] Under such (linguistic) circumstances the "vineyard" may become a figure for the sexual encounter that takes place in it (cf. Song 7:13)—here voiced by the girl, and thus a figure for her own sexuality. There is no similar attempt in these early lines of Isa 5:1–7 to implicate a figurative sense to the vineyard imagery. Indeed, to the contrary, the prophet literalizes the image (esp. in v. 2). It is not precisely as H. G. M. Williamson suggests that the cultivation and upkeep of a vineyard are never topicalized in love poetry. Each of the nine references to a vineyard in the Song (1:6 [2x], 14 [2x]; 2:15; 7:13; 8:11 [2x], 12), for example, arguably has aspects of cultivation and upkeep in view. Perhaps most significant for a reading of Isa 5:1–7 is the line that follows the ascription of a vineyard to Solomon in Song 8:11 mentioned earlier: *nātan ʾet-hakkerem lannōṭĕrîm* "he gave the vineyard to the keepers." Rather, it is that Isaiah takes a common setting in ancient love poems, a vineyard, and makes it the principal subject of his discourse. Indeed, the chief function of this second couplet is to establish the animating scene for the little poem—a vineyard set amid the fertile terraced hills of Judah (cf. Jer 31:5; Amos 9:13)—and to reveal the lover as a farmer. The vineyard only becomes allegorized (and not personified at all) in v. 7—"the vineyard (*kerem*) of Yahweh Sabaoth is the house of Israel."

24. See M. V. Fox, *The Song of Songs and the Ancient Egyptian Love Songs* (Madison: University of Wisconsin Press, 1985) 285–88.

25. E.g., Williams, "Frustrated Expectations," 460; J. D. W. Watts, *Isaiah 1–33* (WBC 24; Waco: Word, 1985) 54.

26. Cf. Fox, *Song of Songs*, 286.

Moreover, though sometimes suggested otherwise,[27] there is no evidence (in the Bible or elsewhere) that the vineyard becomes a literary convention for the beloved woman and/or her sexuality. The often cited imagery of a plowed field (e.g., Judg 14:18; CTU 1.24.22–23) of course is precisely not a vineyard[28] and is an explicitly masculine gendered image of sexuality—if anything in the Song of Songs the metaphorization of the girl as vineyard and vineyard as girl is gendered feminine.[29] In any event, this goes to the same point just made, namely, that in reading Isaiah's love song about the beloved vineyard attention should be paid to the language of the poem and what is accomplished by it and through it.

The language of love, which is explicitly sounded chiefly here in these opening lines (cf. *kerem* and *nĕṭa' ša'ăšû'āyw* in v. 7), accomplishes a number of important things for this song. First, as it clusters in these two short couplets and with the emphasis that such clustering helps muster, tone and expectations are set (up), and given the relatively brief compass of the song as a whole, these are never really left behind at any point. The insistence on a love song (*šîrat dôdîm* with G^{AS}), the naming of a lover (*yādîd*), and the iterative setting in a vineyard (. . . *karmô / kerem* . . . .)—accompanied (in performance) no doubt by a host of non-semantic cues, e.g., rhythm, tune, bodily gestures, scale—more than suffice to set the audience's expectation for love. Second, the lack of an explicit identity for the lover/farmer (cf. *'ănî yhwh nōṣĕrāh*, Isa 27:3) is tolerated in a genre where anonymity prevails, or where identity is ascribed extra-textually (see the Song where only once is the girl given a quasi-sobriquet, "the Shulammite," Song 7:1). Part of the overall force of Isaiah's ditty depends on the catching-out that is effected in v. 7 where the allegorical bent of the prophet's pantomime is revealed. That force is created (in part) by the wait that must endure the intervening lines, which is itself permitted (without frustration) precisely because there is no expectation for a particular identity in such a (love) song. Finally, in specifying the vineyard as belonging to "Yahweh Sabaoth" (through Hebrew's main genitive construction, the construct chain) in v. 7 the poignancy of Isaiah's initial naming of his "beloved" as *yādîd* becomes most fully appreciated:

---

27. E.g., Blenkinsopp, *Isaiah 1–39*, 207; D. M. Carr, *The Erotic Word: Sexuality, Spirituality, and the Bible* (Oxford: Oxford University Press, 2003) 61.

28. Cf. Williamson, *Isaiah 1–27*, 1:335.

29. See J. S. Cooper, "Enki's Member: Eros and Irrigation in Sumerian Literature," in *Dumu-E2-Dub-Ba-A: Studies in Honor of Åke W. Sjöberg* (eds. H. Behrens et al.; Occasional Publications of the Samuel Noah Kramer Fund 11; Philadelphia: University Museum, 1989) 87–89; "Gendered Sexuality in Sumerian Love Poetry," in *Sumerian Gods and Their Representations* (eds. I. Finkel and M. Geller; Groningen: Styx, 1997) 85–97; G. Leick, *Sex and Eroticism in Mesopotamian Literature* (New York: Routledge, 1994) 21, 58.

yādîd is used most frequently in the Bible to figure Yahweh's human adorant (e.g., Deut 33:12; Jer 11:15; Ps 60:7, 108:7, 127:2). While perhaps the term is equally appropriate for either partner in an intimate relationship, and thus entirely kosher as a designation for Yahweh (though it nowhere else occurs), the reversal of the Bible's common usage nonetheless is telling. Not only have Israel and Judah failed in matters of *mišpāṭ* and *ṣĕdāqâ*, they have not acted as a *yādîd*. That is, the approrpiation of the term for Yahweh is telling in its very withholding as a designation for Israel and Judah.

A final observation about the poem's opening couplets is their striking euphony. The high /ī/ sound of *-î* (*hireq yod*) is repeated nine times over and the cluster of root and near-root repetitions, especially involving *y-d-d*, *d-w-d*, *š-y-r*, and *k-r-m*, means that *shin*s, *resh*es, *dalet*s, *kaph*s, and *mem*s clatter and clash pleasantly. Even the press of original *qatl* forms—**karm* (2xs), **qarn*, and **šamn*—all ending with a nasal (*mem* or *nun*; accentuated in the last line of v. 1 by the inclusion of *ben-* lit. "son of")[30] tickle the ear and tongue. In fact, sound turns out to be critical to this song's larger prosody. While Isa 5:1–7, like almost all other biblical poems, does not systematically orchestrate one kind of sound effect to any specific end, a wide use of various kinds of sound patterns nonetheless are prominent and the poem comes closer than many other biblical poems to using sound to effect a rhythmic norm (i.e., beyond the semantically directed mishmash of sounds natural to the language). Beyond the burbles of sound just noted in v. 1 and what is perhaps the Bible's most famous bit of rhyming in v. 7 (*mišpāṭ* // *miśpāḥ* and *ṣĕdāqâ* // *ṣĕ'āqâ*),[31] other plays on sound in the poem include the following: v. 2 opens with three *wayyiqtol* forms from two different *binyanim*, which nonetheless are manipulated to effect a repeated cadence (*way'azzĕqēhû waysaqqĕlēhû* / *wayyiṭṭā'ēhû*), while the component lines of the succeeding two couplets are joined through end-rhyme (*-ô*, *-îm*); a splutter of consonance involving *aleph*s and *ayin*s resounds through the opening couplet in v. 5; and line internal rhyming and chiming punctuates vv. 5–7 (e.g., *lō' yizzāmēr* // *wĕlō' yē'ādēr*, v. 6). This is by no means regularized, but the periodicity of some kind of sound play is sufficient to rival the rhythmic norm of unscripted sounds and to create the anticipation (however non-predictive) of yet further sonic flourishes. So when the rhyming does come in the poem's final couplet auditors are not at all surprised. Indeed, a great deal of felt satisfaction accompanies such a closing, as if the poem was heading to this way of ending all along, even though that could not have been

---

30. Cf. J. B. Couey, *Reading the Poetry of First Isaiah: The Most Perfect Model of Prophetic Poetry* (Oxford: Oxford University Press, 2015) 162.

31. Cf. E. L. Greenstein, "Wordplay, Hebrew," in *ABD* 6:969.

known ahead of time and even though other means of closing the poem equally satisfactorily are imaginable. The glut of these varied sonic effects also increases the felt density of the language material, which enhances aural uptake and, when combined with the semantic opacity of this prophetic song (e.g., who is speaking? who owns the vineyard? why is it trampled? why the love theme?), effectively ensures a slower, more measured pace to the poem.

II

With the exception of the first longish line (10 syllables), v. 2 continues to feature relatively short lines in its three couplets. All are headed by a conjunctive *waw* and *wayyiqtol* forms appear six times, five in line initial position. This allows for a fairly economical narration of the farmer's cultivation of his vineyard and also witnesses the impress of prose writing on this particular poetic production. In fact, this is not the only place that Isaiah's love song betrays a conspicuous debt to prose style. Three more *wayiqtol* forms are present in the song (vv. 4, 6, 7), the phrase *šipṭû-nā' bênî ûbên karmî* in v. 3 appears to be prosaic (see esp. Gen 16:5; Exod 18:16; Num 35:24; Deut 1:16; Judg 11:27; 1 Sam 24:13),[32] and there is a clump of prose particles in the first couplet of v. 5 (*'et-, 'ēt, 'ăšer*) to underscore that couplet's supporting prose syntax. Prose writing in a specifically Hebrew vernacular script likely dates to the latter part of the ninth century BCE (on present evidence),[33] and therefore there is no reason why the poetic prophecies of Isaiah of Jerusalem a century later could not bear the imprint of this new form of (written) discourse. If so note how it has been adapted poetically and acoustically. For example, as noted, the opening sequence of *wayyiqtol* forms in v. 2 have been specifically orchestrated sonically and rhythmically, and that eight of the nine *wayyiqtol*s that appear in the poem are in line-initial position is surely not accidental. The phrase *šipṭû-nā' bênî ûbên karmî* stands out among its hundred plus prose parallels by the intentionality of its sonic shaping: the addition of the first person singular suffix on *kerem* providing the line with internal rhyme (*bênî // ûbên karmî*); *karmî* gets integrated into the patterned repetition of this word throughout

---

32. The only possible poetic use of the *bên . . . ûbên* idiom is in Ruth 1:17, which is clearly under the impress of prose (Judg 5:27; Isa 59:2; and Song 2:2 each has two *bên*s in close succession but they do not employ the typical prose idiom).

33. For my own assessment of this development, see F. W. Dobbs-Allsopp, *On Biblical Poetry* (Oxford: Oxford University Press, 2015), esp. 298–318 (with references to relevant secondary literature).

the song; and the addition of *nā'* helps tie the opening of this section of the poem together with the openings of the sections that precede and follow it where *nā'* also appears. And even the double use of *'et-/ 'ēt* is scripted so as to help articulate line structure. All of which is simply to underscore that the poem's prose touches are artfully deployed. Of course, Isaiah's prosaizing style also benefits his poetry. In the case of the run of *wayyiqtol* forms in v. 2, biblical prose's economy of narration—one of the chiefest gains of written prose—is capitalized on. In a matter of three short couplets the prophet is able to gesture effectively toward the energetic and hard work of the farmer in his care-full cultivation of the vineyard, something in the traditional idiom of oral narrative song (with its characteristic epic—lengthy—repetition) that could well have taken a storyteller many more verses to accomplish. This suits the song which is brief and not interested in a protracted rendering of a farmer's daily routine, the details of which Isaiah's audience with these brief, formulaic hints could easily fill in for themselves from their own practical experience.[34] So even while benefitting from written prose's advantages (e.g., economy of narration) the song remains dominantly indexical in nature and thus tradition bound, where meaning is supplied as much from outside as inside the text, from knowledge shared and broadly familiar— "confirmational discourse falling back on something 'we all know,'" as U. Schaefer terms it in her work on traditional Anglo-Saxon poetry.[35]

The picture briefly evoked by Isaiah of a vineyard sited somewhere on the fertile slopes in the (central) hill country (*běqeren ben-šāmen*)[36] of the

34. Ironically, as Walsh notices, this is also "the most detailed description of vineyard maintenance in the Bible" (*Fruit of the Vine*, 88). For modern readers unfamiliar with the workaday world of an ancient Judahite farmer/vintner, Walsh's book fills in all necessary details.

35. U. Schaefer, "Hearing from Books: The Rise of Fictionality in Old English Poetry," in *Vox intexta: Orality and Textuality in the Middle Ages* (ed. A. N. Doane and C. B. Pasternack; Madison: University of Wisconsin Press, 1991) 123. The Greek translator does not know the first (or second) Hebrew verb used here, from the root *'-z-q* "to dig, break up the ground." This is not surprising as the verb is only used here in the Hebrew Bible (its meaning is established by post-biblical Hebrew (QH, MH) and Arabic (*'azaqa*; see *HALOT*, 810). But even in guessing (καὶ φραγμὸν περιέθηκα, lit. "a wall I placed"; cf. V *et sepivit eam*) the translator is drawing on traditional knowledge, namely, that vineyard's were often fenced in to keep predators away (cf. v. 5: "turning away its hedge").

36. As Song 8:11 (*běba'al ḥāmôn* "in Baal-Hamon") makes clear, Isaiah's figure here is meant to stand in for a geographical location (apparently Ibn Ezra suggests glossing as a place name, Keren Ben Shamen, so Blenkinsopp, *Isaiah 1–39*, 206). The Hebrew itself, *běqeren ben-šāmen*, is surely intended to allude to the high aesthetics associated with royal or sacral anointing (*'et-qeren haššemen*, 1 Sam 16:13; 1 Kgs 1:39; cf. 1 Sam 16:1; Ps 92:11—this is analogous to how the line "your love is better [*ṭôbîm*] than wine [*miyyāyin*]" in Song 1:2 alludes to the best wine, *yên haṭṭôb*, Song 7:10). The phrasing

Cisjordan and of the typical tasks undertaken by a local (eighth-century) farmer in the cultivation and upkeep of such a vineyard—viz. choosing an appropriate site, loosening the soil and clearing it of stones, planting the vines, constructing a guard tower and press—is realistic, so much so, in fact, that C. E. Walsh uses this song to structure the main body of her study of viticulture in ancient Israel.[37] The narrative run is summative and emblematic, only gesturing toward the fuller picture of vineyard work well known to the audience. Much goes uncommented on. And some of what is not mentioned here initially even gets picked up on in later lines, such as the need to enclose terraced vineyards with a wall or hedge (v. 5 cf. Num 22:24; Ps 80:13–14) or the hoeing and pruning that would constitute part of the routine maintenance for a vineyard (v. 6; cf. Lev 25:3; Isa 18:5; *Gez* 1.6). Indeed, all is neatly telescoped. For example, in the real world of ancient Judah it could take from three to four years on average before newly planted vines would bear fruit[38]—the hyper-literal base meaning for the verbal root *q-w-h* "to wait" is to be emphasized in the verb's threefold use in this love song (vv. 2, 4, 7). The point here is the poem's insistence on being taken literally in these early lines. What is heard at the surface of the poem—a farmer's litany of typical tasks for keeping (up) a vineyard—is mostly what is intended to be heard. Mostly. This turns out to be the set up for the rest of the song; the (cultivated) ground against which the remainder of the lines will play. It needs to be (mostly) straightforward. The only tickle in Isaiah's abbreviated farmer's almanac of vineyard care comes sonically and rhythmically. And these clash a bit, at least initially, and perhaps, then, with the intent to bemuse still further. Each of the couplets in v. 2 is marked by sound play. The first couplet involves a run of three *wayyiqtol* forms, each ending with the same object suffix, *-ēhû* (in Tiberian vocalization), while the other two feature end-rhyme, *-ô // -ô* and *-îm // -îm*. The first two sets of like sounds serve to underscore likeness, whether in the acts of cultivation (*-ēhû*) or the site (*bětôkô // bô*) of building, while in the third set, by contrast, the end-rhyme (*-îm*) helps hold together opposites, grapes (*'ănābîm*) and rotten

---

itself is highly euphonic, thus underscores this heightened aesthetic sensibility (cf. Couey, *Reading the Poetry of First Isaiah*, 162), and Walsh (*Fruit of the Vine*, 93–94) is likely correct in thinking that *šāmen* here is used metonymically to figure the fertility of the vineyard (Deut 8:8, 32:13; Job 29:6; cf. Deut 33:24; Isa 28:1, 4; Ps 23:5; *šāmēn*: Num 13:20; Ezek 34:14; *šāmān*: Gen 27:28, 39).

37. Walsh, *Fruit of the Vine*, esp. 87–207. In fact, in an essay derived from the study she even refers to the song as a "vintner's textbook" ("God's Vineyard: Isaiah's Prophecy as Vintner's Textbook," *BRev* 14 [1998] 42–49).

38. Walsh, *Fruit of the Vine*, 93 n.16.

grapes (*bĕ'ušîm*).³⁹ Here, then, is the high euphony of song. Not at all out of character since, as noted, work in the vineyard would have occasionally been accompanied by work songs (e.g., Judg 21:21; Isa 16:10; Jer 48:33; cf. Song 2:12). On the other hand, already beginning in the second couplet of v. 1 and persisting through v. 4 (and reappearing in later lines, too, especially in the poem's final couplet in v. 7) the main rhythm struck is that of the unbalanced couplet, the so-called *qinah* meter, which traditionally accompanies dirges (e.g., Amos 5:2).⁴⁰ Although this couplet type is by no means restricted to dirges (e.g., Ps 19:8–10), I do not think it "absurd," as Williamson, for example, suggests, that in this instance one implication of this rhythmic choice is to foreshadow the song's "denouement."⁴¹ Poetic rhythm means by way of how it is put into play. After the balance of the poem's initial couplet, seven unbalanced, *qinah*-shaped couplets come. Such persistence demands auditorial recognition, especially in a song (*šîr*), the very antithesis of a dirge (*qînâ*; cf. Amos 8:10; Lam 5:15; Ps 30:12; *ANET*, 462). Moreover, each of the couplets where the farmer's failed expectations are sounded (the final couplets in vv. 2, 4, and 7) are unbalanced—a kind of rhythmic underscoring of intent, just in case auditors did not make the immediate (indexical) association. The disappointment of a failed grape crop would have been devastating economically, something truly to be mourned (e.g., Ps 80:13–14). The second mention of failed expectation even mimes the traditional "why" of lament, "why (*maddûa'*) had I waited to make grapes, / but it made rotten grapes?" (v. 4). Here, of course, as in Job 3:12 and Jer 14:19, for example, there is an intentional miss, a flaw if you will in the mime. The word *maddûa'* "why" never occurs in psalmic laments where instead *lāmâ/lāmmâ* is typical (e.g., Ps 22:2, 42:10, 74:11, 80:13; Lam 5:20;

---

39. *bĕ'ušîm* is a *hapax legomenon*. The root has as its basic meaning "to have a bad smell, stink" (e.g., Exod 7:18; Isa 50:2; Ps 38:6; Qoh 10:1), so rotten or spoiled grapes are likely in view here (Aq: σαπριας "rottenness"; see Walsh, *Fruit of the Vine*, 89). There is a cross-linguistic phenomenon known as "rhyming reduplication" in which complex word formations are generated by affixing secondarily derived rhyming elements (e.g., higgledy-piggledy, helter-skelter; BH: *tōhû wābōhû*, Gen 1:2; sometimes called *farragos*; see J. S. Lewis, "'The Earth Was Higgledy-Piggledy': A Proposal for *tōhû wābōhû* as Rhyming Reduplication" [unpubl. ms]). The secondarily derived rhyming elements in these expressions generally do not stand on their own as productive word formations (cf. Isa 34:11 where *tōhû* and *bōhû* are split up in a parallel construction just like compound names or extended epithets). This raises the possibility that *bĕ'ušîm* here (and in v. 4; and also perhaps *mišpāḥ* in v. 7, see below) may not just be an unknown rare word but a made-up rhyme word, albeit one with definite semantic associations through the lexical root (*b-'-š* "to stink"). The versions clearly do not recognize the lexeme (G ἀκάνθας "thorns"; V *labruscas* "wild grapes"; S *ḥrwb'* [pl.] "carob husks, pods").

40. Cf. Wildberger, *Isaiah 1–12*, 179; Williamson, *Isaiah 1–27*, 1:326.

41. Williamson, *Isaiah 1–27*, 1:326.

cf. Jer 14:9). So even here Isaiah seems to signal yet further mystification through his word choice. If there is foreshadowing of the poem's ending, however haunting, it may yet not be quite the expectation anticipated. And finally this succession of limping couplets leads immediately to the announcement of impending destruction—"let me make known to you/ what I am about to do to my vineyard" (v. 5)—which in turn is spelled out to good effect in terms of the undoing of all the farmer's care-full cultivation (e.g., tearing down of the terrace wall, ceasing to hoe or prune). Vineyards, precisely because of their value in the traditional lifeworld of the ancient Levant, figure prominently in biblical depictions of destruction (e.g., Deut 28:30, 39; Isa 32:10, 12–13; 63:3; Jer 12:10; Amos 5:11; Ps 80:13–14). In Isa 16:10 ("in the vineyards no songs are sung [*yĕrunnān*]," NRSV) the absence of song that would normally attend vineyard work is even remarked on, and in Amos 5:17, song is replaced with "lamentation" (*mispēd*; cf. Isa 32:12; Amos 5:16; Mic 1:8), which itself is a consequence of Yahweh's action, viz. "because/for/when (*kî*) I pass through your midst." Thus, it is not absurd at all to follow the feel of the rhythmic contours in these early lines toward their ultimate overturning of the love song Isaiah set out initially singing (cf. Amos 8:10; Lam 5:15; *KAI* 222 A.29–30).

III

In v. 3 the change in line length and the opening *wĕ'attâ* "and now" announce the shift to a new movement in Isaiah's song. This is accompanied by a shift in voice as well. Now the farmer, adopting the first person as his own, addresses a collection of Judahites. The unannounced switch in voice has bothered the (hyper) literate reception of this song, already beginning with the translators of the Old Greek and Targum who level the first person voice throughout (see vv. 2, 7). However, the shift in voice, although textually unmarked, could have been easily managed by the prophet extra-textually in performance, e.g., by a modulation in voice, a nod of the head, or a lifting of the eyebrows. The two central sections of the poem hang together by virtue of this (first person) voice and their like beginnings, *wĕ'attâ* "and now" (vv. 3, 5), which specifically articulate the transition to new material.[42] The farmer asks his neighbors to "judge" (*šipṭû*) between him and his vineyard. The abrupt introduction of forensic language calls attention to itself, especially given the agricultural focus to this point in the poem, not to mention

---

42. Very common in epistolary discourse (e.g., *Arad* 16.3; 21.3; *Lach* 4. obv. 2; *Mur* 1A.2)—a lexical marker (as opposed to graphic meta-script conventions, e.g., punctuation, layout) that betrays its ultimate origin in spoken discourse.

that vineyards, though sometimes the focus of legal theory in antiquity (e.g., Exod 22:4; Lev 19:10), ordinarily were not objectified as a party to a legal dispute.[43] The immediate return to language from the earlier stanza in the two following rhetorical questions smoothes the brief juridical rupture in the poem. But the turbulence is important as it helps the prophetic songster secure his ending when he comes to it. The plays on (the lack of) "justice" (*mišpāṭ*) and "righteousness" (*ṣĕdāqâ*) in v. 7 (cf. Amos 5:7, 24) heard after the call to "judge" (*šipṭû*) are all the more satisfying for having been (briefly) anticipated (cf. Deut 1:16; Lev 19:15; Isa 11:4, 16:5; Jer 5:28; Ps 9:5; Prov 31:9). This brief burst of forensic coloring also sharpens (at least momentarily) the image of the two collectives addressed, framing the *yôšēb yĕrûšālayim* and *'îš yĕhûdâ* more specifically as the community elders and other elites (e.g., Isa 3:14) who would normally sit in judgment and deliberation at the city gate (e.g., Deut 22:13–21; Josh 20:1–9; 2 Sam 15:2; Isa 29:21; Amos 5:10, 12, 15; Zech 8:16; Job 5:4; 29:7; 31:21; Prov 22:22; Ruth 4:1–11; Lam 2:9; 5:14)[44]—an image that shimmers again across the surface of the poem in v. 7, as it is precisely the same group who is chiefly responsible for maintaining social justice in ancient Judah.[45]

The content words (*'ăśôt, karmî, 'āśîtî, qiwwîtî, 'ăśôt, 'ănābîm, wayya'aś, bĕ'ūšîm*) of the two rhetorical questions in v. 4 are all repeats from earlier lines. This tightens the stanza's connection with what precedes—and also with what follows, as some of these (verbs from the root *'-ś-h, kerem*) feature again in the opening couplet of the next stanza (vv. 5–6). As important, the iteration, especially the fourfold repetition of the root *'-ś-h* "to make, do" and the close version of the failed expectation couplet, acts to buttress the picture of care already sketched. In fact, the first question in v. 4, "what more was there to do for my vineyard/ that I did not do in it?," points up the summative and indexical nature of the song's initial depiction of vineyard cultivation. Literally, other pertinent acts of care could be easily formulated (e.g., active guarding, Isa 27:3; Song 1:6), some of which are even referenced in later lines (e.g., building a protective wall, v. 5; hoeing and pruning, v. 6). But a more inclusive rendering is unnecessary given the

---

43. Cf. Willis, "Genre," 350.

44. Cf. S. C. Russell, "Gate and Town in 2 Samuel 15:1–5: Collective Politics and Absalom's Strategy," *JAH* 3 (2015) 2–21.

45. See esp. M. Weinfeld, "'Justice and Righteousness' in Ancient Israel against the Background of 'Social Reforms' in the Ancient Near East," in *Mesopotamien und seine Nachbarn: politische und kulturelle Wechselbeziehungen im alten Vorderasien vom 4. bis 1. Jahrtausend v. Chr. (XXV. Rencontre assyriologique internationale Berlin, 3. bis 7. Juli 1978)* (eds. H. J. Nissen and J. Renger; Berliner Beiträge zum Vorderen Orient 1; Berlin: Reimer, 1987) 491–519.

traditional semiotics of song performance in Judahite culture where auditors, as already mentioned, could easily fill in the details from the stereotyped depiction, and thus would give ready assent to the central thrust of the prophet's question here—yes, no more could have been done. Indeed, the threefold repetition of the root '-ś-h in v. 4 as voiced by the farmer materially underscores the vigor of his effort—I did ... did ... did. It is the break in the pattern that comes with the fourth repetition of the root, "but it [i.e., the *kerem*] made (or "did," *wayya'aś*) rotten grapes" (v. 4) that locates the source of disappointment.[46] This last line is repeated verbatim from the end of v. 2, but in that earlier rendition the intended antecedent (farmer or vineyard) is not made explicit. With the farmer's adoption of the first person voice in vv. 3-4 that ambiguity is resolved in the line's second sounding. Repetition and variation are at the heart of so much of this poem.

IV

The song makes its penultimate turn in vv. 5-6, signaled lexically by a second *wĕ'attâ* ('and now') and rhythmically by a change to more balanced couplets (and one triplet). Some initial word repetition (*wĕ'attâ*, *-nnā'*, *'-ś-h*, *kerem*) in v. 5 eases the transition and continues to build coherence into the song as a whole. Here, too, another outbreak of prosiness is encountered. In the main, the clutter of prose particles (*'et-*, *'ēt*, *'ăšer*) and the syntactic expansion slow the tempo down as a way of setting up and making plain the announcement of what the farmer is now about to do (*'ōśeh*, the only participle in the poem) to his vineyard. And as in the other instances of the prophet's leveraging of prose style in this song the prose touches are also poeticized. Here note the alliteration of *aleph*s and *ayin*s, the staging of *'ôdî'â-nnā'* so that it chimes with *'ăšîrânnā'* from the opening line (v. 1), and the scripting of the markers of direct object (*'et-*, *'ēt*) such as to accommodate and accentuate line structure.

The two couplets and one triplet that follow describe the farmer's decultivation of his vineyard. These lines, now in the farmer's voice, answer to and oppose the set of three couplets in v. 2 where the farmer's labors (of love) on behalf of his vineyard were first narrated. In fact, these lines appear as the material undoing of those earlier lines. The formal elegance of three unbalanced, *qinah*-shaped couplets, with each line headed by a conjunctive *waw* and the *wayyiqtol* form repeated six times over, is in vv. 5-6 completely unraveled. The run of couplets this time is exploded by the song's lone

---

46. Williamson (*Isaiah 1-27*, 1:339-40) well appreciates the sevenfold repetition of the root '-ś-h "to make, do" in vv. 2-5—"unlikely to be accidental."

triplet (v. 6), none of the line groupings pattern alike in this later material, and the dominantly parallelistic strategy in v. 2 gives way to the song's most strikingly enjambed couplet, "and the clouds I will command/ from raining upon it rain" (v. 6)—the non-normative, tortured syntax here seeming to be the final ruining of the smooth run of *wayyiqtol*s in the earlier lines.[47] And just to underscore the point, the lone *wayyiqtol* form—*waʾăśîtēhû* (v. 6)— mimes the sonic pattern of the poem's first three *wayyiqtol*s (*wayʿazzĕqēhû, waysaqqĕlēhû, wayyiṭṭāʿēhû*, v. 2), only now apocopated and as an act of unmaking, de-cultivation (*bātâ* "wasteland"[48]).

The semantics follow suit. In place of the digging, clearing, planting, and building of cultivation the farmer announces his intention to destroy the vineyard hedge/wall, to cease hoeing and pruning (emblematic of the routine tasks of care grape growing demands, cf. *Gez* 1.6), and even to withhold the vital life giving rain that all agriculture depended on in this part of the world—this last, like the positioning of the vineyard as a party to a legal dispute, jars a bit; this is no ordinary farmer. As already noted, these aspects of vineyard care were not specifically mentioned in v. 2 but we may assume that they draw on the community's large store of common knowledge about viticulture. In other words, here again we have good evidence of the poem's informing traditional, indexical semiotics. These lines also feature sound and word play as throughout the song. In particular, the line-internal plays prepare auditors for the song's final punchlines, which depend on line-internal rhyming (*mišpāṭ // miśpāḥ* and *ṣĕdāqâ // ṣĕʿāqâ*, v. 7). There is a run of these: *hāsēr // bāʿēr, lōʾ yizzāmēr // lōʾ yēʿādēr*, and *mĕhamṭîr // māṭār*—with the alliterative pairing *šāmîr wāšāyit* (cf. Isa 7:23, 24, 25; 9:17; 10:17; 27:4) and the sequence of *wĕʿālâ* ... *wĕʿal* ... *ʿālāyw* punctuating the last three lines in v. 6.

V

The song's concluding movement in v. 7 is marked, initially, by *kî* ("for, because"), a particle that commonly appears at the end of biblical poems

---

47. In fact, the stanza starts out with the song's other pronounced bit of enjambment (v. 5), so the two together form a nice inclusio by which this section of the poem is set apart, and thus given formal shape.

48. *bātâ* is a *hapax legomenon* (MH *bātâ* "destruction") with no obvious cognates. The sense seems clear enough from context—waste, ruin, desolation, destruction (cf. S *wʾbdywhy dnḥrb* "and I will make it so that it is desolated, destroyed"; V *et ponam eam desrtam*). G (καὶ ἀνήσω τὸν ἀμπελῶνά μου) is interpreting in light of the previous imagery—though its gloss ὡς εἰς χέρσον "as in a dry land" later in the verse is perhaps closer to the mark (there it is a gloss for BH *šāmîr* "thorn," as also in Isa 7:23–25).

and sections of poems (e.g., Isa 1:20; Amos 4:13; Ps 1:6, 82:8, 100:5, 133:3; Job 3:10; Lam 1:22c), and a change in line length, shifting to slightly longer lines (nine to eleven syllables) than that which typifies the immediately preceding stanza (v. 6: seven to nine syllables). The return to the third person perspective of the song's beginning (vv. 1–2) completes a version of the ring structure that so often contains and thus closes traditional songs. And then there is the change-up to verbless clauses. Most of the poem's clauses to this point consist of verbal predicators—often involving finite verb forms. However, at poem's end in v. 7 the identity of the players in the allegory are finally revealed in a (longer-line) couplet consisting of verbless clauses:

> kî kerem yhwh ṣĕbā'ôt bêt yiśrā'ēl
> wĕ'îš yĕhûdâ nĕṭa' ša'ăšû'āyw
> For the vineyard of Yahweh Sabaoth is the house of Israel
> and the people of Judah are the planting of his delight.

The actional flow of verbal clauses momentarily stops in the stasis created by the two verbless clauses for the allegory's unveiling. The final couplet, as well, though set up verbally (*wayqaw* "and he waited/hoped"—the language reaching back to and echoing the end of the first two stanzas, *wayqaw* and *qiwwîtî*, vv. 2, 4), derives its punch through the contrasting verbless clauses at the ends of both lines (*wĕhinnê miśpāḥ* ... *wĕhinnê ṣĕ'āqâ*). Here the stasis underscores the damning disappointment and contrary reality and quite literally stops the poem. This last bit of justly celebrated rhyming helps to cinch and thus close the poem forcefully, emphatically:

> wayqaw lĕmišpāṭ wĕhinnê miśpāḥ
> liṣdāqâ wĕhinnê ṣĕ'āqâ (Isa 5:7)
> He hoped for justice but instead there was bloodshed,
> for righteousness but instead there was outrage.

The missed expectations are mimed sonically and formally in the consonantal mismatches in the pairs *mišpāṭ* // *miśpāḥ* and *ṣĕdāqâ* // *ṣĕ'āqâ*—the rhyming holds the pairs together so that auditors can hear (and readers see)[49] the mismatch.

---

49. 1QIsa[a] mistakenly adds the preposition *l-* "to, for" (*lmśpḥ*) under the influence of the preceding *lmšpṭ*. The word *miśpāḥ* (often glossed as "bloodshed") is another *hapax legomenon* (cf. Ar. *safaḥa* "to spill, pour out, shed"; *saffāḥ* "shedder of blood, murder"; Wildberger, *Isaiah 1–12*, 185), which the versions, not recognizing, gloss from context: G (ἀνομίαν "lawlessness"), V (*iniquitas* "iniquity"), S (*ḥṭwpy'* "violence"), T (*'ānôsîn* "robbers"). As with *bĕ'ûšîm* in vv. 2 and 4 *miśpāḥ* here may be another made-up rhyme word. Indeed, if the root derives originally from *ṣ-p-ḥ* (cf. *mispaḥat* "skin rash," *sappaḥat* "scab"; cf. *śippaḥ* in Isa 3:17), then perhaps even the spelling has been

The allegorization itself is brief and tightly focused. The realistic depiction of vineyard care takes a commonplace image from the agrarian world of eighth century Judah and figures it to symbolize the kind of love and care required socially. *kerem* is the poem's chief *Leitwort*, repeated six times over and at least once in each of the poem's four component stanzas. The vineyard is the main focus of the allegorical move here at poem's end, viz. "the vineyard of Yahweh Sabaoth is the house of Israel." The citizenry of Israel and Judah (especially the elders and ruling elites), who already in vv. 3 and 5 are staged as stand-ins for Isaiah's (live) audience, as a consequence of being identified as the vineyard and the "planting" of Yahweh's "delight" in v. 7 is shifted from onlooker and judge to participant and target. The poetics of the poem work to catch the citizenry out,[50] to reveal in the language of the song the prevalence of *miśpāḥ* and *ṣěʿāqâ* where there should be *mišpāṭ* and *ṣědāqâ*. No wonder the song closes shortly thereafter. This is to recall that the poem is a temporal art form. And although scholars have a habit of reading this poem from the perspective of their knowledge about how it ends, there does not appear to me to be strong impetus in the poem itself for going back and trying to map out a full blown allegory.

Moreover, and by contrast, the allegorization of Yahweh Sabaoth as lover and farmer is not scripted in the same way at the surface of the poem, but chiefly comes off obliquely—grammatically, Yahweh Sabaoth is the *nomen rectum* and not the *nomen regens* in the construct chains in the first couplet of v. 7. Ancient allegories frequently make explicit their participants (e.g., Ezek 23:4; cf. 2 Sam 12:7; Isa 54:5) but here there is no corresponding identification of Yahweh as farmer or lover (cf. Isa 27:3: "I Yahweh am its keeper"). Indeed, the farmer's assumption of the divine powers to control the rain (see esp. Job 38:25–28; cf. Gen 2:5) suggests that the punch at the poem's end is not principally fixated on Yahweh. That is, again, the allegorizing in this poem is mainly limited and local and not wholesale.[51]

---

altered. The spelling with a *sin* graphically enhances and underscores the aural play—which also implies an anticipation of readers (and not just listeners) for this text.

50. Though such "catching out" need not be accompanied by "surprise," as assumed in so much of the commentary tradition (see. esp. J. Schipper, *Parables and Conflict in the Hebrew Bible* [Cambridge: Cambridge University Press, 2009] 113–15)—the contestation with the vineyard (v. 3) and the farmer's putative ability to control the rain (v. 6), in particular, in a song on the lips of a well-known prophet would be sufficient to elicit certain expectations on the part of an audience.

51. Thus R. E. Clements speaks appropriately of "allegorical features" (*Isaiah 1–39* [NCBC; Grand Rapids: Eerdmans, 1980] 56); cf. Blenkinsopp, *Isaiah 1–39*, 207; Schipper, *Parables and Conflict*, 112 ("limited allegory"); Couey, *Reading the Poetry of First Isaiah*, 162 n. 89.

The slight unbalance in the length of lines in the final couplet (four words, three words) alludes to the *qinah* rhythm that shaped the run of couplets in vv. 2–4. This adds to the poem's ending an undertone of sadness, lament, mourning. But of course the prophets in particular were fond of using the dirge (*qînâ*) ironically as a kind of condemnatory critique that, among other things, proclaims the impending downfall of some person or polity, as in Ezekiel's famous dirge over the king of Tyre (Ezek 27:1–36) or in Isaiah's own *māšāl* (*cum* dirge) over the king of Babylon (Isa 14:3–23; cf. Isa 47:1–15; Amos 5:1–3). So there is also a bite to Isaiah's lament over the lack of *mišpāṭ* and *ṣĕdāqâ*. Indeed, the whole point of the little ditty is quite simple, to underscore this lack. Whatever specificity might accompany the terms *mispāḥ* "bloodshed" and *ṣĕʿāqâ* "outcry"—the first is a *hapax legomenon* and the second a general cry of despair or suffering (e.g., Gen 18:21; Exod 3:9; Ps 9:12; Job 27:9; Lam 2:18)—they chiefly mark (especially sonically and formally) a rupture in the unquestioned (and thus traditional) norms of *mišpāṭ* "justice" and *ṣĕdāqâ* "righteousness" (the terms are paired on more than forty occasions in the Bible, e.g., Gen 18:19; 2 Sam 8:15; Isa 1:27; 9:6; 32:16; Amos 5:24; Ps 72:1–2, 106:3; Prov 21:3; cf. *KAI* 4.6–7; Akk. *kittum u mīšarum*, *CAD* K, 470–71).[52] This is yet another point at which this poem makes plain its extra-textual appeal to shared experiences and interpretations. The song does not so much explicate the wrongs that have generated *mispāḥ* and *ṣĕʿāqâ* as expose and name them for what everybody already knows them to be, namely, not *mišpāṭ* and not *ṣĕdāqâ*. Indeed, refusing a fifth itertion of the verb *ʿ-ś-h* "to do, make" (M, 1QIsaᵃ) only adumbrates the complaint, a figural erasure of the traditional exhortation to do "justice" and "righteousness" (esp. Gen 18:19; Jer 22:3; Ps 99:4, 119:121; Prov 21:3; 2 Chr 9:8; cf. 1 Kgs 3:28; Isa 56:1; Jer 5:1; Mic 6:8; Ps 106:3; Prov 21:15).[53]

What is at stake here is the very foundation of the cultured—or better, the cultivated (see Gen 2:8)—world as the ancients knew it. The gods were responsible for establishing the foundations of the earth (e.g., Isa 54:11; Job 38:4) and the lack of justice on earth could threaten to topple those foundations (esp. Amos 8:4–8; Ps 82:5). Or as S. Paul observes (commenting on Amos 5:24), "The proper divine-human relationship is based upon a correct

---

52. An analogous play on *ṣĕdāqâ* and its lack or absence appears in Isa 54:14: "In righteousness [*biṣdāqâ*] you will be established,/ and you will be far from oppression [*mēʿōšeq*]" (cf. Prov 16:8). And Isa 32:16 specifically associates the traditional norms of *mišpāṭ* and *ṣĕdāqâ* with the image of a flourishing "fertile field" (*karmel*).

53. G (ποιῆσαι κρίσιν), V (*faceret iudicium*), and T (*dyʿbdwn dynʾ*) resort to periphrastic renderings that supply the expected idiom that M (and 1QIsaᵃ) so artfully resists, thus ramifying the erasure itself and the damning critique it reveals, viz. the very absence of doing "justice" and "righteousness."

human-human relationship."[54] Ancient love songs were sung to many ends, including as means for securing divine blessing and ensuring fecundity, fertility, and human flourishing. The latter is most obviously at issue in the so-called sacred marriage texts from ancient Mesopotamia. Two inscriptions from Assurbanipal provide some of the most explicit explication of the underlying ideology of divine love in first-millennium Mesopotamia.[55] The first is an inscription dating to 655 BCE that references the celebration of divine love involving Marduk and his consort Zarpanitu:

> [For the sake of] my [li]fe and for the lengthening of my days I gave them [i.e., chariot and bed of *musukkannu* tree] as a present. / [When] they perform the ritual of love and enter the house of love, may the divine couple talk to each other of my [...]! / May they bless my kingship [by the ut]terance of their pure mouths which is not to be countermanded! / May they make me, who looked for their dwellings, attain my heart's desire! / May they suppress my enemies, (I) who fulfilled their ardent wish ... May Marduk, king of the gods, weaken his potency and destroy his seed, May Zarpanitu pronounce a bad word about him on the bed of her boudoir.[56]

The second comes from a colophon addressed to Nabû (referencing the divine couple Nabû and Tašmetu):

> [Tašme]tu, the Great Lady, your beloved spouse, who intercedes (for me) [daily] before you in the sweet bed, who never ceases demanding you to protect my life. [The one who trusts] you will not come to shame, O Nabû.[57]

As M. Nissinen explains, "This telling piece of evidence makes plain the earthly ramifications of the divine lovemaking. The goddess, while gratifying her beloved in the 'sweet bed,' intercedes with him on behalf of the king—and, through him, the community of worshippers."[58] The third century BCE Aramaic text in Demotic script (Papyrus Amherst 63) even preserves a sacred marriage text where Levantine deities (e.g., El, Baal Shamayin) appear to be invoked and where the purpose of the divine lovemaking is to bestow divine blessing on a deported people and their

---

54. S. M. Paul, *Amos* (Hermeneia; Minneapolis: Fortress, 1991) 192.
55. For details, see Nissinen, "Akkadian Rituals and Poetry," 93–136, esp. 110–13.
56. Nissinen, "Akkadian Rituals and Poetry," 104.
57. Ibid., 98; cf. 106 (a prayer to Shamash by Nabonidus).
58. Ibid.

land—"Rebuild, man, Ellipi. A cursed land rebuild, a city of ruins rebui[ld]; ... Keep alive the pauper." (*COS* 1.99:322).

That the erotic was also an appropriate vernacular means for giving expression to similar themes in ancient Israel and Judah (and even in Persian period Yehud) is indicated by texts such as Hosea 2, Jer 3:1–5, Ezekiel 16 and 23, and Isaiah 54.[59] This suggests that Isaiah's choice to riff on a love song likely was not innocent but intended to trade on these extra-textual associations of the genre all along. That is, the final upshot of the small poem is to point up the failure to maintain traditional norms of justice and rightness in Israel and Judah, a theme that was commonly enough inflected in the language of love. In the Bible (especially in the prophets), the staging of the erotic mythologically (i.e., involving Yahweh) is usually negative (sometimes pornographic and/or misogynistic) and in service of critique. Yahweh is imagined as the jealous and wronged husband—the so-called jealousy poems from Mesopotamia (Si 57; MS 3285) use the erotic to give expression to a related range of feelings and worries. Nowhere in Isa 5:1–7 is divine love elaborated narratively. No personification is ever evoked. There is no mention of marriage or adultery, no mention of sex at all. The thematic touch is light and weighted toward the very beginning of the short song. Nevertheless, the love song genre is entirely appropriate as a means to expose the rift in the divine-human relationship that emerges when basic norms of social justice falter.

H. Wildberger, who authored what was surely the most influential commentary on Isaiah of Jerusalem from the last third of the twentieth century, in his initial assessment of the form of Isa 5:1–7 reports that "it is frequently suggested that Isaiah wants to get the attention of his listeners by playing the part of a popular singer."[60] While Wildberger never totally disavows this idea, he does seem to distance his own thinking about the song from it, ultimately stressing the song's formal resemblances to an "accusation speech"—something, one suspects, felt to be just a bit more serious than a simple love ditty.[61] For me, however, Wildberger's initial impression

---

59. Carr rightly reads these texts together with Isa 5:1–7, sensing their broad literary kinship (*Erotic Word*, 65–72). If anything, when this group of biblical texts is read comparatively with Mesopotamian love poetry, especially that of the sacred marriage texts and the so-called jealousy poems, this kinship becomes all the more apparent.

60. *Isaiah 1–12*, 177.

61. Ibid., 178. Cf. the image of Isaiah at a city gate in Jerusalem presenting "what sounds like a legal case," as imagined by Carr (*Erotic Word*, 60).

seems spot on. I do think Isaiah is posing (in a way) as a popular singer and spoofing a love song. Prophets were traditional performers of whom we may presume a range of performative competencies (e.g., acting, 1 Kgs 20:35–43), including singing,[62] which is specifically the image (however unflattering) struck in the simile in Ezek 33:32. And the repurposing (e.g., through parody, irony) of (verbal) art forms—here a love song—to different ends is well attested already in antiquity (e..g., Isaiah's mock dirge over the king of Babylon, Isa 14:3–23; the Joban poet's parody of Deuteronomy 32, e.g., Job 12:7–8[63]). Besides, as I have tried to indicate above, the vernacular of love in antiquity could be put to various uses (e.g., to secure divine blessing), including critique, and staged mythologically, even in Israel and Judah. Thus Isaiah's pose here (as a singer of love songs) is not at all innocent. Indeed, the lyric medium of the love song is itself crucial to Isaiah's exposé of the breakdown in *mišpāṭ* and *ṣĕdāqâ*. How he does it—as much through word and sound play, manipulation of rhythm, line-structure and form, as through semantics—is very much to point. The love song, like many of the Bible's other nonnarrative poetic genres, is much more than its thematic bits. In the end, then, Isaiah's song of love in behest of beloved divinity and about a much loved vineyard proves to be a most congenial vehicle for his prophetic critique.

---

62. D. Pardee, in his brief comments on Isa 5:1–7 at the end of his *The Ugaritic Texts and the Origins of West Semitic Literary Composition* ([Oxford: Oxford University Press, 2012] 123), presses this point even further. He argues that "the oldest Hebrew data on the prophets [i.e., the abundance of poetry collected in their names] reveal these persons to have been poets in the fullest sense of the term"—poets, and thus singers, who also "happened to be prophets" and "not so much prophets who knew something about poetry."

63. E. L. Greenstein, "Parody as a Challenge to Tradition: The Use of Deuteronomy 32 in the Book of Job," in *Reading Job Intertextually* (eds. K. J. Dell and W. Kynes; LHB/OTS 574; London: Bloomsbury T. & T. Clark, 2012) 66–78.

Appendix: Isaiah 5:1–7

Transcription, Translation, and Notes

1. ʾāšîrâ nnāʾ[i] lîdîdî[ii]
   šîrat dôdîm[iii] lĕkarmô[iv]
   kerem hāyâ lîdîdî[v]
   bĕqeren ben-šāmen[vi]

   Let me sing of my love(r)
   a song of love about his vineyard
   a vineyard belonged to my love(r)
   on a fertile spur[vii]

2. wayʿazzĕqēhû[viii] waysaqqĕlēhû[ix]
   wayyiṭṭāʿēhû śōrēq
   wayyiben[x] migdāl bĕtôkô
   wĕgam-yeqeb ḥāṣēb bô
   wayqaw laʿăśôt ʿănābîm
   wayyaʿaś[xi] bĕʾūšîm[xii]

   and he dug it and cleared it of stones
   and planted it with *soreq* vines[xiii]
   and he built a tower[xiv] in the middle of it
   and even hewed out a winepress[xv] in it
   and he waited to make grapes
   but made rotten grapes.[xvi]

3. wĕʿattâ yôšēb[xvii] yĕrûšālayim wĕʾîš yĕhûdâ[xviii]
   šipṭû-nāʾ[xix] bênî ûbên karmî[xx]

   And now inhabitant(s) of Jerusalem and citizen(s) of Judah
   judge between me and my vineyard

4. mah-llaʿăśôt ʿôd lĕkarmî[xxi]
   wĕlōʾ ʿāśîtî bô
   maddûaʿ qiwwîtî laʿăśôt ʿănābîm
   wayyaʿaś[xxii] bĕʾūšîm

   what more was there to do for my vineyard
   and I did not do in it?
   why had I waited to make grapes
   but it made rotten grapes?

5. wĕʿattâ[xxiii] ʾôdîʿâ[xxiv]-nnāʾ[xxv] ʾetkem[xxvi]
   ʾēt ʾăšer-ʾănî ʿōśeh[xxvii] lĕkarmî
   hāsēr[xxviii] mĕśûkātô[xxix] wĕhāyâ[xxx] lĕbāʿēr[xxxi]
   pārōṣ gĕdērô wĕhāyâ[xxxii] lĕmirmās

   And now let me make known to you
   what I am about to do to my vineyard
   removing its hedge and it will be devoured[xxxiii]
   breaking down its wall[xxxiv] and it will be a trampled place

6. *waʾăšîtēhû bātâ*[xxxv]
lōʾ yizzāmēr wĕlōʾ yēʿādēr
wĕʿālâ šāmîr wāšāyit
wĕʿal heʿābîm[xxxvi] *ʾăṣawweh*
mĕhamṭîr ʿalāyw māṭār

and I will set it as a wasteland
it will not be pruned and it will not be hoed
and it will grow up thorns and thistles
and the clouds I will command
not to rain on it rain.

7. *kî kerem yhwh ṣĕbāʾôt bêt yiśrāʾēl*
wĕʾîš yĕhûdâ nĕṭaʿ šaʿăšûʿāyw[xxxvii]
wayqav[xxxviii] *lĕmišpāṭ wĕhinnê miśpāḥ*[xxxix]
liṣdāqâ[xl] *wĕhinnê ṣĕʿāqâ*

For the vineyard of Yahweh Sabaoth is the
house of Israel
and the citizen(s) of Judah are the planting
of his delight
and he waited for justice but there was only
bloodshed
for righteousness but there was only outcry.

ENDNOTES FOR THE APPENDIX

i. The particle does not appear in QIsa[a], which may have resulted from what is traditionally described as parablepsis (homoioteleuton), especially if the particle was spelled *nh* (as elsewhere in 1QIsa[a] three times, Isa 5:3, 7:13, and 64:8)—though the loss could have also been trigged or aided by aural/oral interference, i.e., the one time writing of segments that sound the same. Or perhaps *ʾšyrh lydydy* is just a good variant (see *ʾāšîrâ l-* without *nāʾ* in Exod 15:1; Judg 5:3; Ps 13:6, 101:1, 144:9). Nevertheless, it would seem that the particle was originally present, since it punctuates the opening sets of lines of each of the next two sections in the poem as well.

ii. This is the reading of M, supported by QIsa[a] (*lydydy*) and all the versions except G, which has only τῷ ἠγαπημένῳ, lacking an explicit reflex of the first person suffix (Aq, Sym, and Theod add μου as they correct back towards M). Greek in certain circumstances, especially "when the relationship between two entities . . . is obvious" and "when the 'owner' forms the subject of the clause," has the capacity "to communicate that a thing or a person belongs to something or someone else" through the use of the article alone (without the explicit use of a genitive pronoun, though the latter is more typical; see M. van der Vorm-Croughs, *The Old Greek of Isaiah: An Analysis of Its Pluses and Minuses* [SBLSCS 61; Atlanta: Society of Biblical Literature, 2014] 109; cf. 114). Both of the circumstances noted seem relevant to the material reading presupposed by all the other witnesses, and thus G here is likely a translation variant and does not reflect a different material reading in its *Vorlage*.

iii. This is the (conjectural) emendation (presuming M has resulted from a scribal writing error) suggested already by R. Lowth, who compares *šîr yĕdîdōt* 'love song' in Ps 45:1 (R. Lowth, *Isaiah*; cf. Roberts, *First Isaiah*, 70, n. b). M, QIsa[a], and all the versions except GAS preserve a different material reading, *šyrt dwdy*, which most construe after M, *šîrat dôdî* lit. 'a song of my beloved' (e.g., Emerton, "The Translation of Isaiah 5, 1," 18–30; Williamson, *Isaiah 1–27*, 1:317–18); others (e.g., Roberts, *First Isaiah*, 70, n. b; cf. Blenkinsopp, *Isaiah 1–39*, 205, 206, 207) advocate vocalizing *dwdy* as *dôday* "my love," resulting in an explicit reference to a love song: *šîrat dôday* "(my) love song." That ᾆσμα τοῦ ἀγαπητοῦ in GAS may reflect a different (and even preferable) material reading appears not to have been closely considered, in part perhaps because in Greek under certain circumstances, as mentioned in an earlier note, the genitive form of a personal pronoun may be replaced by an article, which "can equally serve to communicate that a thing or a person belongs to something or someone else, or that a necessary relationship exists between the two things or persons" (van der Vorm-Croughs, *Old Greek of Isaiah*, 109; cf. 114). LXX Isaiah has plenty of examples where the attributive suffix of the Hebrew is not reflected in the Greek translation (van der Vorm-Croughs, *Old Greek of Isaiah*, 109, 109–15). In this instance, however, unlike with the preceding τῷ ἠγαπημένῳ, the pertinent circumstances—"when the relationship between two entities . . . is obvious" and "when the 'owner' forms the subject of the clause" (van der Vorm-Croughs, *Old Greek of Isaiah*, 109)—seem not to obtain. Indeed, who the beloved is and what song is being referenced is precisely at issue. Moreover, the rendering of G at Ps 45:1 (LXX Ps 44:1), ᾠδὴ ὑπὲρ τοῦ ἀγαπητοῦ "a song for the beloved," suggests that GAS in Isa 5:1, ᾆσμα τοῦ ἀγαπητοῦ "a song of the beloved," could reflect the very material reading posited by Lowth as a conjectural emendation, *šîrat dôdîm*. That the Hexaplaric (e.g., GB, Aq, Sym, Theod), Lucianic, and Catena groups all have μου (see J. Ziegler, *Isaias* [Septuaginta Vetus Testamentum Graecum 14; 3d ed.; Göttingen: Vandenhoeck & Ruprecht, 1983] 137) only underscores the uniqueness of GAS here (especially note the presence of μου in the non-Hexaplaric groups)—as M. van der Vorm-Croughs also stresses, "LXX Isaiah contains many genitive pronouns that are *plusses* [more than 60x], probably additions by the translator to make his text more explicit," *Old Greek of Isaiah*, 109, n. 31; cf. 33–36). Indeed, the addition of the pronominal suffix (-*î*) in M may itself be viewed as an explicating gloss that makes clearer whose love song is being referenced, i.e., the lover's/farmer's and not the singer's (on such explicating glosses from a traditional text-critical perspective, see McCarter, *Text Criticism*, 34–35, 36). The awkwardness ("decidedly odd," Blenkinsopp, *Isaiah 1–39*, 206) of the threefold reference to the lover/farmer (so esp. Roberts, *First Isaiah*, 70, n. b) that results from this explication is perhaps yet a further sign of its secondary derivation. In sum, there are good warrants for seriously considering the materiality of G's reading here.

iv. G's τῷ ἀμπελῶνί μου is consistent with this translation's decision to level through the distinction between the third and first person references to the farmer/lover throughout the song, and thus is likely secondary to the third person reference reflected in all the other textual witnesses (cf. Williamson, *Isaiah 1–27*, 1:318), if it is not simply a scribal reading error (*yod* and *waw* are often graphically confused in many scripts used to write Hebrew). Aq, Sym, and Theod read back toward M, providing the expected αυτου for μου.

v. G (τῷ ἠγαπημένῳ, viz. a vineyard belonged to "the beloved"), presumably under the influence of the earlier τῷ ἠγαπημένῳ in G (and τοῦ ἀγαπητοῦ in GAS), is lacking any reflex of M's first person pronominal suffix (-*î* "my"; cf. QIsaᵃ, V, T, S), which Aq, Sym, and Theod correct.

vi. G's ἐν τόπῳ πίονι is a periphrastic rendering, as often when translating non-literal uses of Hebrew *bēn* in Isaiah (van der Vorm-Croughs, *Old Greek of Isaiah*, 136–37; cf. 350). Aq and Theod literalize, viz. *filio olei*/υιω ελαιου.

vii. Literally, "horn" (BH *qeren*; cf. G κέρατι; V *cornu* [cf. Aq, Sym, Theod]; S *qrnʾ*), though used here to indicate a cultivatable ridge or spur (Syr. *qren* "peak of a moutain," cf. modern Arab. *qarn*) in the hilly topography of ancient Judah where vines were planted in terraces (so T's hyperliteral *bṭwr rm* "on a high mountain"; cf. Amos 9:13:

"the mountains shall drip sweet wine,/ and all the hills flow with it," NRSV; Jer 31:5: "Again you shall plant vineyards/ on the mountains of Samaria," NRSV; cf. Walsh, *Fruit of the Vine*, 93–97). Though the use of *qeren* in reference to a ridge or spur is unique, the term's frequent (26x) use as a designation for the up-turned corners of an altar (e.g., Amos 3:12) shows that such a geographical denomination (especially when viewed on the horizon) is at least not entirely implausible. ("Horn" in English can be used with a similar sense, which the Oxford English Dictionary treats under the general rubric, "a horn-shaped or horn-like projection"). As Song 8:11 (*běbaʿal ḥāmôn* "in Baal-Hamon") makes clear, Isaiah's figure here is meant to stand in for a geographical location (apparently Ibn Ezra suggests glossing as a place name, Keren Ben Shamen, so Blenkinsopp, *Isaiah 1–39*, 206). The Hebrew itself, *běqeren ben-šāmen*, is surely intended to allude to the high aesthetics associated with royal or sacral anointing (*ʾet-qeren haššemen*, 1 Sam 16:13; 1 Kgs 1:39; cf. 1 Sam 16:1; Ps 92:11; *CTU* 2.73.29–31—this is analogous to how the line "your love is better [*ṭôbîm*] than wine [*miyyāyin*]" in Song 1:2 alludes to the best wine, *yên haṭṭôb*, Song 7:10). The phrasing itself is highly euphonic, thus underscores this heightened aesthetic sensibility (cf. Couey, *Reading the Poetry of First Isaiah*, 162), and Walsh (*Fruit of the Vine*, 93–94) is likely correct in thinking that *šāmen* here is used metonymically to figure the fertility of the vineyard (Deut 8:8; 32:13; Job 29:6; cf. Deut 33:24; Isa 28:1, 4; Ps 23:5; *šāmēn*: Num 13:20; Ezek 34:14; *šāmān*: Gen 27:28, 39).

viii. The root ʿ-z-q only occurs here in the Bible, but its meaning ("to dig, break up the ground," cf. S *wplḥw* "and he worked/cultivated/plowed") is established by post-biblical Hebrew (QH, MH) and Arabic (*ʿazaqa*; see *HALOT*, 810). G (καὶ φραγμὸν περιέθηκα) and V (*et sepivit eam*) do not recognize the root, perhaps interpreting in light of v. 5. G (also T) uses first person forms throughout this verse and in v. 7, assimilating to the voice used in the middle sections of the song (vv. 3–6).

ix. Again G (καὶ ἐχαράκωσα) uses the first person (cf. T) and misunderstands the underlying Hebrew (cf. S *wʾhdrw sygʾ* "and he surrounded it with a hedge"—both again are probably influenced by v. 5).

x. QIsaᵃ *wybnʾ* for M's *wayyiben*. As E. Y. Kutscher (*The Language and Linguistic Background of the Isaiah Scroll (QIsaᵃ)* [Studies on the Texts of the Desert of Judah 6; Leiden: Brill, 1974] 328–29), notices, QIsaᵃ prefers the long form of the imperfect after *waw*. For the variation in spelling /e/ with either a *he* or an *aleph* at Qumran, see Kutscher, *Isaiah Scroll*, 163–64; E. Qimron, *The Hebrew of the Dead Sea Scrolls* [HSS 29; Atlanta: Scholars, 1986] 23.

xi. Only here does G (cf. T) use the third person (cf. G at v. 4), as a means of distinguishing the lover's/farmer's expectation (still voiced in the first person: καὶ ἔμεινα τοῦ ποιῆσαι σταφυλήν "and I waited to make grapes") from its ultimate frustration—the responsibility for the failure explicitly assigned to the vineyard, viz. ἐποίησεν δὲ "but it made" (cf. T *wʾynwn ʾbʾyšw ʿwbdyhwn* "but they made their deeds evil"—the explicit disjunctive syntax in T points up the ambiguity of M's use of the *wayyiqtol* here). M (and presumably the *Vorlage* of G) is not so explicit. Only after v. 4 and especially v. 7 is the allegorized vineyard's culpability more specifically implicated. G interprets in light of the whole. T is even more explicit: *ʾmryt dyʿbdwn ʿwbdyn ṭbyn* "I said they should do good deeds" (see also v. 3 where T glosses M's *karmî* as ʿ*my* "my people"). Many modern translations follow G and T, as, for example, NRSV: "he expected *it* to yield grapes,/ but *it* yielded wild grapes" (emphasis added). But BH ʿ-*ś-h* may be used of the farmer's production (e.g., Amos 9:14) and that of the plant or tree or vine (e.g., Gen

1:11; Job 14:9). In Ps 1:3, for example, the language in the last line of the simile (wĕkōl ʾăšer-yaʿăśeh yaṣlîaḥ) needs to have both the righteous man and the flourishing fruit tree in view: "and all which he/it does thrives." Isaiah in 5:2 appears to be counting on the same semantic breadth of the term. Songs are a performative art form that evolve temporally, in and through time. They happen. The full unraveling of Isaiah's allegory does not come till the end. The Hebrew here remains intentionally opaque as to the ultimate antecedents for the verbs. Indeed, the audience does not yet know that the lover/farmer is Yahweh—though with Isaiah doing the singing/spoofing such an identity may well have been anticipated.

xii. The root has as its basic meaning "to have a bad smell, stink" (e.g., Exod 7:18; Isa 50:2; Ps 38:6; Qoh 10:1), so rotten or spoiled grapes are likely in view here (Aq: σαπριασ 'rottenness'; see Walsh, *Fruit of the Vine*, 89). There is a cross-linguistic phenomenon known as "rhyming reduplication" in which complex word formations are generated by affixing secondarily derived rhyming elements (e.g., higgledy-piggledy, helter-skelter; BH: *tōhû wābōhû*, Gen 1:2; sometimes called farragos; see Lewis, "'The Earth Was Higgledy-Piggledy.'" The secondarily derived rhyming elements in these expressions generally do not stand on their own as productive word formations (cf. Isa 34:11 where *tōhû* and *bōhû* are split up in a parallel construction just like compound names or extended epithets). This raises the possibility that *bĕʿušîm* here (and in v. 4; and also perhaps *mišpāḥ* in v. 7, see below) may not just be an unknown rare word but a made-up rhyme word, albeit one with definite semantic associations through the lexical root (*b-ʾ-š* "to stink"). The versions clearly do not recognize the lexeme (G ἀκάνθας "thorns"; V *labruscas* "wild grapes"; S *ḥrwbʾ* [pl.] "carob husks, pods").

xiii. BH *śōrēq* seems to be some kind of grape vine (Jer 2:21; cf. Gen 49:11; Isa 16:8; S *šbwqʾ* [pl.] "shoots, sprigs, suckers"; T *gpn bhyrʾ* "choice vine"; cf. Sym εκλεκτην). Etymologically the term is associated with the color red (*HALOT* 1362), so perhaps in reference to dark red grapes (P. King and L. Stager, *Life in Biblical Israel* [Library of Ancient Israel; Louisville: Westminster John Knox, 2001] 98)—"all grapes and vine leaves of *Vitis vinifera* turn red in autumn" (Walsh, *Fruit of the Vine*, 107). Or the term may reflect a vine common to a particular region, such as the Soreq Valley southwest of Jerusalem (*HALOT* 1362; Walsh, *Fruit of the Vine*, 109–10; King and Stager, *Life in Biblical Israel*, 98; Lowth, *Isaiah*, 2:58). My translation takes its cues from G (cf. Aq, Theod), which also transliterates (σωρηχ), and Lowth's "vine of Sorek" (*Isaiah*, 1:13).

xiv. The reference is likely to a field tower that served as a guard post for the vineyard, affording a raised vantage point from which to scan the vineyard and its surroundings and providing shelter from heat and cold for the vineyard workers as well as a convenient storage area for newly pressed wine (see Walsh, *Fruit of the Vine*, 123, 132–36).

xv. Winepresses in ancient Israel and Judah were hewn out of bedrock (often within the vineyard) and consisted (prototypically) of two vats, the higher and larger one (*gat*) for the treading and the lower and deeper one (*yeqeb*) for collecting the pressed juices. The two were connected by a channel (see Walsh, *Fruit of the Vine*, 142–65; King and Stager, *Life in Biblical Israel*, 98–101). *yeqeb*, strictly the lower vat, here is used as a metonym for the entire press (e.g., Judg 7:25; Isa 16:10; Zech 14:10; Job 24:11; cf. Walsh, *Fruit of the Vine*, 163).

xvi. Lineation in biblical poetry generally, as in many traditional (and aboriginally performative) corpora (cf. R. Finnegan, *Oral Poetry: Its Nature, Significance, and Social Context* [Cambridge: Cambridge University Press, 1977] 106, 130), is a "relative phenomenon," as Couey notes specifically in reference to the poetry of Isaiah of Jerusalem (*Poetry of First Isaiah*, 25–26). Multiple construals will sometimes be equally defensible and the placement of line breaks may have even varied from performance to performance (e.g., compare *ʾănî lĕdôdî* in Song 7:11 as a singular line in a couplet to the same phrase which only makes up part of a line in Song 2:16 and 6:3, viz. *ʾănî lĕdôdî wĕdôdî lî*)—inscription in a running format, as with this song (and prophetic poetry more generally), requires active readerly performance/construal of line ends. For variation in the construal of these opening lines, see, for example, Wildberger, *Isaiah 1–12*, 175; Williamson, *Isaiah 1–27*, 1:316; Blenkinsopp, *Isaiah 1–39*, 205; Roberts, *First Isaiah*, 70. Generally here I have opted for the short-line construals because otherwise the resulting lines are abnormally long and/or comprised of rare or even non-attested syntactic configurations (for one statement of the basic syntactic constraints relevant to Hebrew line structure, see M. O'Connor, *Hebrew Verse Structure* [Winona Lake, IN: Eisenbrauns, 1980] 87, 315–16 [summary], 297–360 [detailed analysis]).

xvii. QIsa^a (*ywšby*), Mmss, and several of the versions (G ἐνοικοῦντες; S *ʿmwdyh* [pl.]; T *ytby*) read a plural instead of the singular preserved in MAL (*yôšēb*) and V (*habitator*). Both readings are equally well explained by mechanical error (dittography or haplography). Preference, however, may be given to MAL (and V) as the more original reading. The plural version of the phrase, *ywšby yrwšlm*, is likely secondary, either because it is far more common (occurring thirty times, e.g., 2 Kgs 23:2; Jer 4:4, 11:9, 17:25, 32:32; Dan 9:7; 2 Chr 34:30), and thus the less difficult reading; or because *yôšēb* is a collective (e.g., Isa 8:14, 22:21; Zech 12:8, 10), and thus the plural renderings may be interpretive in nature (this certainly is the tendency of T and S; see Williamson, *Isaiah 1–27*, I, 320). The addition of ἐν in G results either from dittography (double writing of final *bet* in a shorter text) or is interpretive, since *yôšēb* GN and *yôšēb b*-GN are alternative phrasings (see F. W. Dobbs-Allsopp, "The Syntagma of *bat* Followed by a Geographical Name in the Hebrew Bible: Reconsideration of Its Meaning and Grammar," *CBQ* 57 [1995] 451–70, esp. 465). QIsa^a and the other versions support M (without the preposition).

xviii. GAS (ἄνθρωπος τοῦ Ιουδα καὶ οἱ ἐνοικοῦντες ἐν Ιερουσαλημ) and S (*gbrʾ dyhwdʾ wʿmwdyh* [pl.] *dʾ wršlm*) invert the order of the phrases in M, QIsa^a, GB, V, and T. This does not appear to be any obvious kind of graphic copying mistake but perhaps is a "good variant" arising from oral (performative) interference (see D. M. Carr, *The Formation of the Hebrew Bible: A New Reconstruction* [Oxford: Oxford University Press, 2011], esp. 13–36).

xix. Spelled -*nh* in QIsa^a. For the variation in spelling /a/ with either a *he* or an *aleph* at Qumran, see Qimron, *Hebrew of the Dead Sea Scrolls*, 23. The lack of a corresponding δή (or νυν) in G is marked by an *asterikos* in Origen's *Hexapla* and added by Aq, Sym, and Theod. Of the seventeen times in Isaiah that M has *nāʾ* G mostly fails to provide a quantitative counterpart (fourteen times); a Greek equivalent appears only in 5:1 (δή), 7:13 (δή), and 47:12 (νυν; van der Vorm-Croughs, *Old Greek of Isaiah*, 135).

xx. Whether to construe v. 3 as a single, unbalanced couplet (as I have done; so also Lowth, *Isaiah*, I, 14; Roberts, *First Isaiah*, 70) or to break it up into two (very) short-line couplets (e.g., BHS) remains open to a performer's discretion (see broadly Couey, *Reading the Poetry of First Isaiah*, 21–54). The first line (on my construal) is admittedly long (14 syllables), both for this poem and for biblical poetry in general, and thus is amenable to being broken up into two shorter lines. However, breaking v. 3 into two sets of short lines moves to the other extreme, where the lines are exceedingly short by biblical poetic standards. In favor of construing as a single couplet is the following: the difference in line length with the preceding lines helps to signal a new movement in the poem (which almost all commentators recognize—now the farmer/lover is speaking); the resulting unbalanced *qinah* couplet is consistent with the other two unbalanced couplets in this section of the poem (vv. 3–4); and the poetic awkwardness of the whole may be due to its pronounced prosaic bent—the second line, *šipṭû-nāʾ bênî ûbên karmî*, in particular is indebted to prose phrasing (see esp. Gen 16:5; Exod 18:16; Num 35:24; Deut 1:16; Judg 11:27; 1 Sam 24:13). Still, construing as two couplets remains a viable option (e.g., Wildberger, *Isaiah 1–12*, 175–76; Williamson, *Isaiah 1–27*, 1:316)—Blenkinsopp (*Isaiah 1–39*, 205) construes as a triplet.

xxi. QIsaᵃ reads *bkrmy* instead of M's *lĕkarmî* (also G, V, T, S) likely under the influence of the use of the preposition *b-* that follows immediately at the end of the next line (*bô*) and that was used previously in v. 2 (*bĕtôkô, bô*).

xxii. QIsaᵃ has *wyśh*, which as Roberts (*First Isaiah*, 70, n. n) notices appears to be a defective form of *wyʿśh* /*wayaʿaśeh*/ (cf. QIsaᵃ at v. 2 and 48:14) where the *ayin* has elided in light of the tendency for gutturals to weaken in Qumran Hebrew (Qimron, *Hebrew of the Dead Sea Scrolls*, 25; cf. in QIsaᵃ *-nh* for M's *nāʾ*, v. 3; *wʾth* for *wĕʾattâ*, v. 5; *ʿwśʾ* for *ʿōśeh*, v. 5). A good example of aural/oral interference. QIsaᵃ prefers long forms of the imperfect after *waw*, see Kutscher, *Isaiah Scroll*, 328–29.

xxiii. QIsaᵃ has *wʾth* for M's *wĕʾattâ* (cf. G νυν δὲ; V *et nunc*; T *wkʿn*; S *hšʾ*), which, as Roberts observes is an auditory error (*First Isaiah*, 70, n. o).

xxiv. QIsaᵃ has *ʾwdyʿ* for M's *ʾôdîʿâ*. As Qimron notes, the long and short forms of the first person imperfect are in free variation at Qumran (when not following a *waw*; *Hebrew of the Dead Sea Scrolls*, 44).

xxv. G again lacks a δή corresponding to M's *-nnāʾ*, which is marked by an *asterikos* in Origen's *Hexapla* and added by Aq, Sym, and Theod. Of the seventeen times in Isaiah that M has *nāʾ* G mostly fails to provide a quantitative counterpart (fourteen times); a Greek equivalent appears only in 5:1 (δή), 7:13 (δή), and 47:12 (νυν; van der Vorm-Croughs, *Old Greek of Isaiah*, 135).

xxvi. QIsaᵃ has the long form of the second person suffix, *-kmh*.

xxvii. Spelled *ʿwśʾ* in QIsaᵃ (for the variation in spelling /e/ with either a *he* or an *aleph* at Qumran, see Kutscher, *Isaiah Scroll*, 163–64; Qimron, *Hebrew of the Dead Sea Scrolls*, 23.). T's gloss, *dʾnʾ ʿtyd lmʿbd*, "what I am about to do," captures perfectly the use of the participle in BH to depict imminent action.

xxviii. The versions all render the infinitive absolutes in M, *hāsēr* "removing" and *pārōṣ* "breaking down," *ad sensum* with first person forms. *ʾsyr* /*ʾāsîr*/ in QIsaᵃ, construed as a Hiphil imperfect 1cs from *s-w-r* "I will remove," would appear to reflect the same trajectory of interpretation as is evident in the versions (N.B. Qimron notes the relative non-usage of the infinitive absolute in late biblical Hebrew and at Qumran, *Hebrew of the Dead Sea Scrolls*, 47). However, it is not inconceivable that *ʾsyr* /*ʾāsēr*/ could be an oral/aural variant for *hāsēr*, especially in light of the use of the infinitive absolute in the following line in support of M (*prṣ*; cf. Qimron, *Hebrew of the Dead Sea Scrolls*, 19–20 (and n. 19), 25; Williamson, *Isaiah 1–27*, 1:321).

xxix. S has *mgdlh* "its tower," presumably under the influence of v. 2. G (τὸν φραγμὸν αὐτοῦ) and V (*sepem eius*) support M (*mĕśûkātô*) and QIsa^a (*mswktw*; see Qimron, *Hebrew of the Dead Sea Scrolls*, 24, for the occasional spelling of *ś* with *s* at Qumran).

xxx. QIsa^a has *wyhyh*, which perhaps is not an incorrect gloss of M (*wĕhāyâ*), given that both converted perfects and unconverted imperfects are used (depending on genre) at Qumran to express future time (see M. S. Smith, *The Origins and Development of the Waw-Consecutive: Northwest Semitic Evidence from Ugarit to Qumran* [HSS 39; Atlanta: Scholars, 1991] esp. 59–60). On the preference for the long form of the imperfect of III-weak roots (2nd/3rd person) with *waw*, see Kutscher, *Isaiah Scroll*, 328–29; Qimron, *Hebrew of the Dead Sea Scrolls*, 45 n. 8.

xxxi. QIsa^a lacks the preposition *l-*, which normally precedes the infinitive construct at Qumran, and thus represents a variant of note (if not a simple mistake—though there appear not to be any obvious mechanical triggers for such a mistake).

xxxii. As in the preceding line, QIsa^a has *wyhyh*, again likely not an incorrect gloss of M (*wĕhāyâ*), given that both converted perfects and unconverted imperfects are used (depending on genre) at Qumran to express future time (Smith, *Origins and Development of the Waw-Consecutive*, esp. 59–60). On the preference for the long form of the imperfect of III-weak roots (2nd/3rd person) with *waw*, see Kutscher, *Isaiah Scroll*, 328–29; Qimron, *Hebrew of the Dead Sea Scrolls*, 45, n. 8.

xxxiii. Williamson rightly problematizes the etymology of *b-ʿ-r* here (*Isaiah 1–27*, 1:266, 321–22), but it is less clear that its usage in Isa 3:14 and 5:5 must be understood similarly, or that "grazing" as a specific means of devouring or destroying is not immediately in view here (see Exod 22:2; so Wildberger: "grazed bare" [*Isaiah 1–12*, 176]; the versions are of no help). After all, vineyards were enclosed specifically to prevent such kinds of devastation.

xxxiv. In a mountainous vineyard plot, terrace walls served as revetments for stopping water runoff and as barriers to keep intruders out of the vineyard (Ps 80:13–14; see Walsh, *Fruit of the Vine*, 96, 123).

xxxv. *bātâ* is a *hapax legomenon* (MH *bātâ* "destruction") with no obvious cognates. The sense seems clear enough from context—waste, ruin, desolation, destruction (cf. S *wʾʿbdywhy dnḥrb* "and I will make it so that it is desolated, destroyed"; V *et ponam eam desrtam*). G (καὶ ἀνήσω τὸν ἀμπελῶνα μου) is interpreting in light of the previous imagery—though its gloss ὡς εἰς χέρσον "as in a dry land" later in the verse is perhaps closer to the mark (there it is a gloss for BH *šāmîr* "thorn," as also in Isa 7:23–25).

xxxvi. Interestingly, the negative idiom "to gather cloud(s) against" (*ur-pí-a a-ka-aṣ-ṣa-ar*, Si 57 i28; cf. MS 3285 obv. 24) appears in one of the Mesopotamian jealousy poems.

xxxvii. QIsa^a's *śʿšwʿw* is either a non-standard spelling of the 3ms suffix on a plural noun, which is not uncommon at Qumran and especially in QIsa^a (Kutscher, *Isaiah Scroll*, 443, 447; Qimron, *Hebrew of the Dead Sea Scrolls*, 59) or suffers from

haplography, given the sequence of graphically similar *waws* and *yods*:
M: *šʿšwʿyw wyqw*
QIsaᵃ: *šʿšwʿw wyqw*

xxxviii. Contrary to the third person form of M and QIsaᵃ, which must be original, all the versions revert to the first person, assimilating to the voice used in the middle sections of the song (vv. 3–6; and in G and T, in v. 2 as well).

xxxix. QIsaᵃ mistakenly adds the preposition *l-* "to, for" (*lmśpḥ*) under the influence of the preceding *lmšpṭ*. The word *miśpāḥ* (often glossed as "bloodshed") is another *hapax legomenon* (cf. Ar. *safaḥa* "to spill, pour out, shed"; *saffāḥ* "shedder of blood, murder"; Wildberger, *Isaiah 1–12*, 185), which the versions, not recognizing, gloss from context: G (ἀνομίαν "lawlessness"), V (*iniquitas* "iniquity"), S (*ḥṭwpyʾ* "violence"), T (*ʾānôsîn* "robbers"). As with *bĕʾûšîm* in vv. 2 and 4 *miśpāḥ* here may be another made-up rhyme word. Indeed, if the root derives originally from **s-p-ḥ* (cf. *mispaḥat* "skin rash," *sappaḥat* "scab"; cf. *śippaḥ* in Isa 3:17), then perhaps even the spelling has been altered. The spelling with a *sin* graphically enhances and underscores the aural play—which also implies an anticipation of readers (and not just listeners) for this text. Further, G (ποιῆσαι κρίσιν), V (*faceret iudicium*), and T (*dyʿbdwn dynʾ*) resort to periphrastic renderings that recall the language of "making" (*ʿ-ś-h*) from vv. 2 and 4, which ramifies the play in v. 7 on the language of "wait, expectation, hope" (*q-w-h*) from these earlier lines, but also from the traditional exhortation to literally "do" (*ʿ-ś-h*) "justice" and "righteousness" (esp. Gen 18:19; Jer 22:3; Ps 99:4; 119:121; Prov 21:3; 2 Chr 9:8; cf. 1 Kgs 3:28; Isa 56:1; Jer 5:1; Mic 6:8; Ps 106:3; Prov 21:15). The absence of the verb in M and QIsaᵃ only adumbrates the closing complaint of the poet, a figural erasure of the traditional exhortation.

xl. The presence of an added conjunction in G, V, and S is likely interpretive in nature (esp. in G and S). As for the unexpected negative particle οὐ in G, it is unclear whether it reflects a misreading of the preposition *l-* as a negative particle or whether it is a part of G's periphrastic rendering of the last two lines of the song.

Simon Bruce Parker
A Bibliography

Amy Limpitlaw and Herbert B. Huffmon

A. BOOKS AND MONOGRAPHS

1966   *Enuma Elish: The Babylonian Epic of Creation: The Cuneiform Text.* Text established by W. G. Lambert and copied out by Simon B. Parker. Oxford: Clarendon.

1967   "Studies in the Grammar of the Ugaritic Prose Texts." Ph.D. dissertation. Johns Hopkins University.

1989   *The Pre-Biblical Narrative Tradition: Essays on the Ugaritic Poems Keret and Aqhat.* SBLRBS 24. Atlanta: Scholar's.

1997a   *Stories in Scripture and Inscriptions: Comparative Studies on Narratives in Northwest Semitic Inscriptions and the Hebrew Bible.* New York: Oxford University Press.

1997b   *Ugaritic Narrative Poetry.* Translated by Mark S. Smith, Simon B. Parker, Edward L. Greenstein, Theodore J. Lewis, and David Marcus; ed. by Simon B. Parker. SBLWAW 9. Atlanta: Scholars.

B. CONTRIBUTIONS TO REFERENCE WORKS

1976a "Deities, Underworld" (222–25); "Familiar Spirit" (335); "Rephaim" (739). In *The Interpreter's Dictionary of the Bible, Supplementary Volume*. Edited by Keith Crim. Nashville: Abingdon.

1989 "Amos." In *The Books of the Bible*. Vol. 1, *Old Testament*, edited by Bernhard W. Anderson, 367–74. New York: Scribner.

1994 "The Ancient Near Eastern Literary Background of the Old Testament." In *The New Interpreter's Bible*, edited by Leander E. Keck, 1:228–43. 12 vols. Nashville: Abingdon.

1995a "The Literature of Canaan, Ancient Israel, and Phoenicia: An Overview." In *Civilizations of the Ancient Near East*, edited by Jack M. Sasson, 2399–410. New York: Scribner's.

1995b "Council" (204–8); "Saints" (718–20); "Shahar" (754–55); "Sons of (the) God(s)" (794–800). In *Dictionary of Deities and Demons in the Bible*, edited by Karel van der Toorn et al. Leiden: Brill. 2nd ed. Leiden: Brill and Grand Rapids: Eerdmans, 1999.

2002 "Ammonite, Edomite, and Moabite." In *Beyond Babel: A Handbook for Biblical Hebrew and Related Languages*, edited by John Kaltner and Steven L. McKenzie, 43–60. RBS 42. Atlanta: Society of Biblical Literature.

C. PAPERS AND REPORTS

1966 "A Further Note on the Treaty Background of Hebrew yadaʿ." *BASOR* 184:36–38. (with Herbert B. Huffmon)

1970 "The Feast of Rāpi'u." *UF* 2:243–49.

1971 "Exodus XV 2 Again." *VT* 21:373–79.

1972 "Seating Arrangements at Divine Banquets." *UF* 4:37–40. (with A. J. Ferrara)

1974 "Parallelism and Prosody in Ugaritic Narrative Verse." *UF* 6:283–94.

1976a   "The Marriage Blessing in Israelite and Ugaritic Literature." *JBL* 95:23–30.

1976b   "Revolution in Northern Israel." In *Society of Biblical Literature 1976 Seminar Papers*, 311–21. SBLSP 10. Missoula, MT: Scholars.

1977   "The Historical Composition of KRT and the Cult of El." *ZAW* 89:161–75.

1978a   "Jezebel's Reception of Jehu." *Maarav* 1:67–78.

1978b   "Possession Trance and Prophecy in Pre-Exilic Israel." *VT* 28:271–85. Reprint, in *Prophecy in the Hebrew Bible*, edited by David E. Orton, 124–38. Brill's Readers in Biblical Studies 5. Leiden: Brill, 2000.

1979a   "Some Methodological Principles in Ugaritic Philology." *Maarav* 2/1:7–41.

1979b   "The Vow in Ugaritic and Israelite Narrative Literature." *UF* 11:693–700.

1987   "Death and Devotion: The Composition and Theme of Aqht." In *Love and Death in the Ancient Near East: Essays in Honor of Marvin H. Pope*, edited by John H Marks and Robert M. Good, 74–83. Guilford, CT: Four Quarters.

1988   "The Birth Announcement." In *Ascribe to the Lord: Biblical and Other Essays in Memory of Peter C. Craigie*, ed. Lyle M. Eslinger and J. Glen Taylor, 133–49. JSOTSup 67. Sheffield: JSOT.

1989a   "KTU 1.16 iii, The Myth of the Absent God and 1 Kings 18." *UF* 21:283–96.

1989b   "H. Neil Richardson, 1916–1988." *BRev* 5/2:4.

1990   "Toward Literary Translation(s) of Ugaritic Poetry." *UF* 22:257–70.

1991   "The Hebrew Bible and Homosexuality." *Quarterly Review for Ministry: A Journal of Scholarly Reflection for Ministry* 11/3:4–19.

1993	"Official Attitudes toward Prophecy at Mari and Israel." *VT* 43: 50–68. Reprint in *Prophecy in the Hebrew Bible*, ed. David E. Orton, 245–63. Brill's Readers in Biblical Studies 5. Leiden: Brill, 2000.
1994a	"The Lachish Letters and Official Reactions to Prophecies." In *Uncovering Ancient Stones: Essays in Memory of H. Neil Richardson*, edited by Lewis M. Hopfe, 65–78. Winona Lake, IN: Eisenbrauns.
1994b	"Siloam Inscription Memorializes Engineering Achievement." *BAR* 20/4:36–38.
1995	"The Beginning of the Reign of God: Psalm 82 as Myth and Liturgy." *RB* 102:532–59.
1996	"Appeals for Military Intervention: Stories from Zinjirli and the Bible." *BA* 59:213–24.
1998	Pushing the Limits: Issues in Jewish Bible Translation. In *Hesed ve-emet: Studies in Honor of Ernest S. Frerichs*, edited by Jodi Magness and Seymour Gitin, 73–80. BJS 320. Atlanta: Scholars.
2000a	"Did the Authors of the Books of Kings Make Use of Royal Inscriptions?" *VT* 50:357–78.
2000b	"A Perfect Hymn for Advent." *The Hymn: A Journal of Congregational Song* 51/4:14–16.
2000c	"Ugaritic Literature and the Bible." *NEA* 63:228–31.
2003	"Graves, Caves, and Refugees: An Essay in Microhistory." *JSOT* 27:259–88.
2004	"The Use of Similes in Ugaritic Literature." *UF* 36:357–69.
2006a	"Ancient Northwest Semitic Epigraphy and the 'Deuternomistic Tradition in Kings." In *Die deuteronomistischen Geschichtswerke: Redaktions- und religionsgeschichtliche Perspektiven zur Deuteronomismus. Diskussion in Tora und vorderen Propheten*, edited Mark Witte, et al., 213–27. BZAW 365. Berlin: de Gruyter.
2006b	"Divine Intercession in Judah?" *VT* 56:76–91.

2006c "The Question of Restoration in Epistolary Inscriptions with Special Reference to Arad 40." *IEJ* 56:96–101.

D. SELECTED BOOK REVIEWS

1976 *Baal: A Study of Texts in Connection with Baal in the Ugaritic Epics*, by Peter J. van Zyl. *JNES* 35:143–44.

1978 *The Civil and Sacral Legitimation of the Israelite Kings*, by Tryggve N. D. Mettinger. *JAOS* 98:508–9.

1987 *Psalm 29: Kanaanäische El- und Baaltraditionen in Jűdicher Sicht*, by Oswald Loretz. *JAOS* 107:144.

1988a *God's Conflict with the Dragon and the Sea: Echoes of Canaanite Myth in the Old Testament*, by John Day. *JAOS* 108:152–53.

1988b *Jephthah and His Vow*, by David Marcus. *JAOS* 108:312–14.

1989a *The Ugaritic Hippiatric Texts: A Critical Edition*, by Chaim Cohen. *BASOR* 275:73–74.

1989b *Ugaritic Vocabulary in Syllabic Transcription*, by John Huehnergard. *JBL* 108:320–22.

1990 *Ugaritic and Hebrew Poetic Parallelism: A Trial Cut ('nt 1 and Proverbs 2)*, by Dennis Pardee. *JBL* 109:503–4.

1991 *Samuel and the Deuteronomist: A Literary Study of the Deuteronomic History, Part Two. I Samuel*, by Robert Polzin. *LQ* 5:539–41.

1992a *The Ugaritic Poem of AQHT: Test, Translation, Commentary*, by Baruch Margalit. *BASOR* 288:90–92.

1992b *The Early History of God*, by Mark S. Smith. *HS* 33:158–62.

1993a *Studien zur Ugaritischen Lexikograpie: mit Kultur und Religions- geschicchtlichen Parallelln*, by Kjell Aartum. *RelSRev* 19:344.

1993b *Une bibliotheque au sud de la ville: Les textes de la 34e Campagne (1973)*, by Pierre Bordreuil, et al.; *Arts et Industries de la Pierre*, by M. Yon et al. *JBL* 112:507–8.

1993c   *La trouvaille épigraphique de l'Ougarit, 2: Bibliographie*, by Jesus-Luis Cunchillos. *CBQ* 55:330–31.

1994a   *La religión cananea según la litúrgia de Ugarit: Estudio textual*, by Gregorio del Olmo Lete. *RelSRev* 20:139.

1994b   *The Rise of Yahwism: The Roots of Israelite Monotheism*, by Johannes C. de Moor. *HS* 35:125–28.

1994c   *The Goddess Anat in Ugaritic Myth*, by Neal H. Walls. *RelSRev* 20:139–40.

1995   *Among the Host of Heaven: The Syro-Palestinian Pantheon as Bureaucracy*, by Lowell K. Handy. *CBQ* 57:769–70.

1996   *Ritual and Sacrifice in the Ancient Near East: Proceedings of the International Conference Organized by the Katholieke Universiteit from the 17th to the 20th of April 1991*, ed. J. Quaergebeur. *JAOS* 116:569.

1997   *The Alphabetic Texts from Ugarit, Ras ibn Hani and Other Places* (KTU: 2nd enlarged ed.), by M. Dietrich, O. Loretz, and J. Sanmartin. *JAOS* 117:714.

1998   *The Study of the Ancient Near East in the Twenty-First Century*, ed. Jerrold S. Cooper and Glenn M. Schwartz. *CBQ* 60:181.

1999   *Dicciionario de la Lengua Ugaritica*, Vol. 1, by G. del Olmo Lete and J. Sanmartin. *JAOS* 118:138.

2002   *Ritual in Narrative: The Dynamics of Feasting,Mourning, and Retaliation Rites in the Ugaritic Tale of Aqhat*, by David P. Wright. *JAOS* 122:123.

2005a   *Identifying Persons in Northwest-Semitic Inscriptions of 1200–539 B.C.E.*, by Lawrence J. Mykytiuk. *CBQ* 67:501–3.

2005b   *Manuel d'Ougaritique*, 2 vols., by Pierre Bordreuil and Dennis Pardee. *JAOS* 125:434–35.

2005c   *Biblical Mourning: Ritual and Social Dimensions*, by Saul M. Olyan. *JAOS* 125:478–79.

www.ingramcontent.com/pod-product-compliance
Lightning Source LLC
Chambersburg PA
CBHW071246230426
43668CB00011B/1603